ISLAM AND THE WEST

WORLDS OF ISLAM
WELTEN DES ISLAMS
MONDES DE L'ISLAM

Vol. 4 / Band

Edited by / Herausgegeben von / Edité par

SILVIA NAEF
ULRICH RUDOLPH
GREGOR SCHOELER

PETER LANG
Bern · Berlin · Bruxelles · Frankfurt am Main · New York · Oxford · Wien

ISLAM AND THE WEST

The Limits of Freedom of Religion

HANA SADIK EL-GALLAL

PETER LANG
Bern · Berlin · Bruxelles · Frankfurt am Main · New York · Oxford · Wien

Bibliographic information published by die Deutsche Nationalbibliothek
Die Deutsche Nationalbibliothek lists this publication in the Deutsche Nationalbibliografie; detailed bibliographic data is available on the Internet at ‹http://dnb.d-nb.de›.

British Library Cataloguing-in-Publication Data: A catalogue record for this book is available from The British Library, Great Britain

Library of Congress Cataloging-in-Publication Data

El-Gallal, Hana Sadik,
Islam and the West : the limits of freedom of religion / Hana Sadik El-Gallal.
pages cm. – (Welten des Islams–worlds of Islam–mondes de l'Islam ; bd. 4)
Includes bibliographical references.
ISBN 978-3-0343-0578-5
1. Freedom of religion (International law) 2. Religious minorities–Legal status, laws, etc.
3. Intellectual freedom. I. Title.
K3258.E44 2014
341.4'832–dc23

2014002332

Cover photo: Blue Mosque / Istanbul from iStockphoto.com © by "Lebazele"

ISSN 1661-6278 pb.
ISBN 978-3-0343-0578-5 pb.

ISSN 2235-5766 eBook
ISBN 978-3-0351-0685-5 eBook

Hochfeldstrasse 32, CH-3012 Bern, Switzerland
info@peterlang.com, www.peterlang.com

Printed in Germany

Content

List of Abbreviations

HRC	Human Rights Committee
ICCPR	the 1966 International Covenant on Civil and Political Rights
UDHR	the 1948 Universal Declaration of Human Rights (the Universal Declaration)
ICESCR	the 1966 International Covenant on Economic, Social and Cultural Rights
Religion Declaration	the 1981 Declaration on the Elimination of All Forms of Intolerance and of Discrimination Based on Religion or Belief
Minority Declaration	the 1993 Declaration on the Rights of Persons Belonging to National or Ethnic, Religious and Linguistic Minorities
CERD	the International Convention on the Elimination of All Forms of Racial Discrimination
CRC	the Convention on the Rights of the Child
CEDAW	The Convention on the Elimination of All Forms of Discrimination against Women
UNGA	United Nations General Assembly
ILO	The International Labor Organization
ECHR	European Convention on Human Rights
EctHR	European Court of Human Rights
ECOSOC	Economic and Social Council of the UN
ECRI	European Commission Against Racism and Intolerance
EEOC	the Equal Employment Opportunity Commission (USA)
ISNA,	Islamic Society of North America
ICNA	*Islamic Ci*rcle of North America
CAIR	Council on American-Islamic Relations
OFAC	the Treasury Department's Office of Foreign Assets Control (USA)

List of Arabic Terms

Dhimmi	Non-Muslim Subject
Fatwa	religious decision
Fiqh	the science of the Shari'a or jurisprudence
Ijma	Consensus
Ijtihad	the effort of independent judgment
Imam	Leader of a Muslim community
Isnad	chain of transmitters of a tradition
Istihsan	legal equity
Istislah	aim of Mankind in Law, based on the Public interest
Jizyia	poll tax
Khalifa	Caliph, chief of Muslim state
Madhab	School
Maten	Text
Mujtahid	one who exercises independent reasoning; qualified Scholar
Mutawatir Sunna	well known Sunna, Authentic
Qiyas	Analogy
Riddah	Apostasy
Shari'a	Islamic Law, legal system
Sunna	rules of conduct deduced from the oral precepts, action and decisions of the Prophet or tradition or model behaviors
Sunna ahad	Sunna reported by one or a few people
Ulama	the Religious Scholars of Islam

Introduction

The right to freedom of religion or belief is a fundamental right. It is a broad and a complex right which can be violated in different ways and at different levels. Despite the existence of various constitutional provisions and relevant laws in national and international legal systems to protect this right, manifestations of intolerance and discrimination, based on religion or belief, persists in countries of various political, social, and cultural systems. In fact, it appears that religious intolerance is on the rise. Moreover, religion has been reasserting itself in the politics of the West and the East over the last few years and the name of religion is being invoked by those pursuing specific political agendas or wishing to maintain power. This has led to increased discrimination of religious minorities that live in these respective societies.

Religious intolerance stems mainly from a lack of respect for the beliefs of others and is often associated with domination, exercised by a majority's beliefs, over minorities with different beliefs. Such an attitude leads first to discrimination, then to persecution and sometimes even to the most extreme forms of persecution: the physical elimination of persons. Prejudice, feelings of inferiority and the need to find a scapegoat for social or economic ills are also mentioned among the causes for religious intolerance.

Religions or beliefs originally express tolerant, altruistic, humanistic ideals, but intolerance stems when they are professed in a rigidly dogmatic manner, which divides peoples between believers of the faith and non-believers. Such an exclusivist approach generates prejudice and helps create negative stereotypes. Manifestations of intolerance are not limited to certain regions or religions and they should not be regarded as inherent to a particular social or political system. Thus, both dogmatic theism, as well as dogmatic atheism, can lead to manifestations of intolerance. Today, in many parts of the world, persons belonging to minority religious groups continue to suffer from the worst forms of inequality in all spheres of life.

Of rising concern is the rise of intolerance of Islam in Western society, as well as increased intolerance, in Islamic states, of their religious minority groups. What coverage there is on Islam and Muslims in the West tends to focus predominantly on negative representations, such as conflict and violence in the Middle East and issues relating to terrorism and extremism. Violations of Muslim individual's rights based on counter-terrorism measures adopted in the post 9/11-context have had and continue to show adverse effects on the enjoyment of freedom of religion or beliefs worldwide, sometimes just because they are Muslims. Muslims have been harassed, arrested or deported all over the world. Moreover, the anti-terrorism measures adopted by some states deter Muslims from the enjoyment of virtually all their human rights, be they civil, cultural, economic, political or social. The application of 'terrorist' definitions is being used to outlaw peaceful Muslim religious entities or sometimes to blacklist the entire community and religion, subjecting them to systematic suspicion. Governments, instead of focusing their efforts on the origins of terrorism and on the need to ensure protection and promotion of human rights without bias or selectivity, have aided in increasing and spreading Islamophobia.[1] This attitude is creating an estranged and alienated minority in the West and equating Islam with terrorism is denying the truth that Islamic extremists despite the volume of their voices, make up only a tiny, fringe percent of the Muslim population. Moreover, discriminatory intellectual and media comments have shifted the international debates on religious freedom today to debates on the West versus Islam.[2] In reality, however, the disputes that "divide peoples and nations are not primarily about values

1 It is the experience of Muslim communities of an increasingly hostile environment towards them, characterised by suspicion, deep-rooted prejudice, ignorance, and, in some cases, physical and verbal harassment. A growing number of young Muslims often find themselves caught between their faith and the social expectations placed on them to be "discreet" with their religious practices.

2 Huntington Samuel, *The Clash of Civilizations 'And the Remaking of World Order'*, Simon and Schuster UK Ltd., UK, 1997& 2002, 321.

or civilizations, they are about interests, territory, power, and about the impact of competition for power within particular states on the international system."[3]

Islam has increasingly become labeled as a violent religion responsible for terrorism in the world and human rights violations. This stereotyping and prejudice towards a religion that is considered, as Smith notes, "a vital force in the contemporary world,"[4] and where, as Belt points out, "some 1.3 billion human beings – one person in five – heed Islam's call in the modern world, embracing (it) at a rate that makes it the fasted growing on Earth, with 80 percent of believers now outside the Arab world,"[5] is bound to have repercussions in the global community. Islam today is the "most misunderstood religion on earth."[6] The events of September 11, 2001 seem to have only added to the incomplete or distorted information many Americans and Europeans have about this religion.[7] Thus, a clear and strong political message which rejects the identification of terrorism and extremism with Islam is essential. The Islamic world cannot be held accountable because of the abhorrent acts by a handful of extremists. Prejudices against and misrepresentations of Muslims should be challenged by highlighting the contributions of Muslims to society. Political parties, the media and the honest academia have an important role to play in this field. Like other minorities, such as Sikhs or Jews, Muslims should also be protected by specific laws against discrimination. Law enforcement agencies should be trained to identify, investigate and prosecute various forms of hate crimes against Muslims. In some countries, legal protection from discrimination includes race and ethnicity but not religion.

3 Halliday Fred, *Nation and Religion in the Middle East*, Lynne Rienner Publisher, United States of America, 2000, 10.

4 H. Smith, 'The World's Religions' (New York: HarperCollins, 1991), 267, quoted in Larry A. Samovar, Richard E. Porter, *Communication Between Cultures, 5th edition*, Thomson Wadsworth, Canada, 2004, 98.

5 D. Belt, "*The World of Islam*" National Geographic, January 2002, 77.

6 Ibid, 76.

7 Larry A. Samovar, Richard E. Porter, *Communication Between Cultures, 5th edition*, Thomson Wadsworth, Canada, 2004, 98.

This may create gaps in the legal framework. Finally, the alienation and exclusion of Muslim communities should be addressed by clear and consistent integration strategies and action plans which facilitate inclusion and participation of these communities in public life. "Integration policy for the Muslims" could easily be replaced by "integration policy with the Muslims."[8]

Indeed, today it is important to emphasize harmony and solidarity among the West and Muslim societies by coalescing around common, universal and democratic values. Without this positive climate with respect to Islam and the Muslims, intolerance and discrimination will threaten Muslims in general and the Muslim communities living in the West, in particular. Therefore, one must be careful that the exclusion of Islam and Muslims from the West does not become the new political-intellectual identity of the West. If this happens, it will accentuate unity over diversity at the expense of religious freedoms and religious minorities. Since societies can neither suppress diversity nor dispense with unity, they need to find ways of reconciling their apparently conflicting demands. Deep and extensive cultural diversity is a fact of modern life and every modern multicultural society needs to find ways of accommodating diverse demands without losing its cohesiveness and unity. In a time of religious tension, it is the moment to advocate the ethics and morals of justice, equality and religious liberties which are protected by the human rights standards. These principles are also the moral message of Islam.

Moreover, what is happening in the West should not be a justification for those in Arab states to stop fighting for religious freedoms and other human rights, on the premises that such values are 'Western' by nature. Actually, as Muslims face an increase in discrimination and intolerance because of their religion, it should help them realize the importance of supporting these international standards which protect other

8 Mehmet Aydin, *Fighting Intolerance and Discrimination against Muslims: facilitating integration and respecting Cultural Diversity*, OSCE Conference on Anti-Semitism and on Other Forms of Intolerance, Cordoba, 8 and 9 June 2005, <http://www.osce.org/documents/cio/2005/06/15051_en.pdf> (viewed Sept. 2013).

minorities who are suffering the same violation of their religious freedoms. It is also time for Muslims to realize that the reconciliation between traditional values and the alternative positive values resulting from the evolution of modern societies do not contradict with Islamic teaching which focuses mostly on *the welfare of humanity.*

The aim of this thesis is to remind the reader that it is in the greater interest of mankind to put an immediate end to religious persecution and manifestations of religious prejudices and discriminations. Discussion and analysis of the right to freedom of thought, conscience and religion can only take place in an atmosphere of freedom and equality in dignity and rights of all human beings and this can be done only by respecting the principle of tolerance.

Outline of the Study

This study sets out a framework, founded upon international and regional legal instruments, relating to religious discrimination, racism and intolerance, in order to accentuate the role of the international standards in creating harmony between states, communities, and individuals regarding religious freedoms. The study reviews the different ways to promote respect of freedom of religion, especially, the protection of religious minorities at various levels through the evaluation and implementation of these international instruments, while at the same time, stressing the positive contributions of religious and cultural diversity to the world.

This thesis is divided into four parts:
The first part sets out the right of freedom of religion or belief under international human rights standards. It outlines the right to freedom of religion or belief by focusing on the definition of religion and what the term 'religion' actually encompasses; examining the main provisions protecting freedom of religion or belief, the scope of this right, which includes the freedom to have and change religion or belief and the right to manifest a religion or belief. Since vulnerable religious minorities are the ones who faces discrimination and intolerance while

manifesting their religion, it is important to define 'minority' in general, the different provisions that protect them, and the role of the state to protect religious freedoms, especially of religious minorities in pluralistic societies, from discrimination and intolerance.

Part two and three address the issue of freedom of religion or belief in practice. It looks at how different states are protecting this right; how the religious freedoms of religious minorities are protected, and in which ways are they violated.

Part two examines the limits on freedom of religion or belief in the West. It will concentrate particularly on limits on religious freedoms of Muslims in France and the United States of America. France has been chosen as a study case because it has a large Muslim Minority. Approximately half of the more than three million Muslims in France have French citizenship, while two to four percent are of French extraction. Islam has long been a presence in France-the Mosque of Paris was built in the 1920s and was financed in part by public funds. The USA is chosen as a study case for its important role as a super power in the Muslim world after 9/11, especially in a time that is dominated by the War in Iraq, the War in Afghanistan and the War on Terror.

The primary focus will be on the limitation of the religious symbols law on Muslim in France and the effect of the anti-terrorism measures in the USA on the right of freedom of religion and other human rights, particularly as it applies to Muslims. All along, the section will point to the incitement of hatred against Muslims through some western media (example the Danish cartoons) and focusing on the obligation of the states to protect minorities including religious minorities.

The third part describes limits on the right to freedom of religion or belief as it is practiced in the Arab countries. Countries of focus will be Egypt and Saudi Arabia.[9] It will focus on the several challenges to freedom of religion or belief in the Arab region. These challenges are the restrictions on the right to change religion or belief, especially the accusation of apostasy and religious freedoms of minority groups. This

9 Both Saudia Arabia and Egypt are considered a leading religious states in the Arab and Islamic World.

study will assume that the causes of the existing inconsistencies are rooted, not in Islam as a religion, but rather in domestic politics, constitutional inadequacies and the manipulation of Islam by both the government and militant groups. In fact, this study will establish that equality and justice and respect of all human beings are very crucial tenets of Islam by exploring the religion itself as well as its *Shar'ia* (Islamic jurisprudence).[10]

In each case study, issues discussed will be selected on the basis of the degree of interest they generate internationally. In France, the concentration will be on discrimination against Muslims but especially on the issue of headscarves. France, in 2004, proposed a law banning Islamic headscarves and other visible religious symbols in state schools which created a debate on whether this law violates the rights to freedom of religion and expression. In the US, discrimination against Muslims through anti-terrorism measures will be the focus. The global war on terror declared in the aftermath of the 9-11 attacks has emboldened the US government and other governments around the world to institute sweeping new counter-terrorism measures which have affected fundamental human rights and individual liberties, as well as the impacts on certain communities, predominantly Muslim, that have come under suspicion in a context of anxieties and fears over 'Islamic fascism' which resulted in the rise of Islamophobia. In the Arab Muslim states, discrimination against non-Muslim minorities will be studied as most reports conclude that Arab governments restrict freedom of religion and that there is a further deterioration of the poor status of respect for religious freedom. Another thorny issue in the Arab states is the case of apostasy. In some Arab countries, any attempts to change one's religion are met with the charge of apostasy; which under some interpretations of religious law is punishable by death. Many consider that to stress the com-

10 Yousaf Ali's Translation of the Qur'an is relied on for the purposes of this thesis because of its widespread recognition among scholars of Islam. In citation of Qur'anic verses, first comes chapter number followed by the verse number. Note that any translation of the Qur'an immediately ceases to be the literal word of Allah. The translation is available online at: <http://www.usc.edu/dept/MSA/quran/>.

patibility of Islam with freedom of religion or belief by quoting the Qur'anic verse: "There shall be no compulsion in religion" is a feeble attempt by apologists to disguise the Islamic attitude to apostasy. However, this study stresses that such an opinion is a result of misunderstandings and misconceptions concerning Islam, especially the difference between Islam the religion and its interpretations.

Finally, the concluding remarks will sum up the main challenges to the right to freedom of religion or belief and the vulnerable situation of religious minorities. Thus, in the final part, the reasons for religious intolerance and violence will be contemplated and the importance of the governments' role to ensure an inclusive, plural society characterized by mutual respect and shared democratic values will be stressed.

In this study, two issues have to be taken into account: first, when dealing with specific issues in a particular country, the situation in other countries in the region, in addition to the case study, will be also taken into account and second, dividing the world into the West and Islam, as if they are uniform units is due to the dominance of this division. For practical reasons as well as for simplicity and to avoid being repetitive, the Arab states will be lumped together as will the Western states. Moreover, because the right to freedom of religion is so broad and complex, only certain specific issues will be discussed. It is virtually impossible to include all cases and all categories within the scope of this thesis. Also, it will be difficult to account for all incidents or governmental measures in the chosen states that are incompatible with the international standards. Thus, only specific incidents will be examined. This study will be set against the context of recent changes, in how 'religious diversity', 'politicization of human rights and religion', 'extremism', and mainly the 'war on terror', have led to new challenges to freedom of religion or belief both in the Western and Islamic world.

All along, this thesis will stress that freedom of religion and belief is a precious human right that enables us to reach harmony, safety, and reconciliation. It is significant to accomplish a relationship of tolerance, mutual respect for each other's religions and beliefs to secure peace and prosperity and to fulfill the basic human needs. In order to reach state cohesion, it is important to concentrate on dealing with cultural pluralism, commitment to the equality of all humans and the development of religious sensitivity that is not about power but about justice and an inherent human dignity. This can be done through the international standards, which provide a frame of reference for the measures that should be adopted to combat and eliminate dogmatism and intolerance in the matter of religion or belief.

Part 1

The Right of Minorities to the Freedom of Thought, Conscience, and Religion

We live in an age where changes in technology, travel, economic and political systems, immigration patterns, and population density have created a world in which people increasingly interact with others from different cultures. The history of humankind details an ongoing antipathy and hostility towards those who are different. However, there is no escape from meeting people who are different from us and who adhere to different religions or beliefs. The importance of religion is not only that it helps mankind's quest for a meaning and purpose to their lives, but also gives them clues into the social aspects of a culture. Religion, then, be it theology or the everyday practices of a culture, offers people insight into the identity of the members of that culture. As Lamb observes, "It is clear that religion and culture are inextricably entwined."[1] Religions provide their members with a sense of identity and security. It unites people by asking them to share symbols, values, and norms. For example, there is a strong feeling of security knowing that you are part of a religious family that is feasting on the same day, wearing the same attire when they pray, bowing in one direction or another, or taking Holy Communion. This significance of religion requires from the international community to provide protection for the right to freedom of religion.

1 C. Lamb, 'The Claim to Be Unique', in Eerdman's, *Handbook of the World's Religions*, R. Pierce Beaver et eds. (Grand Rapids, MI; Erdmans, 1982), 358, quoted in Samovar and Porter, 88.

1. The Right to Freedom of Thought, Conscience, and Religion

The world, people, and societies are always in a state of change. These changes, at both the international and domestic levels, have brought us into direct and indirect contact with people of cultural diversity.[1] Consequently, in order to understand others, we have to understand their cultures.

Culture is important because it is everything and everywhere. Hofstede clearly underscores this point when he notes that, "culture is to human collective what personality is to individual."[2] Culture is important to all people because it addresses the basic need of laying out a predictable world in which each of us is firmly grounded and thus enables us to make sense of our surroundings. Culture makes life easy for two reasons:

> First, culture helps facilitate the transition from the womb to this new life by providing meaning to events, objects, and people – making the world a less mysterious and frightening place. Second, culture makes life less confusing because it is automatic and subconscious.[3]

Cultures are subject to fluctuations and seldom remain constant. Luckmann notes that,

> [a]lthough culture provides strength and stability, it is never static. Cultural groups face continual challenges from such powerful forces as environment upheavals, plagues, wars, migration, the influx of immigration, and the growth of new technologies. As a result, cultures change and evolve over time.[4]

1 Samovar and Porter, 3.

2 G. Hofstede, *Culture's Consequences: Comparing Values, Behavior, Institutions, and Organizations Across Nations, 2nd ed.* Thousands Oaks, CA: Sage Publications, 2001, 10.

3 Samovar and Porter, 29.

4 J. Luckmann, *Transcultural Communication in Nursing* (Albany, NY: Delmar Publishers, 1999), 22, quoted in Samovar and Porter, 43.

One element that distinguishes one culture from another is *religion*. Religion is one feature of all cultures. According to Parkes, Laungani, and Young, all cultures posses "[a] dominant, organized religion within which salient beliefs and activities (rites, rituals, taboos, and ceremonies) can be given meaning and legitimacy."[5] The influence of religion can be seen in the entire fabric of a culture. Both consciously and unconsciously and in varying degrees, religion impacts everything from business practices, to politics, to individual behavior. Nanda and Warms note that "[r]eligion is a human universal."[6] The human need to confront important issues is universal and the long history of religion is directly linked to culture. Samovar and Porter affirm this and note that

> [r]eligion as a world view, is a culture's orientation toward God, humanity, nature, questions of existence, the universe and cosmos, life, moral and ethical reasoning, suffering, sickness, death, and other philosophical issues that influence how its members perceive their world.[7]

Most experts agree that religions have endured because they perform a variety of essential needs. Haviland offers a summary of those needs when he notes:

> All religions serve a number of important psychological and social needs. They reduce anxiety by explaining the unknown and making it understandable, as well provide comfort with the belief super-natural aid is available in times of crisis. They sanction a wide range of human conduct by providing notions of right and wrong, setting precedents for accepting behavior, and transferring the burden of decision making from individuals to supernatural powers. Through ritual, religion may be used to enhance the learning of oral traditions. Finally, religion plays an important role in maintaining social solidarity.[8]

Religion has been an important element in the shaping of collective identities in the world in the past. It is again returning to center stage,

5 C.M. Parkes, P. Laungani, and B. *Young, Death and Bereavement Accross Cultures* (New York: Routledge, 1997), 14–15, quoted in Samovar and Porter, 31.

6 S. Nanda and R.L. *Warms, Cultural Anthropology, 6th ed.* (Belmont, CA: Wadsworth, 1998), 6, quoted In Samovar and Porter, 87.

7 Samover and Porter, 85.

8 W. A. Haviland, *Cultural Anthropology*, Belmont, CA: Wadsworth, 2002, 361.

replacing ideologies in a globalized and what is perceived to be an unstable world. It is evident that religion and faith are not going to drift away into a privatized world as many atheists and agnostics had predicted. Consequently, modern societies are going to be increasingly confronted with minority groups demanding recognition of their religious identity and accommodation of their cultural differences. Thus, the new approach to international order and to the safeguarding of societies includes taking seriously the resurgence of religion in all its diversity. It is important to stress that most religions advocate values based on justice and tolerance which can contribute to the eradication of intolerance against religions or beliefs.[9] Most known religions advocate non-discrimination, fraternity, and mutual respect. Moreover, many ideals and values upheld by religions are shared by non-religious beliefs.

The best way to foster cohesive relationships between the dominant culture and the myriad of simultaneously existing co-cultures is the acceptance that human rights are not fictions conferred by governments but are inherent features of our nature as human beings. And while it is clear that "our knowledge and understanding of human rights are relatively modern, human rights themselves are as old as humanity."[10] This view maintains that there is a set of values, standards, morals, and the like that weave their way in and out of every culture. Although there are cultural differences regarding specific ethical behavior that cannot be condoned, there are nevertheless universal codes of conduct that one must believe in which applies to all people and all cultures. In short, one can develop a universal ethic that also grants the relativistic nature of cultures. None likes to be diminished. Everyone wants some level of respect, dignity, and a feeling of worth. An ethical

9 Boyle Kevin, *Chapter III: Models of National or Local Action to Prevent or Combat Intolerance of Religion or Belief*, United Nations Seminar on the Encouragement of Understanding, Tolerance and Respect in Matters Relating to Freedom of Religion or Belief, Geneva, Switzerland 3–14 Dec. 1984, HR/Geneva/1984/CRP, 4–6.

10 R. Grant, *The Social Contract and Human Rights*, (The Humanism, 2000) 18, quoted in Samovar and Porter, 12.

stance gives this respect to every human being.[11] However, on a more universal scale, it is best to turn to the basic aims of the United Nations, as proclaimed in the Charter[12], which is to protect the dignity and worth of the human person by promoting and encouraging respect for human rights and fundamental freedoms, without distinction as to race, sex, language or religion.[13]

1.1 International Instruments for the Protection of Freedom of Religion or Belief

Except for prohibiting the discrimination of persons on religious grounds, the United Nations Charter does not deal specifically with religious rights. However, one of the first acts of the United Nations, in 1945, was to instruct its Human Rights Commission to draw up a set of principles that all member states could pledge to implement. Eventually, the "International Bill of Rights", emerged with the 1948 Universal Declaration of Human Rights (the Universal Declaration)[14], the 1966 International Covenant on Economic, Social and Cultural Rights (ICESCR)[15], and the 1966 International Covenant on Civil and Political Rights (ICCPR)[16]. These three instruments are considered the

11 See: Samovar and Porter, 12–23.

12 *Charter* of the *United Nations*, 24 October 1945. 1 *U.N.T.S* 16 (entered into force 24 Oct. 1945), article. 1.

13 Ibid., *art.* 55.

14 *Universal Declaration of Human Rights*, G.A. res. 217A (III), U.N. Doc A/810 at 71 (1948).

15 *International Covenant on Economic, Social and Cultural Rights*, G.A. res. 2200A (XXI), 21 U.N.GAOR Supp. (No. 16) at 49, U.N. Doc. A/6316 (1966), 993 U.N.T.S. 3, *entered into force* Jan. 3, 1976.

16 *International Covenant on Civil and Political Rights*, G.A. res. 2200A (XXI), 21 U.N. GAOR Supp. (No. 16) at 52, U.N. Doc. A/6316 (1966), 999 U.N.T.S. 171, *entered into force* Mar. 23, 1976.

core norms that protect freedom of thought, conscience and religion. The issue of minority group rights, although not completely ignored, was not addressed in the early United Nations texts mainly because several member states were dealing with minority problems.[17] However, the adoption of these instruments has helped to eliminate various forms of religious discrimination and intolerance. They have set new standards in response to the additional protection requirement of vulnerable population groups such as women, children, and minorities.[18]

In addition to the above mentioned instruments, there is one major international effort to explain the underlying rights protected under the concept of religion or belief and that was done in the 1981 Declaration on the Elimination of All Forms of Intolerance and of Discrimination Based on Religion or Belief (Religion Declaration).[19] The Religion Declaration is considered "the most important global instrument regarding religious rights. It is not binding, but it implies an expectation of observance."[20] Another important instrument is the 1993 Declaration on the Rights of Persons Belonging to National or Ethnic, Religious and Lin-

17 Lerner Natan, *'The Nature and Minimum Standards of Freedom of Religion or Belief'*, 66, in Tore Lindholm, W. Cole Durham, Jr., Bahia G. Tahzib-Lie (eds.), *Facilitating Freedom of Religion or Belief: A Deskbook*, (hereinafter A Deskbook), Koninklijke Brill NV, Netherlands, 2004.

18 Kabasakal Arat, Zehra F., 'Forging A Global Culture of Human Rights: Origins and Prospects of the International Bill of Rights', *Human Rights Quarterly*, 28.2 (2006), 417. Tahzib, Bahiyyih G, *Freedom of Religion or Belief, Ensuring Effective International Legal protection*, The Hague, 1995.

19 *Declaration on the Elimination of All Forms of Intolerance and of Discrimination Based on Religion or Belief*, G.A. Res. 36/55, U.N. GAOR, 36th Sess., Supp. No. 51, at 171, U.N. Doc. A/36/684 (1981).

20 Natan Lerner, in *A Deskbook*, 73. Many see that there is a need for a convention regarding freedom of religion or belief, as observed by Benito "the adoption of the 1981 declaration, however important, should not represent the limits of the international community's aspiration with regard to the complex task of eliminating religious persecution and manifestations of religious prejudice." See: Beneito Odio E., Special Rapporteur of the Sub-Commission on Prevention of Discrimination and Protection of Minorities, *Seminar on the Encouragement of Understanding, Tolerance, and Respect in Matters Relating to Freedom of Religion or belief*, 3–14 December, HR/GENEVA/1984/BP.

guistic Minorities (Minority Declaration)[21]. It addresses the special rights of minorities including religious minorities and it ensures the rights of persons belonging to minorities to maintain and develop their own identity and characteristics and the corresponding obligations of states. This declaration at the same time safeguards the territorial integrity and political independence of a state as a whole.

Moreover, it is important to take into account all other relevant international instruments that have been adopted at the universal or regional level and those concluded between individual States members of the United Nations such as: the Convention on the Prevention and Punishment of the Crime of Genocide, the International Convention on the Elimination of All Forms of Racial Discrimination (CERD), the Convention on the Rights of the Child (CRD), The Convention on the Elimination of All Forms of Discrimination against Women (CEDAW), The International Labor Organization (ILO) Conventions, European Convention on Human Rights, American Convention on Human Rights, Arab Charter on Human Rights[22], etc.

1.1.1 The Universal Declaration of Human Rights

The Universal Declaration of Human Rights (Universal Declaration) is considered the foundation of fundamental human rights standards. It outlines the conditions necessary to guarantee dignity to all humans[23] and it is a legally authoritative source of determining the limits and

21 *Declaration on the Rights of Persons Belonging to National or Ethnic, Religious or Linguistic Minorities, G.A. res. 47/135, annex, 47 U.N. GAOR Supp. (No. 49) at 210, U.N. Doc. A/47/49 (1993).*

22 League of Arab States, Revised Arab Charter on Human Rights, May 22, 2004, *reprinted in* 12 Int'l Hum. Rts. Rep. 893 (2005), *entered into force* March 15, 2008. Available online via University of Minnesota: http://www1.umn.edu/humanrts/instree/loas2005.html?msource=UNWDEC19001&tr=y&auid=3337655 (viewed Sept. 2013).

23 Walker, Scott; Poe, Steven C., *'Does Cultural Diversity Affect Countries' Respect for Human Rights?', Human Rights Quarterly*, 24.1 (2002), 238.

scope of lawful relations between individuals and states. It provides a remedy against abuses of power by states. At the same time, it was the first step in the process of detailing an international system for the protection of freedom of religion or belief. In order to understand the nature of the right to freedom of thought, conscience, and religion, one cannot do better than take as a basis Article 18 of the Universal Declaration. This seminal article "is considered the core standard agreed on by states."[24] It stipulates:

> Everyone has the right to freedom of thought, conscience and religion; this right includes freedom to change his religion or belief, and freedom, either alone or in community with others and in public or private, to manifest his religion or belief in teaching, practice, worship and observance.

Article 18 greatly influenced the 1966 International Covenant on Economic, Social and Cultural Rights (ICESCR), the 1966 Covenant on Civil and Political Rights (ICCPR), regional treaties, and the Declaration on the Elimination of All Forms of Intolerance and of Discrimination Based on Religion or Belief (The Religion Declaration).

Right after the adoption of the Universal Declaration, most authors emphasized its legally non-binding character. They considered it merely the outline of a "human rights project," which became the starting point for the contemporary human rights protection that is now firmly established in a wide range of legally binding conventions.[25] However, many United Nations' experts have emphasized the legally binding nature of the Universal Declaration.[26]

24 Boyle Kevin; Sheen Juliet, *Freedom of Religion and Belief, A World Report*, Routledge, London, 1997, 4.

25 Walter, Kälin, *The Face of Human Rights: What are Human rights?*, Lars Müller Publishers, Baden, Switzerland, 2004, 14.

26 De Jong, Cornelis D., *The Freedom of Thought, Conscience and Religion or Belief in the United Nations* (1946–1992), Intersentia, Oxford, 2000, 38–41.

1.1.2 The International Covenant on Civil and Political Rights

The International Covenant on Civil and Political Rights (ICCPR) is presently the only binding treaty specifically containing a coherent articulation of religious rights. Articles 18, 19, 20, and 27 of the ICCPR are relevant to religious rights. Article 18 (1) of the ICCPR tracks the language in Article 18 of the Universal Declaration with minor changes, as Article 18 of the ICCPR does not explicitly refer to the right to change one's religion. Most specialists interpret the Covenant's article 18 as fully recognizing the right to change religion, as proclaimed by the Universal Declaration. Article 18(1) of the ICCPR provides that:

> 1. Everyone shall have the right to freedom of thought, conscience and religion. This right shall include freedom to have or to adopt a religion or belief of his choice, and freedom, either individually or in community with others and in public or private, to manifest his religion or belief in worship, observance, practice and teaching.

Article 18(2) prohibits 'coercion': No one shall be subject to coercion which would impair his freedom to have or to adopt a religion or belief of his choice.

Article 18 (3) deals with limitations on the freedom to manifest one's religion or belief:

> Freedom to manifest one's religion or beliefs may be subject only to such limitation as are prescribed by law and are necessary to protect public safety, order, health, or morals or the fundamental rights and freedoms of others.

Article 18(4) deals with parental rights in the field of education. States are obliged to respect the liberty of parents, and, when applicable, legal guardians to ensure the religious and moral education of their children in conformity with their own convictions, subject to providing protection for the rights of each child to freedom of religion or belief consistent with the evolving capacities of the child.[27]

27 Article 14 of the *Convention of the Right of the Child* (CRC) adapts article 18(4): 1. States Parties shall respect the right of the child to freedom of thought, conscience and religion.

Although international law adequately addresses racial discrimination, there remains a strongly felt need to protect religious groups from discrimination, persecution, and incitement. Lerner notes that

> [i]nternational and domestic law must also address the defamation and libel of groups or of persons belonging to a group for their membership in the group even though such defamation and libel are less dramatic than physical persecution.[28]

In the international instruments, there are provisions to protect religious groups; the most important is Article 20(2). It imposes upon states, that are parties to the ICCPR, the duty to prohibit by law the advocacy of religious hatred that incites discrimination, hostility, or violence. Many states objected and entered reservations to Article 20(2) seeing in it a limitation on Article 19 of the ICCPR which deals generally with freedom of expression.[29] However, the Human Rights Committee (HRC), in its General Comment on Article 20, stressed Article 20(2)'s mandatory character and full compatibility with freedom of expression.[30] Thus the developing trend is "to make the prohibition of

---

2. States Parties shall respect the rights and duties of the parents and, when applicable, legal guardians, to provide direction to the child in the exercise of his or her right in a manner consistent with the evolving capacities of the child.
3. Freedom to manifest one's religion or beliefs may be subject only to such limitations as are prescribed by law and are necessary to protect public safety, order, health or morals, or the fundamental rights and freedoms of others.

28 Lerner, in *A Deskbook*, 78.

29 Ibid, 71.

30 Human Rights Committee, General Comment 11, Article 20 (Nineteenth session, 1983), Compilation of General Comments and General Recommendations Adopted by Human Rights Treaty Bodies, U.N. Doc. HRI/GEN/1/Rev.1 at 12 (1994), Para 2 states: Article 20 of the Covenant states that any propaganda for war and any advocacy of national, racial or religious hatred that constitutes incitement to discrimination, hostility or violence shall be prohibited by law. In the opinion of the Committee, these required prohibitions are fully compatible with the right of freedom of expression as contained in article 19, the exercise of which carries with it special duties and responsibilities. The prohibition under paragraph 1 extends to all forms of propaganda threatening or resulting in an act of aggression or breach of the peace contrary to the Charter of the United Nations, while paragraph 2 is directed against any advocacy of national, racial or

religious discrimination, like the prohibition of racial discrimination, a peremptory norm of international law or, in other words, *jus cogens*."[31]

The protection of religious minorities' rights could be drawn from Article 27 and 26 of ICCPR. Article 26 specifies the right of non-discrimination on the basis of religion or belief.[32] Article 27 of the ICCPR, grants to minorities the right to national, ethnic, religious or linguistic identity, or a combination thereof, and to preserve the characteristics which they wish to maintain and develop. Article 26, together with Article 27, ensures that religious minorities are not persecuted or discriminated against. Article 27 does not call for special measures to be adopted by states, but states that have ratified the Covenant are obliged to ensure that all individuals under their jurisdiction enjoy their rights. Article 27 stipulates that:

> In those States in which ethnic, religious or linguistic minorities exist, persons belonging to such minorities shall not be denied the right, in community with the other members of their group, to enjoy their own culture, to profess and practice their own religion, or to use their own language.

However, freedom of religion or belief would not be complete without the right of non-discrimination on the basis of religion or belief.[33] Discrimination affects every aspect of people's lives: it leads to exclusion and marginalization. The principles of equality and non-discrimination are

religious hatred that constitutes incitement to discrimination, hostility or violence, whether such propaganda or advocacy has aims which are internal or external to the State concerned. The provisions of article 20, paragraph 1, do not prohibit advocacy of the sovereign right of self-defense or the right of peoples to self-determination and independence in accordance with the Charter of the United Nations. For article 20 to become fully effective there ought to be a law making it clear that propaganda and advocacy as described therein are contrary to public policy and providing for an appropriate sanction in case of violation. The Committee, therefore, believes that States parties which have not yet done so should take the measures necessary to fulfil the obligations contained in article 20, and should themselves refrain from any such propaganda or advocacy.

31 Lerner, 78.

32 Jong, 255.

33 Ibid., 211–248.

central to any system of human rights protection. When based on grounds such as race, sex, religion or belief, it has the status of *jus cogens*.[34] The Covenant contains two all-important provisions on non-discrimination. Articles 2 and 26 prohibit discrimination on grounds of religion.

Article 2 relates to the obligation to ensure the rights recognized in the Covenant to all individuals without discrimination:

> Each State Party to the present Covenant undertakes to respect and to ensure to all individuals within its territory and subject to its jurisdiction the rights recognized in the present Covenant, without distinction of any kind, such as race, colour, sex, language, religion, political or other opinion, national or social origin, property, birth or other status.

Article 2 provides for an accessory right, meaning that it can only be violated in conjunction with some other substantive provision of the Covenant. Article 26, in the other hand, is not similarly accessory in nature and can be applied independently because it contains a free-standing prohibition of discrimination:

> All persons are equal before the law and are entitled without any discrimination to the equal protection of the law. In this respect, the law shall prohibit any discrimination and guarantee to all persons equal and effective protection against discrimination on any ground such as race, colour, sex, language, religion, political or other opinion, national or social origin, property, birth or other status.

Article 26, which is inspired by Article 7 of the Universal Declaration, offers protection against discrimination concerning all legal rights, irrespective of whether these rights represent human rights or fundamental freedoms.[35] The HRC gave an authoritative interpretation in General Comment 18[36]:

> While article 2 limits the scope of the rights to be protected against discrimination to those provided for in the Covenant, article 26 does not specify such limitations. That is to say, article 26 provides that all persons are equal before the law and are entitled to equal protection of the law without discrimination, and that the law

34 Ibid, 211.
35 Ibid, 219.
36 General Comment no. 18(37th), para. 12.

shall guarantee to all persons equal and effective protection against discrimination on any of the enumerated grounds. In the view of the Committee, article 26 does not merely duplicate the guarantee already provided for in article 2 but provides in itself an autonomous right. It prohibits discrimination in law or in fact in any field regulated and protected by public authorities. Article 26 is therefore concerned with the obligations imposed on States parties in regard to their legislation and the application thereof. Thus, when legislation is adopted by a State party, it must comply with the requirement of article 26 that its content should not be discriminatory. In other words, the application of the principle of non-discrimination contained in article 26 is not limited to those rights which are provided for in the Covenant.

Moreover, the ICCPR tasks the UN Human Rights Committee with working to ensure increased compliance with the provisions of the ICCPR. The HRC also gave considerable attention to freedom of religion or belief, as evident by the issuance of the General Comment 22, in 1993.[37] The Human Rights Committee General Comment No. 22 on Article 18 of the ICCPR should be viewed as an authoritative interpretation of the scope of Article 18.[38] Moreover, individuals have the opportunity to appeal directly to the HRC when their rights under the ICCPR are violated and when they have taken all possible steps to obtain a remedy through domestic law and institutions. The first Optional Protocol[39] to the ICCPR aims to enable the HRC to receive and consider communications from individuals claiming to be victims of violations of any of the rights set forth in the ICCPR. Thus, individuals who claim that their rights and freedoms have been violated may call the State in question to account for its actions – if it is a party to the Optional Protocol to the ICCPR.[40] The first Optional Protocol follows logically

37 Human Rights Committee, General Comment 22 (1994), art. 18, UN Doc. HRI/GEN/1/Rev.1 at 35.

38 U.N. Doc and regional documents and others are available online at: <http://www1.umn.edu/humanrts/> (viewed Sept. 2013).

39 Optional Protocol to the International Covenant on Civil and Political Rights, G.A. res. 2200A (XXI), 21 U.N. GAOR Supp. (No. 16) at 59, U.N. Doc. A/6316 (1966), 999 U.N.T.S. 302, *entered into force* March 23, 1976.

40 First Optional Protocol to the International Covenant on Civil and Political Rights, Overview of procedure, <http://www.ohchr.org/english/bodies/hrc/procedure.htm>.

from Article 2 of the ICCPR, which obliges state parties to put in place measures that will give effect to the rights it guarantees and afford remedies where they are violated. To ensure this, Article 2 stipulates that persons who believe their rights have been violated should be able to lay claims before competent judicial, administrative and legal authorities, and that where remedies are granted they should be enforced.

In this way, the ICCPR provides a set of benchmarks against which the growth or degeneration of domestic law and practices may be measured.

1.1.3 The International Covenant on Economic, Social and Cultural Rights

Article 13 of the International Covenant on Economic, Social and Cultural Rights (ICESCR) ensures the right of everyone to education. Education shall be directed to the full development of the human personality and the sense of its dignity. It shall strengthen the respect for human rights and fundamental freedom. States parties to the Covenant further agree that education shall enable all persons to participate effectively in a free society, promote understanding, tolerance, and friendship among all nations of the maintenance of peace. Article 13 recognizes the fundamental role of parents in directing their children's education. States' parties undertake to have respect for the liberty of parents and legal guardians "to ensure the religious and moral education of their children in conformity with their own convictions".

Article 13(3) provides:

> The States Parties to the present Covenant undertake to have respect for the liberty of parents and, when applicable, legal guardians to choose for their children schools, other than those established by the public authorities, which conform to such minimum educational standards as may be laid down or approved by the State and to ensure the religious and moral education of their children in conformity with their own convictions.

1.1.4 Declaration on the Elimination of All Forms of Intolerance and of Discrimination Based on Religion or Belief 1981

The Declaration on the Elimination of All Forms of Intolerance and of Discrimination Based on Religion or Belief (Religion Declaration) is the most comprehensive international statement of the right to freedom of religion and belief. It contains eight articles, three of which (1, 5, 6) define specific rights. The remaining articles act in a supportive role by outlining measures to promote tolerance or prevent discrimination. Taken together, the eight articles constitute a paradigm, an overall concept, to advocate for tolerance and to prevent discrimination based on religion or belief. While human rights are individual rights, the 1981 UN Declaration also identifies certain rights related to states, religious institutions, parents, legal guardians, children, and groups of persons.

The Religion Declaration is a non-binding declaration, and does not have a treaty mechanism. Instead, it has an extra-conventional mechanism. The UN Commission on Human Rights appointed, in resolution 1986/20, an independent expert for the Religion Declaration with the title of 'Special Rapporteur on religious intolerance'.

However, in 2000, the Commission on Human Rights decided to change the mandate title to 'Special Rapporteur on freedom of religion or belief', which was subsequently endorsed by ECOSOC decision 2000/261 and welcomed by General Assembly resolution 55/97.

On 14 December 2007, the Human Rights Council extended, in resolution 6/37 the mandate of the Special Rapporteur for a further period of three years The Special Rapporteur on freedom of religion or belief is an independent expert appointed by the UN Human Rights Council. S/he is invited to identify existing and emerging obstacles to the enjoyment of the right to freedom of religion or belief and present recommendations on ways and means to overcome such obstacles. The Special Rapporteur's mandate includes:

- to promote the adoption of measures at the national, regional and international levels to ensure the promotion and protection of the right to freedom of religion or belief;

- to identify existing and emerging obstacles to the enjoyment of the right to freedom of religion or belief and present recommendations on ways and means to overcome such obstacles;
- to continue her/his efforts to examine incidents and governmental actions that are incompatible with the provisions of the Declaration on the Elimination of All Forms of Intolerance and of Discrimination Based on Religion or Belief and to recommend remedial measures as appropriate;
- to continue to apply a gender perspective, inter alia, through the identification of gender-specific abuses, in the reporting process, including in information collection and in recommendations.

The Religion Declaration is not obligatory. However,

> [...] it contains widely accepted international standards (and) some of those provisions are customary international law, and a few should be seen as *jus cogens*, namely a rule which cannot be altered except by the will of the international community as a whole.[41]

1.2 The Scope of Freedom of Religion or Belief

Worldwide, there is a big variety of religions, sects, cults, philosophies, and other forms of belief. There is also a significant variety of relationships between these religions or beliefs and the state.[42] Krishnaswami classifies countries broadly into three categories: those which have an established Church or state religion, those in which several religions are recognized by the state, and those in which the State and religion are separate.[43] Ghanea points out that,

41 Lerner, in *A Deskbook*, 82.

42 Evans, Carolyn, *Freedom of Religion Under the European Convention On Human Rights*, Oxford Echer Series, Oxford, 2000, 19.

43 Arcot Krishnaswami, *Study of Discrimination in the Matter of Religious Rights and Practices*, E/CN.4/Sub.2/200/Rev.1 (United Nations 1960).

> [...] those countries that provide for 'separation' of religion do so in different formats and to different effects. This can range from the benign neutrality in the USA, through the various types of laïcité or secularism, to the harsh separation that existed in the former socialist bloc regimes. Countries that allow for various degrees of 'establishment' of religion may make legal provisions for significant cooperation with, and financial support of, religious institutions.[44]

International standards do not require the separation of religion and state. Therefore, "many countries do posit a relationship between the political community, which is the state, its institutions and administration and a current or historically predominant religion of its citizens, such as Islamic countries."[45] However, the fact that a certain religion is recognized as an official, traditional or state religion or that its adherents comprise the majority of the population must not result in any discrimination against followers of other faiths or nonbelievers. It has to be remembered that despite the various religious demographics and the perception of the proper relationship between the state and religion or belief, almost all UN member states have adopted constitutional or statuary provisions prohibiting discrimination on the basis of religion and allowing for freedom of religion.[46] Also, all states should recall their obligations to ensure that all persons enjoy their rights to freedom of religion, without any discrimination based on their religion, in accordance with article 26 of the ICCPR.

Increasing diversity in societies, as mentioned above, makes new demands on national policies for tackling intolerance, racism and discrimination of minorities and as religious identities are on the rise, religious discrimination and intolerance is increasing. Protecting minorities was an important aspect in the development of general human rights and still is. However, difficulties exist with regard to religious minorities. In addition to provisions protecting freedom of religion, most international instruments, as shown above, include a prohibition

44 The Editors with Nazila Ghanea, 'The Renewed Salience of Religion and Freedom of Religion or Belief', in *A Deskbook*, xxvii–lxxiv.

45 Boyle & Sheen, 10.

46 Evans Carolyn, 22.

of discrimination on grounds of religion. To ensure the enjoyment of religion and belief the individual must be free from discrimination on the ground of religion and belief in all areas of public life including employment and education especially that, under international instruments, the guarantee of religious freedom is non-derogable under any circumstances, including during times of war.

Despite the fact that freedom of religion is a fundamental right, however, there is no generally accepted definition of 'religion' in international human rights law. Generally, 'religion' followed by the word 'belief' is taken to refer to theistic convictions involving a transcendental view of the universe and a normative code of behavior as well as atheistic, agnostic, rationalistic, and other views in which such elements are absent. 'Beliefs' in this context always relate to 'religious' beliefs, not political or social beliefs that are protected by other substantive human rights provisions.

1.2.1 Defining Religion

The problem with the international instruments, such as the Universal Declaration, the ICCPR, and the Religion Declaration is that they give little guidance or any detailed explanation of what the word religion entailes.[47] Therefore, one reason for the continuing religious ten-

47 Even Krishnasswami did not define religion in his study. (See: E/CN.4/Sub.2/192: 36, para 90). The study of Krishnasswami is considered an important step in the United Nation's identification and protection of religious freedoms, established principles that the Sub-Commission later adopted, and which had considerable influence on future documents. There are many international and regional human rights instruments guarantee rights related to freedom of religion or belief, however, none attempts to define the term "religion." See, e.g.: International Covenant on Civil and Political Rights, art. 18, G.A. Res. 2200A (XXI), U.N. GAOR, 21st Sess., Supp. No. 16, at 51, U.N. Doc. A/6316 (1966); Convention Relating to the Status of Refugees (July 28, 1951), arts. 1 & 4, 19 U.S.T. 6259, 189 U.N.T.S. 137 [hereinafter 1951 Refugee Convention]; Protocol Relating to the Status of Refugees (Jan. 31, 1976), 19 U.S.T. 6223, 606 U.N.T.S. 267;

sions is that it has been difficult to achieve any universally accepted definition of religion.[48] The level of debates that the issue has generated in the United Nations makes it "difficult to claim that the drafters had a common intention in their use of the words."[49] Thus, the term "religion" remains undefined as a matter of international law. A major problem that resulted from not defining religion, as seen by Evans, is that "there (will) always (be) a danger in attempting to apply a concept as complex and controversial as religious freedom, that those charged with applying it will simply draw on their own experiences or notions of 'common sense' and thus give deference to systems of belief with which they are familiar or comfortable, but fail to adequately protect that which seems foreign or strange."[50]

Since 'religion' is difficult to define in legal terms, the best solution for the founders of human rights was "to avoid philosophical and ideological controversy."[51] Instead, "international and human rights law have

---

International Covenant on Economic, Social, and Cultural Rights, art. 2, G.A. Res. 2200A (XXI), U.N. GAOR, 21st Sess., Supp. No. 16, at 49, U.N. Doc. A/6316 (1966); European Convention for the Protection of Human Rights and Fundamental Freedoms (Apr. 11, 1950), art. 9, 213 U.N.T.S. 222; American Convention on Human Rights (Nov. 22, 1969), art. 12, 1144 U.N.T.S. 123; African Charter of Human Rights and People's Rights (June 27, 1981), art. 8, O.A.U. Doc. CAB/LEG/67/3/Rev.5 (1986), reprinted in 21 I.L.M. 58 (1982).

48 The definition of religion in the Shorter Oxford English Dictionary, has frequently been referred to in legal decisions since the middle of the sixteenth century: "Recognition on the part of man of some higher unseen power as having control of his destiny, and as being entitled to obedience, reverence and worship; the general mental and moral attitude resulting from this belief, with reference to its effect upon the individual or the community; personal or general acceptance of this feeling as a standard of spiritual and practical life.

49 Evans, Carolyn, 51.

50 Ibid., 18. However, Donna J. Sullivan considers the omission of definitions of religion and belief proves to be more conducive to the protection of freedom of religion or belief than would any definitions that could be agreed upon. Check her reasons in: Sullivan, Donna J., *Advancing the Freedom of Religion or Belief Through the UN Declaration on the Elimination of Religious Intolerance and Discrimination*, The American Journal of International Law, Vol. 82, 1988, pp. 487–520.

51 Lerner, in *A Deskbook*, 65.

prescribed a catalog of rights and the means of protecting those rights, under the agreed heading of 'freedom of thought, conscience, and religion,' rather than defining the freedoms themselves."[52] Thus, the legal definitions of 'religion' generally appear in the contexts of either: (a) protecting freedom of religion, or (b) prohibiting discrimination (or persecution) of religion. Gunn affirms this point and explains that,

> [t]hese legal definitions do not simply describe the phenomenon of religion, they establish rules for regulating social and legal relations among people who themselves may have a sharply different attitude about what religion is and which manifestations of it are entitled to protection.[53]

Religion, according to Gunn, has three different facets that are of particular importance: religion as *belief*, religion as *a way of life*, and religion as an *identity*:[54]

A. Religion as a *belief* pertains to the convictions that people hold regarding such matters as God, truth, or doctrines of faith. From the perspective of the person who is persecuting or discriminating, the religious beliefs of others are likely to be characterized in such terms such as 'heresy', 'blasphemy', 'apostasy' etc. The clearest examples of persecution for 'false' beliefs are encompassed within the accusation of apostasy against those who convert from one religion to another. There also can be cases where groups as a whole may be considered heretics and suffer persecution, even though they are of the same general ethnicity as their persecutors.[55]
B. Religion as *a way of life* is "associated with actions, rituals, customs, and traditions that may distinguish the believer from adherents of other religions. For example, religion as a way of life may motivate people to live in monasteries or religious communities or to ob-

52 Ibid.
53 Gunn, T. Jeremy, *'The Complexity of Religion and the Definition of "Religion" in International Law'*, Harvard Human Rights Journal, Vol. 16, spring 2003, (hereinafter The Complexity of religion).
54 Gunn, *The Complexity of Religion*, 200.
55 Ibid.

serve many rituals."[56] Religion, in this sense, "is not only a state of mind and it should not be treated as principally belief and principally private as to a modern privatized Christian, but rather for others, like Muslims, it is 'a constituting activity in the world.'"[57] That means it is the salient aspect of their lives. It may demand prayers five times a day, refusal to eat meat and the wearing of certain types of clothes. In this facet, "religion is perhaps the most comprehensive of all human activities."[58]

C. While religion as belief emphasizes doctrines, religion as *identity* emphasizes affiliation with a group. In this sense, religion as identity is experienced as something akin to family, ethnicity, race, or nationality. Religion as identity thus is something which people are born into rather than something to which they have converted to after a process of study, prayer, or reflection. Identity religion, in this basic form, understands co-religionists to be a part of the same group (perhaps even regardless of their personal beliefs). Religion as identity is less likely to emphasize shared theological beliefs and more likely to emphasize shared histories, cultures, ethnicity, and traditions. The classic study of prejudice pointed that,

> The chief reason why religion becomes the focus of prejudice is that it usually stands for more than faith; it is the pivot of the cultural tradition of a group. However sublime the origins of a religion may be, it rapidly becomes secularized by taking over cultural functions.[59]

For example, Islam is more than a religion; it is a well-knit cluster of related cultures carried by ethnic cousins who are sharply demarcated from the non-Muslim world. Christianity, on the other hand, is so locked with western civilization that it is hard to keep in mind

56 Talal Asad, 'Genealogies of Religion: Discipline and Reason of Power in Christianity and Islam', 47 (1993), quoted in Gunn, *The Complexity of Religion*, 304.
57 Ibid.
58 Leonard J. Swidler, 'Religious Liberty and Human Rights in Nations and in Religions', vii (1986), quoted in Gunn, *The Complexity of Religion*, 204.
59 Gordon W. Allport, 'The Nature of Prejudice', 446 (Addison-Wesley Pub. Co. 1979) (1954), quoted in Gunn, *The Complexity of Religion*, 203.

its original core; and sects of Christianity have become tied into sub cultural and national groups so that religious divisions march hand in hand with ethnic and national divisions. Most clear of all is the case of the Jews. While they are primarily a religious group, they are likewise viewed as a race, a nation, a people, a culture. "When religious distinctions are made to do double duty, the grounds for prejudice are laid. For prejudice means that inept, over inclusive categories are employed in place of differentiated thinking."[60] Thus, Gunn concludes that

> [w]hile religion as *belief* is perhaps the most readily understandable facet of religion for the typical adjudicator, religion as *identity* is more likely to be the underlying cause of religious discrimination and persecution as it exists in the world.[61]

Even though, the notion of 'religion' is difficult to define in legal terms, Article 18 of the Universal Declaration includes: First, the right to freedom of thought, conscience, and religion, generally described as the *forum internum*. This includes the right to profess a religion or to profess none. Second, it addresses the right to manifest religion or belief which is described as *the external forum*. Third, it addresses the right to change religion or belief which is the right to conversion.

1.2.2 The Right to Have a Religion

The first part of Article 18 of the Universal Declaration guarantees everyone's right to freedom of thought, conscience, and religion. These freedoms of 'thought' and 'conscience' are closely associated with the freedom of 'religion'. Lerner notes that

> [i]t may be legitimate to consider the freedoms of conscience and religion as included in the freedom of thought. However, freedom of conscience was not

60 Ibid.
61 Gunn, *The Complexity of Religion*, 303–04.

universally considered a consolidated legal concept at the time of the drafting of article 18.[62]

This freedom, he notes, "is frequently discussed under the heading of "conscientious objection," not an exclusively religion-related issue."[63]

The Human Rights Committee (HRC), in its General Comment 22 on ICCPR Article 18, explains the content of this right and states that "the right to freedom of thought, conscience and religion is a far-reaching and profound; it encompasses freedom of thought on all matters, personal conviction and the commitment to religion or belief, whether manifested individually or in community with others." In this sense, the HRC has adopted a broad interpretation of 'freedom of religion or belief' covering freedom of theistic, non-theistic and atheistic beliefs and freedom not to subscribe to any of these beliefs. The Committee has made it clear that minority and non-mainstream religions are no less entitled to the protection of article 18 than majority and traditional religions.[64] Benito notes, "as a result of lengthy discussions

62 Lerner, in *A Deskbook*, 68.

63 Ibid.

64 Compilation of General Comments and General Recommendations Adopted by Human Rights Treaty Bodies, U.N. Doc. HRI\GEN\1\Rev.1 at 35 (1994) Para.1. Also, *General Comment 22, Para.2.* States: "Article 18 protects theistic, non-theistic and atheistic beliefs, as well as the right not to profess any religion or belief. The terms "belief" and "religion" are to be broadly construed. Article 18 is not limited in its application to traditional religions or to religions and beliefs with institutional characteristics or practices analogous to those of traditional religions. The Committee therefore views with concern any tendency to discriminate against any religion or belief for any reason, including the fact that they are newly established, or represent religious minorities that may be the subject of hostility on the part of a predominant religious community." United Nations Rapporteurs have also taken the view that religion or belief encompasses theistic, non-theistic and atheistic beliefs. *Boyle confirms* that "in international law, freedom of thought, conscience, religion and belief are highly interrelated freedoms and all must be protected. Protection is not limited to religion, but extends to non-theistic and atheistic beliefs as well as the right not to profess any belief." Boyle and Sheen, 5. *Cornelis* affirm the same point, "It is not recommended to break up the right to freedom of thought, conscience and religion into its constituent parts does not seem to be very fruitful. The very fact that the elements

in various international bodies, it is now generally accepted that "religion or belief" includes theistic, non-theistic, and atheistic beliefs."[65]

On the other hand, while favoring a broad interpretation of belief, the Committee is of the view that there are some limits to its breadth for the purpose of Article 18. This was illustrated in *M.A.B.; W.A.T. and A.Y.T. v Canada*, a 1993 communication to the Committee.[66] The authors of the communication were Canadians; they submitted that the actions of the Canadian authorities violated a number of their rights under the ICCPR, including the right to freedom of thought, conscience and religion in Article 18. The Committee concluded that the

---

are grouped together in all major human rights instruments makes it impossible to try to establish three separate rights. Moreover, the interaction between the various elements is most important: religion may have to be interpreted in a broader sense, since it has been linked to conscience and thought: by the same token, now that the notion of thought has been associated with conscience and religion, not all thoughts are to be included." De Jong, Cornelis D., *The Freedom of Thought, Conscience and Religion or Belief in the United Nations (1946–1992)*, Intersentia, Oxford, 2000, 22. One explanation to Article 18 came in the study commissioned by the Sub-Commission on Prevention of Discrimination and Protection of Minorities in 1954, Halpern agued that the formulation of Article 18 comprises the following: "…The right is not only to freedom of religious belief but also to freedom of thought and conscience. This includes the right to entertain a belief, which may be regarded as a system of philosophy rather than a formal religion. It also includes the right of the individual to adopt atheism as his belief." In the same line, Tahzib explains "Freedom of thought and conscience are read as supporting freedom of religion rather than as separate concepts worthy of independent analysis and development" Tahzib, Bahiyyih G, *Freedom of Religion or Belief, Ensuring Effective International Legal protection*, The Hague, 1995, 73. Also, See: T C Van Boven, Elimination of All Forms of Intolerance and Discrimination Based on Religion or Belief, UN Doc. E/CN.4/Sub.2/1989/32 1989, paragraph 5; E Odio Benito, Study of the Current Dimensions of the Problems of Intolerance and of Discrimination on Grounds of Religion or Belief, UN Doc. E/CN.4/Sub.2/ 1987/26 1986, paragraph 13, reprinted in Human Rights Study Series No.2, UN Sales No. E.89.XIV.3, 1989; A Krishnaswami, Study of Discrimination in the Matter of Religious Rights and Practices, UN Doc. E/CN.4/Sub.2/ 200/Rev.1, page 1 n.1, UN Sales No.60.XIV.2 (1960) .

65 Benito, HR/GENEVA/1984/BP. 2, Para, 13.

66 M.A.B.; W.A.T. *and* A.Y.T. v Canada, a 1993 communication to the Committee.

beliefs and practices of this organization did not fall within the scope of Article 18. The Committee pointed out that the expression of religion or belief does not encompass a belief which consists primarily or exclusively of the worship and distribution of a narcotic drug. While it is difficult to extract general principles from this decision, the Committee made it clear that the scope of religion or belief is not without limits. It imposed an element of objectivity by demonstrating that a situation does not automatically fall within religion or belief simply by assertion such as through the use of language such as Church, sacrament and so forth. At the same time, not every opinion is being protected, only those are of fundamental importance to one's way of living.[67]

Article 18 of the Universal Declaration and the ICCPR do not only protect the right to have a religion or belief but also the freedom to manifest that belief in practice and expression.

1.2.3 The Right to Manifest Religion or Belief

In describing the scope of the right to freedom of thought, conscience and religion, Article 18 of the Universal Declaration makes a distinction between "freedom to change religion or belief" on the one hand and "freedom, either alone or in community with others, and in public or in private, to manifest religion or belief in teaching, practice, worship and observance". While, the majority rights and freedoms set forth in the Universal Declaration take into consideration only the individual aspect, however, Article 18 explicitly affirms that freedom to manifest a religion or belief may be exercised either "alone" or "in a community with others". Kälin notes that

> [t]he freedom of religion or belief is an individual right with a strong collective component, which includes the right to exercise one's faith together with others; the right to find and establish a religious community; the right of such commu-

67 Jong, 7.

> nities to organize themselves and to appoint their leaders, to look for and admit new members, and to collect financial contributions from them. These rights can be limited under the same conditions as those of individual believers.[68]

Some activities of the freedom to manifest one's religion or belief are listed in Article 6 of the Religion Declaration. However, the listing of what constitutes the practice of a faith or belief was not intended to be exhaustive.[69] The manifestation of religion or belief may take the following forms:

- Right to worship, assemble, and to establish and maintain places of worship
- Right to establish and maintain appropriate charitable or humanitarian institutions
- Right to make, acquire and use materials related to rites and customs
- Right to write, issue and disseminate relevant publications in these areas
- Right to teach a religion or belief in places suitable for these purposes
- Right to solicit and receive voluntary financial and other contributions
- Right to train, appoint, elect or designate appropriate leaders
- Right to observe days of rest and celebrate holidays and ceremonies
- Right to establish and maintain communication with individuals and communities at national and international levels.

These elements are also mentioned in the Human Rights Committee, General Comment 22, which provides:

> The freedom to manifest religion or belief may be exercised 'either individually or in community with others and in public or private.' The freedom to manifest religion or belief in worship, observance, practice, and teaching encompasses a broad range of acts. It is important to stress that the concept of worship extends to ritual and ceremonial acts giving direct expression to belief, as well as various practices integral to such acts, including the building of places of worship, the use of ritual formulae and objects, the display of symbols, and the observance of holidays and days of rest. Hence, the observance and practice of religion or belief

68 Kälin, 2004, 405.
69 Boyle& Sheen, 7.

may include not only ceremonial acts but also such customs as the observance of dietary regulations, the wearing of distinctive clothing or head coverings, participation in rituals …, the freedom to establish seminaries or religious schools and the freedom to prepare and distribute religious texts or publications.[70]

The major concerns with this right that are usually raised are those regarding the need for legislation to protect the right to manifest religion and belief, especially since there are permissible restrictions on this right. While the international instruments call for unconditional protection of the "internal" right to freedom of religion, the 'external' right to manifest one's beliefs is subject to limitations. Article 18(3) subjects' manifestation of religion or belief to such limitations as are prescribed by law and are necessary to protect public safety, order, health, or morals or the fundamental rights and freedoms of others.

However, states often abuse this latitude and overstep the bounds of legitimate governmental interference in manifestations of religion and belief. In a number of cases "there are doubts whether these restrictions were really necessary for the protection of public safety, order, health, or morals, i.e., whether the proportionality test has been applied in an appropriate manner."[71] Thus, in a delicate area such as religious rights, Jong notes "limitations must be interpreted narrowly."[72] In order to achieve this, limitation must satisfy two essential criteria: it must be 'determined by law'" and it must be enforced solely for one or several of the purposes mentioned in the article. Thus, HRC in its General Comment 22, paragraph 8 observes that:

- "Article 18.3 permits restrictions on the freedom to manifest religion or belief only if limitations are prescribed by law and are necessary to protect public safety, order, health or morals, or the fundamental rights and freedoms of others."
- "The freedom from coercion to have or to adopt a religion or belief and the liberty of parents and guardians to ensure religious and moral education cannot be restricted."

70 General Comments 22, Para. 4.

71 Manfred Nowak and Tanja Vospernik, 'Permissible Restrictions on Freedom of Religion or Belief', in *A Deskbook*, Ch. 6, 171.

72 Jong, 85.

- "In interpreting the scope of permissible limitation clauses, states parties should proceed from the need to protect the rights guaranteed under the Covenant, including the right to equality and non-discrimination on all grounds specified in Articles 2, 3 and 26."
- "Limitations imposed must be established by law and must not be applied in a manner that would vitiate the rights guaranteed in Article 18."
- The limitation clause must be "strictly interpreted: restrictions are not allowed on grounds not specified there, even if they would be allowed as restrictions to other rights protected in the Covenant, such as national security."
- "Limitations may be applied only for those purposes for which they were prescribed and must be directly related and proportionate to the specific need on which they are predicated."
- "Restrictions may not be imposed for discriminatory purposes or applied in a discriminatory manner. The Committee observes that the concept of morals derives from many social, philosophical and religious traditions; consequently, limitations on the freedom to manifest a religion or belief for the purpose of protecting morals must be based on principles not deriving exclusively from a single tradition."

The burden of justifying a limitation upon the freedom to manifest one's religion or belief lies with the state. The chosen measures should promote religious tolerance and avoid stigmatizing any particularly religious community. Furthermore, the principles of appropriateness and proportionality need to be thoroughly respected both by the administration and during possible legal review. This is why Article 29[73] of the Universal Declaration of Human Rights, after setting forth the grounds on which limitations are permissible, uses the term "in a democratic society"; a term which should, of course, be construed as referring to a society in which human rights and fundamental freedoms are ensured.

73 *Article 29* "1. Everyone has duties to the community in which alone the free and full development of his personality is possible. 2.In the exercise of his rights and freedoms, everyone shall be subject only to such limitations as are determined by law solely for the purpose of securing due recognition and respect for the rights and freedoms of others and of meeting the just requirements of morality, public order and the general welfare in a democratic society. 3. These rights and freedoms may in no case be exercised contrary to the purposes and principles of the United Nations."

Article 30[74] of the Universal Declaration prohibits not only public authorities, but also "any group or person" from engaging in activities aimed at the destruction of a human right or fundamental freedom. The expression 'in democratic society'" in Article 29 in addition to Article 30 of the Universal Declaration may be said to constitute restrictions on the permissible limitations.[75] A limitation, thus, must be regarded as proportionate to the legitimate aim pursued, and, accordingly, as necessary in a democratic society.

1.2.4 Freedom to Change Religion or Belief

The Universal Declaration is the only UN instrument that explicitly recognizes the right to change religion. Article 18, states that: "this right includes freedom to change religion or belief." However, Article 18 of the ICCPR does not state this clearly. It differs from Article 18 of the

74 *Article 30* "Nothing in this Declaration may be interpreted as implying for any State, group or person any right to engage in any activity or to perform any act aimed at the destruction of any of the rights and freedoms set forth herein.

75 Jong, 81–62. Also, the European Convention on Human Rights (ECHR) lists the same conditions as the ICCPR as to acceptable limitations, with the addition that all restrictions must be "necessary in a democratic society." According to the European Court of Human Rights, in order to meet this requirement, any restriction must correspond to a "pressing social need" and must be "proportionate to the legitimate aim pursued." European Court of Human Rights, *Serif v. Greece*, December 12, 1999 (00038178/97).The court has observed that it does not only involve that a restrictive measure should be based on domestic law, but also that the law in question "should be both adequately accessible and foreseeable, that is, formulated with sufficient precision to enable the individual – if need be with appropriate advice – to regulate his conduct." *Hasan and Chaush v. Bulgaria*, October 26, 2000 (00030985/96). In the 1989 Concluding Document of Vienna, the OSCE states recognized that "the exercise [...] of the rights relating to the freedom of religion or belief may be subject only to such limitations as are provided by law and consistent with their obligations under international law and with international commitments. They will ensure in their laws and regulations and in their application the full and effective exercise of the freedom of thought, conscience, religion and belief." A similar statement was included in the 1990 Copenhagen Document. Copenhagen, 1990, para. 9.4.

Universal Declaration in that it speaks "of the freedom to have or to adopt a religion or belief of his choice' instead of 'the freedom to change one's religion or belief." The codification history of the Covenant also indicates that the freedom to adopt a religion or belief of one's choice should be broadly interpreted as to include the freedom to change one's religion or belief.[76] This is also the opinion of the HRC, in General Comment 22, as it observes that, "the freedom to 'have or to adopt' a religion or belief necessarily entails the freedom to choose a religion or belief, including the right to replace one's current religion or belief with another or to adopt atheistic views, as well as the right to retain one's religion or belief.'[77] Even though Article 1 of the Religion Declaration copies, to a large extent, the text of Article 18 of the ICCPR, its language contains textual differences where the right to change one's religion or belief is concerned. In the Religion Declaration, the reference to the right to adopt a religion or belief of one's choice has been deleted. Instead, it merely refers to the right 'to have a religion or whatever belief of his choice'. The Third Committee in 1981[78], after adopting this change of wording, has also adopted a general safety clause in Article 8 of the Religion Declaration which reads: 'Nothing in the present Declaration shall be construed as restricting or derogating from any right defined in the Universal Declaration of Human Rights and the International Covenant on Human Rights.' Benito, after examining the texts of the Universal Declaration, ICCPR, and the Religion Declaration concluded that: 'these provisions although they varied slightly in wording, all meant precisely the same thing. That everyone has the right to change one's religion or belief and to adopt another, or to remain without any at all."[79] In her view, "this meaning is implicit in the concept of the right to freedom of thought, conscience, religion, and belief, regardless of how that concept is presented."[80] The most practical argument

76 Jong, 47.
77 General Comment 22, Para. 5.
78 A/C.3/36/SR.43: Para. 40.
79 E. Odio Benito Report, E/CN.4/Sub.2/1987/26: p. 4. paras. 21, 201.
80 Ibid.

defending the right to change one's religion was used by the Netherlands, in 1973, when its representative stated that "freedom to change religion was a fundamental right, and it was better that men should have the right to change their beliefs than that they should be obliged to live in a lie."[81]

No limitations whatsoever on the freedom of thought and conscience or on the freedom to have or adopt a religion or belief of one's choice are permitted,[82] and that is what distinguishes them from the freedom to manifest religion or belief.

1.2.4.1 The Right to Change one's Religion in the Muslim States

Saudi Arabia's proposal to omit the phrase 'freedom to change religion or belief' and its abstention on the United Nations General Assembly (UNGA) vote to approve the Universal Declaration, is arguably the Muslim world's best known connection to the mid-century efforts to create international human rights standards.[83] Its attitude was mainly due to fear of the repercussions which such a provision would have upon the Muslim world. Baroody, the representative of Saudi Arabia, argued that such sentiments had led to crusades and religious wars, charging that "throughout history missionaries had often abused their rights by becoming the forerunners of a political intervention, and there were many instances where peoples had been drawn into murderous conflict by the missionaries' efforts to convert them."[84] Waltz explains that "It must not be forgotten that in the course of history missionaries had often abused their rights. Political propagandists were taking the place of religious missionaries, but the methods used varied little."[85]

Because of this abstention, some considered the text of Article 18 to run counter to Islamic precepts. Susan Waltz sees this as "unfortunate

81 A/C.3/SR2012, 202, quoted in Jong, 35.

82 General Comment 22, Para. 3.

83 Waltz, Susan, 'Universal Human Rights: The Contribution of Muslim States', *Human Rights Quarterly*, 26.4 (2004), 815.

84 Ibid.

85 Ibid.

for several reasons, mainly because the Saudi abstention led some to infer that Saudi Arabia was disengaged from the human rights project."[86] To the contrary, the Saudi representative was one of the few diplomats to have seen the Universal Declaration through, from the start of the Third Committee debates in 1948, to the end. Muslims role on other issues[87] such as gender equality in marriage, Waltz affirms that,

> It will perhaps come as a surprise to some readers that the Muslim world was not united on this issue, and at various moments, differences were aired in open forum. While most Muslim diplomats sought to limit gender equality, some strong voices advocating women's rights were also lifted from among representatives of the Muslim world, including delegations from Iraq and Pakistan.

It should be remembered that

> [...] some of the most difficult social issues faced by Western society at the time (such as divorce) were removed from or finessed in the text, with no great fanfare. If the Muslim concerns about changing religion had initially been handled in this manner, Saudi Arabia might have joined other Muslim states in casting its vote for the UDHR.[88]

Moreover, the attention to the Saudi abstention directs attention away from the substantial diversity of opinion among delegations from the Muslim world. The Saudi view, from the beginning, was not shared by all Muslim delegates. Indian delegate Mohammed Habib pointed out that the Indian constitution provided the right to convert or be converted, a provision that applied to the forty million Muslims of India.[89] Sir Mohammed Zafrullah Khan of Pakistan felt it necessary to explain that the teaching of Islam, and in this sense the Qur'an, stated that neither faith, nor conscience which gave birth to it, could have an obligatory character. The Qur'an expressly said, "Let he who chooses

86 Ibid., 816

87 Moreover, Muslims played an important role on other issues such as the issue of the right to Self-Determination, the "Colonial Clause", and the issue of measures of implementation and the right to petition.

88 Walz, 816.

89 Jong, 36.

to believe, believe, and he who chooses to disbelieve, disbelieve." [Islam] formally condemned not lack of faith, but hypocrisy.[90]

All Muslim states, other than Saudi Arabia, voted in favor of the Universal Declaration. However, the representative of Saudi Arabia did not contest the individual's freedom to change one's religion or belief. The Universal Declaration was adopted by forty-eight votes in favor, none against, and eight abstentions. Saudi Arabia, South Africa, and six Eastern European states abstained from voting. Egypt did register its objection to the freedom to change one's religion or belief clause in Article 18. Its objection was based on the same fear the Saudi Arabian delegation had and that is "the activities of missionaries in the Orient."

Freedom to change one's religion or belief is one of the thorny issues that is being used by some in the West to emphasize the incompatibility of Islam with the international human rights standards and whose efforts to stress the negative stereotypes of Muslim societies as being essentially backward and uncivilized. Unfortunately, Muslims have not been successful in overcoming "an image that is imposed on them"[91] by people not directly exposed to the work of Islam who have forgotten that "the protracted process of elaborating and negotiating the text of the provisions concerning freedom of religion is more an illustration of the rule than demonstration of an exception."[92] For example, in the Third Committee debate, Egypt expressed the view that economic, social, and cultural rights had become "an essential part of the structure of civilized society."[93] In its December 1950 plenary session, the UNGA affirmed these views, deciding to include socioeconomic rights in a single covenant by a vote of 35 to 9, with 7 abstentions. However this did not happen, because the US was resolved not to have socioeconomic rights included in the legally binding instrument. Hence, "con-

90 See: A/PV. 182: p. 890. A/C.3/SR.571, p. 152, para. 45 and A/C.3/SR.1024, p. 211, paras. 21–23, quoted in Jong, 37.

91 Hicks, Neil, 'Does Islamist Human Rights Activism Offer a Remedy to the Crisis of Human Rights Implementation in the Middle East?', *Human Rights Quarterly* 24.2 (2002), 374.

92 Waltz, 815.

93 Ibid.

structing and negotiating the international human rights standards involved stubbornness, demagoguery, and power plays as much as it did principled argument and legal reasoning."[94]

1.2.4.2 The Right to Non-coercion

The right to freedom of religion or belief is related to the right to non-coercion that impairs the freedom to have or adopt a religion or belief of one's choice (art. 18.2 of the ICCPR). The text does not define coercion[95] but coercion includes the use of threat of physical force or penal sanctions to compel believers or non-believers to adhere to their religious beliefs and congregations, to recant their religion or belief or convert.[96] Policies or practices having the same intention or effect, such as those restricting access to education, medical care, employment or the rights guaranteed by Article 25 and other provisions of ICCPR, are similarly inconsistent with Article 18.2. Natan asserts that coercion "should be read as meaning not only the use of force or threats but also more subtle forms of illegitimate influence, such as family considerations, public standing, and social relations."[97]

Jong, on the other hand, notes that, "it is dangerous to interpret the term 'coercion' in a broad sense."[98] For him

> It would be all too easy for those wishing to limit the right to freedom of thought, conscience, and religion to consider behavior as inducement: Could not a sermon, in public, be seen as moral inducement? Could not the distribution of a leaflet be regarded as material inducement?[99]

The prohibition of coercion in the 1981 Religion Declaration is worded in article (1) exactly the same way as Article 18(2) of the ICCPR.

94 Ibid.
95 Lerner, in *A Deskbook*, 70.
96 Tahzib, 26.
97 Lerner, in *A Deskbook*, 70.
98 Jong, 51.
99 Ibid.

Throughout the codification process, both broad and narrow interpretations were given of the term 'coercion' as there is no clear understanding, however, of what constitutes coercion.[100]

In 1952, Egypt submitted to the Commission of Human Rights an amendment concerning the interpretation of the term 'coercion'. This amendment, provided by Egypt, made it plain that

> [...] this delegation did not aim at the prohibition of a normal exchange of ideas. The Egyptian representative explained that this phrase could be construed as not in any way limiting the person who sought to maintain or change his religion or belief, but was designed solely to safeguard him against coercion by any party.[101]

That is what the Secretary General confirmed in 1955, on this issue, in his annotation to the draft ICCPR: 'It was understood that the word "coercion" in this context should not be construed as applying to moral or intellectual persuasion, or to any legitimate limitation of freedom to manifest one's religion or belief.'[102] Accordingly, Jong concludes that "Codification history of the Covenant therefore shows that the term 'coercion' in Article 18 should be narrowly interpreted."[103]

However, between activities that clearly will be proper and activities that clearly will be improper, there are activities that are hard to place.[104] It follows from the judgment that in assessing such activities,

100 See: Sullivan, Donna J., 'Advancing the Freedom of Religion or Belief Through the UN Declaration on the Elimination of religious intolerance and Discrimination', *The American Journal of International Law*, Vol. 82, 1988, 493.

101 E/CN.4/SR.319, 6, quoted in Jong, 45.

102 A/2929: 48, para, 110. In Jong, 45.

103 Ibid.

104 As an example: religious clothing may be thought to have a proselytizing aspect and may be not, consequently, two cases regarding students' right to wear hijab have received different outcomes. A ban on hijab was accepted by the European Court of Human Rights in the case Sahin v. Turkey, while this was not accepted by the UN Human Rights Committee in the case Hudoyberganova v. Uzbekistan (931/2000). It follows from the jurisprudence of the European Court of Human Rights that only proper proselytism is protected by the international human rights instruments, and that in deciding the properness of the act of proselytism, one has to take into consideration the rights and freedoms of others, and how

it is not just the activity in general that has to be assessed, but all the concrete aspects of the situation, including the characteristics of the parties of interest that are involved. Some important factors are the strength (cultural, financial, mental etc.) of the proselytizer compared with the strength of the object, the way the message is delivered (choice of media, the words used etc.), the belonging of the parties to a majority or minority belief (including indigenous beliefs), and where the activity takes place (military, prison, hospital, school etc.).

The issues of conversion and religious proselyting are controversial matters. However, regarding proselytism,[105] the question will often be how to balance the right to engage in faith persuasion against the right to maintain one's religion or belief?

1.2.5 Non-derogable Right

According to Article 4(2) of the ICCPR[106], the freedom of thought, conscience, and religion cannot be derogated from, not even in times

---

the state may ensure diversity without coercive measures. The European Court of Human Rights has remarked, inter alia, that freedom of thought, conscience, and religion comprises the right of a believer to bear witness about his or her convictions – in words and in deeds – and the right of religious communities to function without arbitrary state intervention. European Court of Human Rights, *Kokkinakis v. Greece,* May 25, 1993 (00014307/88); and *Hasan and Chaush v.Bulgaria,* October 26, 2000 (00030985/96).

105 Other important cases of proselytism that have been decided by the European Court of Human Rights are of interest in this context: Kokkinakis v. Greece, judgment of 05/25/1993, A 260-A and Larissis and others v. Greece, judgment of 02/24/1998, RJD 1998, 362.

106 ICCPR, Article 4 provides that "In time of public emergency which threatens the life of the nation and the existence of which is officially proclaimed: 1. The States Parties to the present Covenant may take measures derogating from their obligations under the present Covenant to the extent strictly required by the exigencies of the situation, provided that such measures are not inconsistent with their other obligations under international law and do not involve discrimination solely on the ground of race, colour, sex, language, religion or social origin. 2. No derogation from articles 6, 7, 8 (paragraphs 1and 2), 11, 15, 16

of war or public emergency.[107] In July 2001, the UN Human Rights Committee adopted General Comment No. 29,[108] concerning ICCPR Article 4, in which it clarified the scope of non-derogable rights and identified elements, which cannot be subject to lawful derogation. Paragraph 7 of the General Comment 29 provides:

> Article 4, paragraph 2, of the Covenant explicitly prescribes that no derogation from the following articles may be made: … (Including) article 18 (freedom of thought, conscience and religion). The rights enshrined in these provisions are non-derogable by the very fact that they are listed in article 4, paragraph 2…The reference in article 4, paragraph 2, to article 18, a provision that includes a specific clause on restrictions in its paragraph 3, demonstrates that the permissibility of restrictions is independent of the issue of derogability. Even in times of most serious public emergencies, States that interfere with the freedom to manifest one's religion or belief must justify their actions by referring to the requirements specified in article 18, paragraph 3. On several occasions the Committee has expressed its concern about rights that are non-derogable according to article 4, paragraph 2, being either derogated from or under a risk of derogation owing to inadequacies in the legal regime of the State party.

Jong notes that "all paragraphs of Article 18 have been excluded from derogation. This implies that neither the freedom to have or to adopt a religion or belief, nor the freedom to manifest, can be suspended in times of public emergency."[109]

---

and 18 may be made under this provision. 3. Any State Party to the present Covenant availing itself of the right of derogation shall immediately inform the other States Parties to the present Covenant, through the intermediary of the Secretary-General of the United Nations, of the provisions from which it has derogated and of the reasons by which it was actuated. A further communication shall be made, through the same intermediary, on the date on which it terminates such derogation."

107 Vospernik, Tanja, 'Permissible Restrictions on Freedom of Religion or Belief', Ch. 6 in *A Deskbook*, 148.

108 Human Rights Committee, General Comment 29, States of Emergency (article 4), U.N. Doc. CCPR/C/21/Rev.1/Add.11 (2001).

109 Jong, 100.

1.3 Intersection of Freedom of Religion or Belief with Freedom of Expression

The right to freedom of religion or belief is a complex right, containing sub-elements that overlap with a variety of values protected by other human rights norms. The freedom of manifestation can embrace a range of activities and essentially concerns the guarantee of other freedoms to believers, including freedom of expression, assembly, and association. Benito observes that,

> The right to freedom of religion or belief is so closely linked to all other human rights and fundamental freedoms, and so intimately interconnected with them, that it is not possible to enjoy freedom of religion or belief if full realization of other rights and freedoms is restricted or denied.[110]

In almost all situations, involving freedom of religion or belief similar intersecting values and concerns will inevitably arise.

The interaction between freedoms of religion or belief and other basic human rights, according to Vyver,

> is a recurring theme: on the one hand is the need to afford meaningful protection to freedom of religion or belief by also protecting rights and freedoms that complement the free exercise of religion or belief, and on the other is a certain tension between basic rights and freedoms perceived by proponents of a particular religion or belief as violating the norms upon which their convictions are founded. Freedom of religion or belief cannot prosper on its own; it requires protection of these collateral rights such as freedom of expression and of assembly.[111]

Freedom of peaceful assembly and association, as an example, allows groups bound by a particular religion or belief to be able to meet or to organize themselves effectively. It is very important for religious com-

110 E/CN.4/Sub.2/1987/26, Para. 23.

111 Vyver, Johan D. van der, 'The Relationship of Freedom of Religion or Belief Norms to Other Human Rights', in *A Deskbook*, 86–87.

munities to have standing and institutional rights to represent their rights and interests as communities.[112]

However, the intersection of freedom of religion or belief with other human rights can be illustrated best by the relationship to freedom of expression.

1.3.1 Freedom of Expression

Freedom of expression is important to freedom of religion or belief, without which it may not be possible to reveal and denounce instances of intolerance and discrimination based on religion or belief when they occur. Moreover, Article 18 protects not only the freedom to believe but also the freedom to manifest that belief in practice and expression. Freedom of expression is a fundamental right which lies at the core of civil and political rights. The right is often viewed as a touchstone for all other rights protected by the ICCPR. Article 19 guarantees the right to hold opinions without interference. Article 19.2 states that it includes the 'freedom to seek, receive and impart information and ideas of all kinds, regardless of frontiers, either orally, in writing or in print, in the form of art, or through any other media'. The Special Rapporteur on freedom of religion or belief Asma Jahangir, notes that the right to disseminate or propagate one's religion in a peaceful fashion is an important element of freedom of religion or belief and is also supported by the right to freedom of expression.[113]

While international law requires that freedom of expression be guaranteed without qualification (ICCPR Article 19.1), freedom of expression is not an absolute right.[114] A state can impose certain restrictions

112 See Vyver, 85–123.

113 A/61/340, Report of the Special Rapporteur on freedom of religion or belief, para. 69.

114 Ambeyi Ligabo, *Report of the Special Rapporteur on the Right to Freedom of Opinion and Expression*, E/CN.4/2006/55, para. 44.

on the exercise of freedom of expression, but these restrictions may not put in jeopardy the right itself. There are a few legitimate limitations on the exercise of the freedom of expression, which, as set out in Article 19 freedom of expression, "carries with it special duties and responsibilities". Accordingly, it may be subject to certain restrictions, provided by law and necessary for respect of the rights or reputations of others and for the protection of national security or of public order, or of public health or morals. Moreover, Article 19 must be read in conjunction with Article 20, which prohibits "any propaganda for war," and of crucial importance for present purposes, "any advocacy of national, racial or religious hatred that constitutes incitement to discrimination, hostility or violence."

1.3.2 The Balance between Freedom of Religion or Belief and Freedom of Expression

The right to freedom of expression is probably the most striking example of the difficult balance between protecting freedom of expression and protecting religious vilification, incitement to discrimination, hostility, and violence. Important aspects to take into consideration when discussing defamation issues are the right to criticize and the right to be protected from religious hatred and discrimination. The right to criticize is a fundamental part of freedom of expression and of the correct functioning of a democratic society, especially on matters of public interest. Of course this exercise can also involve criticism of individuals, particularly states' high-ranking officials and political personalities.[115] However, it is important to remember the legitimate limitations on the exercise of the freedom of expression:

1. This right is subject to certain restrictions, provided by law and necessary for respect of the rights or reputations of others and for the protection of national security or of public order, or of public

115 E/CN.4/2006/55, Para. 47.

health or morals. Yet the restrictions should not put this 'right' in jeopardy'.[116]

2. The right to express or criticize should not reach to a point of inciting hatred and religious discrimination against minority groups.

The Human Rights Committee has commented upon the relationship between Articles 19 and 20 by emphasizing that the limitations required by Article 20 'are fully compatible with the right of freedom of expression as contained in Article 19, the exercise of which carries with it special duties and responsibilities'.[117] The 1981 Declaration does not guarantee specifically a right to be free from religious vilification. However, Article 4 requires all states to 'take all appropriate measures to combat intolerance on the grounds of religion or other beliefs'. In this sense, freedom of expression is a fundamental and important right but it is not superior to the other fundamental rights protected by the international instruments.

116 Ibid, para. 48.

117 Human Rights Committee, General Comment 11, Article 20 (Nineteenth session, 1983), para. 2.

2. Religious Minorities

In every society there is a dominant culture. The term 'dominant culture', note Samovar and Porter, "indicates that the group we are talking about is the one in power."[1] Whether (minorities) within a society like it or not, this power allows this segment of the population to speak for the whole while setting the tone for the culture. The people in power are "those who historically have controlled, and who still control, the major institutions within the culture: church, government, education, military, mass media, monetary system, and the like."[2] However, "a national culture is never a homogeneous thing of one piece. In every culture there are internal contradictions or polarities."[3] Thus, in every society there are (minorities) who interact with the dominant culture. Simultaneously, these groups that, for numerous reasons, remained silent for years, now ask (and at times demand) to be heard. The members of these groups, like the members of the dominant culture, share perceptions, values, modes of communication, and lifestyles that make them unique. Minorities often hold affiliations that lead to behaviors and perceptions, values, beliefs, and practices that are significantly different enough to distinguish them from the other groups, communities, and the dominant culture. However, minorities, because they live within the dominant culture, often share many patterns and perceptions found within the larger dominant culture.

Almost all states, consequently, have one or more minority groups within their national territories, characterized by their own ethnic, linguistic or religious identity which differs from that of the majority population. The protection of minorities has not, until recently, attracted the same level of attention as that accorded other rights which the United

1 Samovar and Porter, 9.

2 Ibid., 11.

3 S. Victor, "Election 2000 and the Culture War," *The Humanist*, January/February, 2001, 5.

Nations considered as having a greater urgency. In recent years, however, there has been a heightened interest in issues affecting minorities as ethnic, racial and religious tensions have escalated, threatening the economic, social and political fabric of States, as well as their territorial integrity.[4] One reason for these tensions is that some people see the best society of all as one where all people share the same, true religion or the same true belief. However, today religious diversity is a fact of life. Since the end of the Cold War, a new world order emerged which created a global transition where previously

> [...] isolated peoples are being brought together voluntarily and involuntarily by the increasing integration of markets, the emergence of new regional political alliances, and remarkable advances in telecommunications, biotechnology and transportation that have prompted unprecedented demographics shifts.[5]

This rapid result of globalization has created a world full of tension, confusion, destabilizing one's sense of identity and resulting in religious resurgence. Consequently, peaceful co-existence of religions in a pluralistic society, which should be founded upon respect for equality and for non-discrimination between religions and other beliefs, is still difficult to achieve. This climate of change and acute vulnerability has raised new challenges in the pursuit of universal human rights and has brought us back to the clash of cultures debate that has come to characterize our time.

In this time, religious identities are increasing in importance and "the rise of religion as a national identity is on the rise."[6] Religious

4 Office of the High Commissioner for Human Rights, *Fact Sheet* No. 18(Rev.), Minority Rights. The human rights Fact Sheet Series is published by the Office of the United Nations High Commissioner for Human Rights (OHCHR) in Geneva, February 1998. The individual booklets deal with topical human rights issues and explain the structure and procedures of United Nations human rights treaty monitoring bodies and special mechanisms. The goal is to help readers understand basic human rights and the international machinery that has been established to promote and protect them.

5 Diana Ayton-Shenker, The Challenge of Human Rights and Cultural Diversity, United Nations Background Note, <http://www.un.org/rights/dpi1627e.htm>.

6 Samuel P. Huntington, *The religious Factors in World Politics, Religion and Politics,* Schweizerisches Institut für Auslandforschung, Zurich, 2001, 147–159.

minority groups are struggling for equality and tolerance within a modern nation state[7] and are trying to acquire some sense of belonging to the state; this cannot happen except by gaining equal participation in its institutions and economic justice. Even though the Charter of the United Nations and the Universal Declaration of Human Rights emphasize the protection of freedom of religion or belief and the principles of non-discrimination and equality and the ICCPR Article 27 recognized religious minorities, it is evident, however, that further measures are needed in order to better protect persons belonging to minorities from discrimination and to promote their identity. To this end, the Declaration on the Rights of Persons Belonging to National or Ethnic, Religious and Linguistic Minorities (Minority Declaration) was adopted in 18 December, 1992, and special rights for minorities were elaborated and measures adopted to supplement the non-discrimination provisions in international human rights instruments.

2.1 Defining 'Minority'

What is a minority?[8] No definite answers have been found and no satisfactory universal definition of the term "minority" has proved to be acceptable. The difficulty in arriving at an acceptable definition lies in the variety of situations in which minorities exist. Some live together in

7 Rex, J. (1996) 'National Identity in the Democratic Multi-Cultural State', *Sociological Research Online*, vol. 1, no. 2, <http://www.socresonline.org.uk/socresonline/1/2/1.html> (viewed Sept. 2013).

8 There are a number of studies by experts of the Sub-Commission and lengthy debates in many forums in which minority protection have been addressed. See the studies of Mr. Jules Deschênes, Mr. Asbjørn Eide and Mr. Stanislav Chernichenko: "Proposals concerning a definition of the term minority", by Mr. Jules Deschênes, E/CN.4/Sub.2/1985/31 of 14 May 1985; "Definition of minorities" by Mr. Stanislav Chernichenko, E/CN.4/Sub.2/AC.5/1996/WP.1 and E/CN.4/Sub.2/AC.5/1997/WP.1; "Classification of minorities and differentiation in minority rights", by Mr. Asbjørn Eide, E/CN.4/Sub.2/AC.5/1996/WP.2.

well-defined areas, separated from the dominant part of the population, while others are scattered throughout the national community. Some minorities base a strong sense of collective identity on a well-remembered or recorded history; others retain only a fragmented notion of their common heritage. In certain cases, minorities enjoy, or have known, a considerable degree of autonomy. In others, there is no past history of autonomy or self-government. Some minority groups may require greater protection than others, because they have resided for a longer period of time in a country, or they have a stronger will to maintain and develop their own characteristics. In socioeconomic, the term 'minority' typically refers to a socially subordinate ethnic group (understood in terms of language, nationality, religion and/or culture).[9] International law has so far provided us with no universally accepted and binding definition of a minority, and efforts by the United Nations to define a minority have proved unsuccessful, but two definitions have been proposed within the framework of Article 27 of the ICCPR.

The first effective definition was provided by UN Special Rapporteur on the rights of persons belonging to ethnic, religious and linguistic minorities, Francesco Capotorti, and has undoubtedly contributed to clarifying certain aspects of what constitutes a minority. In his view

> [...] minority is a group, numerically inferior to the rest of the population of a state, in a non-dominant position, whose members-being nationals of the state-posses ethnic, religious or linguistic characteristics differing from those of the rest of the population and show, if only implicitly, a sense of solidarity, directed towards preserving their culture, traditions, religion or language.[10]

A second definition worth noting was put forward by Jules Deschênes:

> A group of citizens of a State, constituting a numerical minority and in a non-dominant position in that State, endowed with ethnic, religious or linguistic

9 Other minority groups include "people with disabilities", "economic minorities" (working poor or unemployed), "age minorities" (who are younger or older than a typical working age) and "sexual minorities" (whose sexual orientation or gender identity differs from the sociological norm).

10 Study on the Rights of Persons belonging to Ethnic, Religious and Linguistic Minorities, UN Document E/CN.4/Sub.2/384/Add.1–7 (1977).

> characteristics which differ from those of the majority of the population, having a sense of solidarity with one another, motivated, if only implicitly, by a collective will to survive and whose aim is to achieve equality with the majority in fact and in law.[11]

Despite the difficulty in arriving at a universally acceptable definition, various characteristics of minorities have been identified, which, taken together, cover most minority situations. The most commonly used description of a minority in a given State can be summed up as "a non-dominant group of individuals who share certain national, ethnic, religious or linguistic characteristics which are different from those of the majority population."[12]

11 Proposal Concerning a Definition of the Term 'Minority' UN Document, E/CN.4/Sub.2/1985/31 (1985). Other definitions that are often referred to in international and human rights law are: The *Permanent Court of Justice:* "The criteria to be applied to determine what is a community within the meaning of the articles of the Convention ... is the existence of a group living in a given country or locality, having a race, religion, language and traditions of their own, and united by the Identity of such race, religion, language and traditions, maintaining their own form of worship, securing the instruction and upbringing of their children in accordance with the spirit and traditions of their race and mutually assisting one another." PCIJ Series B, No. 17 pp. 19, 21, 22, 23. The quote relates to the emigration of Greco-Bulgarian communities concomitant to a Convention adopted between Greece & Bulgaria in 1919. *Council of Europe, 1993*: A group of persons in a state who: (a) reside on the territory of that state and are citizens thereof; (b) maintain longstanding, firm and lasting ties with that State; (c) display distinctive ethnic, cultural, religions or linguistic characteristics; (d) are sufficiently representative, although smaller in number than the rest of the population of that state or of a region of the state; (e) are motivated by a concern to preserve together that which constitutes their common identity, including their culture, their tradition, their religion or their language. Council of Europe Parliamentary Assembly, Recommendation 1201 (1993) on an additional protocol to the European Convention on Human Rights (adopted February 1, 1993).

12 Halida Nasic, Minority Rights Instruments and Mechanisms:Minority Protection along the Conflict Continuum, EURAC Research, Bozen-Bolzano, 2007, 8, <http://www.eurac.edu/NR/rdonlyres/0AD072B0-460E-4C3E-A7C2-783B388EC275/0/ReportonHRinstrumentsWEB.pdf> (viewed Sept. 2013).

2.2 The Rights of Religious Minorities in the UN System

A 'religious minority'[13], as understood from the definition of 'minority', consists of a group that is numerically smaller than the rest of the population of a country and displays religious characteristics different from those of the rest of the population. They are also committed to safeguarding their religion, religious culture and traditions. For the protection of their rights, religious minorities, as it has been mentioned, can draw upon the freedom to manifest one's religion or belief in community with others in Article 18 of the ICCPR, which constitutes "a firm basis for the exercise of their religious rights".[14] This provision, together with the right of non-discrimination on the basis of religion or belief, also ensures that religious minorities are not persecuted or discriminated against, in addition to article 27 of the ICCPR.

2.2.1 International Covenant on Civil and Political Rights

Article 27 of the ICCPR protects minorities. It recognizes the right of minority to profess and practice their own religion or belief. It is the most widely-accepted legally-binding provision on minorities[15] and

13 See thensection on 'The Rights of Religious Minorities' in Jong, 254–358.

14 Jong, 254.

15 Several international human rights instruments refer to national, ethnic, racial or religious groups and some include special rights for persons belonging to minorities. These include: the Convention on the Prevention and Punishment of the Crime of Genocide (art. II); the Convention on the Elimination of All Forms of Racial Discrimination (arts. 2 and 4); the International Covenant on Economic, Social and Cultural Rights (art. 13); the International Covenant on Civil and Political Rights (art. 27); the Convention on the Rights of the Child (art. 30); the UNESCO Convention against Discrimination in Education (art. 5); the United Nations Declaration on the Rights of Persons Belonging to National or Ethnic, Religious and Linguistic Minorities; and the UNESCO Declaration on Race and Racial Prejudice (art. 5). Regional instruments which contain special rights for minorities include the Framework Convention for the Protection of

provides that in those states in which ethnic, religious, or linguistic minorities exist, persons belonging to these minorities shall not be denied the right, in community with the other members of their group, to enjoy their own culture, to profess and practice their own religion, or to use their own language. In 1994, the Human Rights Committee adopted General Comment No. 23 on Article 27, in which it states that "[t]he existence of an ethnic, religious or linguistic minority in a given State party does not depend upon a decision by that State party but requires to be established by objective criteria."[16] However, General Comment No. 23, makes clear (at paragraph 1) that Article 27 does not establish collective rights but rather establishes and

> [...] recognizes a right which is conferred on individuals belonging to minority groups and which is distinct from, and additional to, all the other rights which, as individuals in common with everyone else, they are already entitled to enjoy under the Covenant.[17]

National Minorities, the European Charter for Regional or Minority Languages (Council of Europe); and the Document of the Copenhagen Meeting of the Conference on the Human Dimension of the CSCE 1990 (Conference on Security and Cooperation in Europe).

16 Human Rights Committee, General Comment 23, Article 27 (Fiftieth session, 1994), Compilation of General Comments and General Recommendations Adopted by Human Rights Treaty Bodies, U.N. Doc. HRI\GEN\1\Rev.1 at 38 (1994), para. 5(2).

17 See also: Economic and Social Council resolution 1995/31 which established the Working Group on Minorities. This Group is a subsidiary organ of the Sub-Commission on the Promotion and Protection of Human Rights (previously called the Sub-Commission on Prevention of Discrimination and Protection of Minorities). Economic and Social Council resolution 2005/79: This established the United Nations independent expert on minority issues. The work of the independent expert on minority issues complements and enhances the work of other United Nations bodies and mechanisms that address minority rights and minority issues, including the Working Group on Minorities and the treaty-monitoring bodies.

In a different paragraph the Committee does recognize the potential need for affirmative action to protect the identity of the minority as such:

> Although the rights protected under article 27 are individual rights, they depend in turn on the ability of the minority group to maintain its culture, language or religion. Accordingly, positive measures by States may also be necessary to protect the identity of a minority and the rights of its members to enjoy and develop their culture and language and to practice their religion, in community with the other members of the group.[18]

This tension on recognizing the collective rights of religious minorities reflects the concern of many states with the creation of group rights. However, according to the report of the Working Group[19]

> […] the wording of article 27 of the Covenant on Civil and Political Rights, that is the collective element contained in the phrase 'in community with other members of their group', was mentioned repeatedly as a possible bridge between the individual and collective rights approaches.

However, Danilo Türk, as a member of the Sub-Commission on Prevention of Discrimination and Protection of Minorities, in 1989, emphasized that the community aspects is essential when it comes to the freedom of thought, conscience and religion[20]:

> It was important to bear in mind, that, unlike the freedom of opinion, religion was not a rational individual's choice, but rather a matter of culture, common and inherited values, and tradition; second that religion was often a crucial component of ethnic identity, and as such, had to be protected; and last, that the exercise of religious rights, even at individual level, often required a collective effort. To confine the right to practice a religion to the individual level would be to, as it were, privatize the issue, and could lead to the limitation of religious freedoms.

States that have ratified the Covenant are obliged to ensure that all individuals under their jurisdiction enjoy their rights; this may require

18 Ibid, para. 6(2).
19 E/CN.4/1991/53, paras. 12–13.
20 E/CN.4/Sub.2/1989/SR.14: 4, para. 9, quoted in Jong, 254. For the work of the Sub Commission see online: http://www.unhchr.ch/html/menu2/2/sc.htm

specific action to correct inequalities to which minorities are subjected. Ryszard Cholewinski argues that this provision (Article 27 of ICCPR) imposes "a positive duty on states to assist...minorities in preserving their culture, rather than merely a negative duty of noninterference or nonrepression."[21] Cholewinski believes, further, that there is "an increasing recognition on the part of states with minorities that positive action is indeed necessary to live up to the conditions of Article 27."[22] General Comment No. 23 provides that

> [...] although Article 27 is expressed in negative terms, that article, nevertheless, does recognize the existence of a 'right' and requires that it shall not be denied. Consequently, a State party is under an obligation to ensure that the existence and the exercise of this right are protected against their denial or violation. Positive measures of protection are, therefore, required not only against the acts of the State party itself, whether through its legislative, judicial or administrative authorities, but also against the acts of other persons within the State party.[23]

2.2.2 The Declaration on the Rights of Persons Belonging to National or Ethnic, Religious and Linguistic Minorities

Despite the importance of Article 27 of ICCPR, it was very soon evident that further measures were needed in order to better protect persons belonging to minorities from discrimination and to promote their identity. The only United Nations instrument which addresses the special rights of minorities in a separate document is the Declaration on the Rights of Persons Belonging to National or Ethnic, Religious and Linguistic Minorities (Minority Declaration).

The Minority Declaration was inspired by the provisions of Article 27 of the ICCPR concerning the rights of persons belonging to ethnic,

21 Ryszard Cholewinski, 'State Duty Towards Ethnic Minorities: Positive or Negative?', *Human Rights Quarterly*, 10.3 (1988), 344, quoted in Joel E. Oestreich, 'Liberal Theory and Minority Group Rights', *Human Rights Quarterly* 21.1 (1999), 114.

22 Ibid.

23 General Comment 23, para. 6.1.

religious and linguistic minorities.[24] Again, the Declaration focuses on individual rights for persons belonging to minorities. Article 2 (1) states: Persons belonging to national or ethnic, religious and linguistic minorities have the right to enjoy their own culture, to profess and practice their own religion, and to use their own language, in private and in public, freely and without interference or any form of discrimination.

Although the Declaration is not a legally binding convention, it expresses the international community's understanding of minority rights protection.

- Article 1 obliges States to protect the existence and identity (national or ethnic, cultural, religious and linguistic) of minorities.
- Article 2 grants minorities the right to enjoy their culture, profess and practice their religions and languages freely and without interference and without any form of discrimination. It also grants minority groups the right to participate effectively in cultural, religious, social, economic and public life.
- Article 3 provides that those rights may be exercised individually and in community with other members of the group and without discrimination.
- Article 4 obliges States to take positive measures to protect minority culture, language, etc.

24 Declaration on the Rights of Persons Belonging to National or Ethnic, Religious and Linguistic Minorities, Adopted by General Assembly resolution 47/135 of 18 December 1992. Other provisions related to the issue of minorities: Art. 30 of CRC: "In those States in which ethnic, religious or linguistic minorities or persons of indigenous origin exist, a child belonging to such a minority or who is indigenous shall not be denied the right, in community with other members of his or her group, to enjoy his or her own culture, to profess and practice his or her own religion, or to use his or her own language." *General Assembly Declaration 47/135:* Art. 1 (1): "States shall protect the existence and the national or ethnic, cultural, religious and linguistic identity of minorities within their respective territories and shall encourage conditions for the promotion of that identity." Art. 2 (1): "Persons belonging to national or ethnic, religious and linguistic minorities have the right to enjoy their own culture, to profess and practice their own religion, and to use their own language, in private and in public, freely and without interference or any form of discrimination."

- Article 8 provides that measures taken to further the aims of the Declaration shall not be considered prima facie contrary to the principle of equality.
- Article 8(4) provides that nothing in the Declaration shall permit any activity contrary to the purposes and principles of the UN, including sovereign equality, territorial integrity and political independence of States.

It is important to understand that the promotion and protection of the rights of minorities is the only way to contribute to the political and social stability of States in which they live. The independent expert on minority issues, Gay McDougall, believes that there is a lack of knowledge and understanding regarding minority rights as set out in the Minority Declaration, as well as regarding the value of diversity in general. She notes that,

> [...] states must understand that respect for minority rights benefits States and societies in terms of securing the richness of cultural diversity, reflecting their full heritage, and contributing to social cohesion. It also advances the conditions for political and social stability and peace. Rather than promoting segregation and separation, minority rights are based on the principle of an integrated society, where each can use one's own language, enjoy one's culture and practice one's religion but still feel part of a broader, inclusive national identity.[25]

The Minority Declaration remains one of the most comprehensive international documents of its kind, setting out both the rights of minorities and the duties of states. The five rights of persons belonging to national or ethnic, religious and linguistic minorities, specified in the Declaration, are a reaffirmation of rights appearing in other international instruments rather than a statement of new rights. These are Minorities' rights to:[26]

25 Gay McDougall, *Annual report of the Independent Expert on minority issues, specific Groups and Individuals: Minorities*, E/CN.4/2006/74, Para. 83.

26 Deon Geldenhuys and Johann Rossouw, The International Protection Of Minority Rights special report complied for the F W de Klerk Foundation, August 2001, 18.

- enjoy their own culture, profess and practice their own religion, and use their own language freely in public and private;
- participate effectively in cultural, religious, social, economic and public life;
- participate effectively in decisions on the national and, where appropriate, regional level concerning their minority group or region;
- establish and maintain their own associations, and
- establish and maintain free and peaceful contacts with other domestic minorities and with citizens of other states to whom they are related by national or ethnic, religious or linguistic ties.

Positive action or affirmative measures (also known as 'special measures') are proactive measures taken by a government or private institution to remedy the effects of past and present discrimination by providing reverse preferences favoring members of classes previously disadvantaged. These 'special rights' are not privileges, but they are granted to make it possible for minorities to preserve their identity, characteristics values and traditions. Special rights are just as important in achieving equality of treatment as non-discrimination. Only when minorities are able to use their own languages, (practice their religion), benefit from services they have themselves organized, as well as take part in the political and economic life of states can they begin to achieve the status which majorities take for granted. Differences in the treatment of such groups, or individuals belonging to them, are justified if it is exercised to promote effective equality and the welfare of the community as a whole.[27]

However, Lerner argues that "the 1992 Declaration is a rather timid approach to the issue of minorities' rights,"[28] and for religious minorities, the Special Rapporteur on freedom of religion or belief, Asma Jahangir calls attention to that:[29]

27 Sub-Commission on Prevention of Discrimination and Protection of Minorities (first session) – E/CN.4/52 (certain articles), E/CN.4/52, Section V. in Fact Sheet No. 18.

28 Lerner, in *A Deskbook*, 71.

29 A/61/340, paras. 49–51.

- Religious minorities remain, by and large, the main victims of violations of the right of freedom of religion or belief and other acts of religious intolerance. In this respect, one must take into account that while a certain religion may be a minority in one part of the world and suffer accordingly, it may constitute the religion of the majority of the population in another part of the world.
- The problems related to the existence of religious minorities remain as important as ever and the rules pertaining to the principles of freedom of religion or belief have to be constantly re-emphasized. In addition to lack of respect, ignorance of these principles is often at the source of violations.
- Moreover, when religious minorities are groups that follow a so-called non-traditional or newer religion, the members of these communities may be the object of suspicion and, consequently, suffer greater limitations to their right to freedom of religion or belief.

2.3 Prohibition of Discrimination against Religious Minorities

The right to freedom of religion or belief is a fundamental right. The right of minorities to freedom of religion details the particular activities which amount to freedom of religion, including: the right to receive or impart instruction of the religion or belief of the minority; the right to freely change one's religion or belief; to publish and disseminate religious materials; to establish, manage and maintain religious institutions; to train, appoint, elect or designate by succession appropriate religious leaders; and to observe religious holidays. The right of minorities to profess and practice their own religion is of particular relevance in the regions where religious issues and factionalism have come to dominate much of the political discourse, and have sharpened the expression of identity. However, it is clear that religious discrimination exists in many societies.

The principle of equality and non-discrimination is both a human right of its own and a constitutive element of all human rights. The first step taken was the adoption of the 1965 Convention on the Elimination of all Forms of Racial Discrimination (CERD). However, the CERD does not explicitly prohibit discrimination on grounds of religion. However, in many instances discrimination on grounds of race, ethnic or national origin may also constitute discrimination on grounds of religion or racial discrimination may arise together with discrimination on grounds of religion, such as in the case of multiple discriminations.

The ICCPR contains two all-important provisions on non-discrimination. In addition to Article 2 of the ICCPR which provides for an accessory right, meaning that it can only be violated in conjunction with some other substantive provision of the Covenant, Article 26 of the ICCPR provides for the free-standing prohibition of discrimination. Unlike Article 2, however, Article 26 employs the concept of "discrimination". While the ICCPR does not itself define "discrimination", the Committee has in its General Comment No 18 on discrimination provided such a definition:

> [...] the Committee believes that the term "discrimination" as used in the Covenant should be understood to imply any distinction, exclusion, restriction or preference which is based on any ground such as race, colour, sex, language, religion, political or other opinion, national or social origin, property, birth or other status, and which has the purpose or effect of nullifying or impairing the recognition, enjoyment or exercise by all persons, on an equal footing, of all rights and freedoms.

Discrimination on the basis of religion or belief is prohibited under the legally binding ICCPR; however, the Religion Declaration is the most comprehensive international statement of the right to freedom of religion and belief elaborating on the ICCPR guarantees. Article 2.1 proclaims that 'no one shall be subject to discrimination by any State, institution, group of persons, or person on grounds of religion or other beliefs'. Article 2.2 defines religious discrimination as:

> [...] any distinction, exclusion, restriction or preference based on religion or belief and having as its purpose or as its effect nullification or impairment of the

> recognition, enjoyment or exercise of human rights and fundamental freedoms on an equal basis

Article 3 of the Religion Declaration proclaims discrimination on the ground of religion or belief 'an affront to human dignity' which is to be condemned as a violation of fundamental rights and freedoms. Some of the elements of the freedom to manifest one's religion or belief are listed in article 6 and include the freedom to assemble for worship, freedom to use the articles and materials related to the rites or customs, freedom to write and disseminate publications and freedom to teach the religion. Like the CERD[30], the Religion Declaration prohibits intentional as well as unintentional acts of discrimination and actions, which have a discriminatory effect. But Boyle notes that

> It is of interest to compare the duties imposed by the Religion Declaration and CERD in terms in combating intolerance and discrimination. The CERD requires the use of penal law to combat racial hatred whereas the Religion Declaration is not specific.[31]

Discrimination usually occurs at all levels of society; it can be practiced by governments, or by one community against another; it can result from active, direct, and deliberate actions, and it can happen unconsciously through insensitivity, ignorance, or indifference. The global experience of discrimination indicates a predisposition in all communities to reject those who are different in a negative manner (politically, socially, culturally or economically), and that is a major source of tension in many parts of the world.

Discrimination can be based on the following means:

1. Legislation: Laws can directly or indirectly discriminate against particular group. Often, equal treatment legislation exists, but is not

30 The 1965 International Convention on the Elimination of all Forms of Racial Discrimination, Adopted and opened for signature and ratification by GA Res. 2106 (XX) of 21 December 1965.

31 Boyle Kevin, *Working Paper, United Nations Seminar on the Encouragement of Understanding, tolerance and Respect in Matters Relating to freedom of religion or Belief*, Geneva, Switzerland, 3–14, 1984, HR/Geneva/1984/WP.5, 10.

effectively implemented and many incidents, cultural traditions outweigh the law. The lack of protective legislation may give implicit messages of legitimacy to discriminatory actions; and government inaction or negligence can feed individual prejudice.[32]

2. Institutionalized Attitudes: These kinds of prejudices are often unquestioned or even unrecognized throughout society. It is often rooted in fear of unfamiliar people who look different, have another language, culture, and religion. They are seen as a threat to their security and cultural identity of the majority population.[33] Widespread prejudices and discriminatory practices that prevail over a long period usually have a devastating impact on the life of the discriminated people. Moreover, what determines a person's attachment to a given group is essentially the influence of others, especially, the influence of those on the other side, who do their best to exclude him. In the same sense, Amin Maalouf noted, "[p]eople often see themselves in terms of whichever one of their allegiance is most under attack."[34]
3. The Media: It can, and often promotes, discrimination. It can reinforce traditional hostilities toward some groups, stimulate, and encourage contempt and hatred towards others. When a group is seen as a threat to the society, the media's representation of them will be hostile, demeaning, degrading and will propagate negative stereotypes. At its most extreme, the media can be responsible for orchestrated campaigns to mobilize hatred and dehumanize particular groups.[35] Discriminations, direct or indirect, are prohibited by international discrimination provisions. In the same sense, religious discrimination can be characterized as direct or indirect. Direct discrimination is based on the idea of formal equality. It may be defined as less favourable or detrimental treatment of an individual or

32 Muscroft, Sarah, Ed., *Children's Rights: Equal Rights?* The International Save the Children Alliance, United Kingdom, 2000, 32–33.

33 Ibid., 35–36.

34 Maalouf Amin, *On Identity*, Harvill Panther, Great Britain, 2000, 21–22.

35 Muscroft, *Children's Rights*, 35.

> group of individuals on the basis of a prohibited characteristic or ground such as race, sex, or disability.This means applying special treatment (generally unfavorable) to an individual solely on the basis of the person's religion. Indirect discrimination occurs when a practice, rule, requirement or condition is neutral on its face but impacts disproportionately upon particular groups, unless that practice, rule, requirement or condition is justified. Prohibitions of indirect discrimination require a State to take account of relevant differences between groups.[36]

However, it is important to note that "not every unequal treatment means automatically discrimination. Only unequal treatments and degradation of the person because of particular characteristics in the person's identity are to be classified as discrimination."[37] Tahzib makes a distinction between 'open' and 'structural' forms of intolerance and discrimination.[38] The former form of intolerance may be described as discriminatory or intolerant behavior on the part of individuals; by openly advocate or practice violence or to harass and discriminate others or by pressure exercised through subtle methods of exclusion from social life, or other forms of social ostracism. The latter form of intolerance may be characterized as the propensity towards intolerance, which exists in some political, cultural and religious, public service or private institutions, in the mass media and, in general, in the communication system, and in some traditions of society.[39]

Experiences of discrimination and vilification on the basis of religion and belief infringe the rights of individuals and groups, thus, it is important, in order to ensure the enjoyment of religion and belief, that the individual must be free from discrimination on the grounds of religion and belief in all areas of public life, including employment, education, the provision of goods and services and accommodation.

36 Kevin Kitching, *Non-Discrimination in International Law, A Handbook for Practitioners*, Interlights, London, January 2005, 20–21.

37 Kälin, 1999, 87.

38 Tahzib, 24.

39 Ibid., 15.

Moreover, vilification, insults, threats or abuse against a person on the basis of religion or belief impair that person's right to freedom of religion and belief. Benito notes that the

> [...] term intolerance and discrimination based on religion or belief encompasses not only discrimination infringing upon or negating the right to freedom of thought, conscience and religion and belief, but also acts which stir up hatred against, or persecution of, such persons or groups.[40]

Any such advocacy of religious hatred that constitutes incitement to discrimination, hostility or violence must be prohibited by law (art. 20.2 ICCPR).

Minority rights approaches incorporate an element of substantive equality, in addition to formal equality and therefore recognize the need for special measures to remedy the disadvantages of minority groups and preserve their characteristics. Consequently, rights of religious minorities include:

- The prevention of discrimination, i.e., the prevention of any action that denies to individuals or groups of people equality of treatment; and
- The protection of minorities: protection of non-dominant groups which, while seeking equality of treatment with the majority, also require a measure of differential treatment in order to preserve basic characteristics which they possess and which distinguish them from the majority of the population.

Tolerance, as Boyle notes,

> [...] must mean that the goal is equality of treatment. This goal requires a firm acceptance that differences in religious orientation are to be first, respected by the state, and by all in society; secondly, differences in religious belief are not to be the source of any discrimination whether by penalizing or favoring one belief over another, and third of all, discrimination is unacceptable, whether it emanates from the state, or from any institution, group of persons, [or] persons.[41]

40 Beneito, E/CN.4/Sub.2/1987/26, Para. 18.

41 Boyle Kevin,HR/Geneva/1984/WP.5; 6.

2.4 Integration of Religious Minorities

As mentioned above, religion is one of the most important elements in culture and there are a wide variety of religions and beliefs. Diversity of religions and beliefs, both at the international level and national level, can be a source of knowledge and understanding, an impetus and challenge to development and improvement, a broadening of human horizons and an enrichment of human life. On the other hand, religious diversity can, as history abundantly demonstrates, be a source of national disharmony and disunity and international distrust, ill-will and dispute and the cause of, or excuse for, national or international conflict and even war.

Today, societies are multicultural. They are the outcome of historical processes, which, owing to the way in which they evolved, brought different peoples, cultures, and religions into contact with each other.[42] This cultural diversity derives from a number of sources, such as the process of globalization and immigration.[43] Samovar and Porter note that "[g]lobalism and multiculturalism have become guiding international and national developments during the last several decades,"[44] and this challenge of religious diversity is highlighted by recent processes of globalization, since it intensifies the awareness of fundamental differences between religious world-views.

42 In 1971, Canada became the first country in the world to adopt an official Multiculturalism Policy. In 1982, Canada became a constitutional multicultural state that sees multiculturalism as a way to "ensures that all citizens can keep their identities, can take pride in their ancestry and have a sense of belonging. Acceptance gives Canadians a feeling of security and self-confidence, making them more open to, and accepting of, diverse cultures. The Canadian experience has shown that multiculturalism encourages racial and ethnic harmony and cross-cultural understanding, and discourages ghettoization, hatred, discrimination and violence." See: Canadian Multiculturalism: An Inclusive Citizenship, <http://www.pch.gc.ca/progs/multi/inclusive_e.cfm>.

43 Bhikhu Parekh, *Unity and Diversity in Multicultural Societies*, International Institute for Labor Studies, Geneva, March 2005, <http://www.test-red.pucp.edu.pe/ridei/wp-content/uploads/biblioteca/Parekh_multiculuralismo.pdf> (viewed Sept. 2013).

44 Samovar and Porter, 232.

Thus, one of the most common dominant characteristics of the modern societies is multiculturalism.[45] Clearly enough, both at the international and on the domestic scene, the key to real success lies in mutual and genuine understanding, tolerance and respect of and for different religious traditions, practices and beliefs. However, there are a variety of policies to deal with religious diversity. Some policies, developed to manage religious pluralism, may stress assimilation, integration or multiculturalism.

– *Cultural Assimilation:* This concept describes the process of growing participation in the culture and values of the host society. It leads to the cultural absorption of minorities into the host society, making cultural differences disappear to a large extent. This requires minorities to give up their cultural identity and take on, in the sense of acculturation, the values and behaviors of the (majority) society.[46] Assimilationism argues that a society cannot be cohesive and stable unless its members share a common national culture, including a common system of meaning and significance, a shared conception of the good life at personal and collective levels, and a shared body of customs, practices, habits, attitudes and collective memories. In the absence of such a shared culture, they would disagree deeply about the meanings of different human activities and relations and the values to be assigned to them and would simply not be able to cooperate and sustain a shared life. The choice for religious minorities is stark and simple. If they want to be accepted as full and equal citizens, they should assimilate into the national culture and show exclusive and undivided loyalty to their country

45 Alves Lindgren Jose, 479. Multiculturalism as a term is used in three distinct senses: as a description of the state of cultural diversity in a society, as an ideology aimed at legitimizing the incorporation of ethnic diversity in the general structure of society, or as public policy designed to create national unity in ethnic diversity. See: *International Journal on Multicultural Societies* (IJMS), Vol. 5, No. 2, 2003: 119–134.

46 Kälin, "Human Rights and the Integration of Migrants", Ch. 16, 272, in Aleinikoff T. Alexander & Chetail, Vincent, Ed., *Migration and International Legal Norms*, T. M. C. Asser press, The Hague, 2003, 272.

of settlement. Conversely, if they hold on to their (religion), retain close ties with their country of origin, and thus remain different; they must not complain if the rest of society refuses to identify with them and treats them unequally.[47] Parekh notes that:

> [...] the assimilationists' obsession with moral and cultural uniformity springs from and leads to a deep suspicion of moral and cultural differences. For them these differences are departures from the norm, they are abnormal, deviant, sources of disorder. Once they have eliminated some of them, they turn their attention to others. And since differences are constantly generated by human ingenuity, creativity and choices, the assimilationists are forever at war with their fellow citizens.[48]

He further notes that, "This is hardly the way to hold a society together, which they say is their basic objective. By demanding far more than what is possible, they fail to secure even what is necessary."[49]

– *Social integration:* Narrowly defined by Kälin, social integration "denotes the incorporation of minorities into, and their participation in the structures of the host society at all levels." He explains that

> This so called structural or social integration takes place in various areas. One can speak of the economic integration as access to economic opportunities, in particular labor, of all kinds and on all levels; of integration into the educational system as access to non-segregated primary schools and to higher education at all levels, or of social integration as access to the status system of the host society. The opposite of structural and social integration is exclusion or marginalization.[50]

Thus, social integration is absent if minorities are

> [...] marginalized in three interrelated ways: *economically*, through social unemployment or low-status work that is insecure; *socially*, through poor edu-

47 Bhikhu Parekh, *Unity and Diversity in Multicultural Societies*, 5.
48 Ibid.
49 Ibid.
50 Kälin, 2003, 272.

> cation and vulnerability to crime, drugs, and household disintegration; and *politically*, by their powerlessness to influence decision-making.[51]

For Parekh, integration is primarily a socio-political rather than a cultural concept. It implies that no individual or group of individuals should be excluded from society or treated as inferior, as was the case under racial segregation in the United States. However, it involves far more than inclusion and equality. It implies that those included should be incorporated or integrated into the social structure so that they become an integral and indistinguishable part.[52]

– *Multiculturalism:* The opposite of cultural assimilation is cultural diversity or, as it is often called, multiculturalism. Multiculturalism, as an ideology, advocates that society should consist of, or at least allow and include, distinct cultural groups, with equal status. The aim of these collective rights is to protect the specific cultural traits of minorities through the authorization of certain practices (e.g. private and public use of mother tongue; practicing one's religion in public space, etc.), the institutionalization of mechanisms that protect these groups against discrimination based on these practices, and the active promotion of minority cultures.[53] According to Joseph Raz

> [l]iberal multiculturalism…affirms that in the circumstances of contemporary industrial or postindustrial societies, a political attitude of fostering and encouraging the prosperity, cultural and material, of cultural groups within a society, and respecting their identity is justified by considerations of freedom and human dignity. These considerations call on governments to take action that goes beyond that required by policies of toleration and nondiscrimination.[54]

51 N. Van Haer, 'Migration, displacement and social Integration', UNRIS. Occasional Paper No. 9, World summit for social Development, Geneva 1994, n. 21, quoted in Kälin, 2003, 272.

52 Bhikhu Parekh, *Unity and Diversity in Multicultural Societies,* 7.

53 Juan-Díez Medrano and Matthias Koenig, "Nationalism, Citizenship and Immigration"; in Social Science Research – Editorial Introduction, *In International Journal on Multicultural Societies (IJMS),* Vol. 7, No. 2, 2005, 85.

54 Joseph Raz, 'Multiculturalism: A Liberal Perspective', DISSENT 78 (1994), quoted in Jovanović, Miodrag A. 'Recognizing Minority Identities Through Collective Rights', *Human Rights Quarterly* 27.2 (2005), 625.

Multiculturalism ensures that

> [...] as far as possible, it reflects the cultural values of all various ethnic groups that now constitute contemporary [...] society, and it promotes effective, genuine equality before the law (not just formal equality) and is administered so that it does not have an unintended discriminatory impact on the members of ethnic minority groups.[55]

Multiculturalism, thus, is concerned with establishing cultural connections that transcend national experience. This new multiculturalism requires that appropriate consideration be given to racial and cultural diversity.

This diversity will not threaten the unity of the State, but it will enrich it. Will Kymlicka explains the significance of diversity as follows:

> The protection of minority rights need not occur at the expense of national unity or loyalty. Instead of being mutually exclusive, group and national loyalties can be mutually reinforcing. In multinational states recognizing cultural uniqueness of minorities, such groups' loyalty towards the state may actually be strengthened. They can be expected to develop a common patriotism, rather than a shared national identity.[56]

Parekh affirms this and notes that "the language of citizenship and common belonging meets this requirement better than any other."[57] He explains that "if dominant society does not want to alienate minorities, then the rest of society needs to do all it can to ensure that they are able to do so."[58] Equal citizenship in his view is not enough. Thus, citizenship needs to be grounded in and nurtured by "a common sense of belonging." He, further, explains that

> [c]ommon belonging is a two-way process. Religious minorities cannot belong to the society in which they live in unless it is prepared to accept them as full mem-

55 The Law Reform Commission, Multiculturalism and the Law 2, 3 (1990), quoted in Jovanović, Miodrag, 625.

56 Deon Geldenhuys and Johann Rossouw, *The International Protection of Minority Rights*, the F W de Klerk Foundation, August 2001, 8.

57 Parekh, *Unity and Diversity in Multicultural Societies*, 10.

58 Ibid.

> bers, and conversely it can not do that unless they wish to belong, with all that this entails. Common belonging therefore can only be achieved if each party respects the terms of the relationship and discharges its obligations.[59]

Multiculturalism recognizes the personal worth and dignity of each individual. Singh believes that everyone deserves equal respect and equal opportunity for self-realization by virtue of their humanity and human potential as rational beings.[60] There are universal values shared by everyone, and there are particular values that are shared within various minorities. Multiculturalism, thus, serves what Singh refers to as "an overarching value that requires the acceptance of cultural diversity as a shared value"[61] by both the dominant culture and the various minorities) of a society in order to establish a multicultural society. There are several good reasons why society should respect the cultural differences that minorities have. Athanasia Åkermark, approaching minority protection from an international law perspective, presents three 'justificatory grounds'[62]: peace, human dignity, and culture.

- As far as peace is concerned, the link with minority protection is obvious from the frequency of treaty stipulations regarding minorities in peace treaties over a long period of time. The politically destabilizing effect of the insufficient recognition of minorities is evidenced by the number of conflicts engendered by this kind of situation.
- The second link flows from the fact that human rights have always been regarded as fundamental to human dignity and that minority rights today are increasingly viewed as a further development of human rights.

59 Ibid.

60 B.R. Singh, "Multicultural Education: Education-Social Aspects," 11–25 (1995), quoted in Samovar and Porter, 233.

61 Ibid.

62 Åkermark, Athanasia S, *Justifications of Minority Protection in International Law*, Kluwer Law International, The Hague, 1997, quoted in Deon Geldenhuys and Johann Rossouw, *The International Protection of Minority Rights*, F W de Klerk Foundation, August 2001,5.

– The dignity of the individual is in the third instance intertwined with his cultural context. If one understands human dignity as 'a right to self-preservation (existence), accompanied by a right to develop one's own personality according to an own plan of life (self-fulfillment)', "then the legitimacy and necessity of minority cultures as 'contexts of choice' seems to be well founded."[63]

According to Kälin, however, "international law, in most cases, does not require states to adopt a particular course of action in integrating and assimilating (minorities)".[64] Nevertheless, it limits state policies through the prohibition of discrimination which is probably the most important safeguard in the area of integration as it prohibits the exclusion of minorities and the denial of their access to labor, education, health services etc., on the basis of their religion. Moreover, "non-discrimination prevents governments from utilizing cultural arguments to justify disadvantages for some groups. Authorities must, in this regard, not only be 'color blind' but also 'culture blind'.[65] The equal treatment of religious minorities without regards to their religion facilitates their integration in most cases. However, equal treatment leads to segregation if rules of general application cause disadvantage of certain minority groups because their situation is very different from that of the majority of population. Kälin gives examples of

> [t]he dispensation from dress codes at the work place, which allow members of certain minority communities to accept a job without having to sacrifice the demands of their religion, or the availability of special burial grounds for certain religions serve to improve these persons' integration into society.

These cases, he notes,

> [...] clearly show how tolerance toward minorities who want to keep their cultural traditions and belong to cultural minorities can ease their integration into the structures of the majority society. The refusal to take into account these per-

63 Ibid.
64 Kälin, 2003, 274.
65 Ibid, 275.

> sons' religious preferences would force them to either assimilate, and thereby lose an important part of their identity, or, if they hold on to their beliefs nevertheless, to retreat to the outer edges of society and become even more marginalized.[66]

The aim in multicultural and multi-religious societies is the ability of these groups to live confidently together, communicate effectively, and recognize value in their differences and in their society's cultural diversity.[67] To dismiss the Universal Declaration and the other international instruments as ineffective in a multicultural world would mean to abandon the search for human improvement. Without bias and manipulation, the Universal Declaration must be preserved as what it is: *a least common denominator* for a culturally varied universe; a quite precise parameter for the behavior of all; a yardstick of progress for an unjust reality; a tool for the attainment of the other aims of society without losing their human dimension.[68] Benito notes that

> […] a régime of absolute respect for human rights must reconcile unity with diversity, interdependence with liberty. The equal dignity owed to all seeks respect for the differences in the identity of each person. It is in absolute respect for the right to be different that we find authentic equality and the only possibility of the full enjoyment of human rights without racial, sexual, or religious discrimination.[69]

Every society benefits from the full and unhindered practice of religion or belief. Full respect for this basic human right can be a powerful force for preventing, quelling, and ending conflicts. Experience has shown that peaceful coexistence across religious, ethnic, or national borders is only possible if the freedom to have different religious views is ensured, both formally and in practice. Therefore, most governments, today, have to take into account minority positions on spiritual matters where they differ from majority beliefs and values. Judge Voitto Saario stresses "[t]he need to reconcile traditional values and the alternative positive

66 Ibid.
67 Gay McDougall, E/CN.4/2006/74.
68 Alves Lindgren Jose A., 500.
69 Beneito, E/CN.4/Sub.2/1987/26, Para. 17.

values resulting from the evolution of modern societies,"[70] and he recommends the following protective measures[71] to combat intolerance:

- The review, in the light of existing international instruments, of national legislation
- The consequent review of administrative practices
- The guarantee of an effective remedy through judicial institutions or independent mediators against violations of freedom of religion or belief
- The provisions of political, economic and social guarantees for the enjoyment of such freedom.

In addition, he mentions the role of education, the contribution of relevant national institutions in the field of human rights, the establishment of a constructive dialogue between various religious groups, the role of non-governmental organization and mass media in combating attitudes of prejudice.[72] It is the duty of all religions to teach that violence is antithetical to religion. For all religions, an attack on innocents is an assault on religious truth. In every religion, however, there are people who distort teachings of mercy into creeds of violence. In fact, virtually every faith teaches the sacredness of human dignity. The universality of human dignity is at the heart of religious freedom.

70 In Boyle, HR/GENEVA/1984/CRP.4, Para. 2.
71 Ibid.
72 Ibid.

3. Conclusion

The increased importance of religious minorities and the increased religious conflict and violence poses new challenges for the international community. Mainly, religious discrimination generates a failure of recognition of stigmatized persons as citizens, and that the so-called cultural neutrality of the state contributes to their negative symbolic delineation and to their alienation as regards state and society. Freedom of religion is a fundamental human right protected by international law and all states are obligated to respect and protect this right. Freedom of religion or belief is as important to the sanctity and dignity of the human person as it is to the recognition, protection, and maintenance of a free and democratic state. It is predominantly religious minorities who continue to suffer the worst forms of human rights abuses. Today, intolerance of religious diversity has perhaps surpassed racial prejudice as the primary motivation behind human rights violations. The International Instruments are the guidelines to combat these violations.

The Universal Declaration of Human Rights notes that "all human beings are born free and equal in human rights" and that each is "endowed with reason and conscience." It defends the right of every human being to worship and to practice religious faith according to the dictates of conscience. All member states should be committed to eliminate discrimination against people of faith in all fields of civil, political, economic, social and cultural life. Article 18 of the Universal Declaration and Article 18 of the ICCPR are the basic provisions in the international instruments addressing religious freedom. Article 18 of the ICCPR is the binding provision which guarantees to everyone 'the right to freedom of thought, conscience and religion'. One obstacle facing the international instruments is the difficulty to define 'religion'. Instead, the most important international human rights law instruments protect a catalogue of rights relevant to religion under the rubric of 'freedom of thought, conscience, and religion'. Freedom of religion and belief, thus, includes the freedom to have or adopt a religion or belief of one's choice including theistic, non-theistic and atheistic beliefs. Also, it includes freedom to manifest one's religion or belief and freedom of coercion and discrimination.

Main provisions of freedom of religion or belief prohibit coercion which would impair the exercise of this right (art.18.2 ICCPR). It stipulates that freedom to manifest religion may only be subject to those limitations which are prescribed by law and necessary to protect public safety, order, health or morals or the fundamental rights and freedoms of others (art. 18.3 of ICCPR). Like other fundamental human rights, the right to freedom of religion remains primarily an individual right. However, it is often rightly argued that due to the manifestation aspects of the right, the right to freedom of religion or belief is also a collective right.

The freedom of religion or belief is a right of a non-derogable character which can be limited only under restricted conditions. Nevertheless, this right, like other human rights, cannot be used to justify the violation of other human rights and freedoms.

The international instruments ensure the enjoyment of individuals of freedom of religion and belief must be free from discrimination on the ground of religion and belief in all areas of public life including employment, education (article 26 ICCPR). Vilification, insults, threats or abuse against a person on the basis of religion or belief impair that person's right to freedom of religion and belief (art. 20 ICCPR). Moreover, discrimination and vilification on the basis of religion and belief discourages participation in the community and may infringe the right to freedom of religion and belief.

Minority groups are entitled to profess and practice their own religion (Article 27 ICCPR). However, the religions of minorities need special protection. This may involve taking positive action to ensure that people belonging to minority religions are able to exercise their rights. The international instruments positively impose upon states a duty to ensure, as widely as possible, freedom of thought, conscience, and religion to all religions and beliefs and to their followers through eradicating any laws enforcing any unjustified distinctions based on these grounds. Further, they have a responsibility to cut at the very roots of intolerance and prejudice by providing remedies, such as educational measures and cooperation with groups willing to assist in counteracting prejudice and discrimination. The text of the Minority Declaration, while ensuring a balance between the rights of persons belonging to minorities to maintain and develop their own identity and characteristics and the corresponding obligations of states, ultimately safeguards the territorial integrity and political independence of the nation as a whole.

The states' capacity and willingness to guarantee and protect *de jure* and *de facto* freedom of religion of all individuals within its jurisdiction is often the key to developing an appropriate framework for the protection of all human rights. Governments, therefore, should be committed to ensuring that human rights standards are incorporated in legislation, policy and practice. One way to achieve this is by identifying areas where the current protection of human rights and people's understanding of their responsibilities can be improved, especially, in practice, the continuing violations of the right to freedom of thought, conscience, and religion or belief in several participating states and many legal obstacles they are establishing that would infringe on that right. One such barrier is patterns of repressive actions by some countries against unregistered religious believers, including the detention and torture of some just because of their religion or belief. Another barrier is that many governments criminalize religious belief, not violent actions of the believers. The concern, during these times, is that many devout believers in this way are being radicalized and made violent in response to repression. Harassment or discrimination, much less persecution, torture and ill-treatment, against anyone in any country on the basis or religion are unacceptable and those who carry out such acts should be prosecuted to the fullest extent of the law. The proliferation of laws, national security laws, anti-terror measures and registration requirements targeting or limiting religious communities in any region has the potential to cause a chilling effect on religious freedom and is particularly a threat to world peace.

New laws and policies in the West, today, that focus on controlling certain religions, threaten to undermine a host of fundamental freedoms and human rights by contributing to an increase of legal regimes that discriminates against minority religions or beliefs notwithstanding states' commitments found in international documents. Often their reason stated for these new policies and laws is that they are needed to deter terrorism or for state security. However, the ambiguous wording of some of these laws and regulations gives them the potential to jeopardize the right to freedom of religion or belief. At the same time, in many Arab states, there is an increase in the violation of the right to freedom of religion or belief and the persistence of harassment of minority religious groups by some extremists and some officials.

Part 2

Limits of Muslims' Freedom of Religion in the West

Despite international standards that require all member states to protect all people against discrimination (direct and indirect), harassment and victimisation on the basis of religion and belief, the scale and variety of acts of religious intolerance and discrimination are evident in so many countries. The Special Rapporteur on freedom of religion or belief in his report (2004) affirms "the rise in religious extremism, intolerance, and discrimination against religious minorities."[1] He also points out the responsibility of the media for fostering a climate of intolerance towards certain communities, especially those of minorities.[2] The right to freedom of religion obliges the state to encourage tolerance and respect for others' religious practices. This, usually, can be promoted in a variety of ways: through education, especially in schools, through television programming which promotes positive images and role models for a tolerant society, and through celebration of the rich diversity of the nation. All of these are positive strategies to reduce the strangeness of the 'other', and to promote a sense of mutual belonging despite the diversity of cultures and beliefs. In order to achieve that, legislation prohibiting discrimination in all aspects of the life of a shared community is a primary strategy for enforcing tolerance. This section will concentrate on limits on freedom of religion of Muslim minorities in both France and the United States and the role of these legislations in fostering acceptance of incitement of hatred against Muslims and vilification of Islam in some Western States.

1 Report of the High Commissioner for Human Rights, Combating E/CN.4/2004/16, 19 February 2004, para. 12.

2 Ibid.

1. Muslims in France and the United States

Balancing religious positions is far from easy, especially when there is a great deal of discussion in Europe and the US on religious identity and the limits of religious freedom. However, for the sake of society's cohesion, it is important to find a reasonable middle-way. Otherwise the segmentation of society along religious lines with all its detrimental consequences will be aggravated. Today, both France and the USA are criticized for maintaining laws that are used to limit religious rights of Muslim minorities. Since the end of the 1980s, "problems (with religious minorities) have emerged, notably those having to do with Islam".[1] Though Islam is not a new religion, Muslims have become more visible in their presence in the West. In fact, discriminations and intolerance towards Muslim communities have increased since September 11, 2001 and some legislations have had an effect on Muslims minorities, in particular the religious symbols law in France and the legislation of antiterrorism measures and the ensuing of the war on terror by the USA, which helped to trigger the rise of Islamophobia.

1.1 Muslims in France

Muslims in France are a highly diverse mix of ethnicities, religious affiliations, philosophical beliefs, political persuasions, secular tendencies, languages and cultural traditions. They are a product of the colonial era as most come from countries previously colonized or dominated

1 Baubérot, Jean, The Place of Religion in Public Life: The Lay Approach, in *A Deskbook*, 445.

by France. Colonial history still plays a role today and these colonial and postcolonial origins have a direct impact on the French perception of Islam. They help explain, in particular, France's delay in realizing that Islam, present for half a century in France, has become a permanent element of its religious landscape.

The population of the Muslim background in France is comprised mainly of people from Algerian and Moroccan origin, but also consists of people from Afghanistan, Egypt, India, Islamic Republic of Iran, Lebanon, Pakistan, Syrian Arab Republic and Turkey.[2] Islam is now commonly considered to be the second largest religion in France after Christianity. Accepting this demographic reality has never been easy for many French. Questions and doubts on the capacity of these newcomers to become full citizens have been raised consistently since the 1980s. Moreover, the native French often perceive Muslims as a danger and threat due to the fact that the close knit Muslim communities are viewed as being in opposition to the secular tradition of the French Republic and also because of the possibility that these communities may be used as an object of external propaganda and support for terrorist organizations. Too often discussions about Islam in France begin and end with a treatment of Muslims as a social problem. Too often the question is asked: 'Can Muslims fit into French society?' This question presupposes that Islamic values are inherently incompatible with Western ones and that Muslims constitute a 'dangerous class'.[3] The fact is, however, that approximately half of the more than three million Muslims in France have French citizenship, and as Oliver Roy explains it "the second and third generations of Muslims are here to stay".[4]

2 For diversity of Muslim Communities in France, See: Nielsen Jorgen, Muslims in western Europe, second Edition, Edinburgh University Press, Edinburgh, 1995, 8–22.

3 Cesari, Jocelyne, "Islam in France: The Shaping of a Religious Minority," in Yvonne Haddad-Yazbek (ed.), *Muslims in the West, from Sojourners to Citizens*, 2002, Oxford University Press, 36–51.

4 Quoted in Eren Güvercin, Interview with Oliver Roy, "Full Equality before the Law for All Religions", April 29, 2010, <http://www.theamericanmuslim.org/tam.php/features/articles/interview_with_olivier_roy_full_equality_before_the_law_for_all_religions> (viewed Sept. 2013).

To integrate them, France has "used an 'integrationist' or 'assimilationist' model, meaning French citizens are assumed to have no religious, linguistic, or cultural specificity.[5] This method, according to Roy has, 'failed'. Muslims, since colonial times, have not been able to accept the concept of laïcité, consciously or not, especially, in the strict French application; this created the greatest hostility toward North Africans, especially, Algerians. The colonial experience and the immense trauma of the Algerian War help to explain these attitudes. The traditional view that Muslims are difficult, if not impossible to assimilate and the catastrophic failure to create an *Algérie Francaise* are major historical sources of current prejudices.[6] Today, there is a continuous struggle between Muslims and the concept of *laïcité* and their right to freedom of religion or belief. In many ways, this concept gives Muslims and other religious minorities more freedom as the separation from the state is meant to ensure religion is inherently free from intervention. However, in other cases, it limits their freedom of religion or belief. The French laïcité has certainly demanded sacrifices from the Muslim community, especially French Muslim women, in recent years.

5 Ibid.

6 Islam has long been a presence in France-the Mosque of Paris was built in the 1920s and was financed in part by public funds. But since 1975, an "Islam of families" is clearly claiming its place in the polis, having taken the place of an "Islam of celibate of men" constituted of immigrant workers who would often return to their native countries. This legitimate claim to a place in the public arena has met with two obstacles: first, the after effects of decolonization, particularly arising from the Algerian war; next, the social and economic rises that, precisely at the same moment (and in conjunction with the Algerian crises), struck immigrants notably Muslim populations with full force. Baubérot, in *A Deskbook*, 450.

1.2 Muslims in the United States of America

In the United States, religious demography figures are very difficult to make. Muslim Americans number an estimated 6 to 7 million and are increasing steadily. The three largest groups of Muslims in America are the African Americans, the Arabs, and the South Asians.[7] The visibility of Islam in the United States is a recent phenomenon linked to the significant increase in the number of immigrants coming from Muslim countries, with a specific rise in Muslim immigration since 1965 (until the present day) from India, Pakistan, Indonesia and Afghanistan. Immigrants from such countries now outnumber those originating from the Middle East.[8]

Since the 1970s, these new arrivals have given themselves over to building mosques and schools, to founding all sorts of magazines and newspapers, and thus demonstrate a religious vitality that is very distant from the assimilationist attitude of Arab immigrants of the early twentieth century. Islam's visibility within American society is reinforced by the increasing Islamicization of the black community (an estimated 50% of Muslim converts come from the black community). The extreme ethnic and religious diversity of American Muslims means that the boundaries of the Muslim community in America are surrounded by more controversy than in Europe, especially in the post 9/11 context.[9]

7 Karen Leonard, "American Muslims: Race, Religion and the Nation," The International Institute for the Study of Islam in the Modern World (ISIM) Newsletter (June 2004), 16–17.

8 See history of Muslims in America in: Yvonne Yazbeck Haddad, Ed., *The Muslims of America*, Oxford University Press, Oxford, 1991.Jane I. Smith, *Islam in America*, Columbia University Press, New York, 1999. Ron Geaves, Theodore Gabriel, Yvonne Haddad, and Jane Idleman Smith, Editors, *Islam& The West Post 9/11*, Ashgate, USA, 2004.Yvonne Yazbeck Haddad, Ed., *Muslims In The West 'From Sojourners To Citizens',* Oxford University Press, New York, 2002.

9 Cesari, Jocelyne, *American and European Muslims After 9/11: What is Different? French and U.S. Approach to Understanding Islam*, Stanford University, September 12–24, 2004, 3, <http://www.francestanford.stanford.edu/sites/francestanford.stanford.edu/files/Cesari.pdf> (last viewed Oct. 2013).

2. The Western Perception of Islam and Islamophobia

To say that almost every modern society is culturally diverse or multicultural is "to say that its members subscribe to and live by different though overlapping systems of meaning and significance."[1] In practice, however, the West continues to be attached to the idea of the nation state and with globalization and increasing waves of immigrations, a counter-call has come to effect; one that wants to defend 'national identity', against the threat of multiculturalism. Rex explains that "until fairly recently, perhaps until thirty or forty years ago, Western Europeans and Americans did not talk much about national identity. They thought of their states as serving goals of a universal kind reflected in West European political philosophy."[2] Nowadays, however, such complacent self-satisfaction is challenged on two fronts. On the one hand, the nation states find themselves belonging to supranational entities like the European Union or more generally caught up in a process of globalization, involving international economic institutions and international media images. On the other hand, they have had to face an intense process of immigration by minority groups each bringing with them their own culture and forms of social organization. In these circumstances the established nations have been forced to ask whether they have a distinct identity of their own. The rise of new nationalism is essentially a culture of resistance to these forces.[3] This

1 Bhikhu Parekh, *Unity and Diversity in Multicultural Societies,* 3.

2 Rex, J. (1996) 'National Identity in the Democratic Multi-Cultural State', *Sociological Research Online*, vol. 1, no. 2,para. 1.1. <http://www.socresonline.org.uk/socresonline/1/2/1.html> (viewed Sept. 2013).

3 Delanty, G. (1996) 'Beyond the Nation-State: National Identity and Citizenship in a Multicultural Society – A Response to Rex', *Sociological Research Online,* vol. 1, no. 3, <http://www.socresonline.org.uk/socresonline/1/3/1.html> (viewed Sept. 2013). See also, Rex J. (1996) 'Contemporary Nationalism, Its Causes and Consequences for Europe – A Reply to Delanty'

contemporary nationalism or the anxiety about 'national identity' in the West, according to Rex and Delanty, is different from the nationalism of the nineteenth century; whereas the latter was inclusive the former tends to be exclusive.[4]

This return of explicit nationalism as a political force and the revival of national identity are often defined by ethnicity, and concerns about Islam. Thus, the debate on national identity began to focus on Islam and its status in the Western world. Islam became a powerful symbol of Muslim communities' essential difference from the surrounding national community. Conversely, the construction of mosques and the increased adoption of the Islamic scarf, and in a few cases the *burqa*, have made Muslims a distinctly visible minority. The opponents began to appeal to a 'clash of civilizations' perspective, seeing Islam as incompatible with democracy and Western culture. Furthermore, the emergence of what they call 'Islamist terrorism' confirmed, in their eyes, the dangers of multiculturalism and immigration from Muslim countries. American attitudes towards Islam were not out of step with Europe, despite the fact that there was more tolerance in the United States of America. However, this has changed and today many researches and reports show the extent to which prejudice and discrimination against Islam and Muslims have become inherent in American mainstream culture.[5]

This identity crises which has led to the new nationalism, has led to a resurgence of racism, racial discrimination and xenophobia against Muslims, which reflects a major regression affecting democratic progress on account of its traditional political and ideological exploitation by extreme right-wing parties, its intellectual legitimization by intellectuals and influential media, the gradual infiltration of racist and xenophobic rhetoric and platforms in the political programs of democratic

4 Ibid. See also: Rex J. (1996) 'Contemporary Nationalism, Its Causes and Consequences for Europe – A Reply to Delanty' *Sociological Research Online,* vol. 1, no. 4, <http://www.socresonline.org.uk/socresonline/1/4/rex.html> (viewed Sept. 2013).

5 See Yvonne Haddad, and Jane Idleman Smith, Editors, *Islam & The West Post 9/11*, Ashgate, USA, 2004, 218.

parties under the cover of waging war on terrorism and illegal immigration and defending the national identity, and the popular acceptance of racist and xenophobic culture and mentalities.[6] This became to be known as Islamophobia. United Nation's Secretary-General Kofi Annan condemned the rise of Islamophobia and commented in a UN conference in 2004, "[w]hen the world is compelled to coin a new term to take account of increasingly widespread bigotry that is a sad and troubling development. Such is the case with Islamophobia."[7] In his study on the situation of Muslim and Arab peoples in the aftermath of the events of September 11, the Special Rapporteur on contemporary forms of racism, racial discrimination, xenophobia and related intolerance, confirms that, "in various countries, Muslims continue to be subjected to hostility from different sectors of the population and to racial profiling from law enforcement officers."[8]

What is Islamophobia?

The term 'Islamophobia' accurately reflects the largely unexamined and deeply ingrained anxiety many Westerners experience when considering Islam and Muslim cultures. However, it is only in the 1990s that the term became common parlance in defining the discrimination faced by Muslims in the West. The term has been used increasingly amongst

6 Doudou Diène, Political platforms which promote or incite racial discrimination, Updated study by the Special Rapporteur on contemporary forms of racism, racial discrimination, xenophobia and related intolerance; Political platforms. E/CN.4/2006/54, Para. 7. See also, Racism, Racial Discrimination, Xenophobia and all Forms of Discrimination: Situation of Muslim and Arab peoples in various parts of the world Report by Mr. Doudou Diène, Special Rapporteur on contemporary forms of racism, racial discrimination, xenophobia and related intolerance, E/CN.4/2004/19,23 February 2004.

7 SG/SM/9637, HR/4802., Secretary General, Addressing Headquarters Seminar on Confronting Islamophobia, <http://www.un.org/News/Press/docs/2004/sgsm9637.doc.htm> (viewed Sept. 2013).

8 E/CN.4/2004/19, 23 February 2004, Racism, Racial Discrimination, Xenophobia and all Forms of Discrimination: Situation of Muslim and Arab peoples in various parts of the world.

political circles and the media, and even Muslim organizations, especially since the 1997 Runnymede Report (Islamophobia: A Challenge for All).[9] The British Runnymede Trust described Islamophobia as the view that Islam has no values in common with other cultures; is inferior to the West; is a violent political ideology rather than a religion; that its criticisms of the West have no substance; and that discriminatory practices against Muslims are justified. Thus Islamophobia refers to "unfounded hostility to Islam," as well as to "the practical consequences of such hostility in unfair discrimination against Muslim individuals and communities, and to the exclusion of Muslims from mainstream political and social affairs."[10]

Despite miscellaneous differences, the American academy accepted most of the European paradigms for the study of Islam. Islamophobia from an American perspective, explain Peter Gottschalk and Gabriel Greenberg,

> [...] accurately reflects a social anxiety toward Islam and Muslim cultures that is largely unexamined by, yet deeply ingrained in, Americans. Instead of arising from traumatic personal experiences, like its more psychological cousins, this phobia results for most from distant social experiences that mainstream American culture has perpetuated in popular memory, which are in turn buttressed by a similar understanding of current events. This anxiety relies on a sense of otherness, despite many common sources of thoughts.[11]

Nevertheless, there are two factors that make the situation different from within Europe: (a) the social recognition of religious organiza-

9 Early in 1997 the Commission on British Muslims and Islamophobia, under the chairmanship of Professor Gordon Conway, issued a consultative document. The final report, Islamophobia: A Challenge for Us all, was launched in November 1997 by the Home Secretary, Jack Straw. This was the first time that the subject of Islamophobia had been comprehensively tackled in relation to a British Muslim population estimated at between 1.2 and 1.4 million.

10 Runnymede Trust Commission on British Muslims and Islamophobia, *Islamophobia: A Challenge for Us All*, London: Runnymede Trust, 1997, 1.

11 Peter Gottschalk and Gabriel Greenberg, *Islamophobia 'Making the Muslims the Enemy'*, Rowman & Littlefield Publishers, INC., United States of America, 2008, 5.

tions' collective action; (b) the cultural capital of American Muslims. These two factors have meant that, more rapidly that in the European context, a public Muslim voice has begun to emerge (for example ISNA, ICNA, CAIR, etc.) beyond the fact of ethnic diversity.[12] But, while the picture of Islam in the United States seems somewhat different from that in other Western countries, Muslims in North America reveal that there are clear similarities between their experiences and those of Muslims in Western Europe, which has been influenced by issues of stereotyping, discrimination and Islamophobia. It is unfortunate that "American and European attention has focused most readily on divergence instead of convergence."[13]

In this context,

> Islam continues to be identified with terrorism and Muslim religious observance and Muslims themselves continue to be viewed as a security problem not only in law and discriminatory judicial and administrative practice, but also through the intellectual and ideological validation of Islamophobia.[14]

This has led to discrimination against them with regards to access to justice, political participation, and respect of cultures, physical assaults and attacks against their places of worship, cultural centers, businesses and properties.

Islamophobia, thus, has become a topical issue due to the devastating effect it is having on the lives of Muslims and it is debatable whether the term 'Islamophobia' makes sense and is the most adequate term to describe acts and attitudes that are actually unacceptable forms of discrimination and xenophobia. However, it is widely accepted that Muslim communities and people associated with Islam across several Western countries are often exposed to acts of discrimination and hatred

12 Cesari, Jocelyne, *American and European Muslims After 9/11: What is Different? French and U.S. Approaches to Understanding Islam*, Stanford University, September 12–24, 2004, 12.

13 Peter Gottschalk and Gabriel Greenberg, 5.

14 E/CN.4/2006/17, 13 February 2006. Racism, Racial Discrimination, Xenophobia and all Forms of Discrimination: Situation of Muslim and Arab peoples in various parts of the world.

that may vary in degree and dimension but are based on a form of prejudice towards Islam as a religion. In April 2000, the European Commission Against Racism and Intolerance (ECRI) issued its General Policy Recommendation N° 5 on "Combating Intolerance and Discrimination against Muslims", stating that: "religious intolerance towards Islam and Muslim communities is increasing in countries where this religion is not observed by the majority of the population (ECRI 2000 [21])."[15] The ECRI notes the effects of Islamophobia on Muslims are very negative. Muslims are directly affected and, while we should be cautious of any form of victimisation, it is obvious that the negative connotations associated with the practice of Islam may lead to exclusion and self-exclusion, with obvious results in terms of self-esteem and social integration.[16]

The Pew Global Attitude Project affirms the spread of Islamophobia, by observing that, "after a year marked by riots over cartoon portrayals of (Prophet) Mohammad, a major terrorist attack in London, and continuing wars in Iraq and Afghanistan, most [...] Westerners see Muslims as fanatical, violent, and as lacking tolerance."[17] Thus, it could be concluded that in addition to individual acts of intolerance and religious profiling, Islamophobia leads to viewing Muslims as a greater security threat on an institutional, systemic and societal level and perceiving their views to be intrinsically problematic, violent or unethical.

15 ECRI General Policy Recommendation N° 5 on combating intolerance and discrimination against Muslims, European Commission against Racism and Intolerance (ECRI), Strasbourg, 16 March 2000, 3, <http://www.coe.int/t/dghl/monitoring/ecri/activities/gpr/en/recommendation_n5/Rec5%20en21.pdf> (last viewed Oct. 2013).

16 Ibid.

17 The Pew Global Attitudes Project, The Great Divide: How Westerners and Muslims View Each Other, Europe's Muslims More Moderate, 2006, Available online: <http://pewglobal.org/reports/display.php?ReportID=253> (viewed Sept. 2013). The Pew Global Attitudes Project is a series of worldwide public opinion surveys that encompasses a broad array of subjects ranging from people's assessments of their own lives to their views about the current state of the world and important issues of the day. More than 100,000 interviews in 50 countries have been conducted as part of the project's work.

Even though 9/11 jolted Westerners into a new awareness of Islam, it has produced less insight and understanding than caricature and fear. In the minds of many Westerners, Islam is synonymous with the Middle East; Muslim men with violence; and Muslim women with oppression. In the post-9/11 world, a clash of civilizations appears to be increasingly manifest and the 'war on terror' seems to be a struggle against Islam. These are symptoms of Islamophobia which includes false assumptions such as: Islam is static; it has little in common with values and practices of other (especially western) cultures and is thus is inferior to Western culture; it is violent, aggressive, undemocratic, and supportive of terrorism, and therefore represents an enemy.[18]

A growing number of Western Muslims often find themselves caught between their faith and the social expectations placed on them to be 'discreet' with their religious practices.[19] The Special Rapporteur, on contemporary forms of racism, racial discrimination, xenophobia and related intolerance, in his report, affirms that "this is not a new phenomenon, and was in evidence long before the attacks of 11 September 2001; subsequently it has taken on new dimensions, particularly in recent times."[20] These new dimensions are a result of new legislations targeting Muslims indirectly. These new legislations, especially in the United States and France, intended to protect public order, neutrality and national security after September 11, threaten the religious liberty of Muslims.

18 Steven Vertovec, Islamophobia and Muslim Recognition in Britain, Chapter 1, in Yvonne Yazbeck Haddad, Ed., Muslims in the West: From Sojourners to Citizens, Oxford University Press, Inc., 2002, 24.

19 A report by the European Union Monitoring Centre on Racism and Xenophobia, published in May 2002, provided widespread evidence of the multiple forms of Islamophobia in the Member States of the European Union. European Monitoring Centre on Racism and Xenophobia, Anti-Islamic reactions in the EU after the terrorist acts against the USA, 12th September to 31st December 2001, <http://www.pedz.uni-mannheim.de/daten/edz-b/ebr/05/Spain.pdf> (last viewed Oct. 2013)

20 Situation of Muslim and Arab peoples in various parts of the world in the aftermath of the events of 11 September 2001 – Report by the Special Rapporteur on contemporary forms of racism, E/CN.4/2003/23, paras. 31–33.

These legislations, such as the law banning religious symbols and clothing in publicly supported institutions and schools in France and the anti-terrorism measures, in the United States, which have been introduced and adopted following the attacks of 11 September 2001, have increased anti-Muslim sentiments. They have contributed to an increase of Islamophobia, which has led some to question the willingness of Muslims living in the West to accept the political and cultural norms of Western democracies. Islam, more and more, is seen as hampering the integration of Muslims and having a potential to create political disturbance. The dominant negative perceptions of Islam and Muslims are reinforced by the ongoing controversy of Islam and human rights. This has led the Muslim minorities to always be on the defensive, to fight the accentuation of stigma via the linking of Islam, the poor suburbs, and terrorism. Muslims today are facing intolerances, vilifications and stereotyping of their beliefs, which can amount to advocacy of hatred.

In an international context dominated by the fight against terrorism, the situation of Muslim people throughout the world can be viewed in three ways: namely containment of Islam from a security angle, monitoring of places of worship and suspicion of Muslims.[21]

21 E/CN.4/2006/17, Para. 18.

3. Limits on Freedom of Religion of Muslims in the West

One major area of concern in the West is violations of the principle of non-discrimination with regard to the manifestation of one's religion or belief. Martin Scheinin notes that

> [...] states have not considered it difficult to allow their citizens the freedom to think. The difficulties start when we come to the right to *express* one's conviction, the right to *organize* as a community in order to promote a religion or belief and the right to *act* in accordance with one's conscience.[1]

The principle of giving people a 'fair go' irrespective of race, religion, political belief, gender or sexual orientation is a widely held moral value. This principle of non-discrimination is enshrined in various international human rights treaties especially Article 26 of the ICCPR. However, as governments have stepped up their efforts to enhance national security and protect themselves against the threat of religious extremism, pre-existing prejudices against Muslims have been reinforced and has featured prominently in public debate. It is not only certain Muslims in particular, those viewed as 'fundamentalists', or even Muslims in general, who in some aspect of their behavior are questioned, but, Islam is itself now openly and publicly attacked. Generalizations and stigmatization are the common elements in these attacks.

Moreover, there is a direct correlation between official public discourse on issues, such as immigration, integration and multiculturalism and the adoption of legislation and policies that discriminate against Muslim minorities.

1 Scheinin, Martin (1992), 'Article 18'. Asbjørn Eide, G. Alfredsson, G. Melander, L.A. Rehof and A. Rossas, eds. *The Universal Declaration of Human Rights: A Commentary*. Oslo: Scandinavian University Press: 263–4.

3.1 Religious Symbols Controversy in France

There is a great deal of discussion in Europe and the US on religious identity and the limits of religious freedom. In such discussions, symbols such as headscarves, Christian crosses, and the like, play an important role. The most prominent of the religious symbols at stake in current debates over freedom of religion in the Western world is the Islamic headscarf or *Hijab* (e.g. headcover, foulard, or veil). The headscarf in question is worn by a female over her head, generally covering her hair, ears, and neck. However, for some Muslim women, *hijab* may involve wearing a large loose garment that can cover the hands and face – a *chador* or a *burqa*. The headscarf, for many Muslim women, a sign of female modesty, is an integral part of Qur'anic teachings.[2]

France took a decision to ban the headscarf *(Hijab)*, since the beginning of the school year 2004/05. This law has been widely condemned in the United States. Many Americans assume that the wearing of such personal symbols in public schools can be accommodated without violating principles of religious freedom. French supporters of the headscarf ban, however, argue that in the current French social, political and cultural context, they cannot. That is why the government felt it was necessary to pass a new law.

3.1.1 The Law on Religious Symbols in France

The debate over religious symbols in France began over the question of whether denying Muslim girls the right to wear headscarves in public schools constitutes a violation of the right to practice their religion. In 1989, local school officials in Grenoble denied Muslim female students the right to wear their *headscarves* in class due to a law that prohibits

2 Sebastian Poulter, "Muslim Headscarves in School: Contrasting Legal Approaches in England and France," *Oxford Journal of Legal Studies*, Vol. 17, 1997, 45. See also: Sawitri Saharso, "Culture, Tolerance and Gender," *The European Journal of Women's Studies*, Vol. 10, No. 1, 2003, 10.

proselytizing in schools. Their action was upheld in a decision rendered in 1989 by the Conseil d'Etat.[3] In its decision, the Conseil d'Etat,[4] referred to the right to freedom of expression and the right to publicly manifest one's religion or beliefs, decided that "the wearing of symbols intended to show a child's affiliation to a religion in public schools was not necessarily considered incompatible with the principle of the separation of Church and State." The Conseil d'Etat added "it would only constitute a breach of this principle, and therefore be considered illegal, if it was accompanied by proof of proselytizing behavior or provocation." It concluded that an internal code of conduct for schools should ensure that wearing tokens of religious affiliation should conform with (1) respect for the principles of *laïcité* and pluralism; (2) the duty of tolerance and respect for the person and conviction of others; and (3) the obligation of every student to participate in all educational activities (including sports and practical training as in laboratories and workshops).[5]

3 The *Conseil d'État* is one of three high courts in France, the other two being the *Cour de Cassation*, the final venue for appeals of cases involving two private parties, and the *Conseil Constitutionnel*, the tribunal that decides the constitutionality of laws under consideration by the parliament. Together, these three courts serve the roles that in the United States are performed by the Supreme Court, as well as some additional functions.

4 Conseil d'Etat, Assemblée Générale, No 346.893 – 27 November 1989, <http://www.conseil-etat.fr/ce-data/aquoi/avis7.htm>. The French religious symbol guidelines affected not only students, but school employees and teachers as well. In 2000, a Muslim *surveillante* (a type of student supervisor) was dismissed for wearing her headscarf to school. The Conseil d'État dismissed the complaint arising from this case, finding no violation of the woman's freedom of religion. As a member of the public service she benefited from freedom from religious discrimination when hired and must now equally respect the principle of laïcité, which prohibits the free expression of religion within the public service. To wear religious symbols at work, the Conseil stated, is a fundamental violation of one's duties in this French public service setting. "Neutralité," *Le Dalloz*, p. 747; "Éducation: une surveillante d'établissement scolaire ne doit pas porter le foulard durant l'exercice de ses fonctions," *Le Monde*, 9 May 2000.

5 An-Na'im, Abdullahi, 'Human Rights and Islamic Identity in France and Uzbekistan: Mediation of the Local and Global', *Human Rights Quarterly* 22.4 (2000), 921.

Reaffirming its 1989 *avis* in *Kherouaa et autres (1992)*[6], the Conseil also looked to the breadth of the school rule that prohibited headscarves. As this particular rule called for an absolute prohibition on the wearing of religious symbols, the Conseil determined that the rule was invalid due to an *excès de pouvoir*; the girls' freedom to wear their headscarves was upheld.[7] These decisions permitted the wearing of *headscarves* in public schools, accepting that it was a legitimate religious symbol to be expressed and that wearing it was not incompatible with the French system of laïcité. Moreover, the Conseil has emphasized that the principles of laicism and neutrality are not meant to propagate atheism but rather to protect religious freedom in a plurality society.[8]

School administrations found this regime complex and difficult to implement on a case-by-case basis, thus, educational professionals advocated for the adoption of a law on the issue. After much unfavorable media attention to the wearing of the headscarf, the Ministry of Education issued a directive in 1994 that prohibits the wearing of "ostentatious political and religious symbols" in schools. The directive did not specify the 'symbols' in question, leaving school administrators considerable authority and discretion to do so. Despite that, the Conseil d'Etat in 1995 affirmed that simply wearing a headscarf does not provide grounds for exclusion from school and subsequently struck down some decisions to expel girls for wearing their headscarves.[9] Although serious jurists described the Conseil d'Etat's 1989 decision as "nuanced and protective of individual rights,"[10] nevertheless, state officials, at

6 These principles were confirmed by the Conseil in *Kherouaa et autres*, (1992) *Recueil Dalloz Sirey*, 9ième cahier – Jurisprudence, 108, Judgement of 14 March 1994 – N. et Z. Yilmaz, Recueil des Arrets du Conseil d' Etat 1994, 129. Judgement of 20 May 1996 – Ministre d'education nationale v. Ali, Recueil des Arrets du Conseil d' Etat 1996, 187. Judgement of 20 May 1996 – Ministre d'leducation nationale v. Outamghart.

7 *Kherouaa et autres*, (1992) *Recueil Dalloz Sirey*, 9ième cahier – Jurisprudence, 109.

8 Kherouaa 1992, in Dagmar Richter, 209.

9 Conseil d'Etat, 10 March 1995, Fatima et Fouzia Aoukili c. Collège Xavier Bichat de Nantua.

10 Gunn, A Comparison, 457.

both the national and local levels, repeatedly attempted to undermine it. "Led by the right-wing political leader Le Pen, a large part of French society came to perceive the headscarf as a symbol of Muslim conspiracy and extremism. It was seen as a provocative symbol of Muslim identity in the neutral and secularized public sphere."[11] The media seized upon the story and the media was playing a significant role in shaping public opinion. Baubérot notes that,

> [...] the individual does not realize that this spiritual itinerary is, in fact, substantially determined by the media. It is becoming more and clearer, from sociological point view, that it is precisely this media system that establishes the standards for what is a legitimate and what is not, even in matters affecting public religious expression. Thus, in the pervasive influence of the media, we confront a new problem for freedom-a problem in which France is not alone.[12]

Delgado offers an excellent summary of the power of mass media by noting that they "help constitute our daily lives by shaping our experiences and providing the content for much of what we talk about (and how we talk) at the interpersonal level."[13]

In December 2003, a special commission was appointed by the President and headed by the national ombudsman, Bernard Stasi, to analyze the application of the principle of *laïcité* in France. Among other recommendations, the Stasi Commission recommended that a law be drafted banning conspicuous religious symbols (including large Christian crosses, Jewish skullcaps and Islamic headscarves etc.) in state schools.

11 Anna Elisabetta Galeotti, "Citizenship and Equality: The Place for Toleration," *Political Theory*, Vol. 21, No. 4, 1993, 596, quoted in Laura Barnett Freedom of religion and Religious Symbols in the Public Sphere, revised 22 Sempteber 2008, 31. Available online at <http://www2.parl.gc.ca/content/lop/researchpublications/prb0441-e.pdf> (viewed Sept. 2013).

12 Baubérot, in A DeskBook, 453.

13 F. P. Delgado, "The Nature of Power Across Communicative and Cultural Borders," 12 (1993), quoted in Samovar and Porter, 39.

On 10 February 2004, a bill containing proposals for legislation to ban religious symbols, passed its first reading in Parliament.[14] The ban on religious symbols was in application of Law 2004–228 of 15 March, 2004, on "laïcité", and conspicuous religious symbols in public schools *(Loi no 2004–228 du 15 mars 2004 encadrant, en application du principe de laïcité, le port de signes ou de tenues manifestant une appartenance religieuse dans les écoles, collèges et lycées publics.)*[15] The law, which was designed to prohibit students from wearing Islamic headscarves, Jewish skullcaps, and large crosses, was approved by an overwhelming vote of 494 to 36 in the National Assembly, and by a comparably disproportionate vote of 276 to 20 in the Senate, and was strongly supported by popular opinion throughout France.

Whilst the law deals with religious symbols in general, the public debate was mostly concerned with the Islamic headscarf. The headscarf has a stronger symbolic load than a kippah or a Sikh turban for instance. It is as a result of this symbolic overload that the debate has touched questions of identity, community, cultural diversity, religious freedom and tolerance, Islam in Europe, and, not least, gender relations.[16] The question, thus, is whether such a ban would be in violation of the numerous international human rights treaties to which France is signatory.

14 E/CN.4/2006/5. 9 January 2006.Law 2004–228, which amended the Education Act, was adopted by a large majority in the National Assembly and across party lines. In its article 1, it provides that in public elementary schools, middle schools *(collèges)* and secondary schools *(lycées)*, wearing symbols or clothing by which students ostentatiously show a religious Identity is prohibited. School rules are to stipulate that any disciplinary procedure must be preceded by dialogue with the student. The assessment of whether a religious symbol constitutes a conspicuous sign is left to the head of the school establishment, a power that is said to have led in some cases to abuse, including in cases where some of the heads decided to ban all manner of head coverings, with even the slightest religious connotation. Para. 51–52.

15 Law No. 2004–228 of Mar. 15, 2004, J.O., Mar. 17, 2004, at 5190 [hereinafter Law No. 2004–228.

16 Dawn Lyon and Debora Spini, "Unveiling the Headscarf," Legislative note, *Feminist Legal Studies*, Kluwer Academic Publishers, Netherlands 12, 2004, 334.

3.1.2 Religious Symbols and the European Court of Human Rights

When the issue of the headscarf was presented to the European Court of Human Rights in the case of *Dahlab v. Switzerland*[17] and in the case of *Sahin v. Turkey*[18], the Court addressed the issue of whether a ban on religious garb was a violation of Article 9 of the European Convention on Human Right.

In *Dahlab v. Switzerland*, the applicant was a primary-school teacher who has converted to Islam, from Catholicism, in 1991, by which time she had already been teaching at the same primary school for more than a year. She wore an Islamic headscarf for approximately three years, apparently without any action being taken by the head teacher or the district schools inspector or any comments being made by parents.

When the European Court of Human Rights considered whether the requirement was a legitimate restriction of the freedom of religion, it upheld the ban on religious garb worn by teachers. It noted that the Swiss courts had already required the removal of the crucifix from classrooms in order to preserve the principle of denominational neutrality. The headscarf is, according to the Court, "a powerful religious symbol" and "hard to square with gender equality".

> It therefore appears difficult to reconcile the wearing of an Islamic headscarf with the message of tolerance, respect for others and, above all, equality and non-discrimination that all teachers in a democratic society must convey to their pupils.

Thus, according to the Court's reasoning such a measure was justified in order to prevent the possible proselytizing effect of this 'powerful external symbol' where students may be more easily influenced and 'religious peace' must be protected with extreme care, and held that a democratic State should be allowed to limit the right of a teacher in a public school to wear the Islamic headscarf if it found wearing it was

17 *Dahlab v Switzerland* (2001) appln 42393/98 Eur Court HR (15 February 2001).

18 *Şahin v. Turkey*, application No. 44774/98, ECtHR Chamber judgement of 29 June 2004, para. 108 and ECtHR Grand Chamber judgement of 10 November 2005, at 114, 115, 116 and 122.

incompatible with the protection of rights and freedoms of others, public order and public safety.[19]

In the opinion of Torron and Valls "the Court, in Dahlab v. Switzerland, showed too much respect for the state's margin of appreciation. First, the "religious peace" of the school does not seem to have suffered any serious threat, for the applicant wore the Islamic *foulard* during approximately five years until she was prohibited from doing so by the (female) general director of primary schools of Geneva's canton. In all those years there appears not to have been any problem caused at the school by neither the applicant's veil nor a single complaint of the students or of the students' parents. Second, we do not fully understand why the principle of laïcité (neutrality, secularism) should require, in a country enjoying religious peace, as Switzerland, that no religious personal symbols are visible in the teachers' clothes; instead of permitting students to see, in their own school, evidence of the religious pluralism existing in the Swiss society. As long as teachers respect the students' belief and do not attempt to proselytize them, the evidence of religious pluralism seems to be more consistent with a neutral attitude of the state and, on the other hand, more educative for students than the fictional absence of religion on the part of school personnel.[20]

In the case of *"Shin v. Turkey"*, Leyla Sahin, a medical student at the University of Bursa in Turkey, was prohibited from taking examinations and from enrolling in courses while wearing the headscarf. She also refused to remove it in order to continue her studies. The *Sahin* case subsequently was referred to a seventeen-judge grand chamber of the European court. The petitioner did not claim a right for "all women to wear the Islamic headscarf in all places," but rather that university students were "discerning adults who enjoyed full legal capacity and were capable of deciding for themselves what was appropriate conduct,"[21] and what was not. This choice, for Leyla, was based on religious conviction and that she had not sought to influence fellow students or to

19 Kanev, Krassimir, Muslim religious freedom in the OSCE area after September 11, *Helsinki Monitor*, 2004 no. 4, 238.

20 Javier Martinez-Torron and Rafael Navarro-Valls, in A Deskbook, 231 (82n).

21 Kanev, Krassimir, 238.

undermine their rights and freedoms. The petitioner also argued that the ban violated her right to an education, but this argument was rejected by the court.[22]

There was a legal basis for that interference in Turkish law, as the case-law of the constitutional court made it clear that authorising students to "cover the neck and hair with a veil or headscarf for reasons of religious conviction" in universities was contrary to the Constitution. In addition, the Supreme Administrative Court had, for many years, taken the view that wearing the Islamic headscarf was not compatible with the fundamental principles of the Republic. Furthermore, it was beyond doubt that regulations on wearing the Islamic headscarf had existed well before the applicant had enrolled at the university. Students, particularly those who, like the applicant, were studying a health-related subject, were required to comply with rules on dress. In those circumstances, it would have been clear to Miss Şahin, from the moment she entered the University of Istanbul, that there were regulations on wearing the Islamic headscarf and, after the circular was published in 1998, that she was liable to be refused access to lectures if she continued to do so.

In this case, the European Court of Human Rights found that the impugned measure primarily pursued the legitimate aims of protecting the rights and freedoms of others and of protecting public order and it

> [...] considered that, when examining the question of the Islamic headscarf in the Turkish context, there had to be borne in mind the impact which wearing such a symbol, which was presented or perceived as a compulsory religious duty, may have on those who chose not to wear it.

In the case of *Leyla Sahin v. Turkey* the court held unanimously that there had been no violation of Article 9 of the European Convention on Human Rights (freedom of thought, conscience and religion), that they were proportional in a democratic society to maintain public order and to protect the rights and freedoms of others. In its discussion, the European Court of Human Rights granted the state a wide margin

22 TheEuropean Courtof Human Rights judgments are accessible on its website, <http://www.echr.coe.int> (viewed Sept. 2013).

of appreciation and upheld the ban as consistent with the principles of secularism and equality.

In the *Dahlab and Sahin* cases, the Court did not seem to be aware of the fundamental philosophy underlying the protection of religious liberty which is: that the reason why the freedom of each individual must be respected is not that it is objectively correct, rather, the freedom of conscience must be respected because it is considered a fundamental area of the individual's autonomy in democratic societies. Hence, article 9(2) of the European Convention provides that the state may restrict the exercise of that freedom only when it is "necessary in a democratic society." In other words, the government is not obliged to respect and protect religious freedom because it considers the convictions of its citizens to be correct or even convenient. It is obliged to protect the freedom to believe and to act accordingly because this freedom constitutes an essential element of a democratic society. The protection of that freedom is a paramount *public* interest and not merely a *private* interest of individuals and groups.

While in both cases the requirement of a law was not a problem, the decisions raise the question as to whether there are really convincing arguments to say that banning the headscarf is necessary. The debate in France provides a good opportunity to examine this question in detail and to see whether the reasons advanced in favor and against a ban are convincing.

3.1.3 Reasons for Banning the Headscarf

Under French law, the state can limit the exercise of rights-such as wearing religious clothing-only when the restriction can be justified as promoting the 'public order' *(l'ordre public).* This public order doctrine refers to the "traditional function of government, permitting restrictions on individual liberty to be imposed so as to 'maintain public security, tranquility, and health.'"[23]

23 Gunn, A Comparison, 467.

The Stasi Commission justified its recommendation to ban religious attire on two specific public order grounds:

> (1) To respond to the coercion suffered by Muslim girls whose families and communities force them to wear headscarves against their will and because such coercion exacerbates sexual discrimination and religious polarization within France; (2) Religious symbols are "'troubling' the peace in schools."[24]

Thus, another ground invoked to limit this right is that young women were often forced to wear the veil due to pressure from their male relatives or to protect their physical safety in the context of potential violence. The ban, it can be argued, is important because a child's' autonomy is being overridden by parents and communities who are coercing them into wearing the headscarf. The law is considered a mean of protecting young women who were not willing to abide by certain so-called religious norms, including the wearing of the headscarf. As a result, the banning of religious symbols at school would enable those young female children to freely choose the way they conduct their lives.

Moreover, commentators who support the Headscarf Law view it as part of a long tradition of *laïcité*. They use *laïcité* in its narrow definition, as only the separation of church and state; and, thus, they favor the argument that the goal is to provide a religion-free zone where youth are protected from the proselytizing aspect of religion. For the people who are supporting the law, they believe that without banning the headscarf, the French principles of long-established *laïcité* are under threat. *Laïcité*, it is claimed, is crucial to the social harmony and national cohesion of France and its citizens. In essence, the school is a place where children should learn about the elements that unify them rather than the elements that differentiate them.[25]

24 Rapport au président de la République [STASI Report] (2003), at 41, <http://lesrapports.ladocumentationfrancaise.fr/BRP/034000725/0000.pdf> (viewed Sept. 2013), quoted in Gunn, A comparision, 473.

25 E/CN.4/2006/5, para. 58. At a meeting with members of staff of the office of the Minister of National Education, the Special Rapporteur was told that the wearing of religious symbols in schools hurt the freedom of conscience of the other children.

Laïcité, which is often translated into English as 'secular', is a term that is difficult to define and almost impossible to translate. "There is no firm definition of *laïcité*: neither officially established nor generally accepted." *Le Grand Robert* dictionary defines *laïcité* as a "political notion involving the separation of civil society and religious society, the State exercising no religious power and the churches *(Églises)* exercising no political power."[26]

The history of French law on freedom of religion and secularity has its origin in the philosophy of the Enlightenment and the principles invoked in the Revolution of 1789. This concept of *laïcité* was a result of the long French history of religious violence, including the Religious Wars (1562–1598). These religious wars led the French to favor strict separation between the state and religion as a way to make sure that religious competition and religious proselytizing do not create disorder in the public sphere. The secular state evolved as the church's relationship to the state was diminished but its privileges were not entirely removed.[27] On December 9, 1905, the National Assembly adopted the Law on the Separation of Churches and the State.[28] Under the 1905 Act separating the Church and the State, Section 1 declares, '[t]he Republic shall ensure freedom of conscience. It shall guarantee free participation in religious worship, subject only to the restrictions laid down hereinafter in the interest of public order.' This law is the foundation of the principle of *laïcité*, which governs the place of religions in the country and maintains a totally secular public sector. This law removes the principle of recognized religions and stipulates that the State does not subsidize any religion. Articles 3 through 6 effectively expropriated all religious property that had been acquired or built prior to 1905, and established procedures for state officials to conduct inventories of the property. The French state continues to own church build-

26 Paul Robert, 5 *Le Grand Robert de le Langue Françqise*, 915 (2d ed. 1992).

27 Boyle & Sheen, 294.

28 Law on the Separation of Churches and the State of Dec. 9, 1905, J.O. Dec. 11, 1905, 7205. For the current version of the 1905 law, as amended, see: <http://www.laicidade.org/wp-content/uploads/2007/04/loi-1905-fr.pdf> (viewed Sept. 2013); *see also* Baubérot, in A Deskbook, 441–453.

ings constructed before 1905, including all of the famous cathedrals of France, and pays for their maintenance but allows the Church to use them.[29]

Laïcité was confirmed in the 1946 French constitution and in the revised constitution of 1958. Furthermore, the 1958 French Constitution provides, *'France is an indivisible, secular, democratic and social Republic; it shall ensure the equality before the law of all citizens, without distinction as to origin, race or religion. It shall respect all beliefs.'* (A.2).[30] The word *laïcité*, thus, is used in France to summarize prevailing beliefs regarding the proper relationship between religion and the French state.[31] *Laïcité*, in this sense, is a principle of religious neutrality that is intended to create the conditions for religious freedom. The religious symbols law is supposedly to defend this principle of neutrality.

One explanation of the roots of secularism can be found by looking at French society itself. French society is mono-cultural compared to the United States: it stresses assimilation, integration, and shared values. There is an ideal of citizenship that is inscribed in official documents and reinforced by politicians across the political spectrum. Furthermore, the role of government in the lives of citizens is that of the welfare state, which is based on utilitarian notions.[32] As a result, individual rights are seen as less important than those of society as a whole.[33] Religion, in this sense, is considered a personal choice and thus a private affair. As a result, one person's right to exercise his or her faith in certain public contexts is seen as infringing on, and inferior to, the rights of others to exist in a neutral, non-proselytizing sphere.[34]

29 John McManners, 'Church and State in France', 1870–1914 (1972), 152–53, quoted in Gunn, *A Comparison*, 441.

30 Boyle & Sheen, 294–295.

31 Gunn, *A Comparison*, 419.

32 Deshmukh, Fiona, *Legal secularism in France and Freedom of Religion in the United States: A Comparison and Iraq as a Cautionary Tale*, Houston Journal of International Law, 2007, available online at: <http://www.questia.com/library/1G1-175629987/legal-secularism-in-france-and-freedom-of-religion> (viewed Sept. 2013).

33 Ibid.

34 Ibid.

Another line of reasoning for the ban includes that the headscarf is a sign of extremism. Those favoring the ban regard the "headscarf as a symbol of a political Islam"[35] that threatens civil order, seeks to establish a religious regime, and undermines rights acquired by women. This fear of Islam is once again tied to the issue of the headscarf. France is being challenged by militant, radical Muslims, thus, it found that it is sometimes necessary to restrict civil liberties in specific places, like schools, to ensure an atmosphere free of intimidation.[36] Concerns about French identity in the face of an increasing minority of Muslim origin have also played a role in the wide acceptance of the law. Jean-Marie Le Pen, the candidate of the explicitly anti-immigrant *Front National* (FN), received over 5.5 million votes in the French Presidential election 2002, nearly 18% of the vote.[37] Aware of Le Pen's potential appeal among voters concerned by the social effects of immigration, the government at that time has emphasized its willingness to take strong stands on issues such as religious symbols. Gunn notes that,

> The crisis of 2003 seems to have arisen not from particular events, but from statements made by politicians that appealed to latent popular sentiments…it is a combination of popular prejudices, media sensationalism, and exploitation by the political classes.[38]

One can conclude that there are various reasons justifying the ban of the headscarf. One of the main reasons goes to the principles of *laïcité*, neutrality and protecting public order. As it has been noted, the headscarf is seen as a form of religious propaganda, a sign of proselytizing and that is prohibited in public schools. Moreover, headscarves

35 See: T. Jeremy Gunn, *Fearful Symbols: The Islamic Headscarf and the European Court of Human Rights* 28 (July 4, 2005) (conference paper, on file with The Strasbourg Conference), "Fearful Symbols: The Islamic Headscarf and the European Court of Human Rights in Sahin v. Turkey," *Droit et Religion* (2008): 339–367.

36 Tahzib, in a Deskbook, 475

37 Gilles Ivaldi, *Extreme Right Parties in France, An overview*, 8 July 2002, 6. Available online at: <http://www.politik.uni-mainz.de/ereps/download/france_overview.pdf> (viewed Sept. 2013).

38 Gunn, *A Comparison*, 457.

are seen as a provocative symbol of Muslim identity in the neutral and secularized public sphere and that trouble the peace in schools. Furthermore, the headscarf can be read as opposing certain values which are protected in French Republicanism, such as tolerance and equality. In this sense, banning the headscarf is a response to the coercion suffered by Muslim girls whose families and communities force them to wear headscarves against their will and because such coercion exacerbates sexual discrimination and religious polarization within France. Finally, the headscarf ban is, justified as a symbol of Muslim conspiracy and extremism and this and related factors appear to have led to perceptions of an 'Islamic threat' to French cultural identity, political institutions, or legal order.

3.1.4 Arguments Against Banning the Headscarf

The law ignored the Conseil d'Etat's interpretation of the concept of laïcité as an umbrella which also protects free exercise. In its 1989 opinion, the Court balanced French and international human rights concerns with the principle of *laïcité* and ruled that students could wear religious clothing at school as long as it did not constitute a disruption of school activities or an attempt to purvey propaganda. Clearly, for the Court, the principle of laïcité included, and protected, the free expression of religion.[39]

The law singled out the Islamic faith. Women who wear the headscarf are being shunned and excluded and, indeed, so openly and unabashedly that it's almost as if there had been a public appeal to ostracise Muslim women. The debate over the wearing of the headscarf gives the impression that a member of the teaching staff or a student with a headcovering stands in opposition to human dignity, opposes equality, a threat to society or rejects the basic right to liberty and the country's free and democratic constitution. This is a perfect illustration

39 Deshmukh, Fiona, *Legal secularism in France and Freedom of Religion in the United States: A Comparison and Iraq as a Cautionary Tale.*

of how official enemies are constructed: through stigmatisation, moral disqualification and defamation.

3.1.4.1 *Banning the Headscarf for the Protection of Secularity and Neutrality*

In reality, there is a wide variety of practices regarding the headscarf throughout the Muslim world and these practices have changed over time. What is important here, however, is that secular state commissions presumably are not qualified to decide theological questions about what the cross should mean to Christians or what the headscarf should mean to Muslims. Disagreements about the meaning of symbols runs throughout all religions, and what some may believe to be sacred, others, including coreligionists, may see as superstitious. While the state presumably should not decide such matters, it nevertheless should respect-and protect-the right of its citizens to make their own judgments about such matters, just as the Conseil d'Etat determined. Rosalind Higgins opposed the idea that "[s]tates could have complete latitude to decide what was and what was not a genuine religious belief. The contents of a religion should be defined by the worshippers themselves."[40] The European Court of Human Rights [ECtHR], in *Metropolitan Church of Bessarabia v. Moldova*, has affirmed that "the State's duty of neutrality and impartiality is incompatible with any power on the State's part to assess the legitimacy of religious beliefs."[41]

The fundamental philosophy underlying the protection of religious liberty is not that it is objectively correct; rather, freedom of conscience must be respected because it is considered a fundamental area of the individual's autonomy in democratic societies. Hence, Article 9(2) of the European Convention provides that the state may restrict the exercise of that freedom only when it is "necessary" in a democratic society.

40 The Human Rights Committee discussion on 24 July 1992, Summary Records of the 1166th meeting of the forty-fifth session, para. 48. In E/CN.4/2006/5.

41 Metropolitan Church of Bessarabia v. Moldova, 13 December 2001, ECtHR, App. No. 45701/99 para. 123.

In other words, the government is not obliged to respect and protect religious freedom because it considers the convictions of its citizens to be correct or even convenient. It is obliged to protect the freedom to believe and to act accordingly. The protection of that freedom is a paramount *public* interest and not merely a *private* interest of individuals and groups. This is something that is easily understood with regard to other liberties. For instance, the freedom of expression or the freedom of association, but is sometimes inexplicably ignored when dealing with religious liberty. This fact, note Torron and Valls, is even more unacceptable when

> [...] we realize that the [ECtHR] itself has repeatedly emphasized that an adequate protection of these three freedoms (religion, expression, association), enshrined in articles 9–11 of the Convention, is necessary to preserve pluralism, which is in turn indispensable for democracy.[42]

The argument that the ban of the wearing of a Muslim headscarf pursues the legitimate aim of ensuring the neutrality of state primary education, it should be noted that "the evidence of religious pluralism seems to be more consistent with a neutral attitude of the state and more educative for students then the fictional absence of religion on the part of school personnel."[43] Judge Françoise Tulkens,[44] in her dissenting opinion on the case of Leyla Sahin, disagreed with the manner in which the principles of secularism and equality were applied. She underlined that not mere worries, but only "indisputable facts and reasons whose legitimacy is beyond doubt" were capable of justifying interference with a right guaranteed by the Convention.[45]

42 Martinez –Torron and Navarro-Valls, "The Protection of religious Freedom in the System of the Council of Europe, in *A Deskbook*, 234.

43 Tahzib, in *A Deskbook*, 482.

44 Report of the Special Rapporteur on freedom of religion, or belief, Asma Jahangir, Civil and Political Rights, Including the Question of Religious Intolerance, E/CN.4/2006/5, 9 January 2006, para. 47. Also Judge Tulkens dissenting Opinion available at <http://slomanson.tjsl.edu/SahinTurk.pdf> (viewed Sept. 2013).

45 See: Judge Tulkens' dissenting Opinion.

The wearing of the headscarf does not as such constitute a threat to public order and the rights and freedoms of others, especially because there is no real relation between the headscarf and the notion of 'extremism' and there is no evidence that girls with headscarf are involved in any 'extremist activities' other than merely wearing the *headscarf*. Thus, one should not be left with the impression that to equate the headscarf with extremism would be normal. Due to the lack of evidence that wearing the *headscarf is related to extremism, it should not* be used to justify the restrictive measures on freedom of religion.

Moreover, even though the rights of women and the secular way of life are important values in themselves, to prohibit the *headscarf in order* to protect those students who adhere to the rights of women and the secular way of life raises the question as to whether there is any evidence that these rights would remain unprotected if universities (schools) allow the wearing of the *headscarf?*[46] Gunn notes that France "chose to apply a harsh interpretation of laïcité that reflects its confrontational past rather than its mythic values of neutrality, equality, and tolerance."[47] The major problem when dealing with the issue of the headscarf is that in France religion is regarded as a private matter that has to be confined within the individual's conscience and removed from the most significant areas of public life. This idea may have been justified within a specific historical context and dominated by the need to have a free secular society liberated from the burden imposed by large traditional churches, but this is not acceptable today. Torron and Valls note that the "state's failure to facilitate actual religious pluralism in society, and the corresponding external expressions of that pluralism, would be equivalent to support a certain belief (secularism, i.e., no-religion) over the others (religions)."[48] Thus, a direct result of "a too strict conception of state neutrality could easily lead to a sort of 'secular fundamentalism'."[49] According to Lyon and Spini, "in the case

46 Kanev, Krassimir, 'Muslim religious freedom in the OSCE area after September 11', *Helsinki Monitor*, 2004 no. 4, 242.

47 Gunn, *A Comparison*, 472.

48 Torron and Valls, in *A Deskbook*, 235.

49 Ibid.

of France, the relationship between religion and politics it rests on a false separation of public and private."[50] If a secular state is to respect all faiths and ensure free practice of spiritual and cultural activities for all communities, then

> [...] the state must accept publicly visible manifestations of religion, and its ritual expression in public space. Religion cannot be relegated to the private sphere because religious expression is inherently social as well as personal or private.[51]

The French government, however, is known for being reluctant to recognize any diversity on its territory. France continues to be one of the very few European countries that has not acceded to the Council of Europe's Framework Convention for the Protection of National Minorities and thus to implement its standards and to avail itself to international scrutiny with regard to minority rights.[52] France has ratified the International Covenant on Civil and Political Rights with a reservation to Art. 27 stating: "In the light of Article 2 of the Constitution of the French Republic the French Government declares that Article 27 is not applicable so as far as the Republic is concerned". Invoking this principle, France maintains that it has 'no minorities'.[53]

French law protects the individual, but not ethnic or religious minorities:

> The concept of 'minority' is therefore foreign to the Republican grammar. The legal apparatus concerning the protection of minorities put forward by [article 27 of ICCPR] and the European institutions constitute indeed one of the most problematic areas for the French legal order.[54]

50 Lyon and Spini, 336.
51 Ibid.
52 Ibid., 238.
53 Rodley, Nigel S., *Conceptual Problems in Protection of Minorities: International Legal Departments*, Human Rights Quarterly, 17:1 (1995), 51.
54 Amiraux, Valérie (2002) Monitoring de la protections des minorités dans l'Union européenne: la situation des musulmans en France. Budapest: Open Society Institute, quoted in Jocelyne Cesari (ed.), *Securitization and Religious Divides in Europe. Muslims in Western Europe After 9/11: Why the term Islamophobia is more a predicament than an explanation*, 2006, 199 <http://www.libertysecurity.org/IMG/pdf_Challenge_Project_report.pd> (viewed Sept. 2013).

France, thus, is unwilling to "assume any obligation to affirmative action, i.e., to ensure equality in law and *in fact* by appropriate positive measures."[55]

Because France's integration model does not recognize visible minorities, this means discrimination cannot be measured, although it exists, and there is evidence that the integration system is not working. France has adopted a policy of assimilation of citizens from former colonies. This means they are welcome as long as they "submerge their cultural identities within the dominant French secular culture and ideology", while the opposite would result in "ghettoisation".[56] Consequently, it seems that the authorities are also engaging in their own form of proselytism by banning religious symbols to further their own secular agenda and create a society free from religion and intolerant to religious communities. This legislation of banning the religious symbols goes beyond the application of the principle of the separation of church and state, but this legislation is considered as illustrative of the relationship between the French state and religion, and in particular, certain practices of the Muslim community.[57] The French Muslim community was living and continues to live somewhat in isolation in France. The sphere of Muslims social interactions with the rest of society is very narrow and, except at the local level, their plight has rarely formed a significant part of French politics and culture.[58] France has been chang-

55 Alfred de Zayas, *The International Judicial Protection of the Rights of People and Minorities,* Viewed in his personal website available online at: <http://alfreddezayas.com/Chapbooks/AMSTERDAM.shtml#N_1> (viewed Sept. 2013).

56 Boyle & Sheen, 296.

57 E/CN.4/2006/5, para. 53 The French religious landscape has dramatically changed since 1905, in part as a result of the immigration of a large amount of people from Muslim backgrounds. Throughout the years, the population of Muslim background has significantly increased and, in many places, has settled in some of the so-called *banlieues* or housing estates. The *banlieues* are the suburbs surrounding France's larger cities, such as Paris and Marseilles. The population of the *banlieues* is often characterized by poverty, high unemployment rates among young people, growing extremism among Muslim youth and an increasing feeling of alienation from French society at large. Para. 54.

58 Kanev, Krassimir, 238.

ing to secularism-oriented intolerance. This means that France is moving towards adopting an

> [...] aggressive secularism and endeavor to remove any actual reference to religious beliefs and practice from social public life...Secularism then becomes a sort of official 'religion,' and that parallels religious fundamentalism.[59]

The alleged incompatibility between a strong Islamic identity and the French concept of *laïcité* stimulates current fears about the growth of a Muslim population in France and legitimates fervent appeals to the heritage of universalistic assmilationism. Sebastian Poulter notes that laïcité came to

> [...] indicate an active program whereby the country is promoted as fundamentally politically independent of any religious authority and in which a need for public order can be used to justify interference with freedom of religion, a form of anti-religion, to deal with the excesses of religion.[60]

Lindholm cautions and criticizes the modern example of strident laicism as exemplified by modern France,

> While the policy of laicism protests its tolerance and neutrality, laicist politics in these countries tend to be intolerant against public manifestations of religion both traditional and new, acting as if illiberal policing of religion were mandatory for a religiously neutral state. The modern tradition of state laicism is not even consistently tolerant, hovering between religious neutrality and the substitution of antireligious 'rationalism' for hegemonic religion, replacing one hegemony with another rather than achieving genuine neutrality.[61]

3.1.4.2 Banning the Headscarf as a Protection of Public Order

The reasoning that the banning of the headscarf is necessary for protecting 'l'ordre public', especially in the French sense, is too restrictive and inconsistent with the meaning of 'public order' in the English text of

59 Torron and Valls, in *A Deskbook*, 236–37.

60 Sebastian Poulter, "Muslim Headscarves in School: Contrasting Legal Approaches in England and France," Oxford Journal of Legal Studies, Vol. 17, 1997, 50.

61 Tore Lindholm, in *A Deskbook*, 45–46.

Article 18(3) ICCPR and 9(2) ECHR due to the absence of the parenthetical term 'ordre public'. Nowak and Vospernik explain this as follows: "the state should not understand public order in the sense of the French legal expression used in civil and administrative law and private international law, *l'ordre public*, which relates to the fundamental public policies of a society."[62] In this sense, "public order" should be narrowly construed to mean the prevention of public disorder, and not "to protect *ordre public* with its general connotation of national public policy."[63] The state's argument that an employee wearing a headscarf would disrupt order in the workplace or the smooth running of the public sector seems therefore rather untenable. Nowak and Vospernik confirm that, "mere *ordre public* rules, such as dress regulations that prohibit headscarves for Muslim women and girls [...] could not be justified on the basis of 'public order' clause." In their opinion, "case law on this subject from the European Commission of Human Rights seems, therefore, to be way too restrictive".[64] The UN Human Rights Committee has emphasized that the right to manifest one's religion covers a broad scope of activities, including the construction of houses of worship, the observance of religious holidays, the wearing of distinctive clothing or head coverings, and the observance of dietary regulations,[65] and the right to manifest

62 Nowak and Vospernik, in *A Deskbook*, 152.

63 Karl Joseph Partsch, "Freedom of Conscience and Expression, and Political Freedoms," in *The International Bill of Human Rights: The Covenant on Civil and Political Rights,* ed. Louis Henkin (New York: Columbia University Press, 1981), 212–13, quoted in Nowak and Vospernik, in *A Deskbook*, 152n.

64 Nowak and Vospernik, in A Deskbook, 153. The Austrian Constitutional Court in its judgment of 17 December 1998 found "a violation of the freedom to manifest one's religion on the ground that under the heading "public order" only those restrictions are permissible which are essential for the coexistence of human beings such as traffic regulations or provisions for the orderly conduct of burials." (case No. B 3028/97); reprinted in Europäische grundrecht Zeitung 26 (1999): 600. On this issue, see generally Walter Kalin, Grundrechte im Kulturkonflikt, Freiheit und Gleicheit in der Einwanderungsgesellschaft (Zurich: NZZ Verlag, 2000), 192.

65 UN Human Rights Committee, *General Comment 22* – The right to freedom of thought, conscience and religion (Art.18), July 30, 1993.

one's religion may be subject only to such restrictions that "are prescribed by law and are necessary to protect public safety, order, health, or morals or the fundamental rights and freedoms of others."[66] In its decision in the *Hudoyberganova v. Uzbekistan*[67] case, the Human Rights Committee confirmed that

> [...] the freedom to manifest one's religion encompasses the right to wear clothes or attire in public which is in conformity with the individual's faith or religion. Furthermore, it considers that to prevent a person from wearing religious clothing in public or private may constitute a violation of Article 18, paragraph 2, which prohibits any coercion that would impair the individual's freedom to have or adopt a religion.[68]

3.1.4.3 Protection of Muslim Girls against Coercion

What is the significance of wearing the headscarf? As the German Constitutional Court noted in its judgment of 24 September 2003,[69] wearing the headscarf has no single meaning. It is a practice that women engage in for a variety of reasons. It could be seen to symbolize the submission of women to men and it could be seen, in certain cases, as a means of emancipating women. What is lacking in this debate, however, is the opinion of women, both those who wear the headscarf and those who choose not to. This intolerance places Muslim women in a position whereby they must choose between two things that are very important in their life; either they wear the headscarf or they pursue their education. Sociological research on the topic shows that the veiled Muslim women consider learning and education to be a religious duty

66 Article 18.2 of the ICCPR.

67 Views of the Human Rights Committee on the *Hudiyberganove v. Uzbekistan* case, adopted on 5 November 2004, eighty-second session, (CCPR/C/82/D/931/2000).

68 As reflected in the Committee's General Comment No. 22 (para. 5), policies, or practices that have the same intention or effect as direct coercion, such as those restricting access to education, are inconsistent with article 18(2)

69 Federal Constitutional Court of Germany, judgment of the Second Division of 24 September 2003, 2BvR 1436/042.

prescribed by Islam. In this sense, the ban engenders a conflict by forcing them to choose performance of one religious duty over the other.[70] Another conflict for Muslim women is to exercise their freedom to wear headscarves prescribed or motivated by their religion, but not being offered, or losing a job.[71] Muslim women with professional ambitions are now being forced back to the shadows. Thus, this law creates incompatibility between covered women's religious convictions and their desire to be productive members of society through education and employment.[72] Such legislation, according to Ghanea, is causing tensions "that are currently arising in families, schools, employment, and countless other settings, in private and public, both in Europe and (by way of reaction and reverberation) throughout the Muslim World."[73]

After warning everyone about the emergence of a 'parallel society', France has made a big contribution to ensuring that France's Muslims cut themselves off from the rest of the society even more than before. They have neglected that the wearing of the headscarf to many Muslim women is not merely a personal display of faith; it is an obligation imposed by her religion. This means it is simply a matter of personal obedience to God. A large number of these girls endured many difficulties because they had freely chosen to wear the headscarf. Many had been intimidated or humiliated for expressing their personal opinion on the question. Even in cases where young girls were obliged to wear headscarves by their families, the law is said to have provoked particularly painful situations within the families. Lyon and Spini note that:

> [e]ven if banning the headscarf is the only way to "'free' Islamic women from an unjust and intolerable violence, the answer to one constraint (the religious obligation to wear the foulard) cannot be another constraint (the obligation not to wear it)."[74]

70 Özelm Denli, 'Between Laicist State Ideology and Modern Public Religion: The Head-Cover Controversy in Contemporary Turkey', in *A Deskbook*, 503.

71 Tahzib, in *A Deskbook*, 474.

72 Denli, in *A Deskbook*, 503.

73 Ghanea, in *A Deskbook*, xxvii–xxviii.

74 Lyon and Spini, 40–41.

In reality, this is the same freedom of expression advocated by Western countries who criticize states such as Saudi Arabia or Afghanistan for imposing on women how to or how not to observe and practice their religion. International human rights law obliges state authorities to avoid coercion in matters of religious freedom, and this obligation must be taken into account when devising school dress codes. The proposed prohibition on headscarves in France, as with laws in some Muslim countries that force women to wear headscarves, violates this principle. Thus, law No. 2004–228 is sympathetic with Muslim girls who did not want to wear the headscarf, but it did not consider the girls, who chose to wear headscarves; who were treated as if they were invisible or unworthy of being taken seriously. The law condemns coercion that results in the wearing of religious headscarves, however, it never acknowledges the existence of the intense social pressure in France on Muslim girls not to wear headscarves. Schools have been attempting to ban them since 1989, leading French politicians have condemned them, and employers have pressured Muslim women not to wear headscarves.[75] The Stasi Commission never mentions, let alone condemns, such coercion by school teachers, administrators, policemen, or others. The proponents of the law, in Gunn's opinion, "commits exactly the same offense of (coercion) that it freely condemned in others."[76] Especially, there is no evidence or argument that banning headscarves in schools will reduce coercion on girls at home or in their communities.[77]

It would have been better if the Stasi Commission opted for what *the Commission des droits de la personne et des droits de la jeunesse du Québec* reached to in a non-binding report published in February 1995, and that is "public schools were obliged to accept Muslim girls wearing headscarves, provided that this freedom of religious expression did not constitute a real risk to personal safety or security of property."[78] While

75 Gunn, A Comparison, 473.

76 Ibid.

77 Ibid.

78 Pierre Bosset, *Religious Pluralism in Québec: A Social and Ethical Challenge*, Commission des droits de la personne, 29–41, quoted in Laura Barnett.

schools may insist on certain dress codes, they must also seek reasonable accommodations with Muslim students who are discriminated against by the application of such codes. Dealing with the feminist equality argument that a headscarf ban is necessary to protect girls from an overly oppressive religious regime, the Commission was careful to state that:

> Unless it is shown that a specific girl is forced to wear the headscarf against her will, an absolute ban on the headscarf as a religious symbol is not the role of equality laws, and would be an insult to the independence of Muslim women.[79]

It must be recognized that for each individual there is an area of personal liberty immune from state invasion. In recognition of this principle, Article 2 of the First Protocol to the ECHR (1952), to which France is a signatory state that, "[n]o person shall be denied the right to education…the State shall respect the right of parents to ensure such education and teaching in conformity with their own religious and philosophical convictions". The ban on the headscarf is supposed to 'defend' young women from an oppressive and family-enforced tradition, and yet at the same time it submits these same women to another form of tutelage. If the life choices of Muslim women are a concern of the French state,

> […] it is the background social, economic, legal and political conditions in which they live, including the everyday reality of racism, which need to be the focus of attention, to create conditions in which choice can be real.[80]

The Committee on the Rights of the Child, in its concluding observations on the second periodic report of France, expressed its concern that

> […] the new legislation (Law No. 2004-228 of 15 March 2004) on wearing religious signs in public schools may be counterproductive, by neglecting the principle of the best interests of the child and the right of the child to access to

79 Ibid.

80 Lyon and Spini, 340–41.

> education [...]. The Committee recommends that the State party [...] consider alternative means, including mediation, of ensuring the secular character of public schools, while guaranteeing that individual rights are not infringed upon and that "children are not excluded or marginalized from the school system [...]. The dress code in schools may be better addressed within the public schools themselves, encouraging participation of children.[81]

The Committee on the Elimination of Racial Discrimination

> [...] recommend[ed] to the State party that it should continue to monitor the implementation of the Act of 15 March 2004 closely, to ensure that it has no discriminatory effects and that the procedures followed in its implementation always place emphasis on dialogue, to prevent it from denying any pupil the right to education and to ensure that everyone can always exercise that right.[82]

Also, it should not be forgotten that according to Article 13 of the ICESCR that states parties have to respect the liberty of parents and legal guardians "to ensure the religious and moral education of their children in conformity with their own convictions". It would have been a better solution if it has been considered on a case-by-case basis and takes into account the other human right aspects that may be at stake in the situation concerned, especially freedom of expression which is looked upon as the basis of all freedoms in the West.

3.1.4.4 Banning the Headscarf as a Stand against Extremism

It is vital, "to distinguish between those who wear the headscarf and 'extremists' who seek to impose the headscarf as they do other religious symbols,"[83] and it is essential to point that banning the headscarf did not create harmony and tolerance in the society, actually, it has increased the formation of extreme views on both fringes of society.

Recently, the Special Rapporteur, Asma Jahangir, was concerned about the intolerant nature of the supporter of the law arguments. She

81 CRC/C/15/Add.4, paras. 25–26.
82 CERD/C/FRA/CO/16, para. 18.
83 Tulkens Dissenting Opinion.

considers "[l]aws and acts that discriminate, rather than preventing violence, are themselves instigators of religious-based violence,"[84] She goes on to point out that intolerance may be "institutionalized and based on legislation,"[85] the ban of religious symbols, as a result, could be as one example of government action arising from prejudice and bigotry that had given rise to outright hatred…and repression."[86] The law also appears to have sent the wrong message to a certain portion of the population, which has come to believe that the wearing of religious symbols per se, and in particular headscarves, is generally unlawful. Moreover, the stigmatization of the so called Islamic headscarf has triggered a wave of religious intolerance when women wear it outside school, at university or at their workplace. As a result of the new law, "a portion of the population has come to associate the headscarf solely with gender inequality and oppression,"[87] In some instances women were refused access to shops or were insulted in the street because they wore the headscarf, while others were dismissed from their employment, or found it difficult to find employment.[88]

The wide political support for the law has conveyed a demoralizing message to religious minorities in France and the implementation of the law by school establishments has in a number of cases led to abuses that provoked feelings of humiliation, in particular amongst young Muslim women.

> Such public humiliation can only lead to the radicalization of the affected persons and those associated with them. Muslim women (girls) have the right to demand that their connection with one of the religious minorities should be respected and should be enabled to express their characteristics, which may include the right to use their traditional dress or attire with out feeling that they are threat to society.[89]

84 E/CN.4/2006/5, para. 60.
85 Ibid.
86 Ibid.
87 E/CN.4/2006/5, para 64.
88 Ibid., para. 65.
89 Minorities Declaration, art. 4(2).

Wearing the headscarf should be a personal decision that should not be politicised. To consider headcovering a symbol of the oppression of Muslim women by their religion is a perception that is often linked to stereotypes and prejudice. The headscarf has been so over-burdened with meaning that it is becoming hard to deal with it in a neutral fashion. It is viewed as a symbol of what is considered the Islamic oppression of women. It is apparent that the dilemma of retaining the values of the majority while respecting the rights of religious minorities is certainly not an easy one to resolve, regardless whether the laws of the country are defined as religious or not. The religious symbol law led to discrimination against Muslims and the rise of Islamophobia.

For these reasons, it could be argued that France has neglected its obligation to take all appropriate measures, including the modification and rescission of existing laws, to prohibit discrimination on the basis of religion or belief and not taking the appropriate measures to combat intolerance on the grounds of religion or other beliefs.

The wearing of "distinctive clothing or headscarf" has long been practiced as part of the observance or practice of certain religions and beliefs. It is therefore not surprising that such garments have been explicitly recognized as falling within the ambit of external freedom by some human rights bodies. Most notably, this has been recognized by the Human Rights Committee.[90] The Human Rights Committee has emphasized that the right to manifest one's religion covers a broad scope of activities, including the construction of houses of worship, the observance of religious holidays, the wearing of distinctive clothing or head coverings, and the observance of dietary regulations.[91]

90 Further, the UN Declaration on the Rights of Persons Belonging to National or Ethnic, Religious or Linguistic Minorities 1992 provides that 'States shall protect the existence and the…religious…identity of minorities within their respective territories' (A.1). Further, it provides that minorities have the 'right to enjoy their own culture, to profess and practice their own religion…freely and without any interference or any form of discrimination' (A.2).

91 UN Human Rights Committee, *General Comment 22, The right to freedom of thought, conscience and religion* (Art.18), July 30, 1993, para. 4. In its decision in the *Hudoyberganova v. Uzbekistan* case, the Human rights Committee confirmed

The Human Rights Committee has emphasized that any restrictions must be non-discriminatory in character, must relate directly and be proportionate to the aim for which they were introduced and must not be applied in a manner that would violate the right to freedom of religion. The Committee has further pointed out that the grounds listed as permissible grounds for limitations in Article 18.2 must be strictly interpreted, and that restrictions on grounds other than those specified and it should also be noted that restrictions are an exceptional measure which should be strictly interpreted. Article 9.2 of the ECHR adds that all restrictions must be "necessary in a democratic society." According to the EctHR, in order to meet this requirement, any restriction must correspond to a "pressing social need" and must be "proportionate to the legitimate aim pursued."[92] The EctHR has also concluded that the right to freedom of religion as guaranteed by the ECHR "excludes any discretion on the part of the State to determine whether religious beliefs or the means used to express such beliefs are legitimate."[93] The EctHR has consistently stated that there must be a nar-

that "the freedom to manifest one's religion encompasses the right to wear clothes or attire in public which is in conformity with the indivIdual's faith or religion. Furthermore, it considers that to prevent a person from wearing religious clothing in public or private may constitute a violation of article 18, paragraph 2, which prohibits any coercion that would impair the individual's freedom to have or adopt a religion." Views of the Human Rights committee on the *Hudiyberganove v. Uzbekistan* case, adopted on 5 November 2004, eighty-second session, (CCPR/C/82/D/931/2000). It also, considered, with one dissenting and one partly dissenting opinion, that "to prevent a person from wearing religious clothing in public or private may constitute a violation of article 18 (2) of ICCPR, which prohibits any coercion that would impair the individual's freedom to have or adopt a religion. As reflected in the Committee's General Comment No. 22 (para. 5), policies, or practices that have the same intention or effect as direct coercion, such as those restricting access to education, are inconsistent with article 18(2)

92 *Serif v. Greece*, 38178/97, Council of Europe: European Court of Human Rights, 26 January 1999, para. 49.

93 European Court of Human Rights, Manoussakis and others v. Greece, September 26, 1999, para. 47, App. No. (00018748/91).

row construction of these limitations together with a broad interpretation of the freedoms guaranteed. Any restrictions on freedoms must be 'construed strictly' and can be justified only by 'Convincing and compelling reasons.'[94]

The right enshrined in Article 18 of UDHR and ICCPR and Article 9 of the ECHR is so fundamental that the limitations are even narrower than those relating to the freedom of expression, association and assembly contained in all international and regional human rights instruments. The European Court of Human Rights has consistently stated that this right is at the core of a democratic society, claiming that

> [i]t is, in its religious dimension, one of the most vital elements that go to make up the identity of believers and their conception of life, but it is also a precious asset for atheists, agnostics, skeptics and the unconcerned. The pluralism in dissociable from a democratic society, which has been won over the centuries, depends on it.[95]

3.1.5 Conclusion

While proponents of a headscarf ban insist that wearing a headscarf is simply a fundamentalist symbol of subservience of Muslim women and a sign of oppression they face, for many Muslim women wearing a headscarf is a deeply personal choice and a sign of their religious conviction and has nothing to do with Islamic fundamentalism. A headscarf ban would automatically but mistakenly stigmatize all Muslim women wearing the headscarf as fundamentalists. Wearing religious clothing can be an inherent part of manifestation of one's religion. It is not at the discretion of a state to determine which manifestations are legitimate as long as they do not violate other people's basic human rights or

94 *United Communist Party of Turkey and Others v. Turkey*, 19392/92, Council of Europe: European Court of Human Rights, 30 January 1998, para. 46, available at: <http://www.coe.int/t/ngo/source/expert_council_ngo_law_report_2010_en.pdf> (viewed 4/2010).

95 *Kokkinakis v. Greece*, 3/1992/348/421, Council of Europe: European Court of Human Rights, 19 April 1993, para. 31.

do not endanger public safety, health, or morals, as defined by international law. In addition, barring girls and women wearing the headscarf from schools, universities and other public institutions could lead to numerous girls and women staying out of schools and universities – a result contrary to the pronounced aim of the ban, i.e., integration.[96] It is becoming more profound that the French state now promotes secularism and it appears as France is advocating one world-view and so seems to contradict the principle of neutrality to which the state proclaims to be committed.

Thus, it is important today to support 'flexible and tolerant attitudes' in order to allow the variety and richness of garments to manifest themselves without constraints and discrimination against Muslims.

It must be stressed that it should not be acceptable to be discriminated against because of one's religion in the same way that it is no longer acceptable to use skin color as an attribute to distinguish people. Today, religion and culture have become the "markers of seemingly 'natural' kinds of differences." Rudiger notes that Islam has become "the new 'other".[97] Muslims have been forced to take drastic measures in order to comply with the dictates of their religions and while simultaneously not sacrificing their education. The Headscarf Law may lead to greater feelings of alienation on the part of the minority religious groups, and it may actually hamper the desired integration of such groups. The Headscarf Law actually encourages marginalization and discrimination of Muslims and limiting their freedom of religion

96 The Assessment International Helsinki Human Rights Federation (IHF) Concerning the Headscarf Ban, quoted in *Evaluation of the Headscarf Ban in the Light of Surveys and Reports of Human Rights Organization*, p. 14, <http://www.mervekavakci.net/docs/akdereng.doc> (viewed Sept. 2013).

97 Rudiger, Anja. *"Discrimination and Legislation"*, session 5, Conference on "Muslims in Europe post 9/11", St. Antony's-Princeton Conference, St Antony's College, Oxford, April 26, 2004.

3.2 The USA Counter Terrorism Measures and their Effect on Muslims

The United States, similar to France, has political orders characterized by the separation of church and state; 'religious freedom' is the term that plays a similar role as the French *laïcité* in the United States, albeit with a very different meaning.[98] The First Amendment of the U.S. Constitution, written in 1787, guarantees freedom of religion and states that: "Congress shall make no law respecting an establishment of religion, or prohibiting the free exercise thereof..."[99] This freedom has two components: the separation of church and state (the Establishment Clause) and the freedom to worship (the Free Exercise Clause).[100]

The 'Establishment Clause' is broadly worded: "Congress shall make no law respecting an establishment of religion...", but it has been interpreted over time to have a specific meaning.[101] The basic tenets of the Establishment Clause are derived from *Everson v. Board of Education* and *Lemon v. Kurtzman*.[102] Everson lays out a laundry list of actions that are prohibited by the Establishment Clause.[103] Specifically, there can be no: 1) official state church, 2) government coercion to be religious, 3) punishment for one's beliefs, 4) state preference among religions, and 5) government participation in religion.[104] In addition, Lemon sets out a three part test of what must be done in order for a law to satisfy the Establishment Clause. The law can have no: 1) sole religious purpose; 2) primary religious effect; or 3) government entanglement in religious affairs.[105]

98 Gunn, *A Comparison*, 425–26.

99 U.S. Constituion amendment I. <http://www.usconstitution.net/const.html> (viewed Sept. 2013).

100 Ibid.

101 Ibid.

102 Everson v. Bd. of Educ., 330 U.S. 1 (1947); Lemon v. Kurtzman, 403 U.S. 602 (1971).

103 Everson, 330 U.S. at 15–16.

104 Ibid.

105 Lemon, 403 U.S. at 612–13.

The 'Free Exercise' Clause states: "Congress shall make no law prohibiting the free exercise [of religion]." However, it was not until the 1940s[106] that the first powerful and inspiring modern decisions regarding religious speech and other manifestations of religion were published. Perhaps the most impressive of these decisions, *West Virginia, State Board of Education v. Barnette*, came in the wake of widespread violence against Jehovah's Witnesses because of their insistence that their highest loyalty was to God.[107] In the 1960s, with the election of the first Catholic president, John F. Kennedy, the adoption of the Civil Rights Act of 1964,[108] what is now described as "the first freedom" and the founding principle, came to be very widely accepted.

Since, religious freedom is considered to be the first freedom, the United States decided to take the responsibility of protecting specifically the right to freedom of religion all over the world, by enacting the International Religious Freedom Act 1998(IRFA). President Bush has maintained the commitment to protect religious freedoms internationally, stating in his National Security Strategy that the U.S. Government will "take special efforts to promote freedom of religion and conscience and defend it from encroachment by repressive governments."[109] Despite these promises, the scope of discrimination and racial profiling, especially religious profiling and discrimination has dramatically expanded since the attacks of September 11, 2001.

Throughout human history, there have been many threats to the security of nations. These threats have brought about significant losses of life, the displacement of large numbers of people, and devastating economic loss. All along the international community was calling for

106 It was not until 1940 that the Free Exercise Clause was found to be applicable to the states, (Cantwell v. Connecticut, 310 U.S. 296 (1940).

107 West Virginia, State Board of Education v. Barnette, 319 U.S. 624 (1943).

108 1964, 88th Congress, H.R. 7152, The Civil Rights Act, 1964 greatly expanded the rights of minorities in key areas, such as employment, education, voting, and the use of public facilities. It was intended to end discrimination in these areas based on race, color, religion, or national origin. In addition, any form of discrimination on the grounds of religious belief is prohibited under this Act.

109 International Religious Freedom Act of 1998, 22 U.S.C. 6401 et seq. (2000), 352.

strengthening human rights paradigms. However, after 9/11, many governments, led by the US, began to argue that human rights protection is actually an impediment to the campaign against terrorism. As a result, the new counter-terrorism measures and laws have disrupted fundamental human rights and individual liberties as well as the impacts on certain communities, predominantly Muslims. These measures are increasingly used to target Muslims from North Africa, the Middle-East and South Asia[110] and people who appear to be Muslims. This is what could be called the "religious profiling" of Muslims in the context of countering terrorism.

3.2.1 "Religious Profiling" of Muslims in the Context of Countering Terrorism by the USA

As Muslims struggle with issues of personal, cultural and religious identity in Western countries, they are haunted both by various forms in which

> [...] their presence is not fully welcomed in the Western context, and by the legacy of Western colonialism in their own histories which continues as a powerful force affecting the relationship between Muslims and citizens of Europe and America.[111]

However, in the wake of September 11, their struggle, for a better relation with their hosting societies, came to a halt. It is true there have been many positive initiatives aimed at 'building bridges' between Muslim and other communities, promoting tolerance and supporting the participation of Muslims in society, but at the same time it has been pointed out that Muslims have "increasingly experienced hostility, discrimination and exclusion since September 11. The social climate facing Muslims has deteriorated, as the fight against terrorism has been stepped up

110 Profiling here is not related to ethnicity, nationality or race but to what they have all the nationalities in common and that is their religion Islam.

111 See: Gabriel, Theodore, 'Is Islam against the West?', Chapter 2,13–26, in Smith, Jane I., Geaves Ron, Gabriel Theodore, Haddad Yvonne, Eds., Islam & The West: *Post 9/11*, Ashgate, England, 2004, (hereinafter Islam & the West).

and the perceived threat of religious extremism has been given wide attention in public debate and pre-existing prejudice and discrimination against Muslims have been reinforced. Muslims have increasingly felt that they are viewed with distrust and hostility and that they are stigmatized because of their beliefs.

As Theodor Gabriel notes, the perception that Islam is somehow 'against' and even hostile to the Western world has been around for a while, but it has gained ground since 9/11.[112] Few can argue with the reality that Muslims in the West in many ways are worse off since 9/11. In the US, Muslims worry deeply that

> [...] such realities as the US Patriot Act, 'Operation Green Quest' (involving the invasion of Muslims homes and businesses), profiling in airports and other public places, and monitoring the activities and freezing the assets of Muslim charities are resulting in a loss of Muslim civil liberties.[113]

The question which is being asked by many is "are the measures taken by the Bush government ostensibly to counter terrorism really anti-terrorist, "or are they in fact anti-Islam?"[114]

So where have the events of 9/11 and the subsequent 'war on terror' and its ramification left the American public in its understanding and appreciation of Islam?

In this age of the 'War on Terror,' the United States, traditionally characterized by a principle of equality, found that it is much easier to use religious profiling instead of addressing the true problems underlying terrorism. This increase of acts of intolerance against Muslim communities is reported by several nongovernmental organizations and specialized intergovernmental agencies.[115]

112 Smith Jane I., Conclusion, ch. 13, In *Islam & the West*, 211.

113 Ibid., 216.

114 Ibid.

115 See: American Civil Liberties Union, Sanctioned Bias: Racial profiling since 9/11, New York: American Civil Liberties Union, 2004. Amnesty International U.S, Domestic Human Rights Program, Threat and Humiliation: Racial Profiling, Domestic Security, and Human Rights in the United States, New York: Amnesty International USA, 2004.

What is Religious Profiling?

Since September 11, 2001, Congress, the executive departments, and federal agents who are engaged in both terrorism investigations and garden-variety immigration enforcement have become increasingly prone to target individuals thought to be Muslim of Arab or South Asians descents. Christopher Allen points that there is a shift from racism defined by colour, ethnicity or nationalism to what he calls a new strand of racism, one that is defined specifically by religion.[116]

Profiling, which is "the systematic association of sets of physical, behavioral or psychological characteristics with particular offenses and their use as a basis for making law-enforcement decisions",[117] could be either *descriptive*, i.e. designed to those likely to have committed a particular criminal act and thus reflecting the evidence the investigators have gathered concerning this act; or they may be *predictive*, i.e. designed to identify those who may be involved in some future, or as-yet-undiscovered, crime."[118]

"Predictive Profiling" in this sense is "specially targeting individuals who possess identifiable attributes that are believed to bear a positive statistical correlation to particular kinds of misconduct,"[119] in this case, identification of terrorism and violence with Islam and Muslims. The harms that flow from such government-sponsored discrimination are worth emphasizing. They fall into two categories. In the first category are those harms associated with particular substantive deprivations: the person's removal, detention, arrest, questioning, registration, prosecution, and so forth. Second are those harms associated with the discrimination itself. These includes not only the core injustice of be-

116 See: Allen Christopher, Endemically European or European Epidemic? *Islamophobia in a Post 9/11 Europe*, Ch. 9, in Islam & the West, 130–145.

117 Martin Scheinin, Report of the Special Rapporteur on the promotion and protection of human rights and fundamental freedoms while countering terrorism, A/HRC/4/26, 29 January 2007, para. 33.

118 Ibid.

119 Stephen H. Legomsky, The Ethnic and Religious Profiling of Noncitizens: National Security and International Human Rights, Boston College, Boston College, *Third World Law Journal* No. 1, Volume 25, 2005, *18*.

ing treated less favorably than others for inadequate reasons, but also personal feelings of humiliation, unfair treatment, a loss of dignity, a loss of confidence, and the sense of being seen and treated as an outsider.[120]

These harms have been eloquently lived by Muslims since the ratification of the Patriot Act[121]. Discrimination and intolerance against Muslims "Islamophobia" since enacting the Patriot Act led to many distinct and clear manifestations of hate crime and as such generated fear, feelings of stigmatization, marginalization and rejection. The net result is heightened anxiety and rising violence. The second category of harm is endured by Muslims as they faced detention, arrest, questioning, registration, prosecution, and so forth.

These anti-Islamic feelings (Islamophobia) are not new, as they are long-standing endemic responses that European has harboured virtually since the emergence of Islam. Smith notes,

> [...] certainly Islamophobia is a term that has slid across the Atlantic into American parlance and is much used by agencies such as the Council on American Islam Relation (CAIR) to describe what it perceives as anti-Islamic behaviour in public arenas of the US Religious leaders, politicians, employers, public school officials, citizens accused of prejudicial behaviour against Muslims are increasingly identified by CAIR and other Islamic organizations as Islamophobic, and are being called to public account for their discriminatory behaviour.[122]

The range of discrimination and intolerance against Muslims (Islamophobia) could be summarized as follow[123]:

a) ancient hatreds, old prejudices,
b) powerful new trend of anti-immigration,

120 Ibid., 24.

121 Public Law 107–56, 107th Cong., 1st sess. (26 October 2001), *USA Patriot Act*, sec. 507(j) (2)(A). Full text available at: <http://www.gpo.gov/fdsys/pkg/PLAW-107publ56.pdf/PLAW-107publ56.pdf> (viewed Sept. 2013).

122 Smith, Jane I., in Islam & the West, 218.

123 *Ömür Orhun, Dealing With Intolerance and Discrimination Against Muslims: Social and Political Solution, International* Conference on Islamophobia, Istanbul, 8–9 December 2007, last viewed Oct. 2013.

c) antipathy towards Muslims in general, believing that Islam is not compatible with democracy, human rights and contemporary values,
d) Prejudice; negative sentiments and display of such sentiments; negative media coverage and misrepresentation; and adverse political discourse, especially by the far right, but recently by moderates also,
e) identification of terrorism and violence with Islam.

3.2.2 Anti-terror Measures and Religious Profiling

Within weeks of September 11, the United States of America sought a new law to combat terrorism through enhanced federal powers of surveillance and investigation. President George W. Bush signed on October 26, 2001, House Resolution 3162, entitled "Uniting and Strengthening America by Providing Appropriate Tools Required to Intercept and Obstruct Terrorism" Act, which has come to be known as the USA Patriot Act. The USA Patriot Act is an omnibus bill containing numerous reforms to federal criminal procedure, laws relating to foreign intelligence surveillance, wiretaps and interception of electronic communications, laws relating to the gathering of documentary evidence, and DNA and immigration laws.[124] Thus, the act makes it easier for federal investigative agencies to obtain wiretaps on multiple electronic devices, and procure electronic and documentary evidence from sources like internet service providers and cable and telephone companies.[125]

124 Although not all 340 pages of USA Patriot Act are legally controversial, however, for example under sections 215 and 505 of the Patriot Act, law enforcement officials are given broad access to any type of record: sales, library, financial, medical, etc., without having to show probable cause of any crime. The Patriot Act also forbids the holders of this information, such as university librarians and college registrars, from disclosing that they have ever provided such records to federal officials.

125 The "sneak-and-peak" provision of Patriot Act (Section 213) allows law enforcement agencies to conduct secret "sneak-and-peek" searches of anyone's home or apartment without a warrant or even notification to the owner. This means that investigators could potentially enter anyone's place of residence, take pictures, download computer files and seize items without informing them of the search

It also relaxes prohibitions on the sharing of information obtained in investigations by different federal agencies.[126] This act has allowed US security agencies to take invasive measures, including invasive powers of search and surveillance, detention, and seizure of property and its confiscation, which previously had not been allowed because they compromised human rights and basic freedoms.

Moreover, and as amended by the Patriot Act, federal law can impose significant fines and terms of imprisonment for any entity that provides material support or resources knowing or intending that they are to be used in terrorist acts or by foreign terrorist organizations. 'Material support' encompasses an exceptionally broad range of assistance, and would appear on its face, clearly to include grants, microfinance services and many types of technical assistance, if the recipient engages in terrorist acts or is a foreign terrorist organization. This gave the executive branch unchecked power to designate any group as a terrorist organization.[127] Muslim organizations are the ones mostly affected by these procedures.

Moreover, hundreds of Muslim men who were detained in the roundup are deprived of many of their rights and experienced physical and mental abuse at the hands of prison guards in the detention center. These detainees, who are only assumed to be terrorists, were secretly taken to a US Navy detention facility in Guantánamo Bay, Cuba and other secret prisons and many are still being detained there for an un-

---

until days, weeks or even months later. Moreover, the US government has spawned a system of surveillance and control that appears to be stretched beyond what it can or, indeed, should seek to regulate.

126 See: Charles Doyle, CRS Report for Congress, The USA Patriot Act: A Legal Analysis, *Congressional Research Service. The Library of Congress*, April 15, 2002, 1–78.

127 See: Carter, Terrence S., and Carter, Sean S., Worldwide Implications of America's Emerging Policies Concerning NGOS, *Nonprofits and, Anti-terrorism and Charity Law*, No. 5, Carter & associates, Nov. 30, 2004, pp. 1–7. Carter, Terrence S., Claridge, Nancy E., Carter, Sean S., Due Process and Anti-Terrorism Initiatives Worldwide-Recent Developments, Anti-Terrorism and Charity Law alert No. 16, 26 Feburary 2009, pp. 1–4.

limited period of time, without judicial review and without the possibility of meeting and consulting a lawyer. The US claims that these detainees are 'illegal enemy combatants' and are not entitled to the status of prisoners of Wars (POWs) or to the protections set forth in the US constitution and criminal law and, therefore, may be held in detention without trial for an unlimited period of time. These Muslim detainees, including Muslim children, have been held mainly because of their faith.

There have been numerous allegations and extensive evidence of torture and cruel, inhuman and degrading treatment in detention and prison facilities run by the United States. These allegations were denied by the United States' government, but at the beginning of 2003, allegations of abuse of prisoners held in the Abu Ghraib prison in Iraq surfaced, and by early 2004, the media released disturbing photos depicting U.S. military personnel abusing prisoners. In its February 2004 report[128], the ICRC found that "methods of physical and psychological coercion were used by the military intelligence in *a systematic way* to gain confessions and extract information" (emphasis added). The methods cited by the ICRC included:

- Hooding to disorient and prevent detainees from breathing freely;
- Being forced to remain for prolonged periods in painful stress positions;
- Being attached repeatedly over several days, for several hours each time to the bars of cell Doors naked or in positions causing physical pain;
- Being held naked in dark cells for several days and paraded naked, sometimes hooded or with women's underwear over their heads;
- Seep, food, and water deprivation; and
- Prolonged exposure while hooded to the sun during the hottest time of day.

128 This Report is quoted in Human Right Watch Report, The Road to Abu Ghraib, June 8, 2004 <http://www.hrw.org/en/node/12123/section/1> (viewed Sept. 2013).

The classified investigative military report of Major General Antonio Taguba[129] confirmed these findings. Taguba reported that "numerous incidents of sadistic, blatant, and wanton criminal abuses" were inflicted on several detainees. His catalogue was even longer than the ICRC's:

- Punching, slapping and kicking detainees; jumping on their naked feet;
- Videotaping and photographing naked male and female detainees;
- Forcibly arranging detainees in various sexually explicit positions for photographing;
- Forcing groups of male detainees to masturbate themselves while being photographed and videotaped;
- Arranging naked detainees in a pile and then jumping on them;
- Positioning a naked detainee on a box, with a sandbag on his head, and attaching wires to his fingers, toes and penis to simulate electric torture;
- Writing "I am a Rapist" (sic) on the leg of a detainee alleged to have forcibly raped a 15-year-old fellow detainee, and then photographing him naked;
- Placing a dog chain or strap around a naked detainee's neck and having a female soldier pose with him for a picture;
- A male military police guard having sex with a female detainee;
- Breaking chemical lights and pouring the phosphoric liquid on detainees;
- Threatening detainees with a loaded 9-mm pistol;
- Pouring cold water on naked detainees;
- Beating detainees with a broom handle and a chair;
- Threatening male detainees with rape;

129 The "Taguba Report" On Treatment Of *Abu Ghraib* Prisoners In Iraq, Article 15–6 Investigation of the 800th Military Police Brigade, viewed online: <http://news.findlaw.com/wp/docs/iraq/tagubarpt.html> (viewed Sept. 2013). Although the Taguba Report is marked *Secret / No Foreign Dissemination*, it has been widely distributed, and made available to the public worldwide since at least the week of May 2, 2004.

- Allowing a military police guard to stitch the wound of a detainee who was injured after being slammed against the wall in his cell;
- Sodomizing a detainee with a chemical light and perhaps a broom stick;
- Using military working dogs (without muzzles) to frighten and intimidate detainees with threats of attack, and in at least one case biting and severely injuring a detainee;
- Forcing detainees to remove their clothing and keeping them naked for several days at a time;
- Forcing naked male detainees to wear women's underwear.

Testimony before the *ICJ Eminent Jurist Panel* revealed that these abuses represent an affirmative administrative policy to circumvent and disregard fundamental principles of U.S. and international law," and that "these practices have been shown to be a direct result of decisions and orders given by the administration and specifically, the Secretary of Defense."[130]

Religious humiliations of Muslims, detained in the context of the war on terror, have been widespread in many other US prisons as well. Muslims, just because of their faith and before being proved guilty were deprived from many rights: the right to equal protection of the law, the right not to be ill treated and tortured, and the freedom to practice their religion with out discrimination

The anti-terrorism investigations and detentions have focused largely on members of the Muslim communities and their organizations. As a result, Muslims have to face an increased risk of religious profiling. In other words, their religion leaves them vulnerable to investigation. One of the major findings of the Amnesty International USA (AIUSA) study

130 Mark W. Vorkink & Erin M. Scheick, *'The "War on Terror" and The Erosion of the Rule of Law: The U.S. Hearings of the ICJ Eminent Jurist Panel', Human Rights* Brief, Volume 14 Issue 1, Winter 2006. See: the International Commission of Jurists ("ICJ"), Counter-Terrorism and Human Rights: *Assessing Damage, Urging Action,* the Eminent Jurists Panel on Terrorism Report, 16, February, 2009, p. 213. Available online at: <http://www.digitalcommons.wcl.american.edu/cgi/viewcontent.cgi?article=1190&context=hrbrief> (viewed Sept. 2013).

"Racial Profiling, Domestic Security and Human Rights in the United States", is that racial profiling of citizens and visitors of Middle Eastern and South Asian descent, and others who appear to be from these areas or members of the Muslim faith, has substantially increased since September 11, 2001.[131]

Thus, profiling of Muslims from the Middle East, North Africa and South Asia often entails detention, intelligence-gathering, expanding the substantive criteria for removing non-citizens, contracting their procedural rights, tightening visa and other overseas policies, and upgrading apprehensions and inspections at ports of entry. Their non-profits organizations have often closed and some of the times, their assets frozen, in addition to being treated with discrimination and prejudice. In practical terms, people who appear to law enforcement officials to be Muslim have been the most thoroughly scrutinized since enacting anti-terrorism measures.

3.2.2.1 Law Enforcement Policies against Muslims

The US anti-terrorism measures, either expressly or at least arguably, entail 'profiling' young Muslim males. Religious profiling occurs, in post 9/11, when "the religious affiliation of persons is wrongly confused with the identification of such persons as potential terrorists."[132] Since September 11, 2001, Congress, the executive departments, and federal agents who are engaged in both terrorism investigations and a garden-variety of immigration enforcement officials have become increasingly prone to target individuals thought to be Muslim either from North Africa, Middle East or South Asia. In this context, officials might consciously and explicitly target people who appear to be Muslim. The same practical results can occur indirectly, or de facto, as the byproducts

131 Amnesty International USA, Threat and Humiliation *(Racial Profiling, Domestic Security and Human Rights in the United States)*, Amnesty International USA Publications, 2004, vi.

132 Martin Scheinin, Report *of the Special Rapporteur on the promotion and protection of human rights and fundamental freedoms while countering terrorism*: Mission to the United States of America, A/HRC/6/17/Add.3, 22 November 2007.

of profiling on the basis of some third attribute that correlates positively with religion.[133] Thus, policymakers or law enforcement agents might target nationals or natives of those countries that "are predesignated as harboring terrorists. The populations of the listed countries are overwhelmingly Muslim."[134]

In September 2002, the U.S. Department of Justice began the 'special registration' program, also known as the National Security Entry-Exit System (NSEERS), which required selected visitors to the United States to be fingerprinted, photographed and questioned. NSEERS's most controversial component, known as 'domestic' or 'call-in' registration, imposed the special registration requirements on men and boys, aged 16 and over, who came to the U.S. as 'nonimmigrants' before NSEERS was introduced. The domestic component, implemented in four phases, applied exclusively to male citizens and nationals of twenty-five countries. With the exception of North Korea, every country designated for special registration was predominantly Muslim and located in the Middle East, South Asia or North Africa. The government never extended domestic registration beyond the initial list of predominantly Muslim countries.[135] This program appeared to use nationality as a proxy for religion and ethnicity.[136]

In June 7, 2003, approximately 16 percent of the 82,000 males required to register had been subjected to removal proceedings, in almost all cases because of immigration status violations.[137] Many of those removed were individuals awaiting priority dates for family reunification; they had often assumed mistakenly that their cooperation in appearing for registration would not precipitate removal proceed-

133 Stephen H. Legomsky, 20.

134 Ibid.

135 Visitors from the following countries were called in for "Special Registration": Afghanistan, Algeria, Bahrain, Bangladesh, Egypt, Eritrea, Indonesia, Iran, Iraq, Jordan, Kuwait, Libya, Lebanon, Morocco, North Korea, Oman, Pakistan, Qatar, Somalia, Saudi Arabia, Sudan, Syria, Tunisia, United Arab Emirates, and Yemen.

136 Amnesty International, United States of America: Amnesty International's Concerns Regarding Post-September 11 Detentions in the USA, March 2002. AI Index: AMR 51/044/2002.

137 Stephen H. Legomsky, 9.

ings.[138] The 82,000 special registrations, combined with the tens of thousands of additional registrations at ports of entry, have, thus far, yielded only eleven terrorism suspects.[139] This mapping of Muslim communities, through the anti terrorism measures seems premised on the faulty notion that Muslims are more likely to commit violent acts than people of other faiths. The result of this approach has been that a large number of totally innocent Muslims have been harassed detained and tortured with out fair trial or equal protection of the law. The American Civil Liberties Union "ACLU" noted that "none of the Muslim detainees have been publicly charged with terrorism."[140]

Muslims, also, had to face anti-Islamic border security policy. In the immediate aftermath of the attacks, Muslims faced discrimination by airlines. Many large U.S.-based airline corporations including American, Continental, Northwestern and United Airlines, discriminated against Muslim men (or men who airline staff perceived to be so). Many of them were summarily ejected from flights based solely on the prejudices of airline employees and passengers and for reasons wholly unrelated to security. Many of these policies have common elements of setting religious features of Muslim life or Muslim religious and political views apart from what is considered normal and acceptable.

At airports, Muslims tend to be singled out the most. They are more likely to be stopped, delayed, and subjected to extended and often humiliating security checks in airports since the enactment of the Patriot Act. These security checks sometimes include unnecessary, degrading and invasive strip searches or forced removal of the religious head coverings worn by Muslim women. Oftentimes, Muslims, after returning to the United States from religious meetings or religious pilgrimages, are singled out in significant numbers. Sometimes they are denied reentry into the United States.

138 Ibid.

139 Ibid.

140 The American Civil Liberties Union, *Sanctioned Bias: Racial Profiling Since September 11*, 2001, Feb. 2004, 5. Available at: <https:/www.aclu.org/sites/default/files/FilesPDFs/racial%20profiling%20statement%20for20%un.pdf> (viewed Sept. 2013).

An example of religious profiling, in the context of American national security practices,[141] is the profile case of Maher Arar, a Muslim, Canadian citizen, of Syrian origin, who was detained in the United States and subjected to an extraordinary rendition to Syria, where he was detained without charge or trial for one year and subjected to severe torture. After more than two years of public inquiry into his case, the Commission of Inquiry into the Action of Canadian Officials issued a report[142] in the fall of 2006, vindicating Mr. Arar and highlighting the wrongdoing, shortcomings and mistakes on the part of the law enforcement and security agencies which were the root of his case. Notably, in his report, Commissioner Dennis O'Connor "raises concerns with respect to religious profiling."[143]

Arar filed a suit in a federal court in the Eastern District of New York in 2004,[144] *Arar v. Ashcroft*, to seek compensatory damages and to prove that the actions of the U.S. government were illegal and violated his constitutional, civil, and international human rights. A year after the case was filed, the U.S. government invoked the rarely-used "State Secrets Privilege" in a motion to dismiss the suit. The government claimed that to go forward in an open court would jeopardize the United States' intelligence, foreign policy, and national security interests. Specifically, the government's invocation of the state secrets privilege asserted that disclosure of "the basis for the rejection of plaintiff's designation of Canada as the country to which plaintiff wished to be removed", "the basis for the decision to exclude plaintiff from this country", and "the considerations involved in the decision to remove him to

141 See: Canadian Council on American-Islamic Relations, *Presumption of Guilt: A National Survey on Security Visitations of Canadian Muslims*, June 2005.

142 Commission of Inquiry into the Action of Canadian Officials in relation to Maher Arar, *Report of the Events Relating to Maher Arar: Analysis and Recommendations*, September 2006, 356.

143 Ibid.

144 US Asserts State Secret Privilege in Arar v. Ashcroft, et al, Civil Action No. 04-CV-249-DGT-VVP (E.D.N.Y.), Eastern District of New York, 18 January 2005.Viewed online at: <http://www.fas.org/sgp/jud/arar-notice-011805.pdf> (viewed Sept. 2013).

Syria" would damage national security interests.[145] Being kidnapped, tortured and held for months for no reason and without any explanation, other than his being a Muslim, is a disturbing experience to say the least. But to suffer that and then receive no justice, not even the hope of justice, because the US government has this overly broad privilege at its disposal, is against humanity and human rights. There's a human cost to protecting the national security of the United States and it is innocent Muslims who, this time round, have had to pay the price as they do not have access to the protection of the rules of law.[146]

Another response to the events of September 11, 2001, was a massive Department of Justice scheme to interview thousands of non-citizens who might have information on potential terrorist activities. The idea was to talk with people whose demographics and immigration statuses resembled those of the nineteen hijackers. The interviews were purportedly voluntary, and the interviewees were to be regarded as potential sources of information, not as suspects. The project was coordinated by the Department of Justice's Executive Office for United States Attorneys (EOUSA).[147]

The rounds of interviews included male non-immigrants ranging in age from approximately seventeen to forty-seven, who had entered the United States between January 1, 2000 and February 27, 2002 and were all Muslim.[148]

145 For understanding '*the State Secrets Privilege*,' see: Memorandum in Support of the US's Assertion of States Secret Privilege, 18 January 2005, Available online at: <http://www.fas.org/sgp/jud/arar-memo-011805.pdf> (viewed Sept. 2013).

146 Mr. Arar "extraordinary rendition" was not an isolated incident; rather it is part of a widespread pattern and practice. Many other victims have come forward in recent years to recount very similar stories. Also see the case of Khaled El -Masri: For a more detailed account, *see El-Masri v. Tenet et al.*, Apr. 6, 2006 (E.D. Va. 2005) (No. 1:05cv1417).

147 U.S. General Accounting Office, Report to Congressional Committees, Homeland Security: Justice Department's Project to Interview Aliens after September 11, 2001, 8 (2003), viewed online <at: http://www.gao.gov/new.items/d03459.pdf> (viewed Sept. 2013).

148 Ibid.

The program was controversial, for at least two reasons. First, although no evidence indicates anyone was coerced into participating, interviewees did not always perceive the conversations to be truly voluntary. They often reported that they "feared there could be [immigration-related] repercussions to them for declining to participate."[149] Second, since the overwhelming majority of the interviewees were Muslim of Arab origin, interviewees often felt "singled out and investigated because of their ethnicity or religious beliefs."[150]

Moreover, the State Department imposed rigorous screening on men seeking visas from twenty-five designated countries. Obviously all were Muslim countries. Many of the students from these countries missed the start of classes; many scientists had to cancel travel to attend a conference; and many students enrolled in universities in other countries because of the cumbersome and burdensome visa screening mechanisms.[151]

Law enforcement used religion, country-of-origin, or religious appearances as a proxy for criminal suspicion.[152] Moreover, Muslim organizations were the focus of suspicion and government efforts to crackdown on terrorist financing. In 2002, the US Treasury Department issued guidelines for the non-profit sector on terror financing that af-

149 Ibid., 8–9.

150 Ibid., 16–17.

151 Report of the AAUP Special Committee on Academic Freedom and National Security in a Time of Crisis, October, 2003. Available online: <http://www.aaup.org/report/academic-freedom-and-national-security-time-crisis> (viewed 2013).

152 Chip Pitts, Committee on the Judiciary, U.S. House of Representatives, Oversight Hearing on *"Reauthorization of the USA Patriot Act"*, Amnesty International USA, June 10, 2005, 3. Also, the American Civil Liberties Union (ACLU) has been busy keeping up with racial and religious profiling cases after 9/11. One example is an Illinois National Guardsman and three private security personnel at O'Hare International Airport engaged in an unnecessary, unjustified, illegal and degrading search of a 22 year old United States citizen of Pakistani descent last November. Ms. Kaukab was identified and subjected to a humiliating search not because she posed any security threat, but only because her wearing of a hijab identified her as a Muslim.

fected a broad swathe of organizations and groups.[153] This involved freezing the assets and closing the offices of several Muslim organizations, as well as drawing up a watch list of terrorist organizations, which were predominantly Muslim. However, the blacklisting of organizations was done outside of a clear legal and policy framework and was based upon an organization's associations rather than its own actions. The USA Patriot Act, along with other related post-9/11 laws, executive orders, and policies are proving to be targeting and profiling mainly Muslims as the only terrorist suspects in the world.

3.2.2.2 Muslim Non-profit Organizations

The effort to quell terrorist financing and money laundering has been identified by the United States as the second phase in its 'war on terrorism'.[154] Executive Order 13224 blocks all property and interests in property of the designated terrorist organizations, known as specially designated global terrorists, or SDGTs. This Executive Order is extremely broad and prohibits transactions with individuals and organizations deemed by the Executive Branch to be associated with terrorism and allow the government to freeze all assets controlled by or in the possession of these entities and those who support them. The Executive Branch has taken the position that it has the authority to freeze assets while it investigates whether an organization is associated with terrorism. Organizations whose property and interests are automatically frozen are: (1) those specifically listed in the annex to the Executive Order itself;[155] (2) those determined by the Secretary of State "to have committed, or to pose a significant risk of committing, acts of terrorism that threaten the security of U.S. nationals or the national security, foreign policy, or

153 Kenneth W. Dam – Deputy Secretary of the Treasury, *"The Financial Front of the War on Terrorism: The Next Phase,"* delivered to the Council on Foreign Relations New York, New York. June 8, 2002. Viewed online: <http://www.treas.gov/press/releases/po3163.htm> (viewed 2013).

154 Ibid.

155 Exec. Order No. 13,224 § 1(a); 31 C.F.R. § 594.201(a)(1).

economy of the United States";[156] and (3) those determined by the Secretary of the Treasury "to be owned or controlled by, or to act for or on behalf of" organizations identified as terrorists.[157]

It is worth noting that so far, only Muslim organizations have been shut down.

As of March 15, 2004, there have been three court cases regarding asset blocking of non-profits under the Executive Order that have produced written opinions from judges. In *Holy Land Foundation for Relief and Development (HFL) v. Ashcroft,*[158] *Benevolence International Foundation (BIF) v. Ashcroft*[159] and *Global Relief Foundation (GRF) v. O'Neill,*[160] the non-profits challenged their designation or pending designation as providing assistance to terrorist organizations. In each case, the asset blocking was upheld.

Once designated as a supporter of terrorism, law enforcement officials simply froze the organizations' assets and seized their property "pending an investigation" without producing any evidence, as authorized by the act. Muslim organizations have sought injunctive relief after being raided and having their assets frozen, citing constitutional issues. These issues include searches and seizures conducted without warrants, the freezing of assets before any criminal charges are filed, and the withholding of evidence from targeted organizations.

The accuracy of such allegations is generally difficult to prove because of the secretive nature of such investigations. Moreover, once all assets are seized and frozen, an organization may be denied access to evidence (the organization's computers, files, documents, etc.) that might prove its innocence. Even if these materials were available, there is no forum where an affected charity can present evidence on its own behalf

156 Exec. Order No. 13,224 § 1(b); 31 C.F.R. § 594.201(a)(2).
157 Exec. Order No. 13,224 § 1(c); 31 C.F.R. § 594.201(a)(3).
157 *Holy Land Found. for Relief & Dev. v. Ashcroft,* 333 F.3d 156 (D.C. Cir. 2003), *cert. denied,* 72 U.S.L.W. 3551 (2004).
159 *Benevolence Int'l Found., Inc. v. Ashcroft,* 200 F. Supp. 2d 935 (N.D. Ill. 2002).
160 *Global Relief Found., Inc., v. O'Neill,* 315 F.3d 748 (7th Cir.), *cert. denied,* 124 S.Ct.531 (2003).

or challenge evidence against it. Appealing Treasury actions to the federal courts is relatively useless, as the court's scope of review is very limited.

Even if there may be legal bases to challenge these preemptory freezes, the government has the practical option simply to designate the entity as an organization identified as terrorist and avoid judicial review.[161] Should the authorities later decide that the designation was improper, or if the designation is challenged in court, the Executive Branch can simply unfreeze the assets.[162] Further, the government does not have to provide any pre-freeze notice or an opportunity to respond to the freeze where this action "would impinge upon the security and other foreign policy goals of the United States."[163] The Executive Order itself states that "there need be no prior notice of a listing or determination" of terrorist status.[164]

In addition, authorities

> […] have failed to produce significant evidence of terror financing by U.S.-based charities. Questionable evidence has been used to shut down the largest U.S.-based Muslim charities. Anti-terrorist financing policies deny charities fundamental due process… Government action has created the perception of ethnic profiling and negatively impacted Muslim giving. Organizations and individuals suspected of supporting terrorism are guilty until proven innocent.[165]

Unlike other international money-laundering prevention statutes, which provide for criminal penalties, the measure does not have either "knowledge" or an "intent" requirement. In other words, an organization can violate the Executive Order, and consequently have its assets frozen, even if it does not *know* it is providing support to individuals or orga-

161 See Global Relief Found., 315 F.3d at 751 (citing 50 U.S.C. § 1702(a)(1)(B)).

162 Ibid., 315 F.3d at 750–51.

163 See Aara Money Wire Serv., Inc. v. United States, No. 02-CV-789, 2003 U.S. Dist. LEXIS 16190 (D. Minn. Aug. 21, 2003).

164 Holy Land Found., 333 F.3d at 163 (quoting Nat'l Council of Resistance of Iran v. Dept. of State, 251 F.3d 192, 208 (D.C. Cir. 2001)).

165 Kay Guinane, *Muslim Charities and the War on Terror, Top Ten Concerns and Status,* March 2006. Viewed on: <http://www.foreffectivegov.org/files/npadv/PDF/MuslimCharitiesTopTenUpdated.pdf> (last viewed Oct. 2013).

nizations identifies as terrorists or has otherwise become "associated with" a terrorist organization as defined in the Executive Order.[166]

The use of secret evidence by the Treasury Department and lack of due process for groups designated as supporters of terrorism has undermined the credibility of the government's anti-terrorist financing efforts. Although the courts have upheld the Treasury's actions in each case, the scope of judicial review on appeals of Treasury action is extremely limited. Courts have granted deference to the executive branch, repeatedly referring to their fear of limiting the president's ability to promote national security. In *U.S. v. Rahmani*,[167] Judge Robert M. Tukasugi of the U.S. District Court for the Central District of California found that the practice of designating terrorist organizations is "unconstitutional on its face." "Accordingly, such designation is a nullity and cannot be relied upon in a prosecution."[168] He added that "the argument for national security should not serve as an excuse for obliterating the Constitution."[169] Nonetheless, this decision has gone largely unnoticed and has not been relied on in other courts. According to the OBM Watch Report,[170] the main concerns about the treatment of Muslim Charities in the war on terror are:

1. Drastic sanctions in anti-terrorist financing laws are being used to shut down entire organizations, resulting in the loss of badly needed humanitarian assistance around the world and creating a climate of fear in the nonprofit sector.

166 See Exec. Order No. 13,224, 66 Fed. Reg. 49,079 (Sept. 25, 2001), *amended by* Exec. Order No. 13,258, 67 Fed. Reg. 44,751 (July 3, 2002) & Exec. Order No. 13,284, 68 Fed. Reg. 4,075 (Jan. 28, 2003) [hereinafter Exec. Order No. 13,224], available at <http://www.ustreas.gov/offices/eotffc/ofac/sanctions/t11ter.pdf>.

167 United States District Court, for the Central District of California, *United States of America v. Roya Rahmani, et al.*, Case NO. CR01-209-RMT, Memorandum order granting defendants' motion to dismiss indictment based on recent D.C. Circuit Case.

168 Ibid.

169 Ibid.

170 Kay Guinane, *Muslim Charities and the War on Terror, Top Ten Concerns and Status*, March 2006.

2. Despite sweeping post-9/11 investigative powers, authorities have failed to produce significant evidence of terror financing by U.S.-based charities.
3. Questionable evidence has been used to shut down the largest U.S. – based Muslim charities.
4. Anti-terrorist financing policies deny charities fundamental due process.
5. There are no safe harbor procedures to protect charities acting in good faith or to eliminate the risk of giving to Muslim charities or charitable programs working with Muslim populations.
6. Government action has created the perception of ethnic profiling and negatively impacted Muslim giving.
7. Organizations and individuals suspected of supporting terrorism are guilty until proven innocent.
8. Charitable funds have been withheld from people in need of assistance and diverted to help pay judgments in unrelated lawsuits, violating the intentions of innocent Muslim donors.
9. There is unequal enforcement of anti-terrorist financing laws.
10. Treatment of Muslim charities hurts, not helps, the war on terrorism.

In KindHearts for Charitable Humanitarian Development, Inc v. Geithner et al., the Federal judge, James G. Carr, issued a temporary restraining order barring the U.S. Department of the Treasury from designating KindHearts for Charitable Humanitarian Development a U.S. charity, as a "specially designated global terrorist" ("SDGT") without affording the organization basic due process.[171] Under the current U.S. regulatory regime, KindHearts didn't have the right to a hearing where it can confront the evidence against it and there are no provisions for independent review of Treasury's decisions. As a result of this,

171 In February 2006, the Office of Foreign Assets Contral ("OFAC"), a department of the Treasury froze the assets of the group "pending investigation" and executed a search warrant at the group's headquarters and the residence of its president, seizing 150 boxes of documents, paper files, computer hard drives, videotapes and other media. The investigation has yet to be completed and Kindhearts' assets remain frozen three years later.

KindHearts initiated a legal challenge on October 9, 2008, in the United States District Court for the Northern District of Ohio[172] challenging the constitutionality of the Treasury Department's process. In his decision released January 30, 2009, Judge James G. Carr of the U.S. District Court granted the motion to vacate, requiring the government to commence producing copies at its expense of all seized materials to KindHearts' lawyers.[173] Judge Carr indicated he had grave concerns with regard to the impact of the protective order on the group's due process and Sixth Amendment rights to enjoy fair and adequate representation by counsel, as a paramount impediment to enjoyment of those rights is legal counsel not having access to all documents and the inability to have meaningful consultation with clients concerning the same.[174] Judge Carr wrote that

> [i]f counsel is to play a meaningful role in opposing and seeking to avoid such designation, and otherwise to protect KindHearts in the face of OFAC's past and potential future actions, they must be able to consult with informed representatives of KindHearts. As long as the current order is in place, they cannot do so.[175]

In a similar decision relating to U.S. charities and terrorism related investigations, a federal judge of the U.S. District Court in Oregon ruled on November 6, 2008 that the Treasury's action in shutting down AlHaramain Islamic Foundation, Inc. in 2004 violated basic due process rights.[176] The judge also ruled that the definition of "material sup-

172 *In re Search of KindHearts for Charitable Humanitarian Development, Inc* v. Geithner et al., 2009 U.S. Dist. LEXIS 9055 (N.D. Ohio Jan. 30, 2009). Available online at: <http://www.aclu.org/pdfs/safefree/kindheartsvgeithner_judges protectiveorderruling.pdf> (viewed Sept. 2013).

173 Ibid., 12.

174 Ibid., 3.

175 Ibid., 9.

176 See: Al Harammain Islamic Foundation, Inc. v. United States Department of the treasury, 585F. Supp.2d1233, 1269–1270 (D.Or.2008), quoted in Carter, Terrence S., Claridge, Nancy E., Carter, Sean S., Due Process and Anti-Terrorism Initiatives Worldwide-Recent Developments, Anti-Terrorism and Charity Law alert No. 16, 26 February, 2009, 4.

port" of terrorist activities is constitutionally vague.[177] This decision represents one of the first successful challenges by an SDGT on the basis that the listing process does not provide for adequate procedural or substantive safeguards.[178]

Moreover, the United States is obliged by international law to protect Muslims from discrimination in freezing assets of charities. Article 6 (b) of the 1981 Declaration states that the right to freedom of thought, conscience, religion or belief includes the freedom, "To establish and maintain appropriate charitable or humanitarian institutions." Moreover, the Resolution 2005/40 of the Commission on Human Rights art. 4 (e) urges States,

> To ensure that, in accordance with appropriate national legislation and in conformity with international human rights law, the freedom for all persons and members of groups to establish and maintain religious, charitable or humanitarian institutions is fully respected and protected.

3.2.3 Preventive Detentions and Religious Discrimination in Prison Settings

In the months directly following 9/11, after the passing of the Patriot Act[179], the US Government rounded up and imprisoned thousands of Muslim men based solely on pretextual immigration violations. The most disconcerting fact about these mass round-ups is the fact that the Justice Department has refused to disclose the identities of the detainees, give them access to lawyers or allow them to have contact with their

177 Ibid

178 Ibid.

179 See: Scheinin Martin, *Report of the Special Rapporteur on the promotion and protection of human rights and fundamental freedoms while countering terrorism*, A/HRC/6/17, 21 November 2007. Scheinin Martin, *Report of the Special Rapporteur on the promotion and protection of human rights and fundamental freedoms while countering terrorism, Mission to the United States of America*, A/HRC/6/17/Add.3, 22 November 2007.

families.[180] According to the Human Rights Watch World Report 2006, these detainees could face one or all of the following measures, ranging from

> [...] secret detention facilities in Europe and elsewhere, illegal holding of terrorist suspects without rights or access to counsel, indefinite or prolonged detention, evidence obtained under torture, refoulement (The return of a person to a country where he or she would be at risk or ill-treatment) with the resort to 'diplomatic assurance' from the countries of origin.[181]

Of the detainees held after 9/11, all were Muslim males.

3.2.3.1 Detention of Muslims as "Unlawful Combatants"

In post 9/11 and in the context of war on terror, Muslims were detained secretly and in secret places for months and years. They were held without the knowledge of the International Committee of the Red Cross. Some Muslim detainees, who are foreign nationals held outside the sovereign territory of the United States, are devoid of any rights, enforceable in either U.S. courts or any court in the world, whether under the U.S. constitution or international law.[182] Moreover, the United States government introduced a dangerous new term "unlawful enemy combatant." Under the new law, anyone who has "purposefully and materially supported" hostilities against the US can be classified as an enemy combatant. The term, as used by the government, does not fit within any category of participants in military hos-

180 See: The September 11 Detainees: A Review of the Treatment of Aliens Held on Immigration Charges in Connection with the Investigation of the September 11 Attacks, U.S. Department of Justice Office of the Inspector General, April 2003. Available online: <http://www.justice.gov/oig/special/0306/press.pdf> (viewed Sept. 2013).

181 See: Human Rights Watch, World Report 2006, pp. 544. <http://www.hrw.org/legacy/wr2k6/> (viewed Sept. 2013).

182 See: White House Press Secretary announcement of President Bush's determination re legal status of Taliban and Al Qaeda detainees (February 7, 2002) *available at:* <http://www.state.gov/s/l/38727.htm> (viewed Sept. 2013).

tilities as those categories have been defined under U.S. or international law."[183]

These measures resulted in ordinary Muslim civilians, who do not have any direct connection to terrorist groups, being placed in military custody and tried before a military commission. The law continued to deprive Muslim detainees held in US custody abroad of the possibility of challenging the legality of their detention *(habeas corpus)*.[184] A variety of challenges have been raised by detainees in Guantánamo regarding conditions of their detention,[185] and lawyers filed dozens of petitions on behalf of the Muslim detainees, where judges reached conflicting conclusions as to whether the detainees have any enforceable rights to challenge their treatment[186] and detention.[187]

Muslims were not protected from coercion to give testimony that may incriminate themselves. They were not granted the absolute right to be summoned and to have their case heard in an open court. They

183 See: Jennifer K. Elsea, The Military Commissions Act of 2006: Analysis of Procedural Rules and Comparison with Previous DOD Rules and the Uniform Code of Military Justice, American Law Division, CRS Report for Congress, September 27, 2007.

184 *The Supreme Court has held that both citizen combatants detained on the U.S. mainland and non-U.S. citizen combatants detained on Guantanamo may use habeas corpus to assert certain procedural due process protections. See Hamdi v. Rumsfeld, 124 S. Ct. 2633, 2643–52 (2004) (citizens); Rasul v. Bush, 124 S. Ct. 2686, 2696–99 (2004) (noncitizens).*

185 Relevant cases: Al-Anazi v. Bush, 370 F. Supp. 2d 188 (D.D.C. 2005). Almurbati v. Bush, 366 F. Supp. 2d 72 (D.D.C. 2005). Abdah v. Bush, 2005 U.S. Dist. LEXIS 4144 (D.D.C. 2005). El-Banna v. Bush, 2005 U.S. Dist. LEXIS 16880 (2005).

186 Muslim detainees have been tortured and ill-treated. An example of a torture case, as been noted by Diène, the Special Rapporteur on racism, is the case of Mohammed C., an 18 years old, Chadian national born in Saudi Arabia who was held at the US naval base in Guantánamo Bay, Cuba and who was freed and found innocent after a long journey of torture and ill-treatment. His only crime was that he is a Muslim. E/CN.4/2006/16/Add.1, Para. 96–100.

187 Such Cases: *Hamdi v. Rumsfeld (*542 U.S. 507 (2004)), *Rasul v. Bush* (124 S.Ct. 2886 (2004)), *Hamdan v. Rumsfeld,* June 29, 2006126 S.Ct. 2749, 2793 (2006). ___ U.S. ___, 126 S.Ct. 2749 (2006). *Khalid v. Bush* (355 F. Supp. 2d 311 (D.D.C. 2005)).

were denied legal counsel and were unable to have their sentence pronounced publically. They were also unable to present evidence in their defense. It is not possible to embrace "a person is innocent until proven guilty" and still deny human beings a hearing under certain circumstances. This right means that no one, absolutely no one, can be denied a trial under any circumstances and that everyone has the right to conduct a forceful defense. However, since 9/11 and the enactment of anti-terrorism measures, Muslims have been denied this right.

The presumption of innocence is, in fact, a legal instrument created by the law to favor the accused based on the legal inference that most people are not criminals. The US Supreme Court, in *Coffin vs. United States,* affirmed that "the presumption of innocence is evidence in favor of accused, introduced by the law in his behalf"[188]. The United Nations incorporated the principle in its Declaration of Human Rights, in 1948, under Article eleven, section one,[189] and it was incorporated into the United Nations International Covenant on Civil and Political Rights [as article 14, section 2]. Despite that, it has been denied to Muslim suspects held in US custody after 9/11.

The international human rights instruments do not leave room for any doubt or uncertainty in respect of torture and ill-treatment.[190] They state clearly that there are absolutely no circumstances in which torture or other cruel, inhuman or degrading treatment or punishment can ever be justified. Torture is defined as any act by which severe pain or suffering, whether physical or mental, is intentionally inflicted on a person, other than that pain or suffering which is inherent in the fact of detention or imprisonment. Governments should ensure that per-

188 Coffin vs. U.S., 156 U.S. 432, 432–463 (1895).

189 Art. 11(1): (1) Everyone charged with a penal offence has the right to be presumed innocent until proved guilty according to law in a public trial at which he has had all the guarantees necessary for his defense.

190 Universal Declaration of Human Rights, Article 5, Convention against Torture and Other Cruel, Inhuman or Degrading Treatment or Punishment, Article 1.1, Article 2, Article 10 (Adopted and opened for signature, ratification and accession by General Assembly resolution 39/46 of 10 December 1984, *entry into force* 26 June 1987, in accordance with article 27 (1)).

sons deprived of their liberty are held in officially recognized places of custody, and that accurate information on their custody and whereabouts, including transfers, is made promptly available to their relatives and lawyer or other persons of confidence.[191] This does not seem to apply to Muslim detainees who, under justifications of the Patriot Act, have been ill-treated and tortured and denied the right to demand justice for this violation of their right because they are Muslims and Muslims are assumed to be inherently terrorists.

There are a number of international instruments that protect prisoners and their conditions of detention. The more detailed standards that are set out in these principles, minimum rules or guidelines, provide a valuable complement to the broad principles contained in the legal treaties. These include: *the Standard Minimum Rules for the Treatment of Prisoners (1957)*;[192] *the Body of Principles for the Protection of All Persons under Any Form of Detention or Imprisonment (1988)*[193]; *the Basic Principles for the Treatment of Prisoners (1990)*[194] and *the Standard Minimum Rules for the Administration of Juvenile Justice (1985)*.[195] There are also a number of instruments that refer specifically to staff working with people who have been deprived of their liberty. They include: the Code of Conduct for Law Enforcement Of-

191 Principles on the Effective Prevention and Investigation of Extralegal, Arbitrary and Summary Executions, Article 6, (Recommended by Economic and Social Council resolution 1989/65 of 24 May 1989.)

192 Adopted by the First United Nations Congress on the Prevention of Crime and the Treatment of Offenders, held at Geneva in 1955, and approved by the Economic and Social Council by its resolution 663 C (XXIV) of 31 July 1957 and 2076 (LXII) of 13 May 1977.

193 Body of Principles for the Protection of All Persons under Any Form of Detention or Imprisonment, Principle 1: All persons under any form of detention or imprisonment shall be treated in a humane manner and with respect for the inherent dignity of the human person.(Adopted by General Assembly resolution 43/173 of 9 December 1988).

194 Basic Principles for the Treatment of Prisoners, Principle 1: All prisoners shall be treated with the respect due to their inherent dignity and value as human beings.

195 ("The Beijing Rules") Adopted by General Assembly resolution 40/33of 29 November 1985.

ficials (1979),[196] the Principles of Medical Ethics relevant to the Role of Health Personnel, particularly Physicians, in the Protection of Prisoners and Detainees against Torture and Other Cruel, Inhuman or Degrading Treatment or Punishment (1982) and the Basic Principles on the Use of Force and Firearms (1990). These international standards are supplemented by a number of regional human rights instruments; in this case of the US, it is the American Convention on Human Rights entered into force in 1978.[197]

It is true that Congress has significant authority over the administration of the judicial system, but it may not exercise its authority over the courts in a way that violates constitutional rights, such as the Fifth Amendment due process clause or precepts of equal protection. Justice Black wrote for the Court, in a different context, that "these granted powers are always subject to the limitations that they may not be exercised in a way that violates other specific provisions of the Constitution."[198] Justice Harlan affirms that, with respect to Congress's power over jurisdiction of the federal courts, "what such exceptions and regulations should be it is for Congress, in its wisdom, to establish, having of course due regard to all the Constitution."[199]

The Fourth Amendment of the US Constitution[200] protects individuals from unreasonable seizure and the Fourteenth Amendment obliges *the State not to deprive any person of life, liberty, or property, without due process of law; nor deny to any person within its jurisdiction the equal protection of the laws.*[201]

Today, the US allowed the assumption that Muslims are guilty of terrorism to take precedence. There is no recourse which to prove the

196 Code of Conduct for Law Enforcement Officials, G.A. res. 34/169, annex, 34 U.N. GAOR Supp. (No. 46) at 186, U.N. Doc. A/34/46 (1979).

197 American Convention on Human Rights, Article 5 (2): All persons deprived of their liberty shall be treated with respect for the inherent dignity of the human person.((Signed at the Inter-American Specialized Conference on Human Rights, San Josi, Costa Rica, 22 November 1969).

198 Williams v. Rhodes, 393 U.S. 23, 29 (1968).

199 United States v. Bitty, 208 U.S. 393, 399–400 (1908).

200 U.S. Constitution amendment IV.

201 U.S. Constitution amendment XIV.

opposite, though the rule is that everyone is presumed innocent, until proven guilty. The United States has established, through its anti-terrorism measures and military tribunals, a measure allows for the detention and prosecution of Muslim suspects (who many of them proved to be innocent) under military rather than civilian law. Thus, they are not guaranteed the full range of constitutional or international human rights safeguards that would normally accrue to criminal defendants. While the Military Order states that "defendants before military commissions shall be granted a full and fair trial,"[202] it does not expressly guarantee, as noted by Orentlicher and Goldman,

> [...] the presumption of innocence or the right of defendants to counsel of their choice; it denies defendants any remedy, including appeal and habeas corpus, to either a U.S. or international court; and it potentially bars defendants from seeking the evidence against them.[203]

3.2.3.2 Religious Humiliation against Muslims in Prison Settings

Religious humiliation of Muslim detainees has been widespread at Guantánamo and in American detention centers around the world. The United States authorities authorized certain interrogation techniques, which were especially degrading for Muslims.[204] These techniques include conduct intended to "soften up" prisoners by abusing items or

202 Military Order on Detention, Treatment, and Trial of Certain Non-Citizens in the War Against Terrorism (George W. Bush, November 13/01), Federal Register: November 16, 2001 (Volume 66, Number 222), Presidential Documents, Sec., 4 C (1)

203 Orenlicher, Diane F. and Goldman,Robert Kogod, "When Justice Goes to War: Prosecuting Terrorist Before Military Commissions" (2002)25, *Harvard Journal of Law & Public Policy* 653 at 661–62, quote in Ramraj, Victor M., The Emerging Security Paradigm in the West: A Perspective from Southeast Asia, *Asia-Pacific Journal on Human Rights and the Law 1*, 2003, 9n. See Also: Report on USA Human Rights After September 2001: Report 6.4: US Muslims Feeling a "Chilling Effect", Meikele John Civil Liberties Institute to the UN Human Rights Committee, August 29, 2005. Available online at: <http://www.ohchr.org/english/bodies/hrc/docs/ngos/liberties.doc> (viewed Sept. 2013).

204 E/CN./2005/61/Corr.1.16 March 2005, Para., 405.

disrupting rituals known to have particular importance for Muslims.[205] The U.S. Secretary of Defense Donald Rumsfeld, in 2002,

> [...] authorized a list of techniques for interrogation of prisoners at Guantánamo, which included 'removal of all comfort items (including religious items),' 'forced grooming (shaving of facial hair, etc.),' and 'removal of clothing.' Each of these practices is considered offensive to many Muslims. These techniques were later applied in Afghanistan and Iraq as well.[206]

Reed Brody, the special counsel for Human Rights Watch, affirms that "The United States has been humiliating Muslim prisoners by offending their religious beliefs."[207]

Many prisoners describe guards and interrogators as regularly defiling the Qur'an by touching it intentionally, dropping it, stepping on it, and throwing it on the ground. In the early days of Camp X-Ray, soldiers repeatedly threw copies of the Qur'an on the ground.[208] The mass suicide attempted in the summer of 2003, was organized to protest the abuse of the Qur'an after an interrogator had thrown a prisoner's Qur'an on the floor, "stepped on it, and kicked it across the room."[209] Abuse of the Qur'an also appears to be used to provoke the prisoners to

205 Report on Torture and Cruel, Inhuman, and Degrading Treatment of Prisoners at Guantánamo Bay, Cuba, Center for Constitutional Right July 2006, 25. Available online at: <http://www2.ohchr.org/english/bodies/hrc/docs/ngos/ccr.pdf> (viewed Sept. 2013).

206 Ibid.

207 U.S.: Religious Humiliation of Muslim Detainees Widespread, (New York, May 19, 2005). Available online at: <http://hrw.org/english/docs/2005/05/19/usdom10981.htm> (viewed Sept. 2013).

208 The most contentious issue .was the way many MPs handled the detainees' Qur'ans. This is an extremely sensitive practice, as the Qur'an is the most respected book in Islam. Muslims believe that the Qur'an contains the actual words of God and therefore is to be treated with the utmost respect. Muslims keep the Qur'an in a high place inside their homes as a show of respect and would never allow it to touch the floor or any place that is even slightly dirty.

209 Fletcher Laurel, Stover Eric & Others, Guantánamo and Its Aftermath: *U.S. detention and interrogation practices and their impact on former detainees,* Human Rights Center and International Human Rights Law Clinic, University of California, Berkeley, November 2008, Sec2: 37.

anger, after which the IRF is called to forcibly punish them. James Yee, the former military chaplain at Guantánamo, describes MPs as "purposely treating the Qur'an with disrespect."[210]

Many Muslim detainees, while they were in custody at Guantánamo Bay, were victims of ill-treatment, such as sexual harassment during prayers (such actions deter Muslims from praying).[211] Religious abuse has also been used "to coerce interrogations, including at *Ramadan* (the Month of fasting in Islam) when guards have withheld food at the break of fast. It can be observed that: "it is the faith of the detainees that is targeted: the religion of Islam."[212]

The right to freedom of religious belief and to observe the requirements of that religion is a universal human right[213] and applies to all prisoners, as well as to free persons.[214] Prison regulations should include the right of qualified religious representatives to visit prisons regularly to meet prisoners. Facilities should be provided to all prisoners who wish to observe their religious duties. This may include the right to pray in private at specified times of the day or night, to carry out various washing practices or to wear particular item of clothing.

Standard Minimum Rules for the Treatment of Prisoners[215], Article 42 states that: So far as practicable, every prisoner shall be allowed

210 James Yee & Aimee Molloy, For God and Country: Faith and Patriotism Under (2005). For a review, see Joseph Lelyveld, *The Strange Case of Chaplain Yee,* N.Y. REV. OF BOOKS, Dec. 15, 2005, available at: <www.nybooks.com/articles/> 18550 (last visited June 20, 2006).

211 E/CN./2005/61/Corr.1.16 March 2005, para. 414. See for the situation of detainees at Guantánamo Bay: E/CN.4/2006/120.

212 See: Report on Torture and Cruel, Inhuman, and Degrading Treatment of Prisoners at Guantánamo Bay, Cuba. Center for Constitutional Right July 2006, 26–28 <http://www.ohchr.org/english/bodies/hrc/docs/ngos/ccr.pdf>.

213 Universal Declaration of Human Rights, Article 18 and ICCPR, Article 18 (1).

214 Article 10 of ICCPR states: All persons deprived of their liberty shall be treated with humanity and with respect for the inherent dignity of the human person.

215 Adopted by the First United Nations Congress on the Prevention of Crime and the Treatment of Offenders, held at Geneva in 1955, and approved by the Economic and Social Council by its resolution 663 C (XXIV) of 31 July 1957 and 2076 (LXII) of 13 May 1977.

to satisfy the needs of his religious life by attending the services provided in the institution and having in his possession the books of religious observance and instruction of his denomination. Deprivation of liberty must not include deprivation of the right to observe the requirements of one's religion. The prison authorities should ensure that:

- Prisoners have the opportunity to pray, to read religious texts and to meet other requirements of their religion, such as clothing or washing, as often as their religion requires.
- Prisoners of the same religion should have the opportunity to gather as a group for religious services on religious holy days.
- Prisoners should have the opportunity to be visited by qualified representatives of their religion for private prayers and group services.

These provisions should apply to all recognized religious groups and should not be restricted to the main religions in any country. Special attention should be paid to the religious needs of prisoners from minority groups.

People who are detained or imprisoned do not cease to be human beings, no matter how serious the crime they have been accused or convicted of. These standards have been agreed to by the international community. The main human rights instruments, such as the International Covenant on Civil and Political Rights and the International Covenant on Economic, Social and Cultural Rights, are treaties which are legally binding for all states which have ratified or acceded to them. Most of them contain references to the treatment of people who are deprived of their liberty.

As far as distinctions according to religion are concerned, there are two sub-tests are generally applicable to determine the existence of an objective and reasonable justification. First, the difference in treatment must pursue a legitimate aim. Second, there has to be a reasonable relationship of proportionality between the difference in treatment and the legitimate aim sought to be realized.[216] This means that, "no profil-

216 Scheinin, para, 45.

ing practice is justified unless it satisfies certain minimum requirements of rationality and weighted cost effectiveness."[217]

Since profiling is premised on "the notion that it is a rational way to allocate limited administrative or enforcement resources, the profiling is irrational if the particular attributes fail to accurately predict criminal conduct."[218] Profiling, thus, is indefensible when its criteria are nothing more than the product of irrational prejudice. Moreover, "even when solid empirical evidence substantiates the assumed correlation between the profile and the criminal conduct, 'rational' does not necessarily mean 'justified'. A balancing is required."[219] On one side of the ledger are the perceived gains in national security from the government's efficient use of limited law enforcement resources. On the other side are the considerable harms associated with government-sponsored discrimination.

The problem here is that religious profiling and discrimination coincides with popular prejudices toward Muslims of Arab and South Asian descent. Some US counter-terrorism strategies have entailed one form or another of religious profiling and many of the national security laws have included serious religious discrimination, some examples are: The immigration authorities have adopted a series of policies and practices designed to counter terrorism that single out Muslim immigrants based on their country of origin or nationality and, indirectly through the choice of the targeted countries, their religion.[220] Under the Voluntary Interview Program, male immigrants, who were not suspected of any criminal activity, were selected for questioning solely because they were of a certain age, had entered the United States after January 2000 and originated from countries that have predominantly Muslim populations.[221] Although the authorities did not identify these countries, almost all the 8,000 men eventually interviewed were Mus-

217 Legomsky, 18.
218 Ibid.
219 Ibid.
220 Scheinin, para. 36.
221 Ibid.

lim. The National Security Entry-Exit Registration System imposed fingerprinting, photographing and registration requirements for all males who are citizens of, or were born in, certain designated countries; all of these countries – except for the Democratic People's Republic of Korea – have predominantly Muslim populations.[222]

Any terrorist-profiling practices that are based on distinctions according to a person's presumed "religion" based on their ethnicity or national origin raise the question as to their conformity with the principle of non-discrimination. This profiling based on stereotypical assumptions may bolster sentiments of hostility and xenophobia in the general public towards Muslims.[223] The anti-terrorism measures enacted by the United States is proven to be just that a "predictive religious profiling" targeting Muslims who are believed to bear a positive statistical correlation to involvement in terrorism.

Thus, by failing to effectively address the problem of religious profiling, the United States is violating its obligations under several international human rights agreements to which it is a party. Any profiling practices that are based on distinctions according to a person's presumed religion raise the question as to their conformity with the principle of non-discrimination. Discrimination on the basis of race and national or ethnic origin is prohibited by the International Convention on the Elimination of All Forms of Racial Discrimination (ICERD).[224] Furthermore, the prohibition against discrimination on the grounds of religion is generally accepted as a peremptory norm of international law, which cannot be set aside by treaty or acquiescence. The guarantees of non-discrimination of Articles 2 and 26 of the ICCPR, prohibit discrimination on the grounds of race, national origin and religion. Even during times of emergency, where states may derogate from certain other rights specified in the Covenant, the prohibition on discrimination remains intact. This view is supported by article 4, paragraph 1, of the ICCPR, which makes clear that the right

222 Ibid.
223 Ibid., 40.
224 ICERD, article 5 (a) and (d) (i); see also articles 1 (1), 2 (1) (a).

to non-discrimination on the grounds of race and religion can never be derogated from, not even in times of an officially proclaimed public emergency. These binding obligations of non-discrimination have been reinforced and supplemented by a range of other international and regional standards.[225] A provision specifically directed against the use of profiles that are based on racial characteristics is to be found in the Programme of Action adopted at the World Conference against Racism in 2000, urging States "to design, implement and enforce effective measures to eliminate the phenomenon popularly known as 'racial profiling'".[226]

At the regional level, the Inter-American Commission on Human Rights, in its Report on Terrorism and Human Rights has cautioned that "any use of profiling or similar devices by a state must comply strictly with international principles governing necessity, proportionality, and non-discrimination and must be subject to close judicial scrutiny".[227]

This is equally applicable to the profiling of persons based upon their religion. International instruments positively impose upon states a duty to ensure, as widely as possible, freedom of thought, conscience, and religion to all religions and beliefs and to their followers through eradicating any laws enforcing any unjustified distinctions based on these grounds. Further, they have a responsibility to cut at the very

225 The Code of Conduct for Law Enforcement Officials, for example, provides that such officials must "maintain and uphold the human rights of all persons", including the right to non-discrimination. Code of Conduct for Law Enforcement Officials, General Assembly resolution 34/169, 17 December 1979, article 2 and its Commentary (a). Basic Principles for the Treatment of Prisoners, Adopted and proclaimed by General Assembly resolution 45/111 of 14 December 1990. Principle 1: All prisoners shall be treated with the respect due to their inherent dignity and value as human beings. Principle 2: There shall be no discrimination on the grounds of race, colour, sex, language, religion, political or other opinion, national or social origin, property, birth or other status.

226 Report of the World Conference against Racism, Racial Discrimination, Xenophobia and Related Intolerance (A/CONF.189/12), Programme of Action, para. 72.

227 American Convention on Human Rights, Article 5 (2).

roots of intolerance and prejudice by providing remedies, such as educational measures and cooperation with groups willing to assist in counteracting prejudice and discrimination. The proliferation of laws, national security laws, anti-terror measures and registration requirements targeting or limiting Muslim communities in any region has the potential to cause a chilling effect on religious freedom and is particularly a threat to world peace. When law-enforcement agents use broad profiles that reflect unexamined generalizations, their practices may constitute disproportionate interferences with human rights. In particular, profiling based on stereotypical assumptions that persons of a certain religion are particularly likely to commit crime may lead to practices that are incompatible with the principle of non-discrimination.

The American Constitution "prohibits selective enforcement of the law based on considerations such as race,"[228] and, the decision of federal prosecutors "whether to prosecute may not be based on 'an unjustifiable standard such as race, religion, or other arbitrary classification."[229] The same is true of Federal law enforcement officers. Federal courts repeatedly have held that any general policy of "utiliz[ing] impermissible racial classifications in determining whom to stop, detain, and search"[230] would violate the Equal Protection Clause. As the Sixth Circuit has explained, "[i]f law enforcement adopts a policy, employs a practice, or in a given situation takes steps to initiate an investigation of a citizen based solely upon that citizen's race, without more, then a violation of the Equal Protection Clause has occurred."[231] "A person cannot become the target of a police investigation solely on the basis of skin color. Such selective law enforcement is forbidden."[232] The same could be said to base investigation or prosecution based solely upon that citizen's religion or other arbitrary classification. Reliance solely

228 *Whren v. United States*, 517 U.S. 806, 813 (1996).

229 *United States v. Armstrong*, 517 U.S. 456, 464 (1996) (quoting *Oyler v. Boles*, 368 U.S. 448, 456 (1962)).

230 *Chavez v. Illinois State Police*, 251 F.3d 612, 635 (7th Cir. 2001).

231 *United States v. Avery*, 137 F.3d 343, 355 (6th Cir. 1997).

232 *Id.* at 354.

upon generalized stereotypes is forbidden. That means the preventive use of this profiling method would only be compatible with the proportionality requirement if it were shown that there was a "concrete danger" to national security or human life, rather than a general threat situation as it existed since 11 September 2001. The US Authorities and advocates of anti-terrorism measures say it's the paramount to enhance the safety of all citizens, however, they have used *predictive* profiling by using suspicion linked to religion which led to a roundup of many innocent Muslims. Such *predictive* profiling violates constitutional freedoms and creates a climate of fear in a pluralistic society. Thus, singling out individuals or organizations for investigation, surveillance, and data-gathering based on their religion constitutes religious profiling that is just as unlawful and deeply offensive as racial profiling.

3.3 Religious Vilification against Muslims in the West

Some sociologists and cultural analysts argue that, during the 1990s, there was a shift in forms of prejudice from race-based prejudice to discrimination based on culture and religion,[233] and since the 9/11 attacks, religion has surpassed race as the primary focus of racism and vilification.[234] *Vilification* is any act that happens publicly and that could incite others to hate, have serious contempt for, or severely ridicule a person or group of people. There are many kinds of vilification of which racial and religious vilification are two types. One definition for religious vilification is the one stated in the *Victorian Racial and*

233 Seabrook, Jeremy. "Religion as a fig leaf for racism", *The Guardian*, July 23, 2004.

234 Rudiger, Anja, European Monitoring Center on Racism and Xenophobia, "Discrimination and Legislation", session 5, Conference on "Muslims in Europe post 9/11", St. Antony's-Princeton Conference, St Anthon's College, Oxford, April 2004.

Religious Tolerance Act[235] that defines religious vilification as "engaging in conduct that incites hatred against, serious contempt for, or revulsion or severe ridicule of, that other person or class or persons' on the grounds of the 'religious belief or activity of another person'. Many consider outlawing vilification on matters of race for equality is a worthy goal at all times in all situations. This is not true of religious vilifications, while many denounce religious hate speech, they do not consider these incidents serious enough to justify religious vilification laws.[236] There have been concerns that such a low threshold could, in practice, be applied to this type of legislation so as to interfere directly with fundamental aspects of freedom of religion, particularly religious practice through teaching and proselytism.

Religious vilification, however, is not less destructive than racial vilification. Both racial and religious vilifications belittle communities, and intimidate and ridicule them. Religious vilification, like racial vilification, includes acts, conduct, behavior, or activity involving the defamation of individuals and groups on the ground of their religion which constitute the incitement or stirring up of hatred or other emotions of hostility and enmity against these individuals and groups. Religious vilification like racial vilification creates and reinforces discriminatory messages and aggravates inequality and encourages acts of oppression and intimidation.[237]

The image of the Muslim population today (who is seen as a primitive, uncivilized sector of society that needs to be controlled) appears to have been deeply entrenched in the history of some Western nations and has been manipulated so that the violence and force used against them can be justified. The French religious symbol law (2004) and the anti-terrorism measures in the US and elsewhere, have helped to increase religious vilification which led to discrimination against Muslim

235 Racial and Religious Tolerance Act 2001 (Vic), s 8(1). See: Evans, Carolyn, "Religious freedom and religious hatred in democratic societies", Monash University, 2006, available at <http://www.law.monash.edu.au/castancentre/events/2006/conf-06-evans-paper.html> (viewed Sept. 2013).

236 Racial and Religious Vilification, 2004, 7.

237 Ibid.

communities and their members, in particular the emergence of increased negative stereotyping, hostile acts and violence against these communities because of their religious beliefs. Muslims began to be seen as 'too different' and are likely to threaten 'community values' and social cohesion.[238] The focus on incompatible differences has been utilized by majorities to exclude Muslims from a society's power and privilege.[239] The xenophobia, intolerance and discrimination towards Muslims, which followed the events of 9/11, has caused the Commission on Human Rights to react with calls for appropriate control of the mass media to prevent incitement to violence and intolerance towards Islam. In his Report, Doudou Diène, the Special Rapporteur on contemporary forms of racism, racial discrimination, xenophobia and related intolerance notes that "in most areas of the world there has been a serious upsurge in manifestations and expressions of discrimination against Muslims … and acts of violence against their places of worship and culture and identifying Islam with terrorism."[240] The central theme of these manifestations is open validation of Islamophobia in political and intellectual discourse, and since then, vilifications against Muslims have become more prevalent.

With regard to xenophobic language in political discourse, two key developments have been underlined: an increase in the use of xenophobic discourse used by *mainstream* politicians since 9/11, and the rise of extremist parties on the Right in both local and national governments. A notable shift has occurred in the way that mainstream politicians and political parties talk about immigration and multiculturalism, and specifically in the way that Muslims have been singled out as an alleged threat to 'Western' societies. There is an increasing penetration of racist political platforms of extreme right-wing parties and move-

238 Racial and Religious Vilification, Short Consultation Paper, Equal Opportunities Commission, Office of Multicultural Interests, Government of Western Australia August 2004, 5.

239 Ibid.

240 'Racism, Racial Discrimination, Xenophobia and all forms of Discrimination: Situation of Muslims and Arab peoples in various parts of the world', E/CN.4/2006/17, 13 February 2006, para. 2.

ments in the political programs of democratic parties and the growing intellectual legitimization of these platforms. This new and particularly alarming phenomenon affects those tendencies through a 'lowering of the guard"' on the part of governments in the fight against racism and the acceptance of open racism in large sectors of the populations of many countries. Racism, therefore, now constitutes the greatest threat to democracy.

Participants of the OSCE-ODIHR Roundtable,[241] pointed to the creation of a discourse of 'the other' and of the 'enemy within' which has been used to publicly justify domestic policies in the fight against terrorism that disproportionately impact particular on Muslims communities and which have effectively resulted in the creation of separate criminal justice systems.[242] Official political discourse which creates a sense of 'us' and 'them' was cited as deepening divides and increasing alienation, just as acts of terror committed under the pretext of religion further increase xenophobia.[243] Nothing better, as an example, than the use of the word *crusade* by US President, George W. Bush, first on September 11, 2001. He spoke of "this crusade, this war on terrorism"[244] In a rally for the troops in Alaska, on February 16, 2002, Bush said, and "I want to tell you something, we've got no better friends

241 Report of OSCE-ODIHR Roundtable: The Representation of Muslims in Public Discourse, OSCE & ODIHR, Warsaw, 2006, 7.

242 It is noted that there is a resurgence of the Neoconservative movement and its powerful role in the Bush administration. As Hugh B. Urban have persuasively argued, election of George W. Bush and the confusion following 9/11 allowed a small but radical group of intellectuals to seize the reins of U.S. foreign policy. Led by figures like Paul Wolfowitz, Dick Cheney, Donald Rumsfeld, and the members of the Project for the New American Century, the Neoconservatives have been able to put into effect a long-held plan for asserting a U.S. global hegemony." See: Hugh B. Urban, America, Left Behind 'Bush, the Neoconservatives, and Evangelical Christian Fiction, *Journal of Religion & Society,* Volume 8, 2006.

243 Report of OSCE-ODIHR Roundtable, 7.

244 From George W. Bush press Conference at the South Lawn, White House, September 16, 2001. Available at: <http://www.whitehouse.gov/news/releases/2001/09/20010916-2.html> (viewed Sept. 2013).

than Canada. They stand with us in this incredibly important crusade to defend freedom, this campaign to do what is right for our children and our grandchildren."[245] Such statements facilitate intolerance and discrimination against Muslim communities, because the memory of the crusade for Muslims is one of a holy war against Islam. The crusaders saw Muslims as: "an accursed race, a race utterly alienated from God… Killing these godless monsters was a holy act: it was a Christian duty to exterminate this vile race from their lands."[246]

Such statements from Bush and other political and influential figures, in addition to legislations (anti-terrorism measures and religious symbol law) targeting Muslims, have helped to increase an anti-Muslim sentiment in Western societies. This has led to more violence against Muslims of Arab and South Asian heritage; even Hispanic Americans and Sikh have suffered from these attacks because of perceived physical similarity to Muslims (United States Commission on Civil Rights, 2001). The Federal Bureau of Investigation (2000–2002) reported a seventeen-fold increase in hate crimes[247] against these groups in the 12 month period following the attacks. Murders, beatings, and attacks on mosques were directed at these people solely because they shared or were perceived as sharing the national background or religious beliefs of the hijackers responsible for attacking the World Trade Center and the Pentagon. The victims of the post-September 11 backlash and perpetrators have included women, senior citizens, shop owners, and even children. These bias-motivated incidents included a high degree of physical violence; with approximately one in five victims suffering bodily injury from physical assaults. Perpetrators used baseball bats, metal poles,

245 President Rallies the Troops in Alaska, Available online: <http://www.whitehouse.gov/news/releases/2002/02/20020216-1.html> (viewed Sept. 2013).

246 Armstrong Karen, "Holy War: the crusade and their Impact on today's World," Anchor Books, New York, 2001, Ix.

247 Hate or bias crimes, as defined by the Federal Bureau of Investigation, are crimes that manifest evidence of prejudice based on race, religion, sexual orientation, or ethnicity (Federal Bureau of Investigation, 1999). Also Check: A History of Backlash Attacks Against Arabs and Muslims in America, available online: <http://www.hrw.org/reports/usahate.usa1102-03.htm# P22_31469> (viewed Sept. 2013).

and guns as weapons (Arab American Institute, 2002). One of the most widely publicized incidents was the September 15, 2001 murder of Sikh-American, Balbir Singh Sodhi, in Arizona, who was assumed to be Muslim.[248]

Penetration of racist political platforms of extreme right-wing parties and movements in the political programs of democratic parties leads to a generalized acceptance of racist and xenophobic statements and writings.[249] The key concepts of this rhetoric are protecting the "national identity," "defending the national interest," safeguarding the "national heritage," giving priority to "national preference in employment," or combating "illegal foreign immigration." Political, social, economic, and cultural discrimination constitutes the natural expression of this defensive and protective national rhetoric. Its legitimacy is assured by the fact that it is accepted and used by the traditional democratic parties.[250]

This democratic normalization of the racist and xenophobic ideology, often for electoral reasons, effectively removes any ethical objections on the part of opponents of racism by making racist and xenophobic

248 Croyn, Chris L. S., Borshuk Catherine, 'The Scope of Justice for Muslim Americans: Moral Exclusion in the Aftermath of 9/11', *The Qualitative Report,* Volume 11 Number 3 September 2006, 589–590. Available online: <http://www.nova.edu/ssss/QR/QR11–3/coryn.pdf> (viewed Sept. 2013). See Also:
- *Hate crimes today: An age old foe in modern dress* [Brochure]. Part of the series "Clarifying the debate: Psychology examines the issues." Washington, DC: Arab American Institute, (2002).
- *Healing the nation: The Arab American experience after September 11, a first anniversary report by The Arab American Institute.* Washington, DC: Coryn, C.L., Beale, J.M., & Myers, K., (2004).
- Response to September 11th: Prejudice, patriotism, and anxiety in the aftermath of terror. *Current Research in Social Psychology,* 9(12), 165–184. Retrieved August 15, 2004, available online: <http://www.uiowa.edu/%7Egrpproc/crisp/crisp.9.12.html> (viewed Sept. 2013).

249 Doudou Diène, Political platforms which promote or incite racial discrimination, Updated study by the Special Rapporteur on contemporary forms of racism, racial discrimination, xenophobia and related intolerance; Political platforms. E/CN.4/2006/54, Para. 7.

250 Ibid.

attitudes commonplace. The most practical illustration of this transition of racist and xenophobic ideas from the outer fringes of the extreme right to democratic normality is the growing sharing of political power by xenophobic parties and their leaders through coalition governments. The bridge has been crossed from a marginal political platform to access to the political institutions of the state and hence to the possibility of taking direct, legitimate action to transform society. Gradually the legal system, public order, education, employment, and social welfare become impregnated with racist and xenophobic ideology.[251]

In addition to xenophobic language in political discourse, many intellectuals legitimize the view that Islam is a violent religion, ignoring the fact that Islam is a fourteen-centuries-old religion practiced by more than one billion people in all countries of the world. They discredit an entire community and malign the entire religion of Islam. For them, Islam is inherently violent and its followers are accordingly addicted to violence; Islam is "bloodthirsty" in all its forms and sects; and Islam is a religion of war. In this context, terrorists from the Muslim world are the products of essentially violent Islamic teachings, culture, theology, and pathos. They assume that a terrorist derives his addiction to violence primarily from Islam and the closer he gets to the puritanical version of Islam, the more likely he will embrace terrorism as an essentialist response to feelings of frustration ad hatred.

The intellectual style is to concentrate on the violence (no difference between aggression and self-defense) committed by Muslims from the time of the prophet. They overlook, however, what happened in their recent history and their past. They conveniently forget or choose to ignore the millions of soldiers and civilians killed in the deadly wars of the twentieth century. They ignore the fact that the massacres in Vietnam, Korea, Cambodia, Laos, Angola, and Rwanda had nothing to do with Islam or Muslims. The nuclear annihilation of Nagasaki and Hiroshima was anything but Islamic. They forget all along that non-discrimination is a fundamental and pervasive feature of international human rights instruments.

251 Ibid., para. 8.

The contribution of the media to anti-Muslim sentiment is also remarkable, since they have privileged the image of a radical Islam and of its alleged incompatibility with Western values, and have hidden the moderated voices of the large majority of Muslims and of the Islamic scholars on this subject. It was found that the use of anti-Islamic terminology in media presentations further supported the negative portrayal of Muslims and fueled the common misconception that all Muslims are terrorists.[252] The impact and reach of the media has meant that misrepresentations and stereotyping of Islam and Muslims have negatively affected public attitudes and contributed to a public climate of hostility towards Muslims. The presence of Islamophobic language and imagery started to spread in the wider media including movies, contemporary literature, comics, cartoons, and computer games. The media reports for a long time kept on identifying Islam as the sole ideological cause of terrorism committed in the name of Islam and that feed "conspiracy theories" through the use of sensationalist images, headlines and comments.

Most Western media do not talk about the enormous cost that civilians are paying, during this war the war on terror. All injuries to noncombatants, including civilians, are unjustified, but somehow they minimize the injuries inflicted on Muslims while highlighting a similar injury suffered by other civilians. They brand Islam as a violent and intolerant ideology determined to destroy Western civilization. They focus on militant groups and extremists and they pay no attention to reformists who talk about Islam's universal and eternal massage of justice, equality, compassion, mercy and dignity and they usually use examples attacking Islam that are often drawn from very limited sources.

They refuse to credit present day causes for present day violence. They keep on crediting Muslim violence to historical civilization de-

252 See, Abrahamian Ervand, 'The US Media, Samuel Huntington and September 11', *Middle East Report*, No. 223, 2002, 62–63. The latest example of the media's role is the position of the New York Post and New York Sun regarding the Khalil Gibran School. The Lebanese-American Christian poet Khalil Gibran is best known for his classic work, "*The Prophet*", written over 80 years ago and translated into over 20 languages

feat. It is easier for some Western Intellectuals and media to accuse Muslims of being violent because they adhere to Islam. It is not an option for them to see extremism and violence in the Middle East as a result of occupation, foreign domination and authoritarian regime. They accredit it to a religion that teaches Muslims to hate freedoms, reject tolerance and despise all dissent and despise free societies.

The political discourse and the intellectual validation of these prejudices, in addition to the impact and reach of the media has meant that misrepresentations and stereotyping of Islam and Muslims have negatively affected public attitudes and contributed to a public climate of hostility towards Muslims. This accentuated the theory of an unavoidable clash of civilizations between the West and Islam and led to some incidents such as the "Danish Cartoons", which led to an important question: is the protection of Muslims from religious vilification is a violation of the right to freedom of expression?

Or is it possible to protect religious minorities from vilification and hatred while stressing that these laws have to be in balance with the protection of freedom of expression as stated in the international standards?

3.3.1 Religious Vilification' against Muslims and Freedom of Expression

Today, the media is circulating the image of the Muslim population, as a primitive, uncivilized sector of society that needs to be controlled. This image appears to have been deeply entrenched in the nation's history and has been manipulated so that the violence and force used against Muslims can be justified.

Increasingly, and particularly among Muslims, "Islamophobia" provides a term to draw attention to a normalized prejudice and unjustified discrimination. However, many in the West have called Islamophobia a myth, arguing that references to Islamophobia confuse legitimate criticism of Islam with discrimination against Muslims, and in this case, the right to freedom of expression is being jeopardized. Undoubtedly,

point Peter Gottschalk and Gabriel Greenberg, that, "this term will elicit the same unease among and even backlash from some of those whose notions of normal it challenges, just as its historical predecessors (sexism, racism, anti-Semitism) have and still do."[253]

The latest example of this view is the Danish cartoon controversy.

3.3.2 The Danish Cartoon Controversy

Discrimination against the Muslim community in Denmark did not start with the Danish cartoons, but it started first in the political discourse. The political debate on .foreigners and minorities has become increasingly harsh since the mid-1980s, when a political fringe movement for the first time warned of the alleged 'invasion of Muslims' in the country. The tone of the current debate has largely been set by the far-right Progressive Party and the Danish People's Party. The Liberal Party, after election, formed a minority government in coalition with a smaller conservative party. Although the People's Party was not included in the new government, it has been able to influence the government's policies considerably. In particular, the government was dependent on support by the People's Party when it introduced new restrictive asylum and immigration legislation in the spring of 2002. Members of these two parties have repeatedly made highly inflammatory statements, including lashing out against Muslims and accusing them of undermining Western values and promoting violence.[254] During the electoral campaign, members of the People's Party lashed out repeatedly against Muslims while advocating tougher immigration policies. During the party's annual meeting in Vejle in late September 2001, the chair of the youth branch of the party, Kenneth Kristensen, stated: *"Just as we Danes share a firm belief in the democratic society, Arab Muslims share a firm*

253 Gottschalk and Greenberg, 11.

254 International Helsinki Federation for Human Rights (IHF), Anti-terrorism Measures, Security and Human Rights Developments in Europe, Central Asia and North America in the Aftermath of September 11 April 2003, 115.

hatred of the Western World and democracy"[255], while another party member, Michael Rex, concluded: *"Islam is not a religion in the proper sense. It's a terrorist organization that strives to obtain world supremacy by the use of violence".*[256] Yet a third party member, Member of the European Parliament Mogens Camre, was quoted as saying: *"All countries of the western world are infiltrated by Muslims. Some of them speak politely to us, whilst they wait until they are enough to kill all of us".*[257]

Thus, it became acceptable for public figures to depict Muslims as prone to violence, religious extremism and terrorism, even though such statements may incite hostility against people belonging to that faith. The Danish cartoons controversy and its defamation of Islam demonstrates this continuous dynamic discrimination and incitement to hatred.

The controversy of the Danish cartoon of Prophet Mohammed (PBUH) was sparked when a regional Danish newspaper, Jyllands-Posten, solicited cartoons of the Prophet Mohammad and published twelve cartoons in the paper and later by other news outlets. The Danish cartoon of the Prophet Mohammed (PBUH), were entries in a com-

255 "Folketingsval 2001: Resultat "(special report published on-line), *Politiken*, November 2001, quoted IHF, *Anti-terrorism Measures, Security and Human Rights, 116.*

256 "Politi afviser racismemesager mod DF", *Politiken*, 26 Oktober 2001, quoted in Ibid.

257 Christian Hüttemeier, "Camre: Islam truer Danmark", *Politiken*, 16 September 2001, quoted in Ibid. The leader of the People's Party, PiaKjaersgaard, later confirmed that all statements made at the meeting were in accordance with party policies. Following the meeting, Kristensen, Rex and Camre were all reported to the police for.allegedly violating paragraph 266b of the country's criminal code, which prohibits public or other statements that serve to "threaten, deride or disparage a group of persons on account of their race, skin colour, national or ethnic origin, faith or sexual orientation". Initially the local police in Vejle refused to open an investigation into the case, arguing that the nature of what can be expressed freely had changed after September 11. However, after an intervention by the Documentation and Advisory Centre on Racial Discrimination (DACRD), the public prosecutor ordered the Vejle police to carry out an investigation, they were all acquitted, see: IHF, *Anti-terrorism Measures, Security and Human Rights, 116.*

petition organized by the newspaper to respond to allegations that Danish cartoonists were too afraid of Muslim fundamentalists to illustrate a biography of Mohammed.[258] Thus, the original intent of the competition was to challenge and express opposition to a defined group, Muslim fundamentalists, who were suspected of creating a climate of self-censorship and the biographical nature of the publication demonstrates the intention to tell the real-life story of the Prophet rather than to give a fictional account.[259]

The dominant theme of the cartoons is to associate Islam and the Prophet (PBUH) with terrorism. The cartoon depicted virgins dispensing sexual favors to suicide bombers harks back to an old cliché of Western Islamophobia, namely the association of Islam and the Prophet with sexual depravity. The most hurting is a portrait of the Prophet Mohammed with a bomb as a turban which relates the Prophet to terrorism. This cartoon is at the heart of this controversy, which seen by many Westerner as a cartoon, while seen by most Muslims as a stereotype and vilification of the Prophet. Peter Gottschalk and Gabriel Greenberg note that

> [i]f the cartoon portrayed Osama bin Laden it would be taken as such. However, because Western audiences recognize Mohammed as a symbol of Islam, they cannot but read this specific caricature as a claim that all Muslims are violent. When a caricature of an individual becomes a symbol used by outsiders to depict a group, the image passes from caricature to stereotype.[260]

The newspaper defended its position on the basis of freedom of speech and said that Islam had, through threats and violence, become immune from the mockery and criticism that every powerful social institution should be subject to in a liberal democracy.[261] However, the debate about the Danish cartoons should not have been about limiting freedom of expression or the use of cartoons as a form of expression

258 E/CN.4/2006/17, 13 February 2006, para. 23.
259 Ibid.
260 Gottschalk and Greenberg, 68–69.
261 See Svenning Dalgaard, 'The Right to Offend: Causes and Consequences of the 'Danish Cartoon Affair'' (2006) 151(2), *RUSI Journal* 28, 28–29.

and criticism, but rather should have been about certain cartoons that cross the boundaries and lead to incitement to religious hatred, discrimination and intolerance against minority groups. The Muslim community is exposed and vulnerable since 9/11 and the Special Rapporteur, on contemporary forms of racism, racial discrimination, xenophobia and related issues, in his report, records

> [...] a clear increase in Islamophobia and religious vilification against Muslims, to which there are two fundamental aspects: intellectual legitimization of increasingly overt hostility towards Islam and its followers by influential figures in the world of arts, literature, media and political discourse.[262]

Thus, it is important to distinguish between different types of expressions: theological analysis, satire, disparaging comments, and incitement to violence against members of a religious group. In response to the offensive publication of representations of the Prophet Mohammed by the media in some countries starting in late 2005, the Special Rapporteur on freedom of religion or belief, Asma Jahangir, the Special Rapporteur for the promotion and protection of the right to freedom of opinion and expression, Ambeyi Ligabo, as well as the Special Rapporteur on contemporary forms of racism, racial discrimination, xenophobia and related intolerance, Doudou Diène, issued a joint press release[263] stressing that,

> [...] peaceful expression of opinions and ideas, either orally, through the press or other media, should always be tolerated. The press must enjoy large editorial

262 European Monitoring Centre on Racism and Xenophobia, Anti-Islamic reactions in the EU after the terrorist acts against the USA, 12th September to 31st December 2001.See also, International Helsinki Federation of Human Rights, Intolerance and Discrimination against Muslims in the EU: Are Muslims "An Enemy Within"?, Available online at: <http://www.ihf-hr.org/viewbinary/view document.php?doc_id=6242>.

263 "Human Rights Experts call for tolerance and dialogue in wake of controversy over representations of Prophet Muhammad", UNOG press release HR06006E of 8 February 2006, full text available online at <http://www.unog.ch/unog/website/news_media.nsf/(httpNewsByYear_en)/54A59D88BFD753FBC125710F005B08A4?OpenDocument>.

freedom to promote a free flow of news and information, within and across national borders, thus providing an arena for debate and dialogue. Nevertheless, the use of stereotypes and labeling that insult deep-rooted religious feelings do not contribute to the creation of an environment conducive to constructive and peaceful dialogue among different communities.[264]

The Danish cartoons not only they discriminate against Muslims and vilify Islam but also, they fall within the criterion of inciting hatred against the Muslim community in Denmark and as an offensive expression which may stigmatize and encourage climate of intolerance. Thus, it was the obligation of the Danish government to take positive steps to create a tolerant and inclusive environment where all religions can be exercised free of discrimination or stigmatization so that they acquire the confidence to refute controversial expressions made against their beliefs.

The Danish government is obliged by its obligation to international laws and the 1981 Religion Declaration:

Art. 3:
Discrimination between human beings on the grounds of religion or belief constitutes an affront to human dignity and a disavowal of the principles of the Charter of the United Nations, and shall be condemned as a violation of the human rights and fundamental freedoms proclaimed in the Universal Declaration of Human Rights and enunciated in detail in the International Covenants on Human Rights, and as an obstacle to friendly and peaceful relations between nations.

Art. 4 (1):
All States shall take effective measures to prevent and eliminate discrimination on the grounds of religion or belief in the recognition, exercise and enjoyment of human rights and fundamental freedoms in all fields of civil, economic, political, social and cultural life.

Art. 4 (2):
All States shall make all efforts to enact or rescind legislation where necessary to prohibit any such discrimination, and to take all appropriate measures to combat intolerance on the grounds of religion or other beliefs in this matter.

264 See Also: Promotion and Protection of All Human Rights, Civil, Political, Economic, Social and Cultural Rights, Including the Right to Development, Asma Jahangir, A/HRC/6/5, 20 July 2007.

The Danish government should have stepped up their efforts to eliminate intolerance and discrimination based on religion or belief, notably by taking all necessary and appropriate action, in conformity with international standards of human rights, to combat hatred, intolerance and acts of violence, intimidation and coercion motivated by intolerance based on religion or belief, with particular regard to religious minorities, in this case the Muslim community.

But in reality, the Danish government refused to adopt an official stance on the content and the publication of the cartoons out of respect for freedom of expression. The Danish government not only refused to take any action, but moreover, its refusal to receive the ambassadors of Muslim countries revealed not just the trivialization of Islamophobia at the political level but also, as events subsequently demonstrated, the central involvement of politicians in the national and international impact of manifestations and expressions of Islamophobia.[265]

It is important to note that Denmark does have limitations on freedom of expression written down in its penal code against libel and blasphemy. It is also important to note that these provisions are not limited to violations against the Christian or Jewish faiths only, but to all people living legally in the country. Thus, section 140 of the Danish penal code states:

> Anybody who publicly mocks or insults any in this country, legally existing religious community tenets of faith or worship, will be punished by fine or imprisonment for up to 4 months.

The Danish government could have also taken action against newspapers over the publication of the offensive cartoons under other sections of its penal code[266], the present Section 266 b of the Danish penal code from 1995 which states that:

265 E/CN.4/2006/17, Para. 24.

266 The Danish Penal Code available in Danish at: <http://www.themis.dk/synopsis/index.asp?hovedramme=/synopsis/docs/lovsamling/straffeloven_indholds fortegnelse.html>. Available translation in English of both section at: <http://en.wikipedia.org/wiki/Freedom_of_speech_and_freedom_of_the_press_in_Denmark>.

> (1) Any person who publicly or with the intention of dissemination to a wide circle of people makes a statement or imparts other information threatening, insulting or degrading a group of persons on account of their race, colour, national or ethnic origin, belief or sexual orientation, shall be liable to a fine, simple detention or imprisonment for a term not exceeding two years.
>
> (2) When handing down the punishment, it is to be considered as an aggravating circumstance that the statement is in the nature of propaganda.

Moreover, there is no shortage of laws that censor speech in many other Western societies. These forms of censorship range from incitement to racial hatred to libel laws, from the official secrets act to incitement to violence, from banning images of child abuse to the proposed glorification of terrorism and graphic details of dead bodies. Hate speech laws mete out punishment for certain types of invective accompanying violence. Unsubstantiated smears denigrating an individual's reputation are grounds for suit. Society defends co-workers from unwelcome verbal advances through sexual harassment codes.

Freedom of speech and expression is very paramount, but, is not unlimited and should not be protected when it causes fear, harassment, or degradation or incites hatred, or serious contempt. However, when incitement to hatred concerns Muslims, freedom of expression becomes absolute and this difference of treatment amounts to discrimination and is unlawful. This conflict as similar to previous outrages in the West, such as the global Christian outrage regarding the release of the cinematic portrayal of Jesus in Martin Scorsese's *The Last Temptation of Christ* in 1989, which led not only to bomb threats at theatres in the United States but also to bans in many nations or similar protests against the satiric critique of Christianity in *Monty Python's Life of Brian* in 1979.[267] In another parallel, "at least nine European nations today outlaw the public denial of the Holocaust or the diminishment of its actuality."[268] Instead of placing the controversy among these similar issues, most of the Western media immediately depicted the debate as yet another emblem of Muslims difference and Islamic threat.

267 Gottschalk and Greenberg, 164.
268 Ibid.

When the awareness of the cartoons became widespread, a global protest soon grew, typified by peaceful gatherings of thousands of protesters in many places but overshadowed by the violence of a group of Muslims who represent not even a fraction of a fraction of the world's more than one billion Muslims.[269] The violence of this tiny percentage of Muslims confirmed in the eye of the West, the image of Muslim intolerance and Islamic otherness. Muslim protests against the Danish cartoons escalated and entwined regionally with divergent political issues from an outrage against the disparagement, not only of them, but of the exemplar of Islam, too. Muslims understand Mohammed as the perfect manifestation of Islam's ideals, as he is the messenger from God and the morality he represents is of a messenger chosen by Him. Thus, he is considered the model of proper human behaviour.[270] Any depiction of him as a terrorist not only denigrates this beloved figure but also stains the character of God and, by default, impugns their own dignity, already sensitive to Western disparagements and suspicions during centuries of Europeans imperial domination followed by today's American hegemony. Westerners, thus, must acknowledge that these particular cartoons exist not in isolation, but as the latest manifestation of more than a millennium of Western portrayals of Mohammed as representing the antithesis of truth, godliness, morality, and freedom.[271] The breadth of the Muslim response demonstrates both a heightened sensitivity to Western denigration of Islam and an increasing sense that the West seeks a war against Muslims through either constant deprecation, as in the cartoon controversy, or outright conquest, as in Afghanistan and Iraq. The violence that has occasionally accompanied the protests of these cartoons cannot be condoned. But no freedom exists without limit.[272] Moreover, the long list of stereotyped features (both physical and behavioural) associated with historically oppressed groups such as African Americans, Jews, women, Latinos, Catholics, and gays and les-

269 Ibid., 2–3.
270 Ibid.
271 Ibid., 146.
272 Ibid.

bians (to name but a few) need no rehearsal here: they have been publically protested and successfully minimized, though not entirely eliminated. Outrage has been the starting point of these groups' efforts to demonstrate that caricatures passing as common knowledge sometimes camouflage, often consciously, malicious stereotypes.[273]

The Religion Declaration calls upon states to take "all necessary measures... to... combat discrimination on the ground of religion or belief." The 1978 UNESCO Declaration on Race and Racial Prejudice urges the mass media and all organized groups to refrain from presenting "a stereotyped, partial, unilateral or tendentious picture of individuals and of various human groups."[274] However, most Western media outlets broadcast a series of repetitive messages regarding Muslims and Islam and they feed their audience's anxieties about Muslims, perpetuating notions of radical difference. The attitude of the newspaper bears out the criticisms that have been made, especially since the tragic events of 11 September, of the responsibility of certain media outlets for conflating Islam with terrorism, which is a major driver of resurgent of Islamophobia throughout the world. The case of the Danish cartoons illustrates such conclusions.[275]

3.3.3 Balance between Freedom of Expression and Freedom of Religion

The problem with the Danish Cartoons is not the limiting of the freedom of expression or the use of cartoons as a form of expression, but the debate is about certain cartoons that cross the boundaries and leads to incitement of hatred against minority groups which in turn may lead to violence. Thus, it is important to distinguish between different

273 Ibid.

274 The 1978 UNESCO Declaration on Race and Racial Prejudice, Adopted and proclaimed by the General Conference of the United Nations Educational, Scientific and Cultural Organization at its twentieth session, on 27 November 1978, Article 5 (3), available online at: <http://www.unhchr.ch/html/menu3/b/d_prejud.htm>.

275 E/CN.4/2006/17, 13 February 2006, para. 28.

types of expressions; theological analysis, satire, disparaging comments, incitement to violence against members of a religious group.

From the Danish cartoons controversy, it could be seen that the right to freedom of expression is more valued when the issue is the right of Muslims to be protected from religious discrimination and hatred based on their religion. The right to freedom of expression is important and values human rights. However, this freedom brings with it important responsibilities and duties to ensure that it is not abused or used to discriminate, particularly against minority groups. Governments of every state, party to the ICCPR, is bound by Articles 18, 19 and 20 in dealing with the relationship between the freedom of religion and freedom of expression. The basic principle embodied in these articles is that any "freedom or right is limited by respect for others and their rights." Respect for other religions does not mean not questioning culturally based practices that are destructive of vulnerable people and may legitimately be discussed. However, the responsibility that comes with freedom of expression must be based on objectively determined facts and should not incite violence, intimidation, or hatred because of race or religion. The most disturbing aspect about these cartoons is the fact that children were the intended readership of such bigotry. This indicates a desire to shape the attitude to religion of a particularly sensitive and vulnerable age group. The newspaper was planning to introduce to these children an Islam that bears the marks of terrorism, sex and intolerance. Where are the objectively determined facts in these cartoons and where is respect for other's right to be protected from religious hatred that constitutes incitement to discrimination, hostility and violence? Unless they considered teaching young children an intolerant massage about Islam as really instructive and really needed in a democratic society?

Moreover, the newspapers' intransigent defense of unlimited freedom of expression is out of step. The newspaper's intention was not a pure protection of free speech. It had, a few years before, refused to publish satirical pictures of Jesus on the basis that they were offensive to their conservative Christian readership.[276] In the 1980s, the news-

276 Gottschalk and Greenberg, 147.

paper thundered against a scandalous mural (which depicted Christ indecently). The editor at the time, who is still actively involved with the paper, demanded the mural's removal and scornfully mocked objections about free speech.

In the case of the protests by Christians, the same newspaper recognized that their rights must be balanced with responsibility[277] while in the case of Muslims; the freedom of expression was given priority and superiority over the protection of religious minority from religious discrimination and vilification. The tiny Muslim population (2 %) in Denmark does not have this luxury of balancing the right to freedom of expression with their right non-discrimination and prejudice to their religion, since it is a minority religion, and is unpopular and misunderstood. It is accepted to incite hatred against them and disparage their beliefs.

Freedom of expression is part of the principles and values of the international human rights instruments, and a fundamental cornerstone in democratic societies. However, freedom of expression does not preclude the protection of people from racist and xenophobic language. Freedom of expression, as mentioned above, is not an absolute right. International laws lay down certain limits in order to protect other fundamental rights. It would have been a better solution if the Danish government emphasized that, "freedom of expression and the protection against racist and xenophobic language can, and have to, go hand-in-hand; the two together make democracy meaningful,"[278] instead of insisting, when dealing with Muslims, on the absolutism of free of speech and giving more value to one fundamental freedom over another and that is the equal protection and nondiscrimination to religious minorities. Finally, the publication of the cartoons came at a time that is marked by the worsening situation of Muslims throughout the world following the events of 11 September, 2001. The upsurge in

277 Ibid., 146.

278 European Monitoring Center on racism and xenophobia Report "Muslims in the European Union: Discrimination and Islamophobia", 2006, available online at: <http://eumc.europa.eu/eumc/index.php> (viewed Sept. 2013).

Islamophobia in particular, has placed the Muslim minority under severe pressure, discrimination and humiliation. The media's consistent disinterest in non-violent Muslim perspectives hardened this view. They consistently overlook the voices of moderation that come from the majority of Muslims.[279]

The Danish government should have respected its obligations, specifically the prohibition of incitement to religious and racial hatred (art. 20 of ICCPR). Muslims, furthermore, are entitled to the right to equal and nondiscrimination treatment that is enshrined in Article 7 of the UDHR and article 26 of the ICCPR which grants everyone "the equal protection of the law" and provides that "the law shall prohibit any discrimination and guarantee to all persons equal and effective protection against discrimination." The UN Human Rights Committee has pointed out that Article 26 prohibits discrimination and noted that the application of the principle of non-discrimination contained in this article is not limited to those rights which are laid down in the ICCPR.[280] Article 4 of the 1981 Declaration calls on states to

> [...] take effective measures to prevent and eliminate discrimination on the grounds of religion or belief in the recognition, exercise and enjoyment of human rights and fundamental freedoms in all fields of civil, economic, political, social and cultural life.

Moreover, states are urged to "make all efforts to enact or rescind legislation where necessary to prohibit such discrimination, and to take all appropriate measures to combat intolerance on the grounds of religion or belief in this matter." The government should have taken into account that Muslim minorities in Western societies are entitled

279 Gottschalk and Greenberg, 8. When violence flared in 2006 over the controversial Danish cartoons, a great variety and number of Muslim leaders in the United States and abroad condemned the violence but received little coverage by the media. The condemnation of the violence issued immediately by the council on American-Islamic Relation (CAIR), one of the most important Islamic organizations in the United states is only one of many decried the attacks.

280 UN Human Rights Committee, General Comment No. 18, 37th session, November 10, 1989.

to protection against discrimination and racially/religiously motivated vilification, incitement to discrimination, hostility or violence. However, the Danish government chose not to respect its obligations. It ignored the fact that hatred, based on racial and religious stereotypes, is based on deeply-rooted attitudes. This behavior can only be changed by addressing the problem on a societal level by engaging in a long and open discussion that aims at getting the parties together and help them see each other's point of view about multicultural society, and not by adopting a stance that promotes hatred and leads to fear, insecurity and alienation. Judge Voitto Saario notes that, "[e]fforts should be made to change or eliminate all stereotyped ideas and prejudices in the field of freedom of thought, conscience and religion." He observed that

> [...] in multireligious societies certain specific limitations may be necessary in order to reconcile the various interests of the different religious groups of the society, and stressed the necessity to decide, in each particular case, the scope of such limitation.[281]

In some cases, intolerance is institutionalized and based upon legislation, but most often it stems from voluntarily intolerant attitudes and conduct derived from habit, prejudice or hatred.[282]

Benito notes that "[i]t is pertinent to remember that the idea of superiority of one group over another and the consequences of such an idea have not disappeared. It is also important to take into account that equality among all human beings means absence of discrimination.[283] Equality however is not uniformity. A régime of absolute respect for human rights must reconcile unity with diversity, interdependence with liberty. The equal dignity owed to all seeks respect for the differences in the identity of each person. It is in absolute respect for the right to be different that we find authentic equality and the only

281 Judge Voitto Saario, quoted in Boyle, HR/GENEVA/1984/CRP.4, Para. 2.
282 E/CN.4/Sub.2/1987/26, Para. 15.
283 Ibid.

possibility of the full enjoyment of human rights without racial, sexual, or religious discrimination.[284] She concludes that the

> [...] term intolerance and discrimination based on religion or belief encompasses not only discrimination infringing upon or negating the right to freedom of thought, conscience and religion and belief, but also acts which stir up hatred against, or persecution of, such persons or groups.[285]

Freedom of expression can definitely be limited if it amounts to religious hatred and incitement to discrimination. Non-discrimination covers not only the usual grounds of non-discrimination, but also those that are specific to minorities, such as language, religion, and culture. In addition, this right ensures full equality of all persons before the law, equal protection of the law and equal benefit of the law, and refers to the enactment of laws prohibiting genocide, hate speech and hate crimes.

284 Ibid., para. 17.
285 Ibid., para. 18.

4. Conclusion

A resurgence of 'national identity' has taken center stage in the politics of the West. This resurgence has led to a re-affirmation of the superiority of the West and the inferiority of others, particularly in this case, that of Muslim cultures. Political parties and groups that have racist and xenophobic platforms have penetrated the political agendas of democratic parties under the pretext of combating terrorism and defending the 'national identity."' The Western view of Islam, thus, has become more and more dominated by prejudices and stereotypes. It is characterized, by reinforcing the image of the militant Muslims and further alienating Muslims who do not match the ""ideal"' image of what a Muslim is 'supposed' to be in a liberal democracy.

An attempt to make liberalism as inclusive as possible used the most conservative Islamic doctrines as a litmus test. Most of Western society, however, fails to notice the regional and cultural diversity among Muslims, the diversity in religious beliefs and interpretations of Islamic texts among them. They fixate on strict interpretations of Islamic texts in the Qur'an as a sign for Muslims in general. In this way, some Westerners accept only a single image of Islamic doctrine that concentrates on particular political aspects, all the while ignoring debates that exist among Muslims vis-à-vis their faith. Regional variation and the contested nature of culture, even within one region, are ignored. Muslims find themselves often represented by their most extreme counterparts. This has resulted in a distorted understanding of Muslims in general and acknowledges only the notion that Muslims are univocal, and their traditions, cultures, and interpretations of Islamic doctrine are unitary.

In this context, Islam's tenets are frequently distorted and taken out of context, with particular acts or practices being taken to represent or to symbolize a rich and complex faith. In too many circles, disparaging remarks about Muslims are allowed to pass without censure so that these prejudices acquire a veneer of acceptability. Stereotypes also depict Muslims as opposed to the West despite a history, not only of conflict, but also of commerce and cooperation and of influencing and enriching each other's art and science. In response to this view that is spread in the West, Kofi Anan, in his address in the seminar on confronting Islamophobia, called for the need "to unlearn the stereotypes that have become so entrenched in so many minds and so much of the media."[1]

Some claim that Islam is incompatible with democracy, or irrevocably hostile to modernity and the rights of women. However, the religious symbol law has affected disproportionately young Muslim women who wear the headscarf. This law has limited the freedom to freely express one's religious beliefs. It has put Muslim women who wear the headscarf as a religious practice and not as a symbol, to be forced to choose between practicing and observing their faith or the pursuit of an education or a chance in the public service.[2]

As for the anti-terrorism measures, history has shown that when societies trade human rights for security, most often they get neither. Instead, minorities and other marginalized groups pay the price through a violation of their human rights.[3] What is remarkable about the legislative response to September 11 is "how quickly many jurisdictions in the West with a longstanding commitment to constitutionalism and human rights have shifted to a security paradigm."[4] Confronted with an 'anomaly' (catastrophic international terrorism) that cannot be explained within the existing paradigm of human rights and constitutionalism, many governments in the West, and particularly the United States, are "starting to articulate and construct a new para-

1 Secretary-General, Addressing Headquarters Seminar on Confronting Islamophobia, Stresses Importance of Leadership, Press Release SG/SM/963, HR/4802, PI/1627. Available at: <http://www.un.org/News/Press/docs/2004/sgsm9637.doc.ht> (viewed Sept. 2013).

2 See: European Monitoring Center on racism and xenophobia Report "Muslims in the European Union: Discrimination and Islamophobia", 2006, available online at: <http://eumc.europa.eu/eumc/index.php> (viewed Sept. 2013).

3 Hoffman Paul, 934.

4 Ramraj, 7.

digm,"[5] much along non-democratic state lines and as more restrictive in the curbing of civil liberties, to cope with it. These legislative measures limited freedom of religion through religious profiling of Muslims, by putting them through tightening immigration and visa requirements, revising and enhancing airline and airport security regulations, adopting anti-terrorist financing and money laundering laws, and introducing new terrorism related criminal offences-all to counter the threat of terrorism, in addition to the enhanced powers of surveillance and information-gathering and preventive detention. All measures have targeted disproportionately Muslims.

Thousands of Muslims have been rounded up and detained in the United States, in Guantánamo and other secretive prisons, in a massive form of preventive detention. As has been discussed, they were detained just because they were Muslims.

These measures treated Muslims as guilty unless they can prove themselves innocent which they did not have the tools to do. Because of these measures, Muslims have been illegally detained, their non-profit organization closed, deported, tortured, discriminated against, solely for their faith, especially most of the detainees were freed with out charges after a long period of detention and ill-treatment and with out even an apology.[6] The disruption to their life and to the lives of their family members was substantial and could have been avoided had international human rights or humanitarian standards been respected.

Although this may change in the future, anti-terrorism investigations at present focus largely on members of the Muslim communities of Arab and South Asian descent. There is therefore an increased risk of religious profiling covered by race or ethnic profiling, in the sense that the race or ethnicity of individuals may expose them to investigation as a proxy to their religion. Profiling in this sense would be at odds with the need for equal application of the law without discrimination.

5 Ibid, 8.

6 Priest, Dana, 'CIA Holds Terror Suspects in Secret Prisons', *The Washington Post*, Nov. 2, 2005 at A1, available online at: <http://www.washingtonpost.com/wpdyn/content/- article/2005/11/01/AR2005110101644.html> (viewed Sept. 2013).

However, the question must be: How far Western societies are willing to adapt to a plural society in which all participants are respected, where everybody's constructive contribution is valued, and where all feel accepted? Still, till today, integration in many parts of the West has, in reality, remained more of a one-way than a two-way process, with the onus placed upon Muslim communities.[7] Muslims have been blamed for not working harder to integrate or participate in the mainstream, and moderate Muslim groups blamed for not being visible or active enough.[8] However, because this is a two-way process, Muslims will also have to adjust their understandings of what it means to be Muslim precisely in order to be able to claim an Islamic identity in a Western state.[9] Thus, the Muslim communities in Western nation states should negotiate with the wider national identity and culture about the meaning and relevance of their Islamic identity in the context of a highly developed and effective national and human rights framework.[10] Consequently, it could be seen that it is quite possible that a Muslim might identify as both Muslim *and* French or American. It is argued that, "[s]tability at the level of social life is not jeopardized by but requires plurality at the foundations of the right to freedom of religion or belief."[11]

States are prohibited from discriminating against minorities. States must ensure that persons belonging to minorities, like all other individuals within their territory or subject to their jurisdiction, enjoy the rights and freedoms guaranteed by law without distinction of any kind and on the basis of equality. Provisions to that effect are found in all the other major human rights instruments, both universal and regional in scope. It is not sufficient, however, that non-discrimination and equality be recognized only as a matter of law, but equality must also be

7 An-Na'im,, *Human Rights and Islamic Identity*, 908.
8 Ibid.
9 Ibid.
10 Ibid.
11 Lindholm Tore, 'Philosophical and Religious Justifications of Freedom of Religion or Belief', in *A Deskbook*, 21.

ensured in fact and that means governments have to take positive measures to protect their minorities.

Historically, 'human rights' has been used by the colonized to free themselves; by the African-Americans in the US; the victims of apartheid, and others. Therefore, there is nothing wrong for Muslims in the West to utilize it too. It should be used by all people who need to gain their rights and this is the real meaning of universalizing the human rights discourse. What would help the Muslims in the West is if the fight for 'human rights' continues in the Muslim world, especially in the Arab states. As much as 'human rights' is needed for religious minorities in the West, it is also needed for religious minorities and majorities in the Muslim (Arab) states. It is a time for Muslims to stress that there is no contradiction between Islamic morals and human rights including the right to freedom of religion or belief. This debate is also relevant to Muslims living in the West.

Muslims do not have to accept the domination of a conservative public discourse on human rights and at the same time they do not have to accept the whole human rights paradigms. Nevertheless, the time has come for Muslims to pay attention to the fact that the international legal system could be used to condemn what happens in Muslim societies and could be an effective tool to point to the violations committed by others against them and to condemn the behavior of states or to express claims toward other states.

ensured in fact and that means governments have to take positive steps to protect their minorities.

Historically, 'human rights' has been used by the minorities to free themselves: by the African-Americans in the US, under apartheid, and others. Therefore, there is nothing wrong for Muslims in the West to utilize it too. It should be used by all people who need to gain their rights and this is the real meaning of universality of the human rights discourse. What would help the Muslims in the West is if the fight for 'human rights' continues in the Muslim world, especially in the Arab states. As much as 'human rights' is needed for religious minorities in the West, it is also needed for religious minorities and majorities in the Muslim (Arab) states. It is a time for Muslims to stress that there is no contradiction between Islamic morals and human rights, including the right to freedom of religion or belief. This approach is also relevant to Muslims living in the West.

Muslims do not have to accept the domination of actors in the public discourse on human rights and at the same time they do not have to accept the whole human rights paradigms. Nevertheless, the time has come for Muslims to pay attention to the fact that the international legal system could be used to condemn what happens in Muslim societies and could be an effective tool to point to violations of rights committed by others against them and to condemn the behavior of states or to express claims toward other states.

Part 3

Limits of Freedom of Religion or Belief in Muslim (Arab) States

Within Islam there exists numerous ways of interpretation of the religion. There exists also a plurality of Muslim positions in the area of human rights. Like other religions or cultures, Islam is a complex reality harboring various, and frequently conflicting, interpretations about its inherent normative demands. In this sense, there is not *one* binding Islamic position but rather *a great variety* of "Muslim voices" offering different views about whether and how the idea of human rights and Islamic normative requirements fit together. This does not mean that there is no tension between human rights and Islamic laws, but by adopting the Islamic revival call of the Islamist and secular scholars, these tensions in the field of freedom of religion and religious minority rights could be eliminated. With reforms to current apostasy laws, in an Islamic framework and according to a contextual interpretation of the Qur'an, Islamic thinkers such as 'Ashmawy, Al Banna, and others believe that Muslims can bring these laws in line with the Qur'an and international human rights standards. Violations of human rights and the right to religious freedoms, in the Muslim world, however, have to be solved within an Islamic framework.

The international human rights law can be used to fight for Muslims rights in the West and within the Muslim states.[1] It is important in this sense to affirm the universality of human rights and the right to freedom of religion or belief despite all the rhetoric that this concept is a secular and western and it has no base in Islam. Human rights, thus, is understood as part of all religions and philosophical doctrine. A growing number of adherents of more and more comprehensive doctrine, both

1 Mayer Anne E., *Islam and Human Rights 'Tradition and Politics'*, Westview Press, United States, 2007, 8.

religious and secular, have adopted these rights, because they represent justice and equalitarian doctrine.[2] What opponents of human rights universality often miss is that treating international human rights as universal implies that peoples in the West and the East share a common humanity and that they are equally deserving of rights and freedoms despite the different culture. The persisting of violations of human rights including the right to freedom of religion or belief, occur in both religious and secular societies. This fact indicates that the fault lies with man himself. Having a theocentric perception therefore does not necessarily accommodate the violation of human rights more than an anthropocentric perception does. The violations are more often political than religious. They are the evils of humans against humans.[3] For God's message to humanity is peace, justice, equality, and the welfare of humanity. Islamic humanism has rarely been employed or stressed, but it is time, as 'Ashmawy stresses, to pay attention to "humanism in Islam."[4] He affirms that, "[c]ontemporary mainstream Islam may be in the midst of a period of review, enlightenment, and renaissance as an outcome of nineteenth-and twentieth-century struggles for direction in every Muslim nation."[5]

The main question therefore, is: are these violations of human rights in Muslim states within the Arab World[6] (Arab States hinandafter) and especially the right to freedom of religion or belief an Islamic perspective? Is the death penalty for abandoning Islam a Qur'anic punishment and the killing of all non-believers is an Islamic duty?

2 Baderin Mashood A., 'Dialogue Among civilization as a Paradigm Achieving Universalism in International Human Rights A Case Study With Islamic Law', *Asia-Pacific on Human Rights and the Law*, 2001, Volume 2, No. 2, 28.

3 Ibid.

4 Fluehr-Lobban Carolyn, Ed., *The Writing of Muhammad Sa'id al-'Ashmawy: Against Islamic Extremism*, University Press of Florida, Gainesville, FL. 1998, 4.

5 Ibid., 5.

6 The Arab World refers to Arabic speaking countries stretching from the Atlantic Ocean in the west to the Arabian Sea in the east, and from the Mediterranean Sea in the north to the Horn of Africa and the Indian Ocean in the southeast. It consists of 25 countries and territories with a combined population of 358 million people straddling North Africa and Western Asia. The Arabic language forms the unifying feature of the Arab World. The majority of people in the Arab World adhere to Islam and the religion has official status in most countries.

1. Historical Background of the Arab States

The Muslim world is usually perceived as a united one. However, this is far from being the case. Regional variations in worship exist in Islam but they have gone largely unnoticed. The Muslim world is also often misconceived as comprising only of the Arab nations. Rather it stretches from Europe to Africa, through the Middle East and into Asia. Most Muslims reside outside of the Arab World and Muslim countries encompass a variety of constitutional arrangements ranging from Islamic States with Islam as the official state religion, to secular states with a strict separation of religion and state.

Saudi Arabia, one of the most conservative Islamic countries, has a legal system almost entirely based on Shar'ia, while the countries in North Africa, such as Tunisia and Egypt are rather secularized. The Arab World is only one region of the Muslim world, extending from Morocco in the West to Bahrain in the East, embracing portions of Africa, Asia, the Atlantic and Indian oceans, the Mediterranean and Red seas, in addition to the Arab-Persian Gulf. It is divided into two areas: the Maghreb (the North African countries), and the Mashreq, or the Levant, (the eastern region consisting of Egypt and the Arab-Asian countries).[1] This region has a lot in common, but at the same time it is very diverse.

1 Democracy in the Arab World, Challenges, Achievements and Prospects, June 2006, available online at: <http://www.hks.harvard.edu/fs/pnorris/Acrobat/stm103%20articles/IDEA%20arabworld.pdf> (viewed Sept. 2013).

1.1 Diversity and Unity of the Arab States

Unity and diversity are two of the parameters of Arab society. The Arab world is a place where diverse cultural, social and political dynamics co-exist, creating both differences and similarities between the countries. It is a region of sharp contrasts. Among the Arab League members are some of the poorest countries in the world (Mauritania, Somalia, and Sudan), as well as some of the richest (Kuwait, Qatar, and the United Arab Emirates). There is also significant ethnic and cultural diversity within each member state, as well as among all of them as a group.[2]

While Islam is often assumed to be a major factor in the presumed unity of 'Arab culture', there are some strong differences in the way it is understood and practiced in various parts of the region, especially in terms of its relationship to the state and public life. Sunni Islam is dominant in the Arab states, except Bahrain where the Shi'a are the majority. The Shi'a may also be a majority in Iraq, and there are important Shi'a minorities in Lebanon, Saudi Arabia, and Syria. It should also be noted that Christians constitute significant percentages of the populations of Egypt, Lebanon, Palestine and Sudan.[3]

The unity in the Arab identity is distinct from Islam. It is based on two components: the Arabic language and history.[4] In modern history the Arab region (with the exception of Morocco), was a part of the Ottoman Empire for more than four centuries. The Ottomans were succeeded mostly by the French and the British colonial powers, under whose hegemony the geo-political borders of most of the countries were drawn (the "Sykes- Picot Agreement" in 1916), and the promise to create a Jewish state in Palestine (the "Balfour Declaration" in 1917).

2 An-Na'im, Abdullhi A., 'Human Rights in the Arab World: A Regional Perspective', *Human Rights Quarterly* 23.3 (2001), 707.

3 Hopkins, Nicholas S. & Ibrahim Saad Eddin, *Arab Society 'Social Science Perspective'*, (hereinafter Nicholas & Saad Eddin), The American University Cairo Press, Egypt, 1985, 12.

4 Ibid, 11.

The origins of the subsequent conflicts in the region are to be found in this history.[5]

Most of the Arab countries achieved independence after the Second World War, although in the case of Algeria, the struggle continued until 1962. By that time, the Arab-Israeli conflict was already prevalent and the region became characterized by war and instability.[6] Moreover, the oil boom in the Arabian Peninsula attracted many contradictory interests, all seeking to control a region rapidly gaining an exceptional strategic significance. A series of foreign interventions and political destabilization factors further complicated the existing conflicts and created explosive regional tensions.[7] As a consequence of emerging from the rubble of colonialism most Arab states were mostly concerned about preserving their political geography and maintaining their national identity. The belief in one Arab nation to which all Arabs belong is still nominally observed-though not always practiced-by most regimes at present.[8] For a long time, there were concentric political-cultural-legal identities for most Arabs. In fact, the broader political-cultural identity as an 'Arab' is readily invoked when the person is outside the Arab world. The particularistic-country-legal identity (Egyptian, Saudi, Iraqi, etc.) is mostly invoked within the Arab world.[9]

The interplay between forces of continuity and forces of change, indigenous forces and external forces is another parameter of the Arab world. In order to assimilate the various religious and ethnic communities into the modern nation-state the Arab world and after the failure of Arabism as a national identity;[10] Arab governments were determined to build the Islamic identity. Thus the main problem behind a lack of

5 Democracy in the Arab World, Challenges, Achievements and Prospects.

6 Ibid.

7 Nicholas & Saad Eddin, 12.

8 Ibid.

9 Ibid.

10 Arabism is a movement for unification among the peoples and countries of the Arab World. It is closely connected to Arab nationalism which asserts that the Arabs constitute a single nation. Arabism has tended to be secular and often socialist, and has strongly opposed colonialism and Western political involvement in the Arab World. Pan-Arabism is a form of cultural nationalism.

acceptance of religious minorities' rights is the desire of the Arab States to forge a nation-state on the basis of a sole homogenous religious identity. The official governmental agenda was to perpetuate the leader's rule and suppress all those who disagreed with his political and ideological framework. Religious minorities were excluded from effective decision-making and parliamentary democracy.[11] Not only that, they also excluded Muslim voices that disagreed with the government's interpretation of religion. In the Arab world, in many instances, the basic rights and freedoms of the Arab citizens, extending from the right to life to civil and political rights, to economic and social rights, continue to be violated. This negative environment, which impedes reform and obstructing implementation of human rights standards, in conjunction with extremism, damages the prospects for a broad revival in the Arab world.

Thus, one feature shaping this region is its tension with the West. The history of colonization is still recent; the memory of European prejudice and racism is still vivid. This, combined with recent American policies, has led to a rise of anxiety about Western interferences. While some in the West attribute this tension to Islam (which they consider a violent religion or one of hate of the Western values) in reality, the main source of tension stems from Western foreign policies and their support of totalitarian regimes in the Arab States.

1.2 The Tension between the West and Muslims in Arab States

The dichotomy, *Islam vs. the West*, has recently gathered impetus as a result of a dual perception arising from the post-Cold War division of the world into East and West. Since the late 1980s, in its search for a new opposite, the West has chosen to confront Islam, considering cul-

11 Rehman, Javaid, Accommodating Religious Identities in an Islamic State: International Law, Freedom of Religion and the Rights of Religious Minorities* *International Journal on Minority and Group Rights*, Vol 7(2), Kluwer Law International, the Hague, 2000,156.

tural issues as the trigger for conflict.[12] This clash of civilizations theory is being developed out of misconception. Munoz notes that,

> [...] this theory gives an interpretation of history based on confrontation and on an ethnocentric conception of coexistence amongst cultures, since it considers such coexistence to be dependent on the extent to which other civilizations on the planet are capable of 'Westernizing'. Furthermore, it ignores the conflicts which result from the disruption caused by the marginalization of established cultural codes in non-Western societies. A case in point would be the drastic civilizations clash caused by the European colonization, the effects which are still being felt.[13]

This dichotomy is based primarily on the false perceptions which have been conveyed traditionally to the different peoples, as a result of a misinterpretation of history. Far from explaining the differences between the sides by using the 'conflict of interests' principle and analyzing cultural relations through the concept of inter-civilizational interpretation, Mohamed Abed al-Jabri shows that "they have focused on the ideological principle of antagonism (Byzantium against the Islamic Empire, the Christian kingdoms against al-Andalus; the Ottoman Turks against Europe, Arab or Islamic nationalism against the West.)"[14] The rivalry for political and economical hegemony between medieval Christendom and the Arab-Islamic Empire was interpreted as a confrontation between civilizations, which led Western consciousness to perceive Islam with hostility and mistrust.[15] Furthermore, the Western observers had a persistent tendency to approach Islamic civilization from the viewpoint of how it differs from, and conflicts with the West, instead of considering it in its own right. When studying the Islamization movements, they see it as a fanatical expression of religious fervor, ignoring all the social, political and economical factors which gave rise

12 Munoz, Gema Martin, Ed., 'Cultural and Political Relations at the End of the Millennium' *Islam, Modernism and the West*, I. B. Tauris Publisher, London, 1999, 3.

13 Ibid., 4.

14 Abed Al-Gabri Mohammed, 'Clash of Civilizations: The Relations of the Future?', 65–81. In Munoz, *Islam, Modernism and the West.*

15 Arkoun Mohammed, 'History as an Ideology of Legitmation: A comparative Approach in Islamic and European Context', 25–38. In Munoz, *Islam, Modernism and the West.*

to these movements. No thought was given as to why it has emerged and spread through the Muslim populations, or to what it means for the societies. Terrorism and warfare when they involve Muslims tend to be explained as a consequence of Islam itself (and its alleged inherent inclination to jihad and not as a result of specific political and socio-economic circumstances.) All this leads to a view of the Muslim world as an immobile universe.

Halim Barakat notes that, "'[t]he static method' used in a large majority of studies conducted by orientalists on Arab and Islamic society has undoubtedly contributed to this view."[16] He adds that

> [a]ny approach to reality must bear in mind that a society is not a complete, constituted finalized entity, but that is in continual evolution, transforming its identity, its conceptions, its culture and its institutions according to new circumstances and situations and that it should not be treated as 'a star turning in its own firmament and on its own axis according to immutable internal laws, which is exactly how some orientalists have perceived, and still do perceive, Arab reality.'[17]

Mayer, in the new edition of her book, *Islam and Human Rights – Tradition and Politics,* affirms that

> [t]he percept of Islam…like other major religions possessed of long and complex traditions are susceptible to interpretations that can and do create conflicts between religious doctrine and human rights or that reconcile the two.

She acknowledges that she too has seen Muslims and Islam as united, and admits that,

> […] by now there should be far greater awareness of the fact that the relationship between Islamic tenets and human rights is intensely contested than there was at the time of earlier (writings). Political developments have illustrated how diverse Muslim's views are regarding the applicability of international human rights law to Muslim societies.[18]

16 Barakat, Halim (1984), 'Al-Mujtama al-arabi al mu'asir. Ba'z istitla ijtima'; Beirut: Markaz dirasat al-wahdaal-arrabiyya, 4–5, In Munoz, *Islam, Modernism and the West.*

17 Ibid.

18 Mayer, xi–xii.

Islam by itself does not determine the attitudes one finds in the Muslim world on human rights issues. Mayer sees "Islam as only one factor in the reception of human rights in Muslim societies." Moreover, she adds that "[o]ne should not speak of Islam and human rights ...as if there (is) one established Islamic human rights philosophy that caused all Muslims to look at rights in a particular way."[19]

The most generic observation, as mentioned above, is that despite the number of Muslims and their visibility across the world, Islam still tends to be a misunderstood religion, often seen through caricatures or through the headline events that focus on the acts of extremists. Esposito explains that "we often fail to see the diversity. We know that [we encompass] a diversity; when Muslims say "the West" we will say, "Wait a minute, there's a difference between Europe and America." Or when they say "the West and Christianity" we will say, "This is isn't Christendom any longer." He adds "we tend not to see the diversity of the Muslim world. Over the years, until recently, we tended to continually equate Islam with Arabs, when they constitute only 23 percent of the Muslims..."[20] Today, there are "different ways that Islam is trying to change itself as it confronts both the constraints posed by the West, on the one hand, but also by the local political situation on the other..."[21]

1.2.1 Supporting the Authoritarian Regimes

The issue of human rights in the Arab world is complicated by the nature of many Muslim governments that are authoritarian and limit dissent and rely on their military and security forces to stay in power. The super powers in the West supported many of these regimes. For them maintaining stability in the Arab world and avoiding uncertainty

19 Ibid.

20 Esposito John L., *Conversations with History*; Institute of International Studies, UC Berkeley,available online at: <http://globetrotter.berkeley.edu/people3/Esposito/esposito-con2.html> (viewed Sept. 2013).

21 Ibid.

carried greater weight for their policy makers where vital national interests, the protection of energy sources, and of Israel, were seen to be at stake. The contradiction of the West in claiming to support democracy, but wishing to have controlled results with only outcomes favorable to Western interests, is not hidden from regional analysts.[22] In some respects, conditions for democracy promotion have changed less in the Arab world than in other regions. The types of concerns that had inhibited democracy promotion during the Cold War have persisted in the Arab world through the nineties. The old fear of left-wing subversion of friendly governments was replaced by a new fear of extremists. These inconsistencies in Western foreign policies have helped to equate advocacy of human rights with service to the hegemonic agenda of Western powers. This attitude tends to emphasize the priority of internal mobilization in confronting the neo-colonial hegemony of the West over issues of internal social and political transformation within the Arab world or its individual countries.[23]

Paradoxically, the peace process launched between the Arabs and Israel, in 1991, provided yet another justification for delaying democratization: the establishment of political and economic stability to attract foreign investment in the period after the peace accord as well as the control of popular reactions against the peace accords which were perceived by many inhabitants of the region as unjust because they were imposed by the existing balance of power. Thus, it is right to presume that the problem between the Muslims and the West are political not religious.

Islam is the spiritual safety for Muslims from their social and economical situation. The double standard of the superpowers that support authoritarian governments in the Arab world, while calling upon Muslims to democractize, is the main source of frustration of the Arab populations. It must not be forgotten, that Muslims suffered from previous

22 Hicks, Neil, 'Does Islamist Human Rights Activism Offer a Remedy to The Crisis of Human Rights Implementation in the Middle East?', *Human Rights Quarterly* 24.2 (2002), 366.

23 An-Na'im, *Human Rights in the Arab World*, 731.

European colonization and recent U.S. foreign policy blunders. With the end of the cold war, the distrust towards liberal secular universalism became even stronger. In fact, the human rights discourse lost prestige because it was associated with the US, a known supporter of the authoritarian regimes. The current war on terror has increased this negative image of the US and the West. With the American intervention in Afghanistan and Iraq and human rights scandals in both states, human rights are increasingly seen, by many Muslims, as an ideological accomplice of American imperialism.[24] For many Muslims, the West, especially the US, vaunts its values of democracy, freedom, the rule of law and respect for human rights, but treats the Muslim world with an ignorant, self-centered disrespect which is contemptible and hypocritical. This tension the average Muslim feels has nothing to do with Islam but has everything to do with politics and US foreign policy.

1.2.2 Foreign Policies of the United States of America in the Region

Recent events and situations causing the tension between the West and the Arab world are:

1.2.2.1 Afghanistan and its Negative Consequences on Muslims and the World

The Soviet government invaded Afghanistan in 1979. When Ronald Reagan came to power in 1981, he was determined to oppose this. He made a pact with the Saudis, the U.S. would provide intelligence, money and materiel (through the CIA), if the Saudis would provide manpower (i.e., mercenaries). In this way the Mujahedeen in Afghanistan

24 Jocelyne Césari, Alexandre Caeiro, Dilwar Hussain, 'Islam and Fundamental Rights in Europe', *European Commission, Directorate-General Justice and Home Affairs Final Report*, October 2004, 6. Available online at: <http://w3.uniroma1.it/jmobservatory/eu_document/eu_doc_rapport/2004islam_fundamental_rights.pdf> (viewed Sept. 2013).

were created. Eqbal Ahmad draws the attention to an American television image from 1985, where on the White House lawn, President Reagan is introducing with great fanfare, to the media members of Taliban, who are supporter of the mujahedeen who later on turned to be members of Al-Qaida, as follows: "These gentlemen are the moral equivalents of America's founding fathers."[25] This, as Mamadani, explains "was the moment when America tried to harness extreme versions of political Islam in the struggle against the Soviet Union." The Pakistanis and Saudis hit upon the idea of attracting recruits under the banner of liberating their Muslim brothers in Afghanistan from atheist-communist invaders. In short, the Saudis sold it as a religious war, a Jihad. The Arab Mujahedeen the Saudis recruited to do Reagan's work became the backbone of the Taliban. For Reagan, the Mujahedeen and the Taliban were 'freedom fighters'. They accepted U.S. guns and missiles and successfully propagated a guerrilla war, eventually driving the Soviets out of Afghanistan. Mahfoud Bennoune, an Algerian sociologist, commented on this event by saying "(The United States) participated in creating a monster. Now it has turned against (Americans) and the world."[26] Thus, as long as those so-called freedom fighters fought the Soviet invader, it was perfectly acceptable to successive U.S. administrations that they used 'irregular methods'. Now they are viewed as 'illegal enemy combatants'.[27] The tension here that is felt by the average Muslim against the West is that super powers create monsters with their authoritarian friends by using Islam as a tool to fight their enemy and then blame it all on Islam and Muslims.

25 Cited in Eqbal Ahamed "Genesis of International Terrorism," Dawn (Karachi), October 5, 2001, (Speech originally given in October 1998), quoted in Mamdani, Mahmood, *Good Muslim, Bad Muslim 'America, the Cold War, and the Roots of Terror*, Pantheon Books, New York, 2004, 119.

26 John-Thor Dahlburg, "Legacy of fear: Afghanistan's Mix of Faith, Terror – A Global Terror," *Los Angeles Times*, August 4,5, and 6, 1996, quoted in Mamdani, 140.

27 See Mamdani, Mahmood, *Chapter Three: Afghanistan: The High Point in the Cold War*, 119–177.

1.2.2.2 The War on Iraq

The September 11 attacks, which the Bush administration associated with Saddam Hussein, provided Bush with an opportunity to execute his plan; the dismantling the regime of Saddam Hussein. In fact, subsequent investigations by several independent commissions have refuted every reason cited by the Bush administration for the invasion of Iraq: there were no weapons of mass destruction; Saddam Hussein had no plans to attack the U.S.; there was no connection between Al-Qaeda and Iraq, and Saddam's government had nothing to do with the attack on September 11th.[28] The number of Iraqi civilian casualties has been higher during the American occupation than during an average year under Saddam's regime without counting the casualties resulting from insurgency activities; the counting comprises of civilian casualties due to actions carried out by American and coalition forces, such as the campaign against Faluja.[29]

1.2.2.3 The Palestinian Crisis

The question of Palestine[30] is by far the struggle most Arabs and Muslims hold dear to their heart. It is one of the main sources of conflict between the Arab world and the West. Without a resolution to this problem, there will continue to be conflict with the West. The United States has been involved in the affairs of the Palestinian territories since the Six-Day War of 1967, when Israel captured Gaza from Egypt and the West Bank from Jordan.

The violence suffered by the native Palestinians and by Israelis will continue as long the roots of the conflict remain: colonization, occupation, displacement, apartheid and the denial of the right of Palestin-

28 See Cook, Robin, The *Point of Departure 'Diaries From the Front Bench'*, Pocket Books, London, 2004. It is his journey during the preparation for the Iraq War, He began his diary from the 8th of June 2001 till 17th of March 2003.

29 See: <http://www.iraqbodycount.org>.

30 See: Mazin Qumsiyeh web pages for detailed informations and evaluation of the Palestinian crises: <http://qumsiyeh.org> and <http://justicewheels.org>.

ian refugees.[31] To see an end to the violence and injustice of war and occupation,

> Americans and the rest of the world must invest in justice and human rights for those living with and living under the occupation and war and as long as the United States continues to support Israel's decades-long practice of illegally appropriating land, destroying homes, and using disproportionate force; a policy which has proven to be both morally bankrupt and self-destructive for Israel; neither Palestinians nor Israelis will ever know peace.[32]

It is true that after decades of struggle, the West has finally grasped that there must be peace between Israel and Palestine; that there shall be a Palestinian state; and that the U.S. is effectively the only country ca-

31 See: Sabeel Ecuminical Liberation Theology Center, A Human Tragedy Called Gaza, Sabeel is an ecumenical grassroots liberation theology movement among Palestinian Christians. <http://www.sabeel.org/statements.php?eventid=5> (viewed Sept. 2013).
- (Video) Bilin Nonviolent Demonstrations and repression by Israeli occupation forces <http://www.youtube.com/watch?v=EzIAYQmIDRU> (viewed Sept. 2013).
- This land was theirs. By Hannah Mermelstein writing in the Jewish Advocate: As an American Jew, I could move to Lajun/Megiddo tomorrow, gain full citizenship rights, and live on the land that Adnan's family has tended for centuries. Adnan, who lives just a few minutes away, is forbidden from doing so. <http://www.palsolidarity.org/2008/03/the-jewish-advocate-this-land-was-theirs/> (viewed Sept. 2013).
- Rachel Corrie's Case For Justice By Tom Wright & Therese Saliba <http://www.countercurrents.org/saliba210308.htm> (viewed Sept. 2013).

32 See: Jewish Voice For Peace, Jewish Voice for Peace Condemns Escalation of Violence in Middle East Calls for US to Support Joint Ceasefire, End its Support of Occupation <http://www.jewishvoiceforpeace.org/publish/article_986.shtml>.
- Gideon Levy, With friends like these, in Israeli paper Haaretz, points out that "The amount of support being shown for Israel these days is almost embarrassing. The parade of highly-placed foreign guests and the warm reception received by Israeli statesmen abroad have not been seen for quite some time. Who hasn't come to visit lately? From the German chancellor to the leading frontrunner for the American presidency. And the secretary-general of the United Nations is on his way. A visit to Israel has become de rigueur for foreign pols. If you haven't been here, you're nowhere. <http://www.haaretz.com/hasen/spages/967055.html> (viewed Sept. 2013).

pable of exerting the necessary pressure on Israel to make the necessary concessions which will lead to the desired result. Nonetheless, the Palestinians, after 60 years and after many ineffective resolutions, have no state and are still the last occupied country in the world.

1.3 Religious Demography and Legal Framework in Egypt and Saudi Arabia

Egypt's large population and its historic influence in the Arab region and the influence of Al-Azhar on Muslims all over the world makes it an important country to study in terms of its human rights record as it pertains specifically to religious belief and practices. On the other hand, Saudi Arabia's role in the international community, a role it has assumed since the time of the oil crisis of the mid 1970s, makes it an important country to analyze. Its dominant position in world oil markets has led to economic and financial influence and the country also exerts religious and political leadership in the Arab world community and among other Islamic countries. Moreover, with Mecca being within the confines of its borders, it is the center of the Islamic faith worldwide.[33]

Egypt is the most populous nation in the Arab world. Although the overwhelming majority of Egyptians are Arabic-speaking Sunni Muslims, there are other religious, ethnic, and cultural minorities. Egypt achieved full independence from British colonial rule in 1953. In 1981, after the death of President Anwar El-Sadat, President Hosni Mubarak became president of Egypt and remains so till this day. Since then Egypt has been under the control of 'Emergency Law'. The ruling National Democratic party (NDP) dominates the People's Assembly and the *Shura* (consultative) Council maintains control over the major media outlets and the state's economic establishments; it also organizes general elections and controls the committee which approves the establishment of any

33 Boyle & Sheen, 452.

new parties.[34] Secular Arab nationalism failed in Egypt leaving two main contending forces: that of a totalitarian government and extremist groups.

Though Egypt had ratified the ICCPR on January 14, 1982, it attached the following declaration: "Taking into consideration the provisions of the Islamic Shari'a and the fact that they do not conflict with the text annexed to the instrument, we support and ratify." The Egyptian Constitution guarantees to all its citizens the freedom of belief and the freedom to practice religious rites. In fact, equality and prohibition of discrimination is clearly stated, Article 8 of Egypt's Constitution: "The state shall guarantee equality of opportunity to all citizens." Also, according to Article 46 of its constitution, the right to freedom of religion or belief is affirmed; this article states that the state shall guarantee the freedom of religion or belief and the freedom of practice of religious rites. The following article of its constitution, Article 47 reaffirms this by stating the freedom of opinion shall be guaranteed and that every individual shall have the right to express his opinion and to publicize it verbally, in writing, by photography or by other means of expression within the limits of the law. Moreover, Article 48 asserts that the freedom of the press, printing, publication and mass media shall be guaranteed as well. Furthermore, Article 151 of the Egyptian Constitution stipulates that international treaties become part of the domestic legal system once ratified and published and as known, under international law, every individual has the right to change his or her religion. Also guaranteed is that its citizens have the right to peaceful and unarmed private assembly, without the need for prior notice. Such private meetings shall not be attended by security men. Public meetings, processions and gatherings shall be allowed within the limits of the law (Article 54). In theory, the Egyptian Constitution of 1971 guarantees the protection of religious freedom, moreover, it has a legal obligation to provide and protect freedom of religion and belief. According to Article 2 of Egypt's constitution, Islam is proclaimed as the religion of the State and Islamic jurisprudence is named the principal source of legislation.[35]

34 Ibid., 26.

35 Constitution of the Arab Republic of Egypt, 1971(as amended to 1980).

In Saudi Arabia too, Islam is the official religion and its tenets are enshrined as law. About 85% of the population is Sunni Muslim and the remaining 15%, primarily on the east coast, is *Shiite* Muslim. Unlike Egypt, Saudi Arabia has no written constitution. King Fahd Ibn Abdulaziz released a decree named A/90, in 1992, whereby he affirmed that the announcement of the basic system of government was only an authentication of regulations already emanating from Shari'a. The Basic System of the Consultative Council (Decree A/90), 1992 states in Article 1 that the Kingdom of Saudi Arabia is an Arab and Islamic sovereign state. Its religion is Islam, and its constitution, the holy Qur'an and the Prophet's Sunna. Article 6 of this decree declares that: the citizens will take allegiance before the monarch in line with the holy Qur'an and the Prophet's Sunna. Article 8 of this decree states that: The rule in the kingdom is based on justice, consultations, and equality in accordance with the Islamic Shari'a. Article 46 establishes the judicial authority as an independent organ and nobody has authority over the judges, except the authority of the Islamic Shari'a. Article 55 asserts that the king will rule the nation according to the rulings of Islam and supervise the application of Shari'a (Islamic laws), the state's general policy and the protection and defense of the country.

Saudi Arabia has ratified three international conventions: those on the elimination of discrimination against women, against torture, and the rights of the child.

The Saudi State adheres to the Hanbali School of Islamic jurisprudence, the strictest of Sunni Islam's four legal schools. In addition, the Kingdom subscribes to the tradition of Muhammad Ibn Abd al-Wahhab, an 18th century Muslim scholar who belonged to the Hanbali School. For this reason, others often refer to these individuals as 'Wahhabis'. Most citizens, however, do not so describe themselves as such, preferring instead to say simply that they are 'Muslims'.[36]

Saudi Arabia's modern history is dominated by the Al Saud family. The clan's origins can be traced to Najd, near Riyadh, beginning in

36 See: Paul Aarts, Nonneman Gerd,eds., *Saudi Arabian in the Balance, Political Economy,Society, Foreign Affairs*, Hurst & Company, London, 2005, footnote (2).

about 1500. The rise of the Al Saud coincided with that of Muhammad Ibn Abd al Wahhab (1703–87). In 1744, Muhammad Abd al Wahhab found the political partner that he had been searching for and he and Muhammad Ibn Saud swore a traditional oath to work together in order to establish a state ruled according to Islamic principles. By 1765, Muhammad Ibn Saud's forces had established Wahhabism and with it Al Saud political authority over most of Najd. After Muhammad Ibn Saud died in 1765, his son, Abd al Aziz, continued the Wahhabi advance. According to the Wahhabi creed, it was imperative to return to a presumed pristine, simple, straightforward Islam, which could be entirely reclaimed by literal implementation of the commands of the Prophet, and by strict adherence to correct ritual practice. Importantly, Wahhabism rejected any attempt to interpret the divine law historically or contextually, with attendant possibilities of reinterpretation under changed circumstances. It treated the vast majority of Islamic history as a corruption of the true and authentic Islam. Furthermore, Wahhabism narrowly defined orthodoxy and was extremely intolerant of any creed that contradicted its own.[37]

Saudi Arabia is thus run by a combination of family ties and religion. The Ulama are

> […] junior partners of the Al Saud family. They enjoyed high prestige, privileges and influence. They were given, in addition to control of religious institutions, key positions in it, including the justice and educational systems In return for these privileges, the religious leaders ensure the legitimacy of the Saudi regime, and also provide religious justification for highly sensitive political decisions while ignoring the excesses of the Saudi family.[38]

Mai Yamani notes that,

> [t]he new Saudi-*Wahhabi* conquerors regarded cultural and religious diversity as chaotic, degenerative, and heretical, and set about resolutely enforcing their nar-

37 Abou El Fadl, Khaled, *The Place of Tolerance in Islam On reading the Qur'an – and misreading it.* Available online at: <http://www.bostonreview.net/khaled-abou-el-fadl-the-place-of-tolerance-in-islam> (viewed Sept. 2013).

38 Ibid.

> row vision of Islam in the name of national unity and religious purification. The political interests of the regime took precedence over the vitality of the *umma and* the ultimate desire of the Saudi *Wahhabi* leaders was to impose their drab, dogmatic politico-religious ideology on the Islamic world as a whole.[39]

Thus, in the course of over 250 years of Saudi history the Wahhabi *ulama* have developed a noteworthy political pragmatism. To preserve their alliance with the rulers, they supported Saudi policy even when it conflicted with their religiously based convictions.

In recent years, a number of critical events have required the ruling Saudi family to make structural reforms in the political, social, educational, cultural and economic domains of the country.[40] Among the most critical of these events are the large number of Saudis who took part in the events of September 11, 2001, the economic decline in the country and the consequent high rate of unemployment, the war in Iraq that made the U.S.A a de facto neighbor, as well as a surge in terrorism inside the kingdom.[41] Not only have these events led to the need for reforms on behalf of the Al-Saud family, but they have also emboldened a growing number of reformists who are seeking changes through peaceful means.

39 Yamani, Mai, *Cradle Of Islam, The Hijaz and the Quest for an Arabian Identity*, I.B. Tauris &CO Ltd, London, 2004, 163–164.

40 Ibid. Yamani characterizes this period by internal and external religious revival, the subsequent recession in Saudi Arabia and the Gulf War in 1990–1, which re-entranced American presence in Saudi Arabia.

41 Raphaeli, Nimrod, Demands for Reforms in Saudi Arabia, MEMRI's Middle East Economic Studies Program, No.247, October 13, 2005. <http://www.memri.org/report/en/0/0/0/0/0/0/1502.htm> (viewed Sept. 2013).

2. Freedom of Religion or Belief of Religious Minorities in Islam and the Refutation of the Misconceived Allegations Associated with this Right

Two important limitations to freedom of religion or belief in the Muslim world are: 1) restrictions imposed on the right to change religion and 2) the accusation of apostasy and the status of religious minorities in an Islamic state. These two issue are the prove to many for the incompatibility of Islam with human rights and the freedom of religion or belief.

2.1 Difference between Islam and Islamic law (Shar'ia)

For Muslims, the Qur'an[1] is God's message to man, a reconfirmation of the eternal message and a summing-up of all that has gone before. The Qur'an, thus, is a record of the exact words revealed by God through the Angel Gabriel to the Prophet Mohammad. For Muslims, the Qur'an is the prime source of every Muslim's faith and practice. The Qur'an which holds the central focus for belief, therefore imperative that all Muslims, regardless of rite, sect or piety, essentially believe in the inerrancy of the Qur'an as the revealed word of Allah."[2] Abou El Fadel notes that,

1 'Mohammedanism' is thus a misnomer because it suggests that Muslims worship Muhammad rather than God.

2 See: 'Ashmawy Mohammed Said, *Usūl al-Shari'a (Roots of Islamic law)*, Sina for publication, Cairo, 1992. 'Ashmawy Mohammed Said Ma'alm Al-Islam, Sina Publication, Cairo, 1989.

> Islam is not simply a national or social identity; it is one of the primary monotheistic world religions. The very raison d'être of the Islamic religion is that it is a universal message that not only speaks to humanity, but that must also construct a way of including humanity in a moral conversation.[3]

The morality which is the most primary important and original features of Islam is that it is the massage of mercy, moderation, knowledge, development, a massage of rationality and continuous change and progress. It is a global massage.

Although Muslims agree on the authenticity and divinity of the Qur'an's revelation, there are different interpretations of the Qur'anic verses and their meanings. Ultimately, the Qur'an, or any text, speaks through its reader. *Accordingly, there is no way of taking the entire text of the Qur'an literally. It has to be interpreted.*"[4] This ability of human beings to interpret texts is considered by Abou El Fadel "a blessing because it provides Muslims with the flexibility to adapt texts to changing circumstances."[5]

While the Qur'anic text is from God, it is man who must apply the law. Between the original divine proposition and the eventual human disposition is interposed an extensive field of intellectual activity and decision, and that is what is known as *Shari'a* in the Muslim world. 'Ashmawy explains that "the term Islamic law is the English translation of the Arabic word *Shari'a*."[6] *In language, Shari'a* can mean "the way to water". Religiously, *it means* 'path', 'method' or 'way' for *Shari'a* believers to reach morality and purification. It was initially used by the first generation of Muslims by its proper meaning. Then it was extended to include the legal rules in the Qur'an. This was expanded over time to cover the legal rules, either in the Qur'an or in the prophetic traditions. Finally, the term incorporated legal rules in all Islamic history. Today, Islamic law or Shar'ia refers to Islamic jurisprudence.[7] However,

3 Abuo El Fadl, *The Place of Tolerance in Islam.*
4 Ibid.
5 Ibid.
6 Fluehr-Lobban, 97.
7 'Ashmawy Muhammad Said, Ma'alm Al-Islam, Sina Publication, Cairo, 1989, 101-03. Also See, Muhammad Said 'Ashmawy, u'sul al-Shar'ia, Sina Publication, Cairo, 1992, 15–32.

it has to be emphasized that "the morality of the Qur'an will always exceed the morality of its interpreters."[8]

The development of a body of positive law has been a task taking up considerable time and effort, the breadth and diversity of jurisprudence allowing it to be adaptable, accommodating and open to varying interpretations. *Shari'a* was constructed by Muslim jurists over the first three centuries, and they "did so in accordance with their personal understanding and comprehension of the Word of God."[9] Judges took into account local values and practices to the extent that these did not violate God's commands. It is thus perfectly within the historical legacy of Islamic reasoning to develop norms that would accord with life in new social situations. One of the most common misconceptions, today, however, is confusing Shari'a (Islamic law) with the Qur'an. It has to be clarified and stressed that *Shar'ia is not the holy book Qur'an.* While, there is no disagreement between Muslims that the text of the Qur'an is divine, there are different interpretations of the Qur'anic texts. 'Ashmawy notes that "[t]oday, Islamic law or *Shari'a* ..., man-made and not sacred at all. To confuse this is to give sacredness to mere human opinions."[10]

The main sources of *Shari'a*[11] or code of law, today, which regulates the diverse aspects of a Muslim's life, are likely to refer to more than one of the following:

2.1.1 Primary Sources of Shari'a

- *The Qur'an:* Muslims believe the Qur'an to be divine, the word of God; it is the highest and most important source of Islamic law.
- *The Sunna:* The second most important source of law in the *Shari'a* is called the *Sunna*. The *Sunna* of the prophet means "the way of

8 Ibid.

9 Rehman, 139–166.

10 Fluehr-Lobban, 97.

11 See: Shaltout, Mahammod, al-Islam 'A qida wa *Shari'a* (No other informations available).

the prophet". The *Sunna,* the living example of the Prophet himself, includes worship rituals: such as, how to pray, cleanliness for worship, how to fast and rules for social etiquette, how to dress, etc. In the terminology of *usul al-fiqh,* or principles of jurisprudence, *Sunna* denotes a saying *(qawl)*, action *(fi'l)* or approval *(taqrîr)*. The *Sunna* also includes *Hadith* (Ahadith pl.), the words and deeds of the Prophet.

All Muslims agree on the use of authentic (Mutawatir) *Sunna* and *Hadith,* but lots of contradictions occur, because the ulama keep on using non-authentic *Sunna* (Ohad) to release *Fatwas*. Abd Al-Sabour Tantawi emphasizes that the

> [...] obedience to the Prophet after his death must be in accordance with the Qur'an and the *mutawatir* traditions and [the main problem with the *Sunna* is that the positions of many clerics regarding the issue of *Sunna* seem to contradict the previous ones.[12]

He explains:

> The problem is that the clerics say things that they do not do and do things that they do not say... They see that the vast majority of the traditions (99.9%) are in the realm of uncertain assumptions, and there is doubt as to whether they [can be] attributed to the Prophet. But [nevertheless], the clerics stress that they must be followed...[13]

The question of non-authentic *Hadith* falling within the abode of the *Sunna* is a disputed one and is highly dependent on the context.

In cases where the *Qur'an* and *Hadith* do not give answers to legal questions, Muslim theologians and jurists have tried to answer these questions and this has resulted in the emergence of different legal schools

12 Dankowitz, A., Egyptian Sheikh Dr. Abd Al-Sabour Tantawi – Islamic Reformist: A Religious and Intellectual Profile, MEMRI, No.287, 13 July 2006. Available online at: <http://www.memri.org/report/en/0/0/0/0/0/0/1741.htm> (viewed Sept. 2013).

13 Ibid.

or *Madhhab.*[14] The main *Madhhab* began with the emergence of the Abbasids rule. They came into power after the Umayyad rulers (661–750 CE) were overthrown. Under their rule, the first real law schools, as we know them today, emerged. They succeeded in systemizing Islamic law and purifying the traditions of false components. There are about twenty different "facets" of speaking and exercising law that could be summarized as *Madhhab.* These finally gave way to four major Sunni Schools of Law. The Abbasids who ceased power from the Umayyad Dynasty in 750 A. D. declared in the 9th century that no further interpretation or Ijtihad in Islam shall be needed. And therefore the Gates for man made 'divine law' was declared closed. This remains the case to the present day.[15]

Thus, most of Shari'a law as a system was developed between the 7th–9th centuries.

The leading jurists of the Abbasid era, followed today by the vast majority of Sunni Muslims, are: *Hanafi,*[16] *Maliki,*[17] *Shafie,*[18] *and*

14 The Sunni community is the largest one and includes approximately 85% of the entire Muslim community, followed by the Shia that represents around 10%. The remaining four groups are dogmatically close to the Shia School and represent the other 5 %: Muotazalah, Kahwarag, Zaydiyah, Jafariah, and Zahiris.

15 For the History of the Abbasid era see: SakneniL Issam, AL-'A bassiuon Fi Sannoate Al-Tassis, Al-mo'asasa Al-arabia L'lderrasat wa Al-nashr, Beirut, 1998.

16 The *Hanafi* in the Near and Middle East was founded by Abu Hanifa (d. 767) and developed in Iraq. It is based on the Hadith, but have rather wide possibilities for interpretation based on "common sense" and analogies.

17 The *Maliki* in North, West and Central Africa is considered of many to be the most liberal school. It has its roots in Medina and the Syrian schools of interpretation and was founded by Malik Ibn Abas (d. 795). It attaches great weight to *vox populi,* the living tradition, rather than what formally is considered the Hadith. In that way the link between law and society is kept alive. Among other things, the Maliki school gives women more individual rights than the others. Countries with the intention to change their laws in a liberal way often seek their support in this school.

18 The *Shafi'i* in east Africa, Malaysia and Indonesia, was founded by the famous theorist Muhammad al Shafi'i (Egypt d. 820), and is a strictly formalistic way of interpreting the Sunna. According al Shafi'i any tradition that isn't directly traceable back to the prophet himself is inadmissible. The most prominent work of those schools in this field is Al Shafii s Usul al fiqh. A great deal of effort was

Hanbali.[19] These schools were responsible for defining the sources of *Shari'a* and for developing the techniques by which general principles and specific rules were derived. In spite of their formal differences and divergences in details, these schools of interpretation grew into agreement on more important matters. They all, in practice, recognized the same sources; *Qur'an, Sunna, Independent juristic reasoning (Ijtihad), Consensus* among Muslim scholars *(Ijima)* and some form of analogical reason *(Qiyas).* They all recognize each other's systems as equally orthodox.

2.1.2 Secondary Sources of Shari'a

Neither the Qur'an nor the *Sunna* offers a system of legal provisions; they only supply the material from which a system could be constructed. In the construction of such a system a science of interpretation was created. The science of *fiqh,*[20] Islamic jurisprudence, has apart from the Qur'an and the *Sunna*, the following roots *(usul):*

---

invested in developing complex techniques for the Sources of Shari'a. To be able to know exactly how to solve a problem the way Prophet Mohammad (PBUH) did, al Shafi'i developed a complicated system of "links of tradition" so called *isnâd.* The isnads have different values, but all have to be satisfactory to not break the chain back to the tradition of the prophet. Every link has to be an approved intermediary of the Islamic tradition, such as a companion of the Prophet or some other approved legal authority. So it became pertinent to understand not only what the Prophet said or did but also what the companions of Mohammed (PBUH) have said or have done to apply the principles of Islam. During the time of the early four Caliphs (Omar until Othman) Muslim's affairs were administered on the basis of the text of the Qur'an and what Prophet Mohamed's surviving companions reported to be his conduct and sayings.

19 The Hanabli was established by Ahmad bin Hanbal (780–855), one of the strictest schools, was the official doctrine of the Abbasid caliphate. It was revived (under the name of Wahhabi) and is nowadays dominant in Saudi-Arabia. It developed from the Shafi'i school, and is often referred to as orthodox extremism.

20 *Fiqh* (Islamic Jurisprudence which is the whole process of intellectual activity which ascertains and discovers the term of the divine will and transforms them into a system of legally enforceable rights and duties).

- *Independent juristic reasoning (Ijtihad):* the Arabic word *Ijtihad* literally means 'strenuousness'and technically means an effort or an exercise to arrive at one's own judgment. To be more precise, *Ijtihad* refers to exercising independent juristic reasoning to provide answers when the Quran and *Sunna* are silent. In a broader sense, it is the use of human reason in the elaboration and explanation of the *Shari'a* law, interpretation of the texts of the Quran, and its application in concrete situations.[21] Soon after the end of the divine revelation with the Prophet's death, *Ijtihad* was needed to answer new questions resulting from the expansion of Islam into new societies and cultures. In the earliest, days it is clear that any adequately qualified jurists was regarded as having the right to go back to the primary sources of the law and make his own deductions. After the closing of the door of *Ijtihad*, and thereby all possibility of re-interpretation, was closed after the tenth century, *Taqlid* [the duty of accepting the conclusions reached by the previous generations of scholars and authoritative, is the sole method open to Muslims.[22]
- *Analogy (Qiyas):* systematic analogical reasoning is a restricted form of *Ijtihad*; it is defined as "establishing the relevance of a ruling in one case to another case because of a similarity in the attribute (reason or cause) upon which the ruling was based. This is the technique in which legal experts sought to incorporate new situations within the divine system.
- *Consensus* among Muslim scholars *(Ijima):* the fourth source of law, *Ijima*, can be defined as the consensus of opinion of the companions of the Prophet and the agreement reached on the decisions taken by the learned Muftis or the Jurists on various Islamic matters.[23]

21 An-Na'im Abdullahi A., Toward *An Islamic Reformation: Civil Liberties, Human rights, and International Law*, Syracuse University Press, New York, 1990, 27.

22 Anderson, Norman, *Law Reform* in the Muslim World, the Athlone Press, University of London, 1976, 7.

23 Mashhour, Amira, *Islamic Law and Gender Equality: Could There be a Common Ground?* A Study of Divorce and Polygamy in Shari'a Law and Contemporary Legislation in Tunisia and Egypt, *Human Rights Quarterly* Volume 27, Number 2, May 2005, 567.

> However, in the course of time, the scope of *Ijima* became virtually all-pervasive.[24]

Today, Muslims are allowed to read the text of the Qur'an, but are required to understand it in accordance with those predetermined interpretations. By turning the calendar to centuries past, a progressive system of principles is transformed into a dogmatic rigid doctrine. In fact, it is advocated that everything should emulate what they allege was the norm in the prophet's times. However, they ignore the fact that

> [...] the Qur'anic text was revealed over a period of twenty-three years. In general, every verse was revealed for a specific purpose, normally in response to a particular incident or question. These incidents are regarded by Islamic jurisprudence as the reasons for revelation, so that each verse has its own historical context. Without understanding the historical context, the verses cannot really be properly understood.[25]

Conservatives do claim that the 'gate to Ijtihad', and thereby all possibility of re-interpretation, was closed after the tenth century. However, *Itjihad* is by many reformists seen as the only way to reinterpret Islamic law to better adjust to modern ideas and society. Thus, over the past years, there are signs of change with civil society groups and individuals in greater numbers and with greater frequency both criticizing and challenging elements of the Shari'a and/or its application, when these elements are deemed to infringe on fundamental liberties. Many Muslim scholars advocate Islamic reform, claiming that the only way to resolve the conflict between Islam and the theory of human rights is through a new interpretation of the Qur'an. A reinterpretation of the Qur'an is seen as the strongest possibility of reconciliating Islam with modern realities. This seeks to return to scriptural Islam as comprised in Qur'an, rather than the popular *Shari'a* dominating most parts of the Islamic world. These calls for reinterpretation have been joined by Islamist reformists.[26]

24 Anderson Norman, 6.

25 Fluehr-Lobban, 95.

26 Check Al-Banna Gamal, 'Call For Islamic Revival', available online at: <http://www.islamiccall.org>(viewed Sept. 2013).

The fact of the matter is that the call for Islamic revival is the only call that offers a comprehensive cultural Islamic plan. It addresses every aspect of society and it is not a call for a partial reform or an attempt at patching up traditional Islamic knowledge. On the contrary, it puts aside all ancient and old knowledge, which is usually considered the reference for all Islamic advocacies and refers directly to the Qur'an without adherence to any of the acknowledged or traditional interpretations.

The main two controversial issues which need to go through radical renovation in the Muslim states are religious minorities' rights and the right for Muslims to change religion. This renovation is Islamic in nature, even if it is based on the international standards of human rights, since the goal is human dignity and human welfare. The right to change religion and the rights of religious minorities are two subjects, which throughout human history, have been sources of profound disagreements and conflict. The situation in modern Muslim states today varies greatly. Some states allow religious freedom with few restraints, while others severely restrict religious freedom, for non-Muslims and Muslims. This may range from not allowing Muslim legal or theological schools, other than those sanctioned by the government, to restricting proselytization, building places of worship, to enforcing the death penalty for apostasy such as in Saudi Arabia and Egypt. However, it would be presumptuous to place blame for the human rights abuses that have occurred (in Arab states) on one factor alone. Rather, a combination of factors accounts for the problem in many states. Among these are historically searing colonial experiences, failures in the leadership of centralized governments, a high level of military involvement in politics, severe economic deprivations, cultural fragmentation, and weak regional means to promote and protect human rights, Western foreign policy interference and considering *Shari'a* a legal system of purely divine source, not to be altered by man.

Consequently, it is important for Muslims to reconcile with themselves and to fight for the dignity of all the citizens of the state and to respect humanity on the basis of justice, equality and tolerance. Proceeding from this message, Muslims can contribute to the discussion of human rights from an Islamic framework, especially that human rights has not reached the stage of completion. Today Muslims can influence the construction of the human rights paradigm, especially, that human rights issues are not static, but evolving. However, Muslims will not be able to do that till they have more democracy, and when that happens, Muslims will protect the human rights standards not because it is a Western demand, but because it is inherent in all humans and that human dignity and human welfare is the ethical message of Islam.

2.2 Islam and the Welfare of Humanity

Islam is often projected, in the West, as an opposing culture that "retards rather than advances human progress in the field of human rights."[27] It is true, for political expediency, some Muslim governments emphasize (as an example) the penal aspects as window dressing to publicize their commitment to *Shari'a* without genuinely being committed to other more important rules about economic and social justice and legitimate political power. 'Ashmawy notes that, "In the Qur'an the term *government* refers to the administration of justice."[28] However, many Islamic jurists have been co-opted by the regimes in power and have contributed to the politicization of Islam.

It is important for religion not to be used as an instrument of intellectual manipulation by those in power in order to achieve its main message and that is the welfare of humanity. Thus, calling for the protection of human rights and for a society free from authoritarianism and religious dogma is the duty of every Muslim. Therefore, promoting freedom of religion or belief, in fact, belongs to the agenda of many Muslim reformers who do not contend themselves with an invocation of traditional Islamic tolerance. Even though not all people enjoy the

27 Baderin Mashood A., *Dialogue Among civilization as a Paradigm Achieving Universalism in International Human Rights A Case Study With Islamic Law*, Asia-Pacific on Human Rights and the Law, 2001, Volume 2, No. 2, 19.

28 Fluehr-Lobban, 73.

same human rights in practice, the basic idea is that they still have the same human rights and hold them equally and inalienably is a universal concept. Mohamed Talbi argues that

> [...] from a Muslim perspective [, ...] religious liberty is fundamentally and ultimately an act of respect for God's Sovereignty and for the mystery of His plan for man, who has been given the terrible privilege of building on his own responsibility his destiny on earth and for the hereafter. [Hence], to respect man's freedom is to respect God's plan.[29]

However, one problem facing this call is that Western scholars argue that the concept of "human rights" emerged from Western culture and these Western norms should always be the universal normative model for international human rights. Donnelly, for instance, presents human rights strictly as a "distinctive set of social practices" of the West and "an artifact of Western Civilization".[30] This view, argues Baderin, "is quite problematic (and controvertible), for a universal conceptualization of human rights."[31]

Even though no direct reference to God is made in the Universal Declaration, one has to see to the essence of the document and judge from the content whether or not it is compatible with Islam, or as Riffat Hassan notes,

> [...] [r]eference to God does not necessarily make sacred, nor does non-reference to God necessarily make profane any human document. [...] document such as the Universal Declaration of Human Rights which, though "secular" in terminology, seems to me more "religious" in essence than many "fatwas" given by Muslims and other religious authorities and agencies.[32]

29 Talbi Mohamed, *Religious Liberty: A Muslim Perspective*, in: Conscience and Liberty, 3rd year, No. 1 (Spring 1991), 31.

30 Donnelly, Jack, Human Rights and Human Dignity: an Analytical Critique of Non-Western Conceptions of Human Rights, 91982) 6, American Political Science Review, pp. 303–316, quoted In Baderin, 6.

31 Baderin, 6.

32 Riffat Hassan, *On Human Rights and the Qur'anic Perspective*, Swidler, A. (ed.) Human Rights in Religious Traditions, NY 1982, Pilgrim Press, 52, quoted in Badrin, 24.

To Baderin, the reference to "inherent Dignity" of human beings in the UDHR represented a compromise language with which every state may feel comfortable, as it is the diplomacy of drafting international instruments. While religiously inclined states may perceive the inherent dignity of the human being as emanating from God, secular-inclined States were equally free to view the same as emanating from whatever source they choose to assign it."[33] However, the problem is more in the school of thought that proposes that every aspect of (Islam) should be reformed to fall in line with present interpretations of international human rights law, such a proposition presumes the present interpretations of international human rights law to be a *fait accompli* that fully satisfies a universalism acceptable in all respects to every culture and civilization. According to Hassan Riffat "it is very utopian to presumes, for instance, that Muslims would want to repudiate every aspect of their legal and moral autonomy for universalism that is not inclusive of their religious sensitivities".[34]

Muslims are entitled, even required, to take advantage of these positive achievements of the West. Al-Banna[35] believes that Islamic revival supports openness and interaction with all cultures and civilizations, not from a position of weakness, imitation, fabrication or selectivity, but on an original Qur'anic base. He demonstrated that the Qur'an considers wisdom to be one of the origins of Islam. He elaborated that this attitude opens up a wide horizon for acquiring knowledge and inspiration from all available sources. It also allows Muslims to draw on all cultures and civilizations, including a different attitude towards women, art, economics and politics. This, he claims, is precisely what Muslims did before the door of *Ijtihad* was closed.[36] This means, Muslims, in their quest to understand God's message, are qualified to use and search all sources to protect human dignity. Islam's main concern, in this sense, is the welfare of humanity. The underlying principle here is that although secular principles cannot easily override Islamic moral

33 Baderin, 24.

34 Riffat Hassan, 55, quoted in Baderin, 24.

35 Al Banna, *Islamic Revival.*

36 Ibid.

and legal values, yet valuable human ideas for the betterment of humanity cannot be prejudicially rejected. Thus, following the Islamic theocentric approach does not mean blindly shutting the door against everything emanating from human thought. It is a Qur'anic injunction upon Muslims to always cooperate for the attainment of the common good of humanity.[37] See e.g. Qur'an 5:2 which says "... *Help ye one another in righteousness and piety, but help ye not one another in sin and rancor: ...* ", thus Khoury has rightly pointed out that

> [...] the contemporary Muslim World must, without loosing its theocentric identity, be able to contribute towards the realization of the universal solidarity of all people and towards the realization of a social order in which all (human beings) are essentially equal before the law and enjoy equal rights in their daily life, and where tolerance is not only practiced, but the irrevocable human rights of all are unreservedly recognized.[38]

2.3 Islam is a Balance between Rights and Duties

One issue that has been used regularly to portray the conflict between Islam and human rights is the argument that Islam stresses an individual's obligations to society rather than individual rights that cannot be violated by governments. Donnelly contends that "Muslims are regularly and forcefully enjoined to treat their fellow men with respect and dignity, but the basis for these injunctions is divine commands that establish only duties, not human rights."[39] Bassam Tibi' affirms this view

37 Baderin, 26.

38 Quoted in Baderin, 26 by Khoury, a. Th. *Toleranz im Islam* (1982), 185 cited in Zakzouk, M. Cultural Relations Between the West and the World of Islam: Meeting Points and Possibilities of Co-operation on the Academic Level, Translated by Walpole, M., (1992), 3 Islam and Christian – Muslim Relations, No. 1, 69 at p. 74.

39 Jack Donnelly, *Universal Human Rights in Theory and Practice,* Ithaca, NY: Cornell University Press, 1989, 51.

and points out that, "Muslims … have duties … but not rights in the sense of entitlement"[40] This statement is a true description of contemporary Muslim society, but not of 'Islam' throughout Muslim history. What is described as collective orientation in 'Islamic culture' is a relatively new phenomenon in Muslim society, resulting from authoritarian regimes established during the post-colonial era, demanding total individual conformity. These assertions only reflect the lack of awareness and possibly access, to the hundreds of voluminous works in Islamic law which elaborate various rights and judicial procedures for protecting these rights, in the historical Muslim society.[41] Contemporary Muslims do not enjoy rights, not because these rights are not written in the Qur'an, but very often because they are ruled by authoritarian regimes in police states that have very little respect for the idea of the rule of law. However, Islam refuses to concentrate on only individual rights without stressing individual duties and that what differentiate the Islamic view with the Western view.

The Western view has historically placed a strong emphasis on the individual, Professors Henry Steiner and Philip Alston affirm this and note in their authoritative text on human rights that

> [o]bservers from different regions and cultures can agree that the human rights movement … stems principally from the liberal tradition of Western thought … [and n]o characteristic of the liberal tradition is more striking than its emphasis on the individual.[42]

Human rights advocates were concerned that duties would be overpowering rather than complementary to rights, that they would be

40 Tibi Bassam, *"Islamic law/Shari'a, Human Rights, Universal Morality and International Relations"*, Human Right Quarterly, 16 1994.

41 SafiLouay M., *Human Rights and Cultural Reform in Contemporary Muslim Society: From the Hegemonic Discourse to Cross-Cultural Dialogue*, available at <http://lsinsight.org/articles/index.html>.

42 Henry J. Steiner & Philip Alston, International Human Rights in Context: Law, Politics, Morals, (2000), 361–62, quoted in Morgan-Foster Jason, Third Generation Rights: *What Islamic Law Can Teach the International Human Rights Movement, Yale Human Rights & Development. Journal*, Vol. 8, 2005, 84.

used as an alternative force for evil, rather than as an additional force for good. However, this fear oversimplifies the respective roles of right and duty, significantly limiting the potential paradigms for societal interaction by excluding all duties-based models. However, Professor Selbourne criticizes this reality as a mutation from the original theoretical balance of rights and duties. Also, contrary to the above critics, Professor Selbourne argues that the principle of duty does not

> [...] represent any serious peril to the moral doctrines which underlie the politics of rights...On the contrary, observance of the principle of duty, by strengthening the civic bond, sustains the *fons et origo* of right itself.[43]

The development of a third generation of human rights (such as the right to peace, healthy environment and development) has begun to point to a balance between rights and duties. With the focus changed to a more collective view, Islam has a chance to teach the International human rights movement the importance of individual duties to the community. The individual duty component of third generation solidarity rights has been de-emphasized by international human rights commentators.[44] Examining Islamic notions of third generation solidarity rights, one finds a very different interpretation of their nature, one which specifically emphasizes their individual duty component. Not only can this add to the understanding of third generation solidarity rights, the strong presence of these rights in Islamic law can also contribute positively to the debate on the universality of human rights. Morgen-Foster in his article, "Third Generation Rights: What Islamic Law Can Teach the International Human Rights Movement,"[45] notes that

> [t]he debate over the universality of human rights has typically focused on the extent to which international human rights law differs from local cultural practices and has generally sought to resolve these differences in favor of the interna-

43 Selbourne David, The Principle of Duty, 33–34 (2001), (arguing that the rights paradigm is more threatened by the misuse of the rights themselves than by any enforcement of the principle of duty), quote in Morgan-Foster, 81.

44 Morgen-Foster, 68.

45 See: Morgan-Foster, 85.

tional paradigm. Less attention, however, has been given to arguments that the international human rights paradigm may have something to learn from non-Western legal systems.[46]

He focuses on one such area: the conceptualization of individual duties to the community. In conventional human rights law, rights are explicit, while corresponding duties are often implicit, controversial, and poorly theorized. In contrast, the Islamic legal tradition offers a sophisticated paradigm of common ideals grounded in individual duties. In his article, he argues that "a reconciliation of the rights-based and duties-based paradigms is both possible and necessary to render justiciable third generation 'solidarity'" rights, such as the right to development, the right to a healthy environment, and the right to peace."[47] Thus, Islamic law can teach the international human rights movement, particularly in the area of individual duties. By attempting this goal, it will help make the case that, as the international human rights movement progressively recognizes the importance of human duties, a core shared universal norm will develop with local (i.e., non-Western) tradition at its roots. This balance between rights and duties will be more acceptable to many, especially that these rights and duties are intrinsically related and historically connected. Viewed functionally, rather than formally, rights and duties are but two different attempts towards the same end: a structure of normative, social, political, and moral order.[48]

This balance between rights and duties will be more acceptable from an Islamic perspective, especially that the moral message of Islam is the welfare of humanity. Mashood Baderin, explains that the object and purpose of Islamic law *(maqâsid al-sharî'ah)* is human welfare and the prevention of harm *(maslahah)*;[49] a goal most certainly in line with the purpose of international human rights. While human rights specifically

46 Ibid., 67.
47 Ibid.
48 Ibid., 72.
49 Mashood A. Baderin, International Human Rights and Islamic Law, 40 (2003), quoted in Morgen-Foster 74. More on the *maslahah al-Mursala (the Public Interest) see: Al-Marzouqy Ibrahim A., Human Rights in Islamic Law, (no Publisher), Abu Dhabi, 2nd Edition, 2001,58–60.*

aim at protecting the rights of individuals, the ultimate aim is equally to guarantee the benefit and welfare of human beings as a whole wherever they may be. Protecting the welfare of individuals does ultimately ensure communal / public welfare and vice versa. This makes the doctrine of *maslahah* very relevant in the discussion of human rights under Islamic law.[50] However, the 'Islamic culture' in which the individual is lost in the crowd of the collectivity is a result of the authoritarian rulers, whose agenda does not include such items as political participation, or constitutional and legal reforms, in their fight against reform ideas and their advocates. Even though Islamic reform has a long way to go before it can ensure individual liberty and equality for all, it has been moving slowly but consistently towards a vision of an open, egalitarian, and tolerant society, and that it has already embraced international human rights as defining principles of its vision of future society. This is happening because there is awareness within the reformists of the attempts to subvert human rights by employing human rights as a tool to justify imposition of external values and choices, rather than an instrument for fighting coercion and imposition. The importance of human rights lies in the instrumental role they play to protect the weak against the powerful, and to liberate the oppressed from their oppressors. However, "the international human rights paradigm has exalted the language of rights while under-developing the concept of duties."[51] Just as 'rights' is such a fundamental word in the Western liberal culture, "duties" is the paradigm-creating fundamental word in non-Western cultures.[52] But, what many call for today is the balance between rights and duties, especially, that the quest for the good society, is in part the search for a healthy balance between rights and duties, between individual freedom and the requirements of the social order. A society can, therefore, get it wrong in either direction. Authoritarian societies usually emphasize obligations at the expense of individual rights. Late twentieth century liberal

50 Ibid, 43, quoted in Morgen-Foster, 75.

51 Morgen-Foster, 72.

52 Douglas Hodgson, 'Individual Duty within a Human Rights Discourse', 41–60 (2003), quoted in Morgen-Foster, 74.

democracies often have the opposite problem, stressing the individual's rights to neglect duties. From authoritarian governments around the world, the demand must be for a greater acknowledgement of the rights and dignity of the individual, and from the modern democracies the demand must be for a greater recognition by citizens of their obligations to society and to one another.

2.4 Problem areas with the Right to Freedom of Religion

2.4.1 Apostasy: Definition and Parameters

In the Orthodox view, Muslims may practice their religion freely as long as they are not in conflict with the local orthodoxy. Once a Muslim converts to another religion or becomes an unbeliever, his position changes and he becomes an apostate. Apostasy, the abandonment of Islam, can be subdivided into the act of apostasy and its legal consequences. The legal consequences of apostasy often extend to death, being unable to inherit, and dissolution of marriage. The term apostasy *(ridda)* is reserved for Muslims. Only a Muslim can "apostate". The Egyptian Administrative Court voiced the general opinion of Egyptian Muslim society that "it is completely acceptable for non-Muslims to embrace Islam but by consensus Muslims are not allowed to embrace another religion or to become of no religion at all."[53] Whether the apostate converts to another religion or merely wants to give up Islam is irrelevant. Hence, apostasy is prohibited and no Muslim is allowed to convert to another religion or commit any of the offences which would make them an apostate. The traditional punishment for an apostate *(murtadd)* set in early periods in the Muslim societies was capital punishment. This punishment was implemented on a large scale

53 Berger, Maurits S., 'Apostasy and Public Policy in Contemporary Egypt: An Evaluation of Recent Cases from Egypt's Highest Courts', *Human Rights Quarterly* 25.3 (2003), 722.

in the period following the death of the Prophet Muhammad (PBUH), when Muhammad's successor Abu Bakr fought the *ridda* wars against the tribes that abandoned Islam. In recent times, there are several cases of apostasy against intellectuals who deviated from the dictates of the orthodox circles. The accusation against Muslims of "unbelief" is an accusation known as *takfir*. Apart from the explicit term *ridda* to cover apostasy, there are a number of associated terms and concepts such as *blasphemy,* heresy, hypocrisy and unbelief that amplify the notion and clarify its scope. There is a substantial amount of overlap between them; at times apostasy appears to be almost synonymous with them.[54]

Another aspect of apostasy and blasphemy is the issuing of *fatwa* either by state *Shari'a* courts, or by individual *Ulama* demanding the death of the apostate: "His blood is permissible". Individual *fatwas* are not legally binding on the state but can be acted upon by any Muslim and many would accept that the assassin is obeying the Shari'a and must not be prosecuted. In some Muslim states, traditional definitions of apostasy, blasphemy and heresy have been broadened to include anyone who disagrees with what the authorities, religious and/or governmental, consider to be orthodox Islam. Given the broad range of divergence within Islam on matters of theology and law, many Muslims now find themselves in danger of being classified as apostates for views which the government or militant groups hold to be heretical.

Who is targeted?

Accusations of apostasy, blasphemy, heresy and all other forms of *kufr* (unbelief) tend to be aimed at several categories of people in Islamic and in other societies:

1. Muslims who convert to another faith.
2. Muslim intellectuals seen as deviating from traditional interpretations (reformers, secularists, modernists, journalists, political opponents). This is what is called heresy.

54 Saeed Abdullah &Saeed Hassan; *Freedom of Religion, Apostasy and Islam*, Ashgate Publishing Limited, England, 2004, 227.

3. Sectarian groups within Islam, such as the *Baha'i* in Iran or the *Ahmadiyya* in Pakistan.
4. Others perceived as insulting Islam and charged under the blasphemy laws.

Today, the problem is the fluidity of definition in apostasy lists. Muslims, who felt that their own position on Islam was the only authentic and true one, began to characterize fellow Muslims as apostate, blasphemers, hypocrites or unbelievers. Some examples of such 'apostasy lists' are the list of Ahmed b. Naqib al-Misri, Abu Baker al-jaza'iri, Ali al-Tamimi and Abd al-Aziz bi. Abd Allah b. Baz.[55] These lists, note Saeed and Saeed, "cover the whole gamut of a Muslim's sphere of beliefs, practices and actions within the purview of apostasy, and hence limit the spiritual freedom and space available to Muslims. Such lists can be used as a basis for total control over their beliefs and actions without making any distinction between 'major sins', 'minor sins', idolatry or unbelief."[56] These modern apostasy lists do not reflect the earliest period of Islam in which the ulama's careful approach to the declaration of other Muslims as unbelievers or apostates adhered to the limits imposed within the Qur'an. Today, there is a surplus of apostasy lists which can only be described as fluid, ambiguous and highly problematic. The rather individualistic nature of these lists seems to stem from the fact that each scholar develops his own list, based on their training and interests. Working from such lists, it is relatively easy to declare one's opponents to be apostates.[57]

2.4.1.1 Apostasy in Saudi Arabia and Egypt

There are different positions on apostasy in the Muslim world. In Saudi Arabia, for instance, apostasy is a crime under Islamic law and is punishable by death. In contrast, contemporary Egyptian jurisprudence refers to the prohibition of apostasy, but not to the death penalty. In Egypt,

55 For detailed discussion of the lists see: Ibid., 43–50.

56 Saeed & Saeed, 49.

57 Ibid., 43–50.

apostasy usually becomes a legal issue only with regard to its consequences, which are limited to the field of personal status. Accusations or self-proclamations of apostasy before the court, therefore, mostly serve purposes that do not necessarily have any relation to the apostate's religious convictions. The 'civil death' incurred by apostasy merely creates several legal impediments as to the validity of the marriage and the inheritance. An apostate, for instance, may not marry, or when already married, should be divorced, and an apostate is not entitled to inherit or to bequeath.[58]

Recently, in Nasr Abu Zayd's case, the Egyptian Court of Cassation in 1996, adopted the very conservative stand that a non-believer, and hence apostate, is also the Muslim who takes a too liberal point of view in interpreting Islamic tenets, or claims that the Islamic Shari'a is not fit for application nowadays.[59] The Court ruled that the writing of Abu Zayd on Islam constituted an act of apostasy. What is new about Nasr Abu Zayd's case, however, is that the conservative Muslim activists exploited the "Hisbah law" enabling anyone to file suit in a court of law against anyone else in the name of society.[60] Thus the charge of *ridda* was filed against several intellectuals; if found guilty, the court could force them to divorce their spouses *(tafriq)* because if one party to an Islamic marriage became an apostate, the marriage was nullified. Thus, according to *traditional Shari'a*, a person, before he becomes a Muslim, is free to adopt or reject Islam. This is based on the verse "There is no compulsion in religion. Truth stands out clear from error…" (Qur'an 2:256). However, once the choice is made, the person assumes certain responsibilities. Accordingly, if one rejects Islam after believing in it, he/she becomes an apostate and is subject to the death penalty. What is disturbing in this case is that the Abu Zayd alleged apostasy was not

58 Saeed & Saeed, 725.

59 Ibid.

60 Berger, 729–30. The unique features of this case are that, the claimants did not have any such direct and personal interest in their accusation of Abu Zayd's apostasy, they referred to the procedure of *hisba,* which allows any Muslim to file a case against a fellow Muslim suspected of violating the so-called "rights of God," or the essential elements of the Islamic faith.

related to conversion on his part, but to blasphemy. This was a matter of legal evidence. Abu Zayd's apostasy was not based on a document or self-pronounced conversion, but on his writings on Islam. In light of Abu Zayd's insistence on being a Muslim and his writings being in conformity with his Islamic beliefs, the court had to embark on the difficult task of evaluating these writings in order to decide whether he was indeed guilty of blasphemy, and consequently, apostasy.

According to the case law of the three highest Egyptian civil courts, neither the act of apostasy, nor its legal consequences,[61] is related to the freedom of religion. Apostasy, in the court's definition, does not pertain to a freedom of belief, which is interpreted as the right to practice one's belief free of any coercion or prejudice. Apostasy is

> [...] part of the *practice* of a belief, the regulation of which is left to the *"internal order"* of that particular religion. It is the freedom of the *"internal order"* of that religion to prohibit or allow apostasy, as it is the freedom of that order to stipulate marriage impediments based on, for instance, the difference in religion between the spouses. While the freedom of belief may not be restricted, conditions can be made on the freedom of its practice. These conditions are related to public policy, albeit in different ways,[62]

and, the Egyptian constitution (in the interpretation of the Supreme Constitutional Court)[63] allow for this freedom to be restricted on the basis of public policy.[64] Apostasy is not prohibited in Egyptian law, but it is deemed a violation of public interest (as indicated in different verdicts of the Court of Appeals for Case No. 20 of 1966).[65]

61 Ibid, 721–22.

62 Ibid, 737.

63 Case No. 20, Year 29, 8 Apr. 1980, cited in Berger, 737.

64 See: Ghanea Nazila, *"Apostasy and Freedom to Change Religion or Belief,"* in *A Deskbook*, 685–88.

65 Berger has a full discussion of various Cassation (Appeals) Cases that shows the problems with the application of *Shari'a* in personal status. Examples include: Court of Cassation Cases No. 9 of Year 44, December 24, 1975; Case No. 162, Year 62, January 19, 1966; and No. 20n of Year 43, March 30, 1966. For a full discussion, see Berger, "Public Policy and Islamic Law: The Modern Dhimmi in Contemporary Egyptian Family Law," *Islamic Law and Society*, Vol. 8, No. 1 (Feb. 2001), pp. 88–136.

However, the ICCPR is more specific in its definition of the grounds which might justify limiting the freedom to practice religious rituals. These are specified in Article 18(3) of the ICCPR, which allows limitations that "are necessary to protect public safety, order, health, or morals or the fundamental rights and freedoms of others." The punishment for apostasy is in violation of the international human rights standards and limitations may be applied only for those purposes for which they were prescribed and must be directly related and proportionate to the specific need on which they are predicated. Restrictions may not be imposed for discriminatory purposes or applied in a discriminatory manner.[66]

In conclusion, most interpretations in Arab states consider conversion by a Muslim to another religion to be apostasy, a crime punishable by death if the accused does not recant. This is considered a violation of the freedom to change religion, which cannot be restricted according to international human rights standards. However, the main question is: is this punishment by death a requirement in the Qur'an or is this punishment one interpretation of the Qur'an at a certain time and under certain circumstances?

2.4.1.2 Islam and Apostasy

In Islamic states, the issue of the freedom of religion is a problem not as much related to the non-Muslim minorities, but to the Muslims who may want to convert to another religion. Shari'a prohibits the conversion from Islam to any other religion. Therefore, this has a negative effect on the freedom of expression for those apostates can find themselves subject to diverse punishments. Under the interpretations of the pre-modern jurists, as it has been mentioned before, apostates were to be punished by death if they didn't repent and return to Islam.

The historical precedent for the law of apostasy is to be found in what is known as 'the wars of apostasy' waged by Abu Bakr against certain tribes in Medina. Following the death of Mohammed (PBUH)

66 UN Human Rights Committee, General Commentary No. 22.

these tribes sought to secede from the *umma* and stop paying the *zakat*. Such secession would have dealt a severe blow to Abu Bakr's authority as the legitimate successor to the Prophet and might have put an early end to the young Muslim state. It was imperative for the caliph to [fight] the secessionist attempts. Sachedina considers

> [...] the treatment of apostasy is thus a purely political matter; it should not, therefore, take precedence over the Qur'anic verse 'no compulsion is there in religion' – which the liberal jurists consider as the clearest affirmation of freedom of belief in Islam.[67]

The accusation of apostasy in the traditional view has three bases: the *Ulama*, the *Hadith* and the Qur'an.

a. Apostasy and the Ulama

Most Muslim states refer to the prohibition of apostasy, but not to the death penalty. However, in his book *Islam and Secularism*, Al-Qaradhawi, representing the traditionalist view, explains:

> The Muslim sages agreed unanimously that anyone who denies something that is known in the religion [...] is an apostate who abandons his religion. The Imam must demand of him to repent, and recant his deviation from the righteous path, or the laws regarding the *murtadd* will apply to him.[68]

Sayyed Al-Qimni notes that,

> [...] according to Al-Qaradhawi, [the *ridda*] punishment does not apply only to someone who decides freely to leave Islam for what satisfies his heart and his conscience – whether this be another religion or nothing at all. It applies in principle [also] to the Muslim who clings to the laws of his religion [...] but

67 Sachedina, Abdulaziz A. (1988), 'Freedom of conscience and religion in the Qur'an'. David Little, J. Kelsay and A.A. Sachedina, eds. *Human Rights and the Conflict of Cultures: Western and Islamic Perspectives on Religious Liberty*. Columbia Un. of South Carolina: 53–90.

68 See: A|l-Qaradawi Yusuf, Secularism vs. Islam, From 'Al-Hulul al Mustawradah wa Kayfa Jaat 'alaa Ummatina', ("How the Imported Solution Disastrously Affected Our Ummah"), pp. 113–114.

> disagrees with those who have appointed themselves the priests of Islam and who call themselves religious sages [...] especially when the disputes concern the understanding of a particular matter in Islam [...] because [the priests of the religion] have determined that their understanding of the holy scriptures is the only [permitted] understanding and the absolute truth, and anything else is absolute falsehood [...]. Any attempt at new thinking in reading the scriptures is thrust away [on the pretext] of [accusations of] abandoning the religion [...] and the punishment for new thought or expressing a different opinion is death.[69]

Sheikh Abd Al-Sabour Tantawi opposes the accusations of heresy *(takfir)* made by *ulama* against other Muslims, and explains that only Allah, who knows the soul of man, can know with certainty whether a man is a heretic and adds that

> [...] handing down a sentence for crimes of heresy and leaving the fold of Islam requires knowing with certainty some things that only Allah alone can determine... and therefore it is forbidden for anyone to sentence for heresy someone who belongs to Islam, someone who attests that he has no God but Allah and that Muhammad is His Prophet, and who observes the rituals of Islam – no matter what he has said and done...Moreover, it is forbidden to kill even a *murtad* [i.e. someone who has abandoned Islam], because the Qur'an has no text that commands [Muslims] to do this.[70]

Besides, in Islam, there is no universally recognized single authority to determine what orthodoxy' was and who represented it.

However, issues about Islamic teaching appear to have been settled by those who had the most power at the time. It was the political authority in collaboration with the official *ulama* that represented the local orthodoxy. Where religious leaders had political power in a particular locality, they could not only label nonconformists as heretics, apostates and unbelievers, but also eliminate them with the support of the political authorities. In this, the collaboration of both the political and religious establishment was essential. If we go back to history, we

69 *Roz Al-Yusouf* (Egypt), September 17, 2004.

70 *Al-Sharq Al-Awsat* (London), April 27, 2006. In Dankowitz, A., Egyptian Sheikh Dr. Abd Al-Sabour Tantawi – Islamic Reformist: A Religious and Intellectual Profile, MEMRI, No.287, 13 July 2006. Available at: <http://memri.org/report/en/0/0/0/0/0/0/1741.htm> (viewed Sept. 2013).

will find many well-known and highly respected Islamic scholars were accused of apostasy, disbelief or heresy, because of the school they belonged to or because of their intellectual orientation. Many of these scholars are respected and revered by Muslims today. However, in their own time, some of the official ulama who were in charge of the protection of local orthodoxy accused some of these scholars of 'denying' Islam and at times considered them to be outside the bounds of faith. Abd Al-Sabour Tantawi speculates: "How will justice prevail in our societies when the clerics monopolize the religion and speak in its name, the politicians monopolize politics and speak in its name?" He, like many Muslims, highlights that, contrary to what many in the West like to propagate that the problem is in Islam, but in reality

> […] the real problem is not Allah, the religions, the holy books, the prophets, logic, modernity, serious thought, secularism or democracy. The real problem is in us, in human beings, and in the evil soul that abides amongst us […] An evil cleric can use the religion in order to spill blood, desecrate honor, and act unjustly […]. Likewise, [intellectuals] whose evil soul has taken over them are likely to use democracy and secularism [in the same way] […].

He adds:

> Clerics, cultured individuals, and intellectuals are only human beings with aspirations, desires, personal considerations, and urges. Religion has not made clerics immune to error, transgression, and committing crimes against others; neither have knowledge, logic, and culture made people immune to error, transgression, and committing crimes against others. Everyone errs, everyone has victims, and everyone has bloodstained hands […]. If our souls heal from the hatred, jealousy, desires, egotism, greed, tyranny, lusts, and base interests […] then our lives will be pleasant […].[71]

Even though, there is no priesthood or clerical class in Islam, today, in almost all Muslim communities, a clerical class does function de facto as the official religious establishment. This class is either the militant groups or the official *ulama*.

71 Dankowitz, A., Egyptian Sheikh Dr. Abd Al-Sabour Tantawi – *Islamic Reformist: A Religious and Intellectual Profile.*

b. Apostasy in the Hadith

There was no attempt to collect the Prophet's sayings (*Ahadith,* pl.) during his life or for a long time thereafter. It was not until 200 years after his death that the attempts to collect his sayings began. It is worth noting the Prophet reversed decisions to collect his Ahadith. The four guided caliphate respected the order of the Prophet and prohibited the writing and collection of Ahadith. This prohibition of collecting Ahadith continued until the reign of Omar Ibn Abdel-Aziz who permitted the writing of Ahadith and Sunna; then many books appeared containing Ahadith. For a Muslim, the prophetic Hadith (oral traditions of Muhammad) is a secondary document after the Qur'an. The texts from various collections of Hadith, comprising varying classifications from *maudu* (fabricated; forged) to *sahih* (authentic; sound) Hadith is being used today irrespective of the authenticity of the *isnad* (chain of narrators) of the identified Hadith, whose chain of transmission could be broken and not reach the Prophet such as Ohad Ahadith. Most people have no background knowledge of the historical facts behind the compilation of the corpus of Hadith and will be more inclined to focus on the *matn* (content of narrative).[72]

The death penalty is specifically mentioned in the Hadith, which says: *"The blood of a fellow Muslim should never be shed except in three cases: That of the adulterer, the murderer and whoever forsakes the religion of Islam."*[73] According to many preachers: Any person or group of people who kill an apostate should not be liable for punishment since they would be fulfilling the legitimate punishments proscribed by Islam and should be treated with leniency. Al-Banna rejects this view and affirms that Islam supports freedom of religion, including the right to change religion. He explains that this Hadith is "an isolated (Ohad) Hadith (not authentic)." He argues that in order to use the import of a Hadith as a fundamental principle, one has to study the Hadith very carefully, considering all aspects of it. One should also establish whether the Hadith

72 All Shari'a books agree on this point whether traditional or modern.

73 Abdullahi Ahmed An-Na'im, *"The Islamic Law of Apostasy and its Modern Applicability: A Case from the Sudan," Religion*, Vol. 16 (1986), 211.

had been narrated properly, that is, in the exact words of the prophet, not just in their general meaning. For him, Muslims should not rely on a Hadith whose text does not correspond to the actual words of the Prophet, in order to execute a person or to restrict their freedom. The meaning of such a text can change with time and one should be cautious in using such Hadith to support the serious penalty under discussion. He also argues that the idea of apostasy during the time of the prophet was linked to enmity and warfare against Islam. It was not merely change of religion that was at issue, as evidenced by several cases where Muslims reverted to their former religions but were not executed.[74]

Moreover, "the material in Islamic Law is amorphous and difficult to handle. Simply to collect the huge mass of variant versions and conflicting reports on a particular subject used to be a laborious task; now it has been rendered practically effortless by searchable databases."[75] The Egyptian scholar, Mohammed Shaltout[76], later rector of Al-Azhar, rejected this method in favor of understanding the Qur'an in the light of the Qur'an itself. He was a religious scholar interested in the religious and moral message of the Qur'an. In his Book *"Al-Islam 'Aqida wa Shari'a"*, he confirms the scarcity of the mutawatir (authentic) from Ahadith and the abuse of the ulama of the careless use of the ahadith.[77] The issue of rejection of the non-mutawatir *Sunna* as a source of legislation was discussed in a workshop on "Islam and Reform," held in Cairo on October 5–6, 2004.[78] The statement pointed to the impor-

74 Al-Banna Gamal, '*Hurriyyat al-I'tiqad fi al-Islam*', Minbar al-Sharq, 10(3), November 1993, 30–38. (Translated) in Saeed & Saeed, 96.

75 Patricia Crone, professor of Islamic history at the Institute for Advanced Study, Princeton, What do we actually know about Mohammed? Available at: <http://www.opendemocracy.net/faitheurope_islam/mohammed_3866.jsp> (viewed Sept. 2013).

76 Shaltout, Mahammod, Al-Islam 3qida wa *Shari'a.*

77 Ibid, 10–66. Also, he talks about that human understanding to Islam is not divine and that Islam is a religion of tolerance, justice and equality.

78 The concluding statement was signed by leading progressives and reformists in the Arab and Islamic world: Dr. Sa'd Al-Din Ibrahim, chairman of the Ibn Khaldun Center in Cairo; Egyptian intellectual Gamal Al-Banna; Egyptian intellectual Dr. Sayyed Al-Qimni; Syrian intellectual Muhammad Shahrour; Dr. Radhwan

tance of "a profound reexamination of Islamic heritage, including all the Islamic sciences established during the past three centuries of Islam: Qur'an commentary, the *Hadith* [Islamic traditions], the roots of the religion, and religious law," and "reliance on the Qur'anic texts as the only authentic source for the purpose of reexamining all of Islamic heritage." The concluding statement further called for "confronting all the institutions that claim a monopoly on the religion and on the proper interpretation of the holy text [the Qur'an]."

The Sheikh of Al-Azhar, Muhammad Sayyed Tantawi, voiced the traditionalist view and attacked those he called 'the *Sunna* deniers' who see the Qur'an as the sole source for religious rulings,

> [...] the attack on the *Sunna* is employed by the enemies of Islam for the [upcoming] attack on the Qur'an, because the *Sunna* is only a clarification of the laws appearing in the Qur'an [...]. Thus, anyone who raises doubts about the prophetic *Sunna* as a source of legislation is acting according to a plan that is hostile to Islam [...].[79]

Al-Azhar University member, Sheikh Mahmoud 'Ashour, another traditionalist, stated:

> Anyone who calls to rely on the Qur'an alone and ignore the *Sunna* of the Prophet is an apostate and has left the fold of Islam, because he has denied a definitely known [aspect] of the religion. Further, he is denying half of the religion. Anyone who says that the *Sunna* should be ignored is beyond doubt an apostate.[80]

Masmoudi, executive director of the Center for the Study of Islam and Democracy in the U.S.; Dr. Najah Kadhim, director of the Islamic Forum for Islamic Dialogue in Britain; Sharifa Macarandas, president of the Mindanao Women's League, the Philippines; Tunisian intellectual Salah Al-Din Al-Jurashi; Dr. 'Abd Al-HamId Al-Ansari, former director of the Faculty of Shari'a Law, Qatar University; Dr. Fabyola Badawi, director of the European Arabian Union for Democracy and Dialogue in France; and Abdallah Ali Sabri, editor-in-chief of the Yemenite *Saut Al-Shura* daily. Dankowitz A., Accusing Muslim Intellectuals of Apostasy, MEMERI No. 208, February 18, 2005. <http://memri.org/report/en/0/0/0/0/0/0/1321.htm> (viewed Sept. 2013).

79 *Al-Sharq Al-Awsat,* London, November 7, 2004.

80 *Al-Masri Al-Yawm* (Egypt), October 25, 2004, as cited in *Al-Quds Al-Arabi* (London), October 26, 2004.

In response to this accusation of apostasy, it should be argued that this view "was not seeking to abolish the *Sunna* of the Prophet, but calling to issue religious rulings based solely on the Qur'an when disputes arose."[81] It must be remembered that "Islam is a universal message to all people, that *ijtihad* is an Islamic duty, and that the gates of *ijtihad* are open to all and no one has the right to close [them] or to monopolize it…" and that this view didn't "disavow the Prophet's *sunna,* but only to base (interpretations) on the unadulterated Qur'an as the sole judicial source [of authority]; that is to say, to rule according to the Qur'an in the event of disagreement."[82] This is an explicit Qur'anic injunction:

> *"Shall I seek for judge other than Allah? – when He it is Who hath sent unto you the Book, explained in detail." They know full well, to whom We have given the Book, that it hath been sent down from thy Lord in truth. Never be then of those who doubt.* [Qur'an 6:114]

Thus, in the event of disagreement with the fact that many traditions and commentaries are of doubtful authenticity and that many of them are responsible for the blaming of Islam [as the cause of] violence, terrorism, and inflexibility, isn't it the supreme obligation of religious people, based on the Al-Azhar Law, to conduct *ijtihad* in order to reveal the truths of Islam and to cleanse it of the lies and distortions which compromise it?[83]

c. Apostasy in the Qur'an

According to the Qur'an, the human being is the most exalted of all creatures, and is therefore especially valuable irrespective of his or her religion. Endowed with reason and the desire for freedom, the human being is the vice-regent of God on earth, which is a human's natural

81 The answer by Ibn Khaldoun Center to Sheik Al Azahr is available online in Arabic at: <http://www.hrinfo.net/egypt/makal/pr041010.shtml>. (Viewed 4/2010). This Translation is by Dankowitz A., Accusing Muslim Intellectuals of Apostasy, MEMERI No. 208, February 18, 2005. <http://memri.org/bin/articles.cgi?Page=archives&Area=ia&ID=IA20805#_edn12#_edn12> (viewed Sept. 2013).

82 Ibid.

83 Ibid.

right from the moment of birth. Being human is the common thread that binds all humankind together before their separation by different faiths,[84] and the first aim of Islam is to maintain justice; all means to achieve justice and public welfare are Islamic in nature. The dynamic nature of Islamic teachings, the evolving character of *Shari'a*, and the direct verses of the Qur'an leave no room for doubt that a common ground can be found between Islam and freedom of religion or belief.[85] Islam is a balance between rights and duties. This balance means a greater duty to protect the human dignity that God bestowed on us. Gamal Al-Banna states that

> [...] freedom of religion or belief is a fundamental human right, and Islam does not force anyone to profess it, and since Islam is from God, this right is in line with the nature (fitrah) of human beings. Islam is the standard religion manifested in all scriptures and revealed to all the prophets. If the basic elements of faith are to believe in one God and in the after-life, it does not matter if the believer is a Jew, a Christian, a Sabian or belongs to any other religion.
>
> *The same religion has He established for you as that which He enjoined on Noah – the which We have sent by inspiration to thee – and that which We enjoined on Abraham, Moses, and Jesus [...].* (42:13)

Moreover,

> *We have sent thee inspiration, as We sent it to Noah and the Messengers after him: we sent inspiration to Abraham, Isma'il, Isaac, Jacob and the Tribes, to Jesus, Job, Jonah, Aaron, and Solomon, and to David We gave the Psalms.* (4:163–164)

It is, therefore, understandable, that all prophets are considered Muslims by definition in the Qur'an (see 6:163; 7:143; 10:72,84,90; 27:31,38,42,91; 39:12; 46:15 etc.).[86] In this context, the freedom of

84 Aral Berdal, *The Idea of Human Rights as Perceived in the Ottoman Empire.*

85 Mashhour, Amira, 'Islamic Law and Gender Equality: Could There be a Common Ground?: A Study of Divorce and Polygamy in Shari'a Law and Contemporary Legislation in Tunisia and Egypt', *Human Rights Quarterly* Volume 27, Number 2, May 2005, 565.

86 Nasr Hamid Abu Zayd, 'The Qur'anic Concept of Justice', <http://them.polylog.org/3/fan-en.htm#s1#s1> (viewed Sept. 2013).

belief is guaranteed. There is no compulsion in religion. The freedom to convert to another faith, after accepting Islam, even to convert back to polytheism or atheism, is left to man's essential free choice.

It is very logical, according to Abou Zaid,

> [...] if freedom of belief is guaranteed and secured against enforcement, the individual's right to change his or her religion is protected. However, it is also expected in a religious text like the Qur'an that such an act will be subject to punishment in the life after. There is no immediate worldly-penalty mentioned for such an act in the Qur'an. Such a penalty as prosecution or execution was later introduced by jurists and institutionalized as part of the faith.[87]

Again, quoting the Qur'an will prove that: *"Say* [Mohammed], *'The truth is from your Lord': Let him who will believe, and let him who will, reject (it): for the wrong-doers We have prepared a Fire ... "* (18:29), or the verse *"O ye who believe! if any from among you turn back from his Faith, soon will Allah produce a people whom He will love as they will love Him, ...*" (5:54), or the verse *"But those who reject Faith after they accepted it, and then go on adding to their defiance of Faith, – never will their repentance be accepted; for they are those who have (of set purpose) gone astray."* (3:90) and verse (4:137): *"Those who believe, then reject faith, then believe (again) and (again) reject faith, and go on increasing in unbelief, – Allah will not forgive them nor guide them nor guide them on the way."*

Al-Banna concludes that "in the modern period the state should not interfere with people's religion and belief under any circumstances." In arguing that belief should be based on freedom and conviction, Al-Banna makes the following points:

> First, the Qur'an makes freedom of belief a basic right; this establishes a fundamental principle of Islam, which corresponds with reason and logic.
>
> Second, there is nothing from the Prophet to suggest that he executed an apostate because of his apostasy.
>
> Third, he specifies that the Qur'an mentions apostasy in many places but does not impose any earthly punishment.[88]

87 Ibid.
88 Al-Banna Gamal,quoted in Saeed & Saeed, 96.

Finally, the door to repentance is open indefinitely as there is no end to God's mercy.

– *Rationality in the Qur'an*

The Qur'an is a source of religious reflection *(tadhakkur)* and intellectual appropriation *(tadabbur)*. In other words, the message of the Qur'an is intimately linked to the expressions of personal piety as much as the intellectual search for the meanings of the divine speech. Both these aspects, of religious reflection and intellectual appropriation have led the Muslims to interact with the Qur'an as the main proof for God's existence and concern for humanity. The search for the divine purposes for humankind, in the Qur'an, has functioned as the most dynamic source for scriptural reasoning in order to reflect on human actions and determine whether they are in conformity with God's will. However, Muslims have also stifled their rational, reflective abilities for fear of introducing innovation in matters derived directly from the revelation. This hesitation in confronting the challenges of rethinking has also resulted in treating the inherited cumulative tradition, propounded and expounded by past Muslim scholars, as sacrosanct as the revelation itself, thereby depriving themselves of approaching the Qur'an afresh through their own contemporary experience of living in a changed time and place.[89] Moreover, the Qur'an refers very often to the universe and to the things and events in it and describes them as symbols, indicators or signs *(ayat)*. It invites the addressee to ponder over the meaning of those signs in order to testify to the veracity of the teachings of the Qur'an. It should be noted that the Qur'an condemns blind imitation. It repeatedly condemns the blind following of the tradition of forefathers,

> *When it is said to them: "Follow what Allah hath revealed:" They say: "Nay! we shall follow the ways of our fathers." What! even though their fathers Were void of wisdom and guidance? The parable of those who reject Faith is as if one were to shout Like a goat-herd, to things that listen to nothing but calls and cries: Deaf, dumb, and blind, they are void of wisdom.* (2: 170–171)

89 *Abdulaziz Sachedina*, 'The Nature of Scriptural Reasoning in Islam', *The Journal of Scriptural Reasoning* Number 5.1, April 2005.

The Qur'an persistently says, "So will you not think?" and refers what it says to reason. It invites those who refuse to consider its proposition as reasonable on its merits to "produce an evidence for what they claim."[90] The believer is over and over invited to think and ponder over the evidences in the universe in order to confirm his *iman* (belief) in the truth of the Qur'anic message. Thus, the Qur'an gives Muslims the right to think and to decide what is wrong and what is right. A strong thread of personal responsibility running through out the Qur'an and each Muslim is given the capacity to discern right from wrong, and it is a personal decision as to which, if any, belief system to follow:

a. verse, 17:15: *"Who receiveth guidance, receiveth it for his own benefit: who goeth astray doth so to his own loss: No bearer of burdens can bear the burden of another: nor would We visit with Our Wrath until We had sent an messenger (to give warning)."*
b. verse 18:29: *Say, "The truth is from your Lord": Let him who will believe, and let him who will, reject (it): for the wrong-doers We have prepared a Fire whose (smoke and flames), like the walls and roof of a tent, will hem them in: if they implore relief they will be granted water like melted brass, that will scald their faces, how dreadful the drink! How uncomfortable a couch to recline on!*
c. verse 6:104: *"Now have come to you, from your Lord, proofs (to open your eyes): if any will see, it will be for (the good of) his own soul; if any will be blind, it will be to his own (harm): I am not (here) to watch over your doings."*

– *The Approach by the Prophet*

A number of Qur'anic passages state clearly that the responsibility of the Prophet Muhammad is to communicate the message of God and not to compel anyone to believe.

90 And yet they choose to worship (imaginary) deities instead of Him! Say: "*Or have they taken for worship (other) gods besides him? Say, "Bring your convincing proof: this is the Message of those with me and the Message of those before me." But most of them know not the Truth, and so turn away."* (21:24).

- 6.107 *If it had been Allah's plan, they would not have taken false gods: but We made thee not one to watch over their doings, nor art thou set over them to dispose of their affairs.*
- Surah 10: Yunus: 99; *"If it had been thy Lord's will, they would all have believed,- all who are on earth! wilt thou then compel mankind, against their will, to believe!"*
- Surah 16: Al-Nahl: 82; *"But if they turn away, thy duty is only to preach the clear Message."*
- Surah 42: Ash-Shura: 48. *"If then they run away, We have not sent thee as a guard over them. Thy duty is but to convey (the Message). And truly, when We give man a taste of a Mercy from Ourselves, he doth exult thereat, but when some ill happens to him, on account of the deeds which his hands have sent forth, truly then is man ungrateful!"*

The Prophet is not responsible for what others do. Each person is responsible for his/her own decisions and the result of such decisions will also be borne by that person. Saeed sees that "in the area of belief, in particular, this personal responsibility is paramount. Since each person, on the 'day of judgment', will be asked about their actions (and not about what other people may or may not have done) it follows that the matter of belief and faith is also left to each individual to decide.

- 10:41, *"If they charge thee with falsehood, say: "My work to me, and yours to you! ye are free from responsibility for what I do, and I for what ye do!"*
- 50:45: *We know best what they say; and thou art not one to overawe them by force. So admonish with the Qur'an such as fear My Warning!*
- 10:108, *Say: "O ye men! Now Truth hath reached you from your Lord! those who receive guidance, do so for the good of their own souls; those who stray, do so to their own loss: and I am not (set) over you to arrange your affairs."*
- 27:92, *And to rehearse the Qur'an: and if any accept guidance, they do it for the good of their own souls, and if any stray, say: "I am only a Warner".*
- 6:66, *But thy people reject this, though it is the truth. Say: "Not mine is the responsibility for arranging your affairs;*

– 4:80, *He who obeys the Messenger, obeys Allah: But if any turn away, We have not sent thee to watch over their (evil deeds).*

The Prophet's task was to explain to people the difference between rights and wrongs, not to coerce them to become believers: 88: 21–22. "*Therefore do thou give admonition, for thou art one to admonish. Thou art not one to manage (men's) affairs.*"[91]

Thus, the Qur'an prohibits conversion by force and there are many verses in the Qur'an, as we have seen, that clearly state that no one should be forced to accept or follow a particular belief or religion:

1. 2:256: *"Let there be no compulsion in religion: Truth stands out clear from Error: whoever rejects evil and believes in Allah hath grasped the most trustworthy hand-hold, that never breaks. And Allah heareth and knoweth all things."*
2. 18. 29: *Say, "The truth is from your Lord": Let him who will believe, and let him who will, reject (it)…"*
3. 109:1–6: *Say: O ye that reject Faith! I worship not that which ye worship, Nor will ye worship that which I worship. And I will not worship that which ye have been wont to worship, Nor will ye worship that which I worship. To you be your Way, and to me mine.*

The right to exercise free choice in matters of belief is unambiguously endorsed by the Qur'an[92] which also states clearly that God will judge human beings not on the basis of what they profess but on the basis of their belief and righteous conduct[93], as indicated by Surah 2: 62 which says:

> *Those who believe (in the Qur'an), and those who follow the Jewish (scriptures), and the Christians and the Sabians,- any who believe in Allah and the Last Day, and work righteousness, shall have their reward with their Lord; on them shall be no fear, nor shall they grieve.*

91 Also See: Surah 10:99, 13:31, 16:9, 6:149, and 6:35.

92 For instance, see Surah 18: Al-Kahf: 29. "*The truth is from your Lord": Let him who will believe, and let him who will, reject (it): […].*"

93 For instance, see Surah 6: Al-An'am: 108: *"Revile not ye those whom they call upon besIdes Allah, lest they out of spite revile Allah in their ignorance. Thus have We made alluring to each people its own doings. In the end will they return to their Lord, and We shall then tell them the truth of all that they did."*

– *No Temporal Punishment for Apostasy*

The Qur'anic dictum, "Let there be no compulsion in religion" applies not only to non-Muslims but also to Muslims. While those who renounced Islam after professing it and engaged in 'acts of war' against Muslims were to be treated as enemies and aggressors, the Qur'an does not prescribe any punishment for non-profession or renunciation of faith. The decision regarding a person's ultimate destiny in the hereafter rests with God. Not only that God recognizes the diversity of religions, but also that God calls for people to come together and know one another. Each person is responsible for his/her own decisions and the result of such decisions will be borne by that person. It is important to emphasize the importance of sincerity in faith, as Shabbir Akhter argues,

> [...] faith should not be based on hypocrisy and coercion: It is the [...] potential risks inherent in the offer of religious freedom are worth taking. Why? Well, if there is a God, I would argue, it can be expected a priori that he wants a voluntary response born of genuine gratitude and humility themselves rooted in reflection and morally responsible choice.

Seen in this light, heresy and even apostasy are morally more acceptable than any hypocritical attachment to orthodox opinion out of the fear of public sanctions. Fortunately for Muslims, they have the evidence in the Qur'an itself in favor of this view: 'there should be no compulsion in religion' (2:256). Unfortunately, however, many learned authorities have sought to cancel this noble sentiment by finding verses within the sacred volume that favor the opposite opinion; "suffice it to say here that even in terms of a pragmatic(as opposed to a moral or religious) outlook, there is much to be said in favor of religious freedom."[94] Thus, Gamal Al-Banna firmly rejects all demands to ostracize any individual or to make charges of apostasy.

94 Shabbir Akhter, 'A Faith for All Seasons: Islam and Western Modernity', London, Bellew Publishing, 1990, 21–22, quoted in Saeed & Saeed; *Freedom of Religion, Apostasy and Islam*, Ashgate Publishing Limited, England, 2004, 96.

> The lawsuits we are seeing today to ostracize and prevent [different] ideas recall previous eras. We must understand that Islam has given man freedom of thought. Islam's history proves that no one is immune to error except the Prophet.[95]

Thus, there is not temporal punishment for unbelievers or apostate. Those who refuse to become believers will receive their punishment on the 'day of judgment'.

a. 4:115: *If anyone contends with the Messenger even after guidance has been plainly conveyed to him, and follows a path other than that becoming to men of Faith, We shall leave him in the path he has chosen, and land him in Hell, – what an evil refuge!*
b. 6:48–49: *"We send the messengers only to give good news and to warn: so those who believe and mend (their lives), – upon them shall be no fear, nor shall they grieve. But those who reject our signs, – them shall punishment touch, for that they ceased not from transgressing."*
c. 72:23: *"Unless I proclaim what I receive from Allah and His Messages: for any that disobey Allah and His Messenger, – for them is Hell: they shall dwell therein for ever."*

It is the duty of all Muslims to respect freedom of religion or belief and to accentuate that these principles are an individual's right and have no relation with public policy. This is what is stated in the Universal Declaration and is also mentioned before it in the Qur'an.[96] There is no punishment specified in this world. It is only when apostasy is coupled with actual engagement in fighting against Muslims that it becomes a crime. These verses that call for Muslims to defend themselves against aggressors are identified as "the verses of the sword". These verses have nothing to do with apostate or a person's belief. At the same time, these verses are not calling for *jihad* against non-Muslims. The relevant verses, discussed above, do not specify any temporal punishment, even if they mention the apostate. These Qur'anic verses, used by the proponents of the death penalty, are mostly indirect verses that are not used in their

95 Al-Banna Gamal, Islamic Revivals.

96 Check Al-Banna Gamal, *Freedom of belief in Islam, Cairo,* Dar al-Ansar, 1977. Our first Demand is Freedom of Belief, Dar AL-Fikr Al-Islami, Cairo, 2000. Many of Gamal Al-Banna articles are found in <www.metransparent.com>.

historical context; besides, the interpretation of these verses as requiring the death penalty for apostate, means that those traditionalists' views are closing the door to repentance, which is considered very important in Islam.

– *The Door to Repentance is Open Indefinitely*

The Qur'an, in Surah 4:137, states that *"Those who believe, then reject faith, then believe (again) and (again) reject faith, and go on increasing in unbelief, – Allah will not forgive them nor guide them nor guide them on the way."* Shaikh Abdur Rahman, the retired Chief of Justice in Shari'a law in Pakistan, argues in no uncertain terms, that

> [...] this is a striking pronouncement and almost conclusive against the thesis that an apostate must lose his head immediately after his defection from the faith. The verse visualizes repeated apostasies and reversions to the faith, without mention of any punishment for any of these defections on this earth. The act of apostasy must, therefore, be a sin and not a crime. If he had to be killed of his very first defection, he could not possibly have a history of conversions.[97]

This verse proclaims that every person is given the choice to accept Islam of their own free will and that every possible way of entering the faith is accessible to all. Muhammad Zafrullah Khan comments:

> It has also been proclaimed that it is possible for everyone to depart from Islam by any of the doors that provide entry into Islam and to proclaim his disbelief and his apostasy. Thus, as the doors of entry into the circle of Islam are open to everyone, the doors of egress from Islam are also open. The person is free to do so a second time and is not subject to any restriction, for there is no compulsion; there is freedom of conscience and freedom of belief. If he disbelieves again and goes on advancing in disbelief and does not repent, Allah would not forgive such a one, nor would guide him to any way of deliverance. He would achieve no spiritual success.[98]

97 Shaikh Abdur Rahman, Punishment of Apostasy in Islam (New Delhi: Kitab Bhavan, 1996), p. 39. In The International Journal of Human Rights, Vol. 5, No. 3 (Autumn 2001) pp. 45–70. Published by Frank Cass, London

98 Muhammad Zafrullah Khan, 'Punishment of Apostasy in Islam' (London Mosque, no date given), 8.

By examining the differences between the international standards on human rights, classical interpretation of Islam and the different Islamic human rights schemes, it is possible to argue that they are indeed conceptually different things. However, contemporary Muslim thought with the reopening of the door of Ijtihad may be able to produce a human rights scheme which could be based on ethical and moral premises but not different to international human rights standards in their outcomes.

2.4.2 The rights of Religious Minorities in Egypt and Saudi Arabia

2.4.2.1 Religious Discrimination

Muslim majorities, in both Saudi Arabia and Egypt, must adhere to the state interpretation of Islam. The majority of Muslims in Egypt must adhere to the Al-Azhar interpretation of the Qur'an and follow their *fatwas*, whereas, in Saudi Arabia, it is the Wahhabi branch that the majority must adhere to. In this sense, Muslims who disagree with these interpretations of the Qur'an, such as the Muslim Brothers or the reformists, their right to freedom of religious expression is violated and most usually they are harassed and detained. Despite of *Article 35 of the Arab Charter on Human rights which states that* "Citizens have a right to live in an intellectual and cultural environment in which … racial, religious and other forms of discrimination are rejected and international cooperation and the cause of world peace are supported", however, there are many issues that the religious minorities in Arab States are discriminated against.

a. Non-Muslim Minorities

For a religious group to be officially recognized in Egypt, it must submit a request to the Religious Affairs Department at the Ministry of Interior which determines whether it would pose a threat or upset national unity or social peace. The Religious Affairs Department also consults the leading religious figures in the country, particularly the Pope of the Coptic Orthodox Church and the Sheikh of Al-Azhar. The registration is then referred to the President, who issues a decree recognizing the new group, according to Law 15 of 1927. If a religious group chooses to bypass the official registration process, participants are subject to detention and could also face prosecution and punishment. Though the constitution provides for religious freedom, the government has a long history of infringements upon this right. Any religious practices that can be considered in conflict to Shar'ia (Islamic law) are prohibited and Article 98 (F)[99] of the penal code allows for prosecution for unorthodox practices and beliefs that are considered to be "insulting heavenly religions." Government discrimination extends to both Muslim fundamentalists and other religious minorities. Members of the recognized religious minorities generally worship without legal harassment and may maintain links with co-religionists in other countries.

The major problem the Coptic Christians face in Egypt is the construction and repair of its churches. The regulations in Egypt are unreasonably restrictive despite, decrees issued by President Mubarak in 1998 and 1999 to facilitate approvals for repairing, renovating, expanding, and building churches. However, some local security and governmental officials have continued to hinder efforts by Christians to obtain the permits required for such construction, an attitude encouraged by the 1856 *Hamayouni decree* and the 1934 *El-Ezabi decree*, an ordinance issued by the Ministry of Interior laid out ten conditions under which churches could be constructed. The contemporary interpretation of the 1856 Ottoman Hamayouni decree, partially still enforced, requires non-Muslims to obtain a presidential decree to enlarge or build places of worship. Judge 'Ashmawy observes that the Hamayouni de-

99 Article 98(f) as amended by Law 147/2006 states: Confinement for a period of not less than six months and not exceeding five years, or a fine of not less than five hundred pounds and not exceeding one thousands pounds shall be the penalty inflicted on whoever make use of religion in propagating, either by words, in writing, or in any other means, extreme ideas for the purpose of inciting strife, ridiculing or insulting a heavenly religion or a sect following it, or damaging national unity.

cree "is the only Ottoman edict that has not been abolished in Egypt",[100] and the application of the regulations to minor church repairs[101] is particularly unreasonable.[102] In January 2004, the National Council for Human Rights (NCHR) was established and entrusted with protecting and improving the status of human rights, including religious freedom, issued its first report in March 2005. Although the Council did not give significant attention to issues of religious freedom, it submitted numerous requests to the Ministry of Interior requesting action on complaints it had received regarding church repair and construction.[103] In some cases, the lack of action over long years on requests for authorization to build or repair churches has amounted to arbitrary denial of permission.[104] Egyptian human rights advocates concur that, by clinging to the old Ottoman edict, the government fuels intolerance and, intentionally or not, sets the stage for anti-Christian violence by extremists, who have attacked churches and also violently halted unauthorized repair work.[105] Judge 'Ashmawy wrote that,

> [...] many Muslims, including myself, have asked the president for this situation to be changed, deeming that the spirit of Islam encourages tolerance for non-Muslims and upholds their right to build and maintain places of worship to practice their religion. I believe that Egypt and her government should reexam-

100 Ashmawy, "Constructing Places of Worship in Egypt," Middle East Times, February 28–March 6, 1994.

101 The requirement that presidential authorization is needed to carry out simple repairs on existing churches – such as painting windows, replacing floor tiles, or renovating bathrooms – appears to Ashmawy and others to be totally unreasonable.

102 Ashmawy, in a letter dated February 10, 1994, Human Rights Watch / Middle East requested copies of the Ottoman decree and the Ministry of Interior guidelines from the Ministry of Foreign Affairs.

103 See: Ibrahim, Saad Eddin, Egypt, Islam, and Democracy, Critical Essays The American University of Cairo Press, Cairo, 2002, 269 pp.

104 See: Civil and Political Rights, Including the Question of Religious Intolerance, Egypt, Paras. 117–121, E/CN.4/2006/5/Add.1, 27 March 2006.

105 "Freedom of Thought and Belief: Between the State's Anvil and the Islamic Groups' Hammer," speech opening EOHR's Third Intellectual Seminar on Freedom of Thought, Belief and Expression," Cairo, May 1–2, 1992.

ine the phenomenon of construction of places of worship and establish an equitable and modern law to regulate their licensing.[106]

This should be the case, especially since the right of private parties to construct and repair property, including religious institutions such as mosques and churches are protected by Article 26 of the ICCPR which sets forth this basic principle: All persons are equal before the law and are entitled without any discrimination to the equal protection of the law. In this respect, the law shall prohibit any discrimination and guarantee to all persons equal and effective protection against discrimination on any ground such as race, color, sex, language, religion, political or other opinion, national or social origin, property, birth or other status. The vastly different legal procedures applied in Egypt to mosque-building on the one hand, and church construction on the other hand, are inequitable and discriminatory in nature, and thus a violation of the spirit of Article 26. Moreover, the special rules that govern church construction and repair and the extremely long periods that some congregations have been forced to wait for presidential permission creates the inevitable suspicion that the state may be purposefully using such procedures to thwart the legal construction and repair of churches that serve Christian worshippers, abridging their right to worship in community with others. Egypt's obligations under international law require the state to guarantee all citizens the freedom to worship publicly in community with others (Article 18 of the ICCPR), and for religious minorities in particular to profess and practice their religion (Article 27 of the ICCPR).

In Saudi Arabia, the situation is more acute for religious minorities. The government prohibits public religious activities that are non-Islamic. Non-Muslim worshippers risk arrest, imprisonment, lashing, deportation, and sometimes torture for engaging in religious activity that attracts official attention.[107] The government officially does not permit non-Muslim clergy to enter the country to conduct religious

106 Ashmawy, in a letter dated February 10, 1994.

107 E/CN.4/2006/5/Add.1, Paras, 327–330, 70.

services, although some do so under other auspices and the government generally has allowed their performance of discreet religious functions. Proselytizing by non-Muslims, including the distribution of non-Muslim religious materials is illegal, and the promotion of non-Wahabbi Islam is restricted. Public worship of other religions is prohibited by law, and is regulated and punished by the state's Committee for the Propagation of Virtue and Prevention of Vice *(Mutawa'ee).*[108]

b. Muslim Minorities

In Egypt, members of other religions that are not recognized by the government, continue to experience personal and collective hardship. For example, the government does not recognize *the Baha'i faith,* and like sects in France, they experience personal and collective hardship. The Law 263 of 1960, which bans Baha'i institutions and community activities, is still enforced, as is a 1961 Presidential decree which stripped Baha'is of legal recognition. In 1997, a human rights activist filed a lawsuit seeking the removal of the religious affiliation category from government identification cards. The plaintiff challenged the constitutionality of a 1994 decree by the Ministry of Interior (MOI) governing the issuance of new identification cards. It had been alleged that the forms currently contain three religious affiliations to choose from: Islam, Christianity and Judaism and that it was impossible for members of other religious groups or non-believers to indicate their religion or leave the space blank.[109] This is contradictory to International human rights instruments specifically recognize ethnic, linguistic and religious minorities, and the distinct set of rights conferred on individuals be-

108 The religious police, known as al-Mutawa'een or Hay'at al-'Amr bil Ma'ruf wan-Nahi 'an al-Munkar, the Committee for the Propagation of Virtue and Prevention of Vice, are mandated to ensure strict adherence to established codes of conduct. They are in theory a semi-autonomous agency, but in practice work closely with the police and the governors of the localities. They have powers of arrest but are required to hand suspects over to the public security police after questioning them.

109 E/CN.4/2006/5/Add.1, 27 March 2006: Egypt, para. 117.

longing to such groups.[110] The U.N. Human Rights Committee made this clear in comments it adopted on April 6, 1994: "The terms used in [Article 27, ICCPR] indicate that the persons designed to be protected are those who belong to a group and who share in common a culture, a religion and/or a language."[111] The Human Rights Committee further noted that the existence of a minority in a country must be determined by objective criteria; a state cannot refuse to recognize a minority group if objective evidence establishes that such a group exists.[112]

In Saudi Arabia, on the other hand, most victims of religious persecution are Muslims. Though the government claims that it permits Shi'a Muslims to use their own version of Shari'a to adjudicate cases limited to family law, inheritance, and endowment management,[113] Shi'a and Isma'ili Muslim communities suffer officially sanctioned political and economic discrimination. Even in Saudi Arabia's Eastern Province, where Shi'a Muslims constitute a majority of the population, virtually no Shi'a is allowed to serve in positions of authority in government, judicial or educational institutions.[114] The government also discriminates against the Shi'a in higher education through unofficial restrictions on the number of Shi'a admitted to universities. Shi'a teachers are not permitted to teach certain courses in schools, such as history or religion, even in predominately Shi'a areas. Moreover, the government controls all mosques, even Sunni ones, and is the direct employer

110 For example, Article 27 of the International Covenant on Civil and Political Rights states: "In those States in which ethnic, religious or linguistic minorities exist, persons belonging to such minorities shall not be denied the right, in community with the other members of their group, to enjoy their own culture, to profess and practice their own religion, or to use their own language."

111 U.N. Human Rights Committee, "General Comment Adopted by the Human Rights Committee Under Article 40, Paragraph 4, of the International Covenant on Civil and Political Rights, Addendum, General comment No. 23(50) (art. 27)," CCPR/C/21/Rev.1/Add.5, April 26, 1994, 2.

112 Ibid.

113 See: AI Reports about Saudi Arabia such as: <http://www.amnestyusa.org/search/node/Saudi%20Arabia> (viewed Sept. 2013).

114 See: Human Rights Watch reports about Saudi Arabia Such as: <http://hrw.org/english/docs/2004/02/17/uzbeki7481.htm> (viewed Sept. 2013).

of imams. Furthermore, The Ministry of Islamic Affairs supervises and finances the construction and maintenance of almost all mosques in order to conform the teaching of the imams, with the Wahhabi interpretation of the Qur'an. A separate government committee defines the qualifications of imams. Sunni Islamic religious education is mandatory in public schools at all levels. Regardless of which Islamic tradition their families adhere to, all public school children receive religious instruction that conforms to the Wahhabi tradition of Islam. Non-Muslim students in private schools are not required to study Islam.

Discussion of religious issues in Saudi Arabia is also limited, and the government has placed temporary or permanent bans on some editors and writers of major local daily newspapers for publication of articles and cartoons critical of the religious establishment. Writers and other individuals who publicly criticized the official interpretation of Islam, including those who favor a more moderate interpretation than the government's view, risk Mutawwa'in sanctions, especially women and their headscarves.[115]

Egyptian law sets no code for clothing. Anyone can dress however he/she chooses. Today, while the *niqab*[116] remains relatively rare in most Muslim countries, the simple headscarf has made a stunning comeback in Egypt as an estimated 70 % to 80 % of Egyptian Muslim women wear a headscarf. This is contrary to the 1970s when headscarves were put on mainly by rural women. The Egyptian government does not encourage the wearing of headscarves or veils – worried they are a sign of Islamic extremism.[117] Many who call for restrictions on headscarf stem from a view that public exhibitions of religious commitment are a political, not a personal, act – and hence a potential threat to the government. While in the West the traditional Muslim dress is seen as a re-

115 E/CN.4/2006/5/Add.1, 27 March 2006, para. 331.

116 The biggest dispute has been over the niqab – a full facial veil that leaves only a slit for the eyes. It re-emerged in Egypt in the late 1980s and has since grown in popularity, both in the Arab world and among Arab Muslims in the West.

117 Nadia Abou El-Magd, In Egypt, renewed and fierce debate surrounds women and veils, Canadian Press, 2007.

fusal by Muslim immigrants to assimilate and accept Western's secular values, in the Arab world, the dispute centers on fears of growing Islamic extremism and concerns by secular governments, like Egypt, that they will lose ground to Islamic opposition groups.

In comparison with France, which requires Muslim women not to wear the headscarf and Egypt which encourages them not to wear it, the practice in Saudi Arabia requires women to identify themselves through the display of religious symbols, including religious headscarf in public. Women in Saudi Arabia can be harassed by religious police, supported by the government, if they do not. Despite that, more women have stopped wearing the face veil in parts of the country. The obligation to wear religious dress in public in certain countries was particularly criticized by Special Rapporteur Amor, who stated that "women are among those who suffer most because of severe restrictions on their education and employment, and the obligation to wear what is described as Islamic dress."[118] There were reports of punishment by whipping and/or a fine[119] and a growing number of women being attacked in the streets,[120] for failing to wear religious symbols.[121]

The general rule in many Muslim states is to dress decently; this does not imply that women be subject to strictly enforced codes of

118 Report submitted by Mr. Abdelfattah Amor, Special Rapporteur, in accordance with Commission on Human Rights resolution 1996/23, Implementation of the Declaration on the Elimination of All Forms of Intolerance and of Discrimination based on Religion or Belief (E/CN.4/1998/6, para. 60).

119 Note by the Secretary-General, Human Rights Questions: Human Rights Questions, Including Alternative Approaches for Improving the Effective Enjoyment of Human Rights and Fundamental Freedoms: Implementation of the Declaration on the Elimination of all Forms of Religious Intolerance and of Discrimination Based on Religion or Belief, A/51/542/Add.2, para. 51.

120 Civil and Political Right, Including the Question of Religious Intolerance, Report by Mr. abdelfattah Amor, Special Rapporteur on Freedom of Religion or Belief, submitted pursuant to Commission on Human Rights resolution 2002/40, (E/CN.4/2003/66/Add.1, para. 59.

121 Report by Mr. Abdelfattah Amor, Special Rapporteur on Freedom of Religion or Belief, in accordance with Commission on Human Rights resolution 1994/18, E/CN.4/1995/91, 36.

dress which provide that in public a woman must always cover her head and face. 'Ashmawy notes that

> Islam recommends that women and girls dress decently, but does not insist that women and girls of the twentieth century don the veil. They may wear the veil, if they so choose, but should in no way be threatened or intimidated into wearing it.[122]

In his book, 'The Responsibility for the Failure of the Islamic State', Al-Banna suggests different ways for Muslim women to integrate into societies including making the headscarf more modern and fashionable and at the same time protect women's modesty.[123]

The essence of the concept of freedom of religion is the right to entertain such religious beliefs as a person chooses the right to declare religious beliefs openly and without fear of hindrance or reprisal, and the right to manifest belief by worship and practice or by teaching and dissemination. But the concept means more than that. Freedom in a broad sense embraces both the absence of coercion and constraint, and the right to manifest beliefs and practices. Freedom means that, subject to such limitations as are necessary to protect public safety, order, health, or morals or the fundamental rights and freedoms of others, no one is to be forced to act in a way contrary to his beliefs or his conscience. It is important to note that, "dress should not be the subject of political regulation,"[124] but at the same time it has to be emphasized that "traditions and customs were worthy of respect."[125]

The history of Islam is not one of a degrading treatment of women. On the contrary, the Qur'an devotes considerable attention to women. In fact, the advent of Islam meant a significant improvement of the

122 Fluehr-Lobban, *The Writings of Ashmawy*, 107–108.

123 Al-Banna Gamal, *The Hijab*, offers a complete study of the issue of the head cover and the veil is found and can be downloaded (in Arabic) from Gamal al-Banna's website <http://www.islamiccall.org>.

124 Report by Mr. Abdelfattah Amor, Special Rapporteur on Freedom of Religion or Belief, in accordance with Commission on Human Rights resolution 1995/23, E/CN.4/1996/95/Add.2, para. 97 and A/51/542/Add.2, para. 140).

125 Ibid.

conditions for women in pre-historic Arabia, enhancing their rights and status. The Qur'an introduced reforms such as the prohibition of female infanticide, which earlier was a considerable problem. It permitted women to inherit, restricted the practice of polygamy and gave women ownership of the dowry, which earlier had been paid to the bride's father. Not only did the Qur'an abolish previous traditions discriminating against women, but it also conferred to women in the seventh century rights that women in the West didn't obtain until recently. Muslim women already at Mohammed's time enjoyed full legal personality, could own and manage property. Contemporary Muslim reformists often argue that it isn't reasonable that a religion which in the beginning aimed to end the suffering of women in prehistoric Arabia, in later interpretations and traditions has been used as a mean to relegate women to an inferior status.

Muslim women, in the Western and Muslim states, should have the right to make their own choices in wearing the headscarf or not. It is not for the state to decide how a Muslim woman ought to practice and observe her religion and what is and what is not a genuine religious belief. Such interference will be unwarranted infringement on the right to religious practice and observance. In reality, however, for most women who cover their hair, in their conviction it's simply a matter of bowing to the will of God.

2.4.2.2 Religious Minorities in Islam

According to some interpretations of Islam, it may seem difficult for non-Muslims to obtain the exact same rights as Muslims in an Islamic society, if traditional Shar'ia rules were to be applied. Therefore, the rights of non-Muslims are often mentioned as a problem area in the human rights discourse.[126] Non-Muslim minorities in Islam can be separated into two categories: people of the book, (*ahl al-Kitáb:* Jews, Christians and Zoroastrians) and other religious minorities. The people

126 An-Naim, "Islamic Foundations of Religious Human Rights," 346.

of the book have always been allowed to keep practicing their religion, without interference, under a certain protection, the so called *dhimmi*, as long as they pay a poll tax called *jizya*. One writer holds that "according to *Shari'a*, pantheists, pagans, and nonbelievers have no rights. In short, they have the options of conversion or death."[127]

Many frequently cite the Qur'anic verse that states:

> *O ye who believe! take not the Jews and the Christians for your friends and protectors: They are but friends and protectors to each other. And he amongst you that turns to them (for friendship) is of them. Verily Allah guideth not a people unjust.*

Qur'an 5:51, as justifying an essentially superiority view towards non-Muslims, traditional views often quote the following Qur'anic injunction. Moreover, many see the verse:

> *Fight those who believe not in Allah nor the Last Day, nor hold that forbidden which hath been forbidden by Allah and His Messenger, nor acknowledge the religion of Truth, (even if they are) of the People of the Book, until they pay the Jizya with willing submission, and feel themselves subdued.*

Qur'an 9:29, as an Islamic duty to be in a state of war with all non-Muslims, except if they pay the *jizyah (poll tax imposed on non-Muslims)*.

Thus, Muslims, according to one interpretation, are required not to befriend or share the normative values of non-Muslims. They read these verses, as pointed by Abou El Fadel, and similar Qur'anic verses, "literally and ahistorically, and therefore reach highly exclusionary conclusions."

According to the traditional view, these verses, many name them the verses of the sword, impose certain obligations on non-Muslims and certain other obligations on Muslims. Some of these obligations are:

1. *Jizyah* imposed on non-Muslims.
2. Muslims have to be in Jihad against non-Muslims
3. Islamic states are only for Muslims

127 Ghanea, Nazila, 'Human Rights of Religious Minorities and of Women in the Middle East' *Human Rights Quarterly* 26.3 (2004), 716.

a. Poll Tax (Jizyah) Imposed on Non-Muslims

The *jizyah* is imposed on the people of the book (Christians and Jews) who live in Muslim territories. When the Qur'an was revealed, it was common, inside and outside of Arabia, to levy poll taxes against alien groups. Building upon this historical practice, classical Muslim jurists have argued that the poll tax is money collected by the Islamic polity from non-Muslims in return for the protection in the Muslim state and for avoidance of any military service. They therefore released from its imposition, women, children, the sick and the handicapped persons as well as priests. Moreover, if the Muslim state was incapable of extending such protection to non-Muslims, it was not supposed to levy a poll tax. In fact, 'Umar' the second Rightly-Guided Caliph and close companion of the Prophet, returned the *jizyah* to an Arab Christian tribe that he was incapable of protecting from Byzantine aggression. They even went further to consider the right of the poor and the needy among non-Muslims; giving them a share of the stipulated *zakat*, which is paid by Muslims alone.

Abou Al Fadel observes that it is important to pay

> [...] attention to historical circumstance [...], especially that the Prophet did not collect a poll tax from every non-Muslim tribe that submitted to Muslim sovereignty, and in fact, in the case of a large number of non-Muslim but non-hostile tribes, he paid them a periodic sum of money or goods.[128]

An-Na'im affirms that,

> There are various indicators that the *jizyah* is not a theologically mandated practice, but a functional solution that was adopted in response to a specific set of historical circumstances. Only an entirely ahistorical reading of the text could conclude that it is an essential element in a Divinely-sanctioned program of subordinating the non-believer.[129]

128 Abou Al Fadel, *The Place of Tolerance in Islam.*

129 Abdullahi A. An-Na'im *Toward An Islamic Reformation: Civil Liberties, Human rights, and International Law*, Syracuse University Press, New York, 1990, 7–8, 74.

Now Muslims live in a world of nation-states, constitutionalism, and international law, and every state imposes taxes on its subjects in order to finance its budget and provide services that the public expects of the state, such as road, infrastructure, hospitals and free education. Therefore, today taxes can be interpreted to support equal citizenship for Muslims and non-Muslims.

The reformists, as it has been mentioned, emphasized the importance of not following exclusionary and intolerant theology by reading Qur'anic verses in isolation, as if the meaning of the verses were transparent; as if moral ideas and historical context were irrelevant to their interpretation. It is impossible to analyze these and other verses, excerpt in light of the overall moral thrust of the Qur'anic message. The Qur'an itself refers to general moral imperatives such as mercy, justice, kindness, and goodness. In a further example, as to justice, the Qur'an states:

> *O ye who believe! stand out firmly for justice, as witnesses to Allah, even as against yourselves, or your parents, or your kin, and whether it be (against) rich or poor: for Allah can best protect both. Follow not the lusts (of your hearts), lest ye swerve, and if ye distort (justice) or decline to do justice, verily Allah is well-acquainted with all that ye do.*

Qur'an 4:135 Abou El Fadel notes that

> Muslims must stand up for justice even against their own self-interests is predicated on the notion that human beings are capable of achieving a high level of moral agency. Moreover, justice in Islam is the basis for belief and all Muslims are required to do justice in every aspect of their life and to all human beings with no difference to gender or religion…[130]

Abu Zaid affirms this by explaining that "the cornerstone of the Qur'anic concept of justice is to be found in the passages where justice is presented as Divine stipulation ordained by God. The example to be analyzed is verse 16:90, *Allah commands justice, the doing of good, and liberality to kith and kin, and He forbids all shameful deeds, and injustice and rebellion: He instructs you, that ye may receive admonition.*

130 Abou El Fadl, Khaled, *The Place of Tolerance in Islam.*

Here, justice is associated with *ihsan*, which means doing the utmost possible good and fine human behavior towards the self as well as towards others." Abu Zaid points out that "in this verse the order to do justice and to do the best is not addressed to any addressee not to man nor to the believers, as is the case in other verses."[131]

As agents, Muslims are expected to achieve a level of moral conscientiousness, which they will bring to their relationship with God. With regards to every ethical obligation, the Qur'anic text assumes that readers will bring a pre-existing, innate moral sense to the text. Hence, the text will morally enrich the reader, but only if the reader will morally enrich the text. The meaning of the religious text is not fixed simply by the literal meaning of its words, but depends, too, on the moral construction given to it by the reader. So if the reader approaches the text without moral commitments, it will almost inevitably yield nothing but discrete, legalistic, technical insights. Similarly, it is imperative to analyze the historical circumstances in which specific Qur'anic ethical norms were negotiated. Many of the institutions referenced in the Qur'an, such as the poll tax or the formation of alliances with non-Muslims, can be understood only if the reader is aware of the historical practices surrounding the revelation of the text. By emptying the Qur'an both of its historical and moral contexts, the traditionalist trend ends up transforming the text into a long list of morally non-committal legal commands.

Moreover, the Qur'anic texts can readily support an ethic of diversity and tolerance. The Qur'an not only expects, but even accepts the reality of difference and diversity within human society:

> *O mankind! We created you from a single (pair) of a male and a female, and made you into nations and tribes, that ye may know each other (not that ye may despise (each other). Verily the most honoured of you in the sight of Allah is (he who is) the most righteous of you. And Allah has full knowledge and is well acquainted (with all things)* Qur'an 49:13.

Elsewhere, the Qur'an asserts that diversity is part of the Divine intent and purpose in creation: "*If thy Lord had willed, He would have made*

131 Nasr Hamid Abu Zayd, *The Qur'anic Concept of Justice.*

humankind into a single nation, but they will not cease to be diverse [...]. And, for this God created them [humankind]."[132]

It is fair to say that Islam is pluralistic and unusually tolerant of various social and religious denominations compared to structure of many of the other religions and beliefs at that time. Historically, Islam has displayed a remarkable ability to recognize possibilities of tolerance, and to act upon these possibilities. Islam has produced a moral and humanistic tradition that preserved Greek philosophy and generated much science, art, and socially benevolent thought. Unfortunately, however, many today are dissipating and wasting this inspiring moral tradition. They are increasingly shutting off the possibilities for a tolerant interpretation of Islam.

b. Jihad against Non-Muslims

The challenge that is most often invoked against Islam is the issue of *jihad*. It is often associated with the idea of a holy war that is propagated in the name of God against the unbelievers. Therefore, *jihad* is often equated with the most unpleasant images of religious intolerance. It is the most sensitive word in the Islamic vocabulary. It is always used, heard and understood in a very emotional way, either positive or negative. To non-Muslims, *jihad* is a holy war against them, a raised sword not easily sheathed. To many Muslims, *jihad* is the religious duty to guide non-Muslims peoples to the right and true faith. Militants believe *jihad* is a divine precept to protect and impose Islam, the ultimate faith, on non-Muslims.[133] They always forget that God stated clearly that HE does not need any one to protect the Qur'an as stated in Surat Al Hejr, [15:9].

We have sent the Message and we shall preserve it.

132 *Qur'an* 11: 118–9 "If thy Lord had so willed, He could have made mankind one people: but they will not cease to dispute. Except those on whom thy Lord hath bestowed His Mercy: and for this did He create them [...]."

133 Fluehr-Lobban, The writings of Ashmawy, 112.

Moreover, jihad in the Qur'an and in the prophetic traditions means self-control and self-refinement. This meaning of the word is reported to have been described by the Prophet Mohammed himself as 'the great *jihad*.' In terms of war, *jihad* is only to be implemented as an act of self-defense alone. In this sense, the most significant and most important *jihad* is continual in life. It is based on the ethical, moral and spiritual *jihad*. 'Ashmawy defines the elements of this aspect as:

> This *jihad* is a struggle, a strenuous effort, or series of efforts, to discipline oneself against greed, avarice, cowardice, fear, tyranny, ignorance, submission to negative elements, yielding to evil desires and giving way to passion. This *jihad* avoids a meaningless existence and an empty, if not easy and comfortable, life.[134]

If *jihad* is interpreted as more than this, 'Ashmawy explains

> [i]t is then not *jihad* but aggression – which has been forbidden by the verses and the very spirit of the Qur'an. As *jihad* is not one of the five pillars of Islam, the one-sided stress placed on 'holy wars' and fighting is a historical distortion of the real concept of *jihad* and is due to political interests.

Moreover, he adds that

> [...] this is the view of a radical... interpretation of the Qur'an and the consequential message: Islam is seen by the militants as the sole, valid and complete faith, abrogating all other faiths. It follows from this that all non-Muslims are infidels and should be converted to Islam, even by force *(jihad)*.[135]

In order to gain legitimacy, Abd Al-Sabour Tantawi points out that

> [...] the extremists use two methods. First, they take the Qur'anic verses out of context and interpret them without connection to the context in which they

134 Mohamed Said Al-Ashmawy; Maalem Al-Islam (Features of Islam); Sina for publication; first edition; Cairo 1989. Mohamed Said Al-Ashmawi, *Usūl al-Shari'a (Roots of Islamic law)*, Sina for publication, Cairo, 1992.

135 See: Muhammad Said Al -Ashmawi, Carolyn Fluehr-Lobban, Against Islamic Extremism: Publisher: University Press of Florida, Gainesville, FL. Publication Year: 1998, 112–18.

appeared. Second, they find in the Sunna and in the books of the Ahadith, material legitimizing (Jihad as a holy war).[136]

In his discussion of the issue of *jihad*, Abd Al-Sabour Tantawi explains that the warlike verses revealed to the Prophet in Al-Madina do not abrogate the verses of tolerance revealed in Mecca, and that the Prophet's *jihad* was not a religious war to spread Islam but a war to defend the rights of the oppressed and weak:

> Whoever reads the verses of war and *jihad* in their full context in the Qur'an, [...] without truncating the verses [...] knows for sure that the Prophet's wars...were not religious wars at all, and were not for the sake of spreading the religion, but were aimed at restoring stolen rights, and stopping the tortures of the weak that were aimed at dissuading them from adopting Islam [...][137]

Thus, in the initial Meccan phase of the Qur'anic revelation (610–622 C.E.) the word jihad was used in an ethical, moral and spiritual sense. Initially, *jihad* meant to maintain one's faith and serenity in the midst of adverse conditions.

In the Meccan period, the Prophet was told, through revelation, to be patient with the Meccans, to suffer quietly, and not meet force with force.[138] However, the Meccans continued to persecute the new Muslim community. The Prophet and the new Muslim community were forced to migrate to Medina. In the Medinan phase of the Qur'anic revelation (622–632 C.E.), and because of the circumstances of the period, the initial spiritual meaning of *jihad*, striving and struggle, gave around to the new material meaning, to struggle against evil and harmful aggression of the people of Mecca. Since the first war *(Bader)*, which began when the Meccans prepared an army of a thousands men to fight against three hundred Muslims, the word *jihad* came to include the struggle of the individual or the community with

136 Dankowitz, A., Egyptian Sheikh Dr. Abd Al-Sabour Tantawi – Islamic Reformist: A Religious and Intellectual Profile, MEMRI, No. 287, 13 July 2006.

137 Ibid.

138 Sura 88:22, Sura 70:5, Sura 29:18, Sura 103:3.

the Meccan. But, the Qur'anic verses stipulate the conditions and limit the fighting: *Fight in the cause of God those who fight you, but do not transgress limits; for God loveth not transgressors* (Sura 2:190.)[139] Ashmawy summarizes the meaning of *jihad* according to the Qur'anic definition and notes that:

> Jihad in its authentic religious meaning is a strong effort or series of efforts against negative or unjust behaviour or unjust conditions in order to keep one's faith strong and one's conscience and then to establish justice and mercy in the community through the individuals and the collective conscience. In its historically determined political meaning, jihad is self defence and nothing more. It is not aggression, hostility or confrontation [...]. Islam is not a nationality, it is a religion and it is not a state for some people but a path of mercy for all people; not an empire for powerful rulers, but a faith for humankind.[140]

So the reformation of Islam must be based on a return to the Meccan message in order to reconcile the Mecca and Medina messages into a single system. The problem, as pointed before, started when Muslim jurists declared that some of the Medina verses have abrogated the corresponding earlier verses from Mecca. Abrogation *(al-nasikh)*, thus, is the method when certain verses of the Qur'an are used to over-rule prior verses. Some Muslim jurists made a comparison of the earliest text of law from the Prophet's time in Mecca with the later laws established in Medina. Any laws from Mecca that appeared to be inconsistent with those in Medina were argued to have been repealed or abrogated to the latter in the legal definitions and interpretations. As the Mecca verses remained within the Qur'an, they were still revered by Muslims and held to represent ethical standards, but for the jurist, these verses were with no weight nor were they legally binding. Many Muslim jurists concluded that this was the situation to be maintained in *Shari'a*.

139 Fluehr-Lobban, The Writings of Ashemawy, 114–9.
140 Ibid.

Mahmoud Taha[141] criticized this view and pointed out that

> Islam in Mecca was presented in terms of freedom of choice *(ismah)* and each individual having the personal responsibility for making that choice. This argument is based on various verses within the Qur'an that also promote the view of personal responsibility for freedom of choice.[142]

In Medina, the various Qur'anic verses were more concerned in building the state and defending aggression from the tribes living in Mecca.[143] Taha's main argument was that the idea of the abrogation of the original Meccan Qur'anic verses was purely a temporary suspension until the appropriate context in the future would allow them to be clearly valid for implementation and enforcement. He based this view on the idea that 'abrogation' should be supported by the rationale supporting it, including the socio-economic and political circumstances within the Arabian region at the time of their revelation. Taha acknowledged that,

> [...] through time, the conditions of societies change and develop; thus, *Shari'a* was established in a way that in modern days, it would be able to respond by deeming the Qur'anic verses of freedom of choice and personal responsibility as authentic and valid. This would uphold the principles of freedom and equality, which would be the basis of modern day *Shari'a*.[144]

141 See: the thinking of Mahmood Tah in O'Sullivan, Declan, The Death Sentence for Mahmoud Muhammad Taha: Misuse of the Sudanese Legal System and Islamic Shari'aa Law? <http://www.alfikra.org/>. Taha developed his concept of understanding Islam and the idea of the Islamic revival through the evolution of certain aspects within Shari'a. He maintained these ideas once released from prison in 1948, while basing his thought pattern on the personal worship practices of the Prophet Muhammad. In the preface of Taha's work, The Second Message of Islam, translated by Abdullahi Ahmed An-Na'im. He eventually achieved a comprehensive understanding of universal Islamic ideology and continued to maintain this position until he was publicly hung in execution on 18 January 1985.

142 Such verses Surah *An-Nahl* 16, verse 125, Surah *Al-Khaf* 18, verse 29 and Surah *Al-Hujurat* 49, verse 13.

143 O'Sullivan, Declan, 'The Death Sentence for Mahmoud Muhammad Taha: Misuse of the Sudanese Legal System and Islamic Shari'aa Law?' <http://www.alfikra.org/article_page_view_e.php?article_id=35&page_id=1> (viewed Sept. 2013).

144 An-Na'im, 'The Islamic Law of Apostasy' (note 2), 205.

There is no mention of abrogation as a tool of interpretation in any document prior to the first century of Islam. This practice is perhaps the most dangerous because it was used to replace moderate general principles of Islam for more specific stringent ones and gave rulers access to modify Islam by suspending substantial parts of the Qur'anic text. In a separate article devoted to the principle of *al-nasikh wa'l-mansukh*, Abd Al-Sabour Tantawi argues that this "method of interpretation is another tool devised by the *ulama* to enable them to play with the Qur'anic verses in accordance with their own biases, tendencies, views, and personal interests."[145]

Although the abrogation did take place and it was logical and valid jurisprudence at one time, it was a postponement, not a permanent abrogation. If we accept the process as a permanent abrogation, notes An'Naim, "we will have lost the best part of our religion-the most humane and the most universal, egalitarian aspects."[146] The Mecca verses, thus, should now be made the basis of the law not the Medina ones. This will result in the total reconciliation between Islamic law and the modern development of human rights and civil liberties. In this sense, comments An'Naim, "we reformers are super fundamentalists. The key to our reformation will be a positive and receptive attitude toward the totality of the human experience. What we find to be consistent with our fundamental principles, we accept, whatever the source."[147]

Islam, hence, does not have a notion of holy war. As was mentioned, *jihad* simply means to strive hard or struggle in pursuit of a just cause, and according to the Prophet, the highest form of jihad is the struggle waged to cleanse oneself from the vices of the heart. Holy war (in Arabic – *al-harb al-muqaddasah*) is not an expression used by the Qur'anic text or Muslim theologians. In Islamic theology, war is never *holy*; it is either justified or not. The Qur'anic text does not recognize the idea of unlimited warfare, and does not consider the simple fact of the belligerent's Muslim identity to be sufficient to establish the just-

145 Metransparent.com, April 13, 2006.

146 An-Na'im, 'The Islamic Law of Apostasy' (note 2), 205.

147 Ibid.

ness of his cause. In other words, the Qur'an entertains the possibility that the Muslim combatant might be the unjust party in a conflict. Moreover, while the Qur'an emphasizes that Muslims may fight those who fight them, it also insists that Muslims may not transgress.[148] Muslims must be constrained by a requirement of proportionality, even when the cause is just. For instance, it states, *"Mandated is the law of equality, so that who transgresses against you, respond in kind, and fear God, and know that God is with those who exercise restraint."*[149]

The verses that are used to prove the intolerance of Islam such as:

- Verse 5:33 *"The punishment of those who wage war against Allah and His Messenger, and strive with might and main for mischief through the land is: execution, or crucifixion, or the cutting off of hands and feet from opposite sides, or exile from the land: that is their disgrace in this world, and a heavy punishment is theirs in the Hereafter; [...]"*, refers specifically to those who are engaged in fighting and 'mischief through the land' and there is no indication that this verse has anything to do with belief. Shawkani explains that "this verse applies to anyone who commits the crimes spelt out in it, be the person a Muslim or an unbeliever."[150] The focus here is the crime against life and property and has nothing to do with a person's belief.

148 *Qur'an* 2:190 "Fight in the cause of Allah those who fight you, but do not transgress limits; for Allah loveth not transgressors." Qura'n 5:2 "[...] But when ye are clear of the sacred precincts and of pilgrim garb, ye may hunt and let not the hatred of some people in (once) shutting you out of the Sacred Mosque lead you to transgression (and hostility on your part). Help ye one another in righteousness and piety, but help ye not one another in sin and rancour: fear Allah: for Allah is strict in punishment."

149 *Qur'an* 2:194 "The prohibited month for the prohibited month, – and so for all things prohibited, – there is the law of equality. If then any one transgresses the prohibition against you, Transgress ye likewise against him. But fear Allah, and know that Allah is with those who restrain themselves."

150 Muhammad b. Ali al-shawkani, Fath al-Qadir: al-Jami bayna Fannay al-Riwayah wa al-Dirayah min Ilm al-Tafsir, vol. 2, Beirut: Dar al-Marifah, (between 1980 and 1993), 438. In Saeed, Freedom of Religion, Apostasy and Islam, 58.

- Contrary to popular belief, "the verses in the Surah (9) of Repentance (al-Tawbah), which took a particular hard line against number of groups, were not aimed at non-Muslims who were at peace with the prophet, but it was aimed at those who were demonstrably in a constant struggle to dominate Islam."[151] These verses appear rather to have been in response to political and security demands of the community. So, these verses were revealed in the context of encouraging Muslims to fight those:

  i. who renegade on their promises of non-aggression
  ii. who violate the terms of the treaties concluded with the Prophet.

The Qur'an insists that Muslims maintain their peace agreements with various groups, as long as the groups keep their side of the bargain. The notion of peace is fundamental to Islamic law and religion. It is present in the salutation exchanged between Muslims at each meeting: *salaam 'alaikum* (peace be upon you). A peace greeting is repeated twice at the end of each of Muslims' five daily prayers. The very word "Islam" shares its root with the word for "peace" in Arabic,[152] and peace is one of the ninety-nine attributes of *Allah*. There are over one hundred Qur'anic verses discussing the importance of peace. This ever-presence of peace in Islam led Professor Mohammed Yessef to state: "The alpha and omega of Islam is peace."[153] Peace in Islam manifests itself in different ways and on different levels, all the way from simple daily acts such as greetings, to kind offerings of food, to financial assistance and charity, to peace on a global scale.[154] According to Al Jirari, "Islam considers that

151 Saeed Abdullah & Saeed Hassan; *Freedom of Religion, Aposasy and Islam*, Ashgate Publishing Limited, England, 2004, 77–78. See also Abdel Sabour tantawi, Al-nasikh wa'l-mansukh between the Fatwas of Bin Baz and the rationality of the zakaria boutros, part I, 13 April, 2006. <http://www.metransparent.com/texts/nehru_tantawi_bin_baz_and_zakaria_boutros_1.htm> (viewed Sept. 2013).

152 Idris Alaoui Abdallaoui, *The Bases of Neighbourliness in Islam,* 1990, 217, 224. In Foster, Third Generation, 95.

153 Mohammed Yessef, *Foundations of Peace and Security in Islam,* 1996, 224. In Foster, Third Generation, 95.

154 Ibid, 222–24.

the basic attitude of man is his inclination toward peace, and that recourse to war occurs only in absolutely necessary situations."[155] Interpreting holy struggle *(jihad)* as recourse to war in the solitary case of self defense makes it the functional equivalent of Article 51 of the UN Charter,[156] a fundamental component of the international understanding of peace and security.[157]

However, despite the prohibition against transgression and the condemnation of unlimited warfare, many classical jurists adopted an imperialist orientation, which divided the world into the abode of Islam and the abode of war. This view was not unanimous, however. Classical Muslim jurists debated whether unbelief is a sufficient justification for warfare, with a sizable number of classical jurists arguing that non-Muslims may not be fought unless they pose a physical threat to Muslims. If non-Muslims seek peace, Muslims should make an effort to achieve such a peace.[158] The Qur'an pronounces a stronger mandate in favor of peace in stating Qur'an 8:61: *"But if the enemy incline towards peace, do thou (also) incline towards peace, and trust in Allah: for He is One that heareth and knoweth (all things)."* Moreover, the Qur'an instructs Muslims not to haughtily turn away unbelievers who seek to make peace with Muslims, and reminds Muslims that,

> *Except those who join a group between whom and you there is a treaty (of peace), or those who approach you with hearts restraining them from fighting you as well as fighting their own people. If Allah had pleased, He could have given them power over you, and they would have fought you: Therefore if they withdraw from you but fight you not, and (instead) send you (Guarantees of) peace, then Allah Hath opened no way for you (to war against them).*[159]

155 Abbas Al Jirari, *The Concept of Coexistence in Islam* (1996) at 43. In Foster, Third Generation, 96.
156 Ibid.
157 Foster, Third Generation, 97.
158 *Qur'an* 60:9 "Allah only forbids you, with regard to those who fight you for (your) Faith, and drive you out of your homes, and support (others) in driving you out, from turning to them (for friendship and protection). It is such as turn to them (in these circumstances), that do wrong."
159 *Qur'an* 4:90.

Abou El Fadl argues: "These discussions of peace would not make sense if Muslims were in a permanent state of war with non-believers, and if non-believers were a permanent enemy and always a legitimate target."[160] Abu Zaid affirms that "equality, in Islam, between all human, regardless of any differences is essentially guaranteed unless a state of war is initiated against Muslims."[161]

The Qur'an instructs the Prophet how to deal peacefully, not only with people of the book, but also with the non-believer in verse 109: 1–6:

> Say: O ye that reject Faith!
> I worship not that which ye worship,
> Nor will ye worship that which I worship.
> And I will not worship that which ye have been wont to worship,
> Nor will ye worship that which I worship.
> To you be your Way, and to me mine.

The Qur'an, as has been mentioned, recognizes the diversity of religions and beliefs and the Qur'an calls for people to come together and to know one another despite this diversity (verse 49:13). According to Qur'anic teaching, non-Muslims living in Muslim territories should have the freedom to follow their own faith-traditions without fear or harassment. The invocation of Islamic ethical injunctions against violence is very important, and there is no scarcity of authority in this respect.

> *[...] if any one slew a person – unless it be for murder or for spreading mischief in the land – it would be as if he slew the whole people: and if any one saved a life, it would be as if he saved the life of the whole people. Then although there came to them Our messengers with clear signs, yet, even after that, many of them continued to commit excesses in the land.* (Qur'an, 5:32).[162]

160 See, Abou El Fadl Khaled, *The Place of Tolerance in Islam.*

161 Nasr Hamid Abu Zayd, The *Qur'anic Concept of Justice.*

162 Amyn B. Sajoo, The Ethics of the Public Square, A Preliminary Muslim Critique polylog. Forum für interkulturelle Philosophie e.V., available online: <http://them.polylog.org/3/asa-en.htm> (viewed Sept. 2013).

The social ethos of

> [...] inclusiveness, compassion and reason is captured in the concept of *hilm*, which deems a dominant feature of the Qur'anic text: The constant exhortation to kindness *(ihsan)* in human relations, the emphasis laid on justice *('adl)*, the forbidding of wrongful violence *(zulm)*, the bidding of abstinence and control of passions, the criticism of groundless pride and arrogance all are concrete manifestations of this spirit of *hilm.*[163]

It is an attribute that derives from the 'traits' of God, and becomes the highest aspiration of the community at large. It also counters the thrust of those inclined to resort to self-serving, decontextualized quotation from scripture and Prophetic tradition in support of political agendas.[164]

c. The Islamic State

Al-Banna, in his book 'The Responsibility for the Failure of the Islamic Nation in the Modern Age',[165] pointed to the difficulties of making the Islamic state a goal. The Hadith about the "Medina State" is, according to Al-Banna, concerned with the exception and not the rule, in addition to the fact that the creation of this state was not on the basis of doctrine, but came as a natural development required by religious circumstances when Quraish[166] conspired against the Prophet and that forced Muslims to immigrate to Medina. Al-Banna, also argues that

> [...] the Medina should not also be taken as an example since it did not have taxes, and there is no country in the modern age that does not have taxes. This

163 T. Izutsu (1964): God and Man in the Quran: Semantics of the Qur'anic Weltanschauung (Tokyo: Keio Institute of Cultural and Linguistic Studies), at 216. In Amyn B. Sajoo, The Ethics of the Public Square.

164 Mohammad Azadpur, 'Interpreting Political Violence in Islamic Philosophy'. Available at: <http://them.polylog.org/5/fam-en.htm> (viewed Sept. 2013).

165 See: Gamal al-Banna, "The Responsibility for the Failure of the Islamic Nation in the Modern Age", 1994.

166 It was the dominant tribe of Mecca. It was both the tribe to which the Prophet Mohammed (PBUH) belonged and his chief antagonist in the Quraish Muslim Wars.

state, therefore, cannot be taken as a standard. More importantly, this state was headed by a Prophet receiving his message (the *Wahi,*) directly from God and none of those calling for an Islamic state have that quality.[167]

Al-Banna pointed to the fact that making the Islamic state a goal to try to achieve so that all people would worship Allah, is an unimaginable thing. The state, according to Al-Banna, is a tool of submission and authority, and therefore when a state is created on religious values, whether Muslim or Christian, or moral values such as socialism and justice and equality, it would corrupt these values. This is because once authority, with its prisons and armies and police, comes into doctrine, it ruins it. He proved this by talking about the corruption of doctrine once authority comes into the picture, since the Islamic "Khelafa", turned into a contemptuous monarchy since Mu'awiya's reign in year 40 of the Hijra.

The reasons vary for the failure of the examples of an Islamic state. One reason, according to Gamal Al-Banna, may be that these trials did not maintain the minimum level of human dignity in their societies without discrimination between men and women or white and black. Another reason concerning the failure of the Islamic state in its different trials is overlooking the most important job of a state which is development.

However, the most important of these reasons, in his view, may be the lack of freedoms in all these trials since the lack of freedom may be the common factor of all these experiences.[168] In this sense, the most important aspect in the Muslim states is to build the state on the essence of Islam which, as mentioned before, is based on justice, mercy, moderation, knowledge, development, rationality and equality. Injustice and inequality to the people, whatever their religion, were not from the Qur'an.

167 Gamal al-Banna, "The Responsibility for the Failure of the Islamic Nation in the Modern Age", 1994. In Dr. Mahmoud Ismail, the founder of the Encyclopedia of the Sociology of Islamic Thought, in his discussion of Al-Banna's work, expresses that Cairo institute for human rights studies (2005), Ibin Roshd Salon: Why Did theIslamic State Fail in the Modern Age? Available at: <http://www.cihrs.org/?p=807&lang=en> (viewed Sept. 2013).

168 Ibid.

Thus, reformation is needed in Islamic theology after long ages of weakness that has stretched from the sixth *hijri* century, until the present day. Islam does not specify any principles for the establishment of an Islamic state, except the principal of counsellorship *(shura)* without any mention of the way the reign should be, and if this principle was truthfully applied without using religion for political authorative causes, solutions can be reached for many of the region problems in a way that would please the majority.[169]

2.4.3 Authoritarian Regimes in Saudi Arabia and Egypt

Egypt has been in a state of emergency since the assassination of President Anwar Sadat in October 1981. Since then, emergency law has been enforced due to the perceived need for punishing terrorists. In 2006, Egypt's parliament approved the renewal of the state of emergency for two years; a controversial measure. The country's premier, Ahmad Nazif, told the People's Assembly that it was "justified with a recent wave of bombings and communal clashes. The sectarian incidents and terrorist operations Egypt has witnessed recently have led us to ask for the extension as of June 1, 2006."[170] For many years now the Egyptian government has used terrorism as a pretext for renewing this state of emergency. The government also invokes the events of 11th September, 2001, to claim that without the proper measures terrorist activity could spread to Egypt. This justification is politically and legally untenable, as was the government use of the Anglo-American War in Iraq as a justification for renewing the state of emergency early.[171] In his speech, Mubarak stressed that terrorism was the only target of the emergency laws. Their implementation, he said, "had to

169 Dr. Mahmoud Ismail, in his discussion of al-Banna's work.

170 Daily Star Egypt, April 29, 2006.

171 The Egyptian Organization on Human Rights, The Situation of Human Rights in Egypt Annual Report 2003, Cairo, Egypt, 2004.

a great extent limited terrorist acts and led to the abortion of several terror plots."[172]

However, what constitutes a state of emergency in Egypt has not been defined. The government has used this lack of clarity to suppress human rights. They have established special courts where the accused cannot receive all of the constitutional protections of the civilian judicial system. The state of emergency also gives state security forces the right to detain individuals for any reason and many of the detainees are subjected to torture.[173] The Egyptian Organization on Human Rights (EOHR) is of the view that, "protecting the rights and freedoms of Egyptian citizens is a primary guarantee for a peaceful society without terrorism… Evidence suggests that the use of exceptional emergency laws only encourages extremism."[174] The state of emergency, in the opinion of Baheieddin Hassan, head of the Cairo Institute for Human Rights Studies, is not just about fighting terrorism, "it quickly became the foundation of the regime's rule…It seeped into the social, political and civil fabric of the country."[175] The emergency law has been shown to not only threaten basic rights and freedoms, but also to play a significant role in hindering the peaceful democratization process in society. EOHR has highlighted, in its reports, the role of the Emergency Law in usurping the role of the legislature and the judiciary and in limiting freedom of religion undermining in that the national constitutional rights and international human rights agreements to which Egypt is a party. Additionally, the authorities have continuously abused the powers of the emergency law, particularly when dealing with Muslim Brotherhood. Muslim Brotherhood members are routinely detained under Egyptian emergency law, which allows for administrative deten-

172 Abdel-Latif Omayma, Beyond the emergency, Al-Aharm Weekly on line, 4–10 August 2005, Issue No. 754.

173 See Reports by Human Rights Watch, <http://hrw.org/press/2003/02/egypt021403.htm>.

174 The FIDH and the Egyptian Organisation for Human Rights (EOHR), The Emergency Law in Egypt, 3 February 2011, <http://www.fidh.org/THE-EMERGENCY-LAW-IN-EGYPT> (viewed Sept. 2013).

175 Abdel-Latif Omayma, Beyond the emergency.

tion in renewable periods of two weeks. The government often cites 'membership of a banned organization' and 'disturbances of public order' as reasons for detaining opposition activists. Moreover, they detain people suspected of links to Islamic militancy. Security sources and a lawyer for some of the detainees said those held were arrested after trying to access militant websites but denied they were linked to al Qaeda. "The state security just arrested some people who were checking militant websites or websites affiliated to Al Qaeda."[176]

The current emergency law grants the authorities extensive exceptional jurisdictions. Upon a declaration of a state of emergency, Article 3 provides that the President may take "appropriate measures to maintain security and public order" through imposing restrictions on individuals' freedom to meet, travel and reside in particular places. Further, the emergency law provides for wide powers of arrest, detention and search, regardless of the protective provisions in the Criminal Procedures Code[177] especially since the Emergency Law has authorized the creation of exceptional courts to hear matters arising under emergency laws. Additionally, military courts have been established by military decree. Exceptional courts do not provide the same protections to individuals as would ordinary courts. For example, the accused has no right of appeal; the prosecutor has greater powers than in ordinary circumstances and the executive power plays an important role in ratifying judgments, in the composition of the courts and in the distribution of jurisdiction. Egyptian security forces have routinely abused the rights of Egyptian by interrogating and detaining them for peaceful and private religious expression and association. The right to freedom of thought, conscience and religion, set forth in Article 18(1) of the International Covenant on Civil and Political Rights (ICCPR), has been abridged each time that intelligence officers have questioned Egyptians about

176 Reuters Foundation, Egypt arrests 95 over suspected militant links, 05 Sep 2006. <http://www.news.oneindia.in/2006/09/05/egypt-arrests-95-over-suspected-militant-links-1157528181.html> (viewed Sept. 2013). See also: Human rights abuses in Egypt, Iraq, Jordan and Syria, Daily Star Egypt, First published: September 9, 2006. <http://www.dailystaregypt.com/article.aspx?ArticleID=2919>.

177 Article 3 of the Emergency Law.

deeply-held personal religious beliefs. In addition, arrest and detention for peaceful religious expression and association violates the right to be free from arbitrary arrest and detention, guaranteed in Article 9(1) of the ICCPR. The state may restrict the right to freedom of religion only if the observance of a religious practice or other form of religious expression constitutes a genuine threat to public safety and public order, and it may do so only to the extent necessary to prevent such a disturbance.

While the Egyptian constitution does offer considerable protection of human rights in theory, there exist significant ambiguities which have made the defense of those rights quite impossible. However, the Egyptian government hides behind the excuse that Islam is the state religion and that the international standards contain rules that are considered incompatible with *Shari'a*. Simultaneously, the war on terror is another excuse the Egyptian government has found to justify its violation of human rights standards, including the standards protecting the right to freedom of religion or belief. In the case of Egypt, not only the right to freedom of religion or belief is violated, but the entire "human rights paradigms" is violated. Both minorities and majority, who do not adhere to the government policy or its interpretations of the Qur'an, are arrested.

In Saudi Arabia, Amnesty International (AI) notes that, "the war on terror has once again resulted in retreat in the struggle for human rights in Saudi Arabia in favor of the old practices."[178] The violations were perpetuated by the strictly secretive criminal justice system and the prohibition of political parties, trade unions and independent human rights organizations. Hundreds of suspected religious activists and critics of the state were arrested, and the legal status of most of those held from previous years remained shrouded in secrecy.[179]

178 AI 2003 Report on Saudi Arabia, <http://www.amnesty.org/en/library/asset/POL10/003/2003/en/9130fc1e-d743-11dd-b024-21932cd2170dpol100032003en.pdf> (viewed Sept. 2013). Also Check: Saudi Arabia: A secret state of suffering, 27 March 2000. In practice, however, these values and rights are consistently violated with impunity in Saudi Arabia to protect the political status quo and the interests of the government. <http://www.amnesty.org/en/library/asset/MDE23/001/2000/en/a1077752-dfd2-11dd-8e17-69926d493233/mde230012000en.pdf> (viewed Sept. 2013).

179 Ibid.

The system perpetuates a wide range of human rights violations: arbitrary arrest and indefinite detention, the incarceration of prisoners of conscience, torture, secret and summary trials, cruel judicial punishments, executions and "disappearances", which are all facilitated by the state's policy of secrecy and the prohibition of the right to express conscientiously held beliefs. Moreover, organizations such as teachers', lawyers' and journalists' associations are increasingly faced with harassment because some of their board members hold "Islamist views".

The "war on terror" is also having effect on non governmental organizations (NGOs) in the region, including legitimate Islamic charities, and has affected families of prisoners and suspect by association. Some relatives have been subjected to detention by security forces in order to force suspected members of their families to hand themselves in. Family members find themselves in emotional turmoil, financial hardship and legal limbo.

Commenting on human rights violations by the Saudi government, Al-'Ubeid, NOHR Chairman, said: "Theoretically, the kingdom sets the laws, and the regime makes sure that these laws do not contradict Islamic *Shari'a.*" He adds

> There are those who consider certain issues a violation of human rights, while we consider them a safeguard to human rights [...]. Therefore, the position of the Saudi Foreign Ministry, and the position of many Islamic countries and even some of the Western countries, is that international proclamations of human rights and their related protocols are [considered only] general principles, and that their implementation is subject to the laws [of each country] [...]. We, in the kingdom, are part of the world insofar as [general principles of] human rights [are concerned]. But domestically we are governed according to Allah's *Shari'a,* so that what [to someone else] seems like a violation of human rights is [in fact] our duty and our right concerning someone who committed a crime or a sin.[180]

However, due to the strict view of wahabism, Saudis are not allowed to hold public gatherings to discuss political, religious or social issues, and petitions are the only means by which people can communicate

180 Raphaeli, Nimrod, Demands for Reforms in Saudi Arabia MEMRI's Middle East Economic Studies Program, No. 247, October 13, 2005, <http://memri.org/report/en/print1502.htm> (viewed Sept. 2013).

with the political leadership. What Muslim Arab rulers tend to forget, however, is that a true Islamic government is "a government of the people, a government in which people share a government that will serve Islam rather than use it, a government based on facts rather than slogans, on realities rather than dreams, on clarity rather than confusion".[181] In Saudi Arabia, it is the religious establishment, that exercises considerable influence on the lives of most Saudis, but what they are doing is not necessarily in accord with the Qur'an which is based on justice, equality, tolerance and mercy.

Since 9/11, many Arab states, when challenged on their human rights records, invoke US practices as justification. Some defend such violations as an attempt to shield their citizens from the harsher treatment by the US authorities. One of the setbacks brought on by the events of 11 September and the subsequent sidelining of the rule of law was the negative impact on civil society and its role as human rights protector. It has also facilitated the implementation with total disregard for international standards of bilateral and multilateral security agreements resulting in the *refoulement* and forcible return of people to countries where they faced great risk of being subjected to serious human rights violations. There have also been cases of people whose fate and whereabouts are unknown.[182]

181 Fluehr-Lobban, The Writings of Ashmawy, 78–9.

182 One example is that of the Abu 'Ali family from the USA. They are US nationals of Palestinian origin. Their 23-year-old son, Ahmed Abu 'Ali has been studying at al-Madina University in Saudi Arabia. On 11 June 2003 he was reportedly sitting his final examination when Saudi Arabian security officers walked into the examination hall and arrested him. The family told AI that five days after Ahmed's arrest their house in Falls Church, Virginia, USA, was raided by 15 FBI agents and that according to the search warrant they were looking for material related to a court case in Virginia involving 11 people charged with terrorism related offences and known as U.S. v Royer. Ahmed has not been charged in the U.S v Royer case, but has been linked to one of the 11 defendants, Sabri Benkahla. During the trial hearings of the 11, the prosecutor referred to Sabri Benkahla as having contacts with Ahmed Abu 'Ali whom he described as an *al-Qa'Ida* member. The prosecutor was also reported to have said that Ahmed was arrested in Saudi Arabia in connection with the bombings which took place in Riyadh on 12 May 2003. However, Sabri Benkahla has been acquitted and neither the US

Governments' lack of democracy and violations of freedom of religion and other human rights in the Arab world have been driven by political concerns and a failure to acknowledge and accommodate competing cultural, ethnic, or religious identities. Even though they claim to act upon the dictates of Islam, in reality, they are strategies for retaining political control and eliminating all forms of opposition. Not only are religious minorities ignored, but moreover, within this nationalistic entity, affairs of the state are managed only by those Muslims who agree with the official governmental interpretation of Islam and the *Shari'a*.

2.4.3.1 Human Rights in Authoritarian States

Muslim dissidents, as well as non-Muslims, are not authorized to have a role in the governance. Mohammed Arkoun notes that "the problem of the relation between Islam and modernity, including human rights, is political rather than scriptural. Islamic elites have mobilized conservative readings of the Qur'an for political purposes. This strategy has had some success because it appeals to those who have suffered from Western intrusions into the Islamic world or from the policies of local Westernized elites.[183] Thus, those who believe that democracy and Islam are incompatible fall in the following categories: first, Westerners who are advocates of war; and second, some Islamic governments that are also dictatorial regimes that violate the rights of their people (and seek legitimacy for doing so).[184]

Muslims are usually accused of hating democracy, however, a survey recently conducted in nine predominantly Muslim countries by

---

nor the Saudi Arabian authorities are understood to have brought any charges against Ahmed. Nevertheless, Ahmed's legal status remains unclear and his family's anxiety is aggravated further by the secrecy which surrounds Saudi Arabia's criminal justice system, particularly the lack of access to legal assistance.

183 Mohammed Arkoun quoted, in Freeman Michael's; 'The Problem of Secularism in Human Rights Theory'; *Human Rights Quarterly*, Volume 26, Number 2, May 2004, 382.

184 Violence, Politics, and Human Rights, Shirin Ebadi in Dialogue with Nermeen Shaikh, <http://them.polylog.org/5/des-en.htm> (viewed Sept. 2013).

two political science scholars, Pippa Norris of Harvard University and Ron Inglehart of the University of Michigan, have disproved this myth. The survey, as reported by the Washington Post, on April 28, 2002, shows that "many Muslims are huge supporters of democracy and may even be slightly more ready for action about democratic values than citizens of Western countries."[185]

However, most of the Muslim regimes are totalitarian regimes and they insist on picturing their way as an application of the Islamic law. Ashmawy refutes this and notes that, "Islam is concerned with people, not with the system; with the conscience, not with the legal rules; with the spirit, not with the letter of the law." He describes a true Islamic government as follows:

> A truly Islamic government will be one based on justice. This government, best described as a civil government will come from the people and will be ruled by the people for the benefit of all people. This government will gather everyone into one community and will exclude no one. This government will care about education, culture, science, art, history, literature and civilization. It will encourage cooperation, understanding, work, planning, constructive labor and self-sacrifice. It will understand Islam as mercy rather than a sword, amity rather than enmity. It will offer Islam to all humankind as a way to God, a method for progress and a path for mercy [...].[186]

Thus, the main reason for religious intolerances and discriminations in Muslim states are political rather than religious. Javaid insists that "the restrictions on religious freedom and violation of the rights of minorities have not been caused by any inherent contradictions between (Islam) and modern human rights norms."[187] He adds, "[s]ubstantial vio-

185 Pippa Norris & Ronald Inglehart, Islam & the West: Testing the "Clash of Civilizations" Thesis, Harvard University and the University of Michigan, available online: <http://www.hks.harvard.edu/fs/pnorris/Acrobat/Clash%20of%20Civilization.pdf> (viewed Sept. 2013).

186 Fluehr-Lobban, The Writings of Ashmawy, 79.

187 Rehman, Javaid, Accommodating Religious Identities in an Islamic State: International Law, Freedom of Religion and the Rights of Religious Minorities, International Journal on Minority and Group Rights 7, Kluwer Law International, the Netherlands, 2000, 139.

lations of minority rights have been a consequence of political and constitutional ineptness and an exclusive emphasis on forging nationhood on the basis of a religious identity."[188] It is possible, hence, to argue that political development, i.e., democracy, is seen as threatening to the majority of Arab regimes. In many Arab countries, the military is the most privileged sector of society, politically, socially and economically. As the histories of other nations indicates, neither the regimes nor the military power that supports them tend to relinquish power easily. This is one of the factors behind the controlled dosage of political freedoms allowed to many Arab peoples today. The Arab Human Development Report III[189] points out that

> [...] choices that individuals in a democracy exercise to enrich their lives are curtailed and even expropriated in this region by authoritarian leaders bent on perpetuating their rule by all means, including the use of instruments of compulsion under their command to insure compliance and to prevent deviation from the narrow paths which they have charted.

From a political perspective, "the powers of the ruler, in the modern Arab state, are absolute; he uses them to tame the judiciary, dominate the media, turn parliament, to the extent that it exists, to a bureaucratic adjunct and use, or misuse, national wealth to enrich himself and a coterie of family members, political associates and friends. The separation of power in the Arab world exists solely on paper. The leader, king, or president, can freely subordinate all these power to his own persona and often to his own whims. Elections are often restricted to a ruling party or to a process of referendum where the voter has no other candidates to choose from. Corruption, which is institutionalized in government and business throughout the region, reinforces this "black hole" phenomenon.[190]

188 Ibid.

189 Third Report on human development in the Arab world issued under the auspices of three organizations: the United Nations Development Program (UNDP); The Arab Fund for economic and social Development; The Arab Gulf Program for the United Nations development Organizations.

190 Ibid., 145.

Some regimes have resorted to new methods to justify their continuation in power. They present themselves as the lesser of two evils or "the last line of defense against fundamentalist tyranny." Such an argument is characterized by the report as the "legitimacy blackmail": *we may be bad but the alternative is worse.* The report points out that this argument has been eroded "by the growing realization that the absence of any effective alternative is itself one of the outcomes of the policies that block all avenues for political and civil activity."[191] Thus, in practice, states not only control the process by which international human rights standards are set in the first place, but are also entrusted with the practical interpretation and implementation of those standards within their own territories.[192] In this light, it is clear that the willingness and ability of communities to use the human rights paradigm is crucial for the ability of this paradigm to influence the course of events on the ground. Willingness and ability to use the human rights paradigm, as is also the case with constitutional rights, are separate but related factors. People may be willing to use this paradigm but be unable to do so because of the structural, institutional, and political limitations.[193]

In most of the Arab countries, an issue generating much debate and tension with governments is the law governing associations; their formal registration, funding and functioning. Whether in Egypt, Tunisia or Morocco etc., non-governmental organizations (NGOs) bitterly complain about repressive laws. Governments tend to counter with the argument that what is at stake ultimately is "national security", and that to allow these organizations to operate without control might render them vulnerable to "manipulation" by external interests.[194] In addition, the governments contend that these organizations need some form of supervision to enhance their own professionalism and ensure that they are serving national concerns rather than those of a particular group or individual. It is the government's obligation, they often claim, to pro-

191 Ibid., 16.
192 An-Na'im, Abdullahi, Human Rights and Islamic Identity, 935.
193 Ibid., 937.
194 Ibid.

tect the people from those who have interests other than those of their own nations in mind, even if these are well intentioned.

Thus, the main problem in the Arab states is democracy, not religion. The problems with freedom of religion and human rights in the Muslim states cannot be separated from the need for genuine freedom and for a new, modern and democratic constitution which establishes a genuine, flexible mechanism for government change. Ebadi points out that "unfortunately the human rights situation is not very good in most Islamic countries. When people object to cases of human rights violations, they are told that Islam and human rights are, in essence, incompatible. It is claimed that governments are observing Islamic rules and regulations. By doing so, that is, by invoking religion, these governments are clearly attempting to silence those who object. This is absolutely incorrect. Islamic studies show us that Islam has no incompatibility with human rights.[195] On the contrary, Islamic culture or religion is insignificant in explaining the violation of human rights in Muslim countries. It is therefore very difficult to use Islamic political culture as a justification for torture or government-sponsored violence against individuals.

In addition to replicating the results of other studies that found religion to be an insignificant determinant of human rights practices, the study of Daniel Price confirmed that "in order to implement human rights practices, the important variable is the democratic nature of the regime."[196] The excuse, leaders of these Arab states proffer, that they are applying the rule of *Shari'a*, is a direct misrepresentation and misinterpretation of Islam especially that the sovereignty of God cannot mean that God comes to earth to rule. On the contrary, the sovereignty of God implies the rule of God's law, (i. e. 'the rule of law'), a cornerstone of modern democratic states and the human rights discourse.[197] The idea of submitting oneself to the sovereignty of God is actually a liberating

195 Violence, Politics, and Human Rights, Shirin Ebadi in Dialogue with Nermeen Shaikh <http://them.polylog.org/>.

196 Price, Daniel (2002). "Islam and Human Rights: A Case of Deceptive First Appearances", *The Journal for the Scientific Study of Religion*, 41(2), pp. 213–225.

197 Ghannouchi, Rachid (1993), *Al-Hurriyyat Al-'Amma Fi Ad-Dawla Al-Islamiyya, (General Freedoms in the Islamic State).*

one; to remove the possibility of despotism, the totalitarian rule of another human being. Using such inventive and creative readings into traditional Islamic thought, makes it possible to remain firmly within the Islamic tradition and at the same time argue the case for Muslims to take notions of human rights, freedom, liberty, democracy, civil society and citizenship very seriously.[198]

2.4.3.2 Extremism in the Arab World

Almost everywhere in the Muslim world, Islam has remained the religion of the state or the religion of the majority. These states are strong enough to repress dissent, but are unable or unwilling to modernize their societies. One of the consequences of this combination of oppression and socio-economic failure was the emergence of political Islam as secular nationalism failed to deliver the goods across the Muslim world. In Muslim countries the development, in later years, has not been in the direction towards secularization or reformism. Instead the extremist's[199] movements have grown stronger in many places. In addition to corrupted governments, extremism is a reaction to Western neo-colonialism and, more significantly, Western cultural domination. The revolt against Western cultural domination is legitimate, but how that revolt develops is the key question for Muslims today.[200]

This pan-Islamic resurgence, however, is not of a single type; it has many voices and expressions throughout the Islamic world. Muslims around the world share some common values, beliefs, codes of ethics, however, as it was mentioned before, their socioeconomic, political, and cultural realities vary considerably. For this reason, reformation

198 Ibid.

199 We will follow the line of many writers who does not use the term fundamentalism to describe what is better understood as extremism. The fundamentals of Islam (usul al-din)-the Qur'an and Sunna and the Five Pillars-are not in dispute. It is important to point out that, no liberal or conservative, is questioning the fundamentals of the faith; matters of interpretation of the sources and application of these ideas in contemporary society are what are at issues. See: Fluehr-Lobban, The writings of Ashmawy, 25.

200 Fluehr-Lobban, The writings of Ashmawy, 28.

and reinterpretation of the Qur'an has been part of the Islamic history. It is necessary to realize that Muslims have neither one unified attitude towards Islamic law, nor one clear understanding about human rights. This is clear, even if one analyzes the classical Islamic jurists' interpretations and the different schools of jurisprudences. One will find that they vary in their interpretations and applications of the texts. This wide scope of schools offers the chance to implement *Shari'a* in different social environments and to allow people, based on the principle of Talfiq, to choose which school they want to follow in a certain incident. Many Muslims, on a number of grounds, are now challenging this position (the divinity of Shari'a in totality). To respond to the demands of modernity, they argue, Muslims needed to return to the original sources of the Qur'an and authentic Sunna (tradition of the Prophet), and engage in *de novo* interpretations of the text.

> The *Shari'a* cannot be understood as a fixed repository of commands and prohibitions. In this way, for the reformists, they will be able to produce modern legislation which will both embody the highest ideals of Islam and be eminently suited to modern life. That does not mean, "*the shari'a's positive precepts are ... to be abandoned lightly – many are still valid, many others are suitable for contemporary society with some modification – but they are not sacrosanct.*[201]

The complete and immediate implementation of Shari'a, which is what extremists demand, is the least Islamic position for a Muslim to adopt today. To try to build a new Islamic identity based on radical ways is equivalent to saying that Islam stands for repression and discrimination at home and aggressive war abroad. Thus, in order to sustain and strengthen the Islamic faith, Muslims need to reassert in a modern context the fundamental truths of the Qur'an and the Prophet's original Mecca message which was based on broad principles of justice and equality. Only by removing the serious inconsistencies between their historical Islamic self-identity and the realities of the modern world can Muslims effectively challenge Western domination. If they fail, they

201 Humphreys in O'Sullivan, Declan, In Defense of Islam-and the Western Misinterpretation of What is Perceived to Be 'Islamic Fundamentalism', <http://stehly.perso.infonie.fr/declan.htm> (viewed Sept. 2013).

will lose their Islamic identity and tradition altogether. However, reformation and calls for Islamic revivals are faced by both the conservative ulama establishment in close alliance with and in the service of the state and by extremist's militant challengers. Both extremes shunned the reformists, and have managed to marginalize them with the help of some Western political agenda.

These forces did not stop and will not stop reformists from calling for Islamic revival. Returning to the divine Qur'anic texts, the main reforming measure agreed upon by reformists is that *Shari'a* is not supposed to be static, but rather evolving, and that the role of Ijtihad, guided by the principles of justice, equity, and public welfare, is crucial in responding to the changing social needs.[202] The evolving nature of *Shari'a* will even allow, based on the principle of public welfare, new questions to be asked and to arrive at new answers not found in classical jurisprudence. Thus, in order to cope with the social changes in different times and places and in different contexts, the *Shari'a* must not be rigid but rather flexible. If *Shari'a* is rigid, how can Islamic law cope with all the social changes that have occurred during the last centuries? Exposing the diversity of practices within different parts of the Muslim world and in different periods of history offers a potent way of challenging ingrained assumptions. The second Caliph, Umar Ibn Al-Khattab, a few years after the death of the Prophet, conducted a revolutionary *ijtihad*, even when compared to the contemporary period. He used *ijtihad* in cases even in which there was a clear, unabrogated text such as that in theft (hadd) and *mo'alafa qolobihem* cases. In the first case, he abolished the application of amputation of the hand as a punishment for theft in times of starvation known as the "the year of famine." In the second one, he refused to pay the new entrants into Islam from the treasury, even though there is a Qur'anic injunction regarding this issue. However, he used his juristic reasoning to conclude that it had become contrary to the public welfare, that Islam was stronger and

202 Mashhour, Amira, Islamic Law and Gender Equality: Could There be a Common Ground?: A Study of Divorce and Polygamy in Shari'a Law and Contemporary Legislation in Tunisia and Egypt, Human Rights Quarterly Volume 27, Number 2, May 2005, 566.

more stable than before, and that there was no need to encourage the new entrants into Islam as before.[203]

Thus, the traditional method of interpretation is challenged by some Muslim jurists on the following points:

1. The divine sources in Islam are the Qur'anic text and authentic Sunna
2. The reopening of the gate of *ijtihad*
3. Islamic law is not static but rather evolving. Thus, one of the crucial steps is to understand the Qur'anic text within its socioeconomic and historical contexts.[204]

This view would help to withdraw the monopoly of interpretation from the political or religious leadership and provide the space for the exploration of alternative interpretations beyond traditional and authoritarian perspectives. Ijtihad, as has been repeated many times by now, is needed to cope with contemporary social change. Abu Zaid explains

> [...] to maintain, in legislating today, commandments laid down 14 centuries ago are invariable and binding for all time is to defy the primordial law of evolution and to ignore the spirit of the Qur'an which attributes the quality of permanence only to spiritual values. All other aspects of life are necessarily subject to change and no enlightened community would legislate on a contrary principle.[205]

There are certain issues that seem to be in contradiction with the concept of justice from modern view at least. Issues like polygamy, the position of women as well as non-Muslims, and freedom of religion are continuously provoked in any discussion about the Qur'an and Islam. There are so many apologetic responses by Muslims trying to tackle such issues, but the historical explanation, as well as textual re-contextualization of the Qur'an, might provide an objective way of analyzing the above mentioned issues.[206]

203 Ghanea, Nazila, 'Human Rights of Religious Minorities and of Women in the Middle East' *Human Rights Quarterly* 26.3 (2004), 727.

204 Mashhour, Amira, 588–591.

205 Nasr Hamid Abu Zayd, The Qur'anic Concept of Justice. <http://them.polylog.org>.

206 See: Gamal Al Banna, *Islamic Revival.*

3. Conclusion

Muslims from all backgrounds refuses to be related to extremism or dictorial regimes, they believe that there is a third way; the way of reform and democracy, one that is designed within an Islamic framework, one that is desired by millions.

In this third way, reformists call for:[1]

1 – "A new intellectual Islamic context, characterized by clarity and unity of perception, that seeks to take into account all the changes and transformations that took place in the social life of the various countries of the Muslim world."

2 – "Implementing a radical revision of the Islamic heritage that involves all Islamic scholarship relating to Islamic Jurisprudence and the *Sunna,* the Traditions of the Prophet – all of which were founded during the first three centuries of Islam, and calling for reliance on the Qur'anic text as the sole authentic source to be utilized for reviewing the entire Islamic heritage."

3 – "Confronting all institutions – whether composed of clerics or lay persons – that claim a monopoly over religion and the proper interpretation of its holy text. Instead, a new spirit should seek to establish the right of *ijtihad* for all, under the banner of an Islamic reformation relevant to in the current century."

4 – "Confronting and refuting the visions and statements of radical religious movements so as to retard their penetration into the Arab society specifically among youngsters many of whom are living in a state of depression under the stress of economic hardship …"

1 Workshop on "Islam and Reform," held in Cairo on October 5–6, 2004, (translated) in Yehoshua, Y., A Cairo Conference Calling for Reform Raises the Ire of the Egyptian Religious Establishment, MEMRI, October 22, 2004, No. 192. <http://freerepublic.com/focus/f-news/1252556/posts> (viewed Sept. 2013).

Today, governments cite the activities of militant groups as justification for the need to "suspend" the protection of human rights in order to safeguard national and regional security.[2] The threat of extremism and domestic terrorism are used in these countries as a pretext to crack-down on opposition political parties, NGOs and reformation movements, and as a means of distracting a potentially disaffected population from more pressing problems faced by these underdeveloped and often destitute nations.[3] Nevertheless, they forget that "extremism" flourishes under political authoritarianism. In some respects, conditions for the promotion of democracy have changed less in the Arab world than in other regions. The types of concerns that had inhibited the establishment of democracy during the Cold War have persisted in the Arab world through the nineties. The old fear of left-wing subversion of friendly governments has been replaced by a new fear of militant groups. The failure of these various ideologies, the accumulation of socio-economic problems and the invasion of the new values of globalization have aggravated an identity crisis among new generations in the Arab region. The resulting vacuum has become a fertile ground for a number of forms of religious extremism. Political Islam already constitutes a viable political opposition and as such must be included in any political dialogue, rather than ignored and marginalized. Ostracism, could lead to further polarization within a number of societies and thus hamper, or obstruct, real democracy.

Egypt and Saudi Arabia have clamped down on its adherents and detained them. One of the questions that arises repeatedly is whether it is possible to include Islamists in any democratic dialogue? Saad E. Ibrahim, in 'Democratization and Islamic Reformation', insists that "the most hardened militants could change toward moderation... The keys to such change are respect (dignity), justice and inclusion."[4] Demo-

2 An-Na'im, Abdullhi A., 'Human Rights in the Arab World: A Regional Perspective', *Human Rights Quarterly* 23.3 (2001), 731.

3 Sethre Ian, The Great Game for the Twenty-first Century: Islamic Extremism and central Asia, *Human Rights & Human Welfare*, Volume 3, 2003, 105.

4 Saad Edin Ibrahim, Democratization and Islamic Reformation, Anti-Terrorism Resources, viewed on: <http://www.freemuslims.org/document>.

cracy, as a form of political association that can accommodate the plurality of communities, is mentioned in Surah 5:48. It does so by allowing for the cooperation and consultation between different groups and individuals such that the virtues of truth and justice are promoted and the vices of corruption and violence are curtailed.[5] Any attempt, thus, at development, which is laid down by governments or experts, without the participation of the masses and is not founded on faith, or which aims to further the interests of the few at the expense of majority, is a development doomed to failure. Thus, in the absence of democracy and freedom for all the citizens of the state, all human rights issues cannot be combated and it will be unrealistic to talk about implementing one of the freedoms and not the other.

Any attempts at development that apply European or American models to Muslim countries, without any thought to the Muslim context, will only bring more backwardness, clashes and conflicts. To learn from their experience is an advantage, but to exchange the *taqlid* [the duty of accepting the conclusions reached by the previous generations of scholars and authoritative,] of the forefathers to the *taqlid* of the West will make the situation worse, not better. Religion is the strongest characteristic of Arab society and it represents history, civilization and conscience. At the same time, however, a society must not avoid the mixing of ideas and dialogue between civilizations and similarities between religions, because justice and equality are the long pursued common goal of humanity.

Thus, what is needes is to first make political reforms. When democracy, justice and the rule of law are fully engrained in a society it is possible to discuss freely and attempt to solve religious issues and defend human rights.

States should ensure that any measure they adopt fully respects the principle of equality before the law and does not amount to discrimi-

5 Abdoulkarim Soroush, "Tolerance and Governance: A discourse on religion and democracy", in *Reason, Freedom and Democracy in Islam: Essential Writings of Abdolkarim Soroush*, trans. and ed. Mahmoud Sadri and Ahmad Sadri (Oxford: Oxford University Press, 2000), 134.

nation on religious grounds and to treat all citizens equally. States should instantly amend, rescind or nullify any laws and practices that have the effect of creating or perpetuating discrimination on such ground.

States should take effective measures to protect persons or groups who may be subject to discrimination, hostility or violence as a result of their religious beliefs including by ensuring that such abuses are effectively investigated, prosecuted and punished. States should take effective measures to promote tolerance among their citizenry and in their action consistently distinguish between those few individuals who commit terrorism in the name of a certain religious or other identity and the vast majority of peaceful representatives of such groups.

Concluding Remarks: Challenges to Freedom of Religion or Belief

Religions and beliefs may embrace the global world or they may resist it. The former, according to James V. Spickard,

> [...] is the path of universalism: a cultural outlook that says, in effect, that we are all in this together and we'd better learn how to co-operate. This may involve supporting cultural diversity which is based on equality and intercultural communication. The other path is a rejection of diversity. This path will lead to extremism, be it religious or nationalistic. Both deny outsiders any worth. This is especially true of people who see themselves as threatened: by outsiders, by economic forces, or by things they do not understand. They find proponents of peace and co-existence as antagonistic to their own ultimate views.[1]

However, the democratic governance of multi-religious societies depends on people's willingness to co-operate with one another and support living in peace, based on the shared principles of justice, human rights, and mutual toleration.

In order to support the universalism of human rights ideals, especially, religious freedoms and to stress the unity of the human family, societies must stand in the face of the following challenges:

Superiority of Religion or Belief

Ethnocentrism, "the notion that one's own culture is superior to any other"[2], can cause the alienation of minorities from the dominant group.

1 James V. Spickard, "Human Rights, Religious Conflict, and Globalization, Ultimate Values in a New World Order", in Exploring Religious Pluralism, *International Journal on Multicultural Societies (IJMS),* Vol. 1, No. 1, 1999, 16–17.

2 W.G. Sumner, Folksway (Boston: Ginnand, 1994), 13. In Samovar and Porter, 297.

When ethnocentrism is excessive, serious communication problems can arise. As Jandt points out:

> *Extreme ethnocentrism leads to a rejection of the richness and knowledge of other cultures. It impedes communication and blocks the exchange of ideas and skills among peoples. Because it excludes other points of view, an ethnocentrism orientation is restrictive and limiting*[3].

Thus, the superiority of one religion or belief over others poses one of the main challenges to freedom of religion or belief. Communities that try to enforce conformity often are characterized by religious intolerance and violence. These intolerances intensify when a religion or belief becomes, not just universalistic, but also exclusivist and expansionistic. Many have long believed that it is the secular, liberal institutions that assuage fears and calm passions with the promise of fair, just, and impartial treatment. However, this view is no longer valid as we are seeing a religious resurgence primarily as a result of the strict concept of secular societies. A secular society, for a long time, was a society where options of religious disbelief and doubt are freely available, along with options of belief. Secular societies were meant to facilitates and safeguard the free exercise, reproduction, and transformation of religion or belief, in a pluralist and radically inclusive sense."[4] However, the process of secularization has brought in its wake the progressive shrinkage, decline, and marginalization of religion in the modern world.

Thus, the only way to combat this challenge is to find solutions for religious pluralism and freedom through ensuring co-existence between the religious minorities and the majority within the national state. The fundamentals should be analyzed which will help the co-existence and the mutual recognition between the minority groups and the majority. Not only should issues of religion be dealt with, but also the ethnocentrism of beliefs and ideas, such as secularism. The multi-faith element of multiculturalism which has long been neglected, despite its impor-

3 F.E. Jandt, Intercultural Communication: An Introduction (Thousand Oaks, CA: Sage, 1995), 43.

4 Tore Lindholm, in *A Deskbook*, 37–38.

tance needs to be taken into consideration. States must elaborate multicultural policies in order to ensure the opportunities for affirming the plural religious identities which can be found within the national state. This is hard to achieve, however, if, the Universal Declaration and other international standards are presented exclusively as Western and secular concepts.

The Western and Secular Origin of Human Rights

Presenting the concept of human rights as a Western and secular concept has led to the exclusion of non-Western societies in the writing of the Universal Declaration and other human rights instruments, and at the same time, they have reduced its interpretation to be only according to Western views and values. It is as though human rights laws and standards have reached the stage of completion with no more work to be done. The reality, however, is that the work is far from being over. Everywhere in the world, be it in the West or in the East, problems of environmental degradation, extreme corruption, racism, religious intolerance, and torture still persist.

To acknowledge the Western origin of the present formulation of 'human rights standards', is to suggest that the concept itself is alien to non-Western cultures. Boyle notes that

> [...] if the emergence of freedom of thought and freedom of religion and belief are linked to the European civilization, how stands the claim that human rights are universal...That these freedoms were first codified from European experience does not mean that the thoughts and values behind them are not reflected in other civilizations and cultures.[5]

It is true that the term human rights is a relatively new one in history, yet human rights issues and finding ways to improve human situations have been around for many centuries. In greater or lesser degree they have long been embraced by the world's major religious and philosophical traditions. However, can we say that the West is the sole coor-

5 Boyle & Sheen, 4.

dinator of the Universal Declaration and they are totally committed to human rights?

Contrary to popular belief, the great powers did not embrace the idea of human rights as they met to lay the foundation for the UN and the United States cannot be considered its great champion, especially when many countries at that time were still under different forms of Western imperialism, which was often justified as an altruistic and civilizing mission,. Western states did not always side with proposals that many would view in keeping with Western values. At various moments, for example, Western states resisted efforts to include liberal provisions for non-discrimination, minority rights, and gender equality.[6] Though the current vocabulary of human rights has more easily detectable references in Western philosophical writings, this does not mean that the notion of human rights was or is alien to other cultures or that the Western cultures and societies have been pro-human rights.

To consider 'human rights' to be an inherently secular moral doctrine challenges the freedom of religion. Most theorists and practitioners commonly assume that the concept of human rights is secular and that it normally takes priority over other values. These assumptions are controversial for those who approach human rights from the perspective of religious beliefs. Perry questioned

> [...] the thoroughly secularized story of the development of human rights, and argued that there exists no secular moral theory capable of intelligibly justifying the doctrine of human rights (and this doctrine) is philosophically insupportable so long as we insist on excluding God. Secular moral reasoning is incapable of justifying our acceptance of the universal validity of the doctrine of human rights. Secular moral reasoning is proven incapable of demonstrating why we should ultimately act in accordance with the principles of human rights.[7]

6 Waltz, Susan, *Universal Human Rights: The Contribution of Muslim States, Human Rights Quarterly* 26.4 (2004), 802.

7 Perry, Michael J., "The Idea of Human Rights: Four Inquires," New York: Oxford University Press, 1998, 162. In Fagan Andrew, Between God and Democracy, Human Rights & Human Welfare, Volume 2:2, Spring/Summer 2002, 20.

Therefore, many believe that only religion is capable of rectifying the moral vacuum created by the failure of secular moral philosophy within the doctrine of human rights and many respect the principles of human rights because, ultimately, they are the manifestation of a force far greater than ourselves and to which are all answerable.[8]

In the case of Muslim states, to commit and subscribe to human rights principles, they must do so "in conformity with Islamic criteria." To do otherwise would be to abandon their religion and the international human rights community, obviously, cannot reasonably require it. Thus, it is more valid to accept the argument that "human rights as a value can be incorporated within a religious framework (including an Islamic framework)." The assumption that human rights standards necessarily need to be "secularized" in order for them to be rendered effective and to base the struggle entirely within a secular framework is extremely unlikely to succeed. This may, Ghanea notes,

> [...] gloss over the complexity of the issue of what is meant by "secularization" in this context...If the claim is for the independence of the judiciary and respect for human rights regardless of religious affiliation, then clearly (she) would support such manifestations of secularization [...]. However, the outright rejection of the possibility of garnering support for human rights from within a religious framework is not supported.[9]

From a Muslim perspective, An-Na'im notes that

> [...] moral or philosophical justifications for the universality of human rights can be found in all major religious and cultural traditions of the world, which should be emphasized through an internal discourse within each tradition that also addresses those features of the religion or culture which are negative or hostile to human rights norms.[10]

8 Ibid., 21.

9 Ghanea, Nazila, 'Human Rights of Religious Minorities and of Women in the Middle East' *Human Rights Quarterly* 26.3 (2004), 720–21.

10 An-Na'im, Abdullhi A., 'Human Rights in the Arab World: A Regional Perspective', *Human Rights Quarterly* 23.3 (2001), 703.

The most obvious foundation of these rights is that they are necessary for the protection of human dignity and the achievement of social justice in the present context of the nation-state and global inter-state system.[11] To achieve these goals, Ramadan urges a dialogical approach, but notes that "imposing one's norms on others will inevitably mean conflicts. But to call each religion and culture to develop from within spaces of protection for the dignity of woman, man and child is… the choice of the future."[12]

What counts today is not whether religious people appreciate other beliefs and practices, what really matters is whether each, on sound internal grounds, supports the public doctrine of the equal inherent dignity and inalienable freedom of all human beings, irrespective of their religion, life stance, or any other differences, and that each reasonably understands or else trusts that others similarly support general freedom of religion or belief.[13]

> It is important to emphasize that it is not the task of human rights theory to determine ultimate religious or philosophical truths, but to identify the rules that ought to govern the relations among persons with different beliefs. Human rights theory therefore has the task of reconciling religion and human rights so far as it is possible.

It is true that defining a global ethic is an extremely complex and delicate exercise, particularly in the light of the debate on the universality of human rights versus cultural relativism. However, Professor Kälin affirms the universality of human rights, since "every country in the world has now ratified at least one human rights convention and as a result human rights have become a truly universal legally binding concept."[14] Moreover, at the Second U.N. World Conference on Human

11 Ibid.
12 Ramadan, Tariq (2003), *Western Muslims and the Future of Islam.* Oxford: Oxford University Press.
13 Lindholm, in *AR*, 50.
14 Walter, Kälin, *What are Human rights?,* In: Lars Müller, Walter Kälin, Judith Wyttenbach (Eds.), *The Face of Human Rights* Lars Müller Publishers, Baden, Switzerland, 2004, 19.

Rights (Vienna, June 1993), the states of the world agreed by consensus that "the universal nature of these rights and freedoms is beyond question."[15] They agreed "all human rights are universal, indivisible and interdependent and inter-related."[16] They also proclaimed that "national and regional particularities and various historical, cultural and religious backgrounds must be borne in mind."[17] However, none of the stipulations were envisaged as really offensive to any cultural or sociopolitical system. Had they been so envisaged, the document would have faced stronger opposition and negative votes at the United Nations General Assembly. Bobbio notes that "[t]he fundamental problem with human rights is not, nowadays, how to justify them, but rather how to protect them. The problem is not philosophical, but rather political."[18] This was affirmed by the UN Secretary General Kofi Annan in the year 2000, when he pointed out that, "it was never the people who complained of the universality of human rights, nor did the people consider human rights as a Western or Northern imposition. It was often their leaders who did so."[19] Thus, justifications for the universality of human rights can be found in all major religious and cultural traditions of the world; this should be emphasized through an internal

15 The Vienna Conference was the largest international gathering ever convened on the theme of human rights. Its final document, the Vienna Declaration and Program of Action – adopted by consensus without a vote or reservations, although with some interpretive statements – unambiguously affirms, in Article 1 that: "The universal nature of these rights and freedoms is beyond question." Article 5 of the Vienna Declaration states: "While the significance of national and regional particularities and various historical, cultural and religious backgrounds must be borne in mind, it is the duty of States, regardless of their political, economic and cultural systems, to promote and protect all human rights and fundamental freedoms."

16 Vienna Declaration and Program of Action, U.N. Doc. A/CONF. 157/23, pt. I, paras. 1 and 5 (1993).

17 Ibid.

18 Quoted in Alves Lindgren Jose A., The Declaration of Human Rights in Postmodernity, Human Rights Quarterly 22.2 (2000), 497.

19 Kofi Annan, United Nations High Commissioner for Human Rights, (last modified 22 Feb. 2000) <http://www.unhchr.ch>.

discourse within each tradition that also addresses those features of the religion or culture which are negative or hostile to human rights norms.

The most obvious foundation of these rights is that they are necessary for protection of human dignity and achievement of social justice in the present context of the nation-state and global inter-state system.

Overcoming these factors will help, within the democratic perspective, to recognize the personal worth and dignity of each individual and to recognize that everyone deserves equal respect and equal opportunity for self-realization by virtue of their humanity and human worth. There are universal values shared by everyone, and there are particular values that are shared within various minorities.

So the question is how can religious minorities become equal citizens and be bound to the rest by the ties of mutual commitment and attachment? Any minority group cannot belong to the society in which it has chosen to settle in unless it is prepared to welcome them, and conversely it cannot accept them as full members unless they wish to belong, with all that this entails. Common belonging therefore can only be achieved if each party respects the terms of the relationship and discharges its obligations. People of various religions or beliefs can live together in harmony, with political freedoms in states that are able to provide for persons' basic needs, because, almost all religions and beliefs have an Ethic of Reciprocity. This is what is called the *Golden Rule*: to do onto others as one would wish to be treated in return. One can recognize the worth of each human being, and the importance of guaranteeing fundamental human rights to all. This includes the freedom by which individuals can follow their own spiritual and religious path. Valuing the rights of other people to hold diverse beliefs can lead to an appreciation of their beliefs." The argument should be that our similarities, not our differences, often can serve as part of common values. The credo of similarity is important to the study of ethics in that it helps us look for common ground as a way of deciding how to treat other people regardless of their religion. What is important is that in a multicultural world we begin to see our commonalities. We must all begin to realize that diversity can be rich without being threatening, for in the end, people of all cultures long for the same things: a place to raise their children, ply their trade, and express themselves aesthetically and socially. When those forms of expression differ from our own, we must respect the rights of people.

In a world that can destroy itself with powerful bombs, toxic gases, or global pollution, it should be important to remember that it is not easy to know how to create wholeness incorporating diversity, but we owe it to the world, as well as ourselves, to keep trying,[20] and share one view and that is: the welfare of humanity.

A multicultural society based on equality of treatment in the sense of equal citizenship stance implies a positive stance towards the different religions and world-views, which complement each other and have something to teach each other, whilst they co-exist in our world. For example, an exclusively Islamic frame of reference will probably be confronted with an exclusively Western one, thus, the human rights paradigm offers the possibility of common ground between these competing ethnic and cultural claims. In addition, it will encourage of all state parties to examine the question of the interpretation of existing norms on freedom of expression, religious freedom and non-discrimination, and reflect on whether additional standards are needed for that purpose.[21]

There are three lines of action, which supporters of religious freedom and human rights are pursuing and advocating:

– The starting point has to be education aimed at spreading the understanding of the sheer diversity of fundamental beliefs in the world and that all such beliefs are entitled to respect, especially that ignorance is the true enemy of freedom. Therefore, there is need for ever more effort at interfaith and intercultural dialogue.

20 Samovar and Porter, 336.

21 E/CN.4/2006/17, 13 February 2006. See also, Doudou Diène Updated study by the Special Rapporteur on contemporary forms of racism, racial discrimination, xenophobia and related intolerance, Political platforms which promote or incite racial discrimination, E/CN.4/2006/54, 13 January 2006, CHR 62 session para. 23.

- The second factor, associated with religious intolerance, is the fact of legal political economic and social inequalities. Prejudice and discrimination lead to, and reinforce structural intolerance and as such, can be the trigger for conflict as the victims seek to challenge inferior status and reactions to the threat of loss of power and privilege turn also to violence.
- Finally, the real challenge now for all states and religious entities is to find a language, which without diminishing the integrity of their own beliefs, recognizes the entitlement of all other beliefs to equal moral dignity. Thus, an essential concept to religious freedoms is *dialogue,* not in any pedestrian sense, but in the sense of a deep dialogue, a transformative kind of consciousness that seeks to primarily *learn* from rather than teach those who think differently from us.

Bibliography

English Books

Arts Paul, Moneyman Gird, Ed., Saudi Arabian in the Balance, Political Economy, society, Foreign Affairs, Hurst &Company, London, 2005.

Anderson, Norman, Law Reform in the Muslim World, the Athlete Press, University of London, London, 1976.

An-Maim, Abdullah A. Toward an Islamic Reformation: Civil Liberties, Human Rights, and International Law, Syracuse University Press, New York, 1990.

Armstrong Karen, Holy War, the Crusades and Their Impact on Today's World, Anchor Books, New York, 2001.

Audi Robert & Wolterstorff Nicholas, Religion in the Public Square 'The Place of Religious Convictions in Political Debate,' Rowman & Littlefield Publishers, INC. Lanham, MD, 1997.

Boyle K. and Sheen J., *Freedom of Religion and Belief: A World Report,* Routledge, London & New York, 1997.

Carr, E. H., The Twenty Years' Crisis, Palgrave, Great Britain, 2001.

Cook, Robin, The Point of Departure 'Diaries From the Front Bench', Pocket Books, London, 2004.

Coulson, N. J., A History of Islamic Law, Edinburgh University Press, Edinburgh, 1964.

Donnelly, Jack, Universal Human Rights in Theory and Practice, Ithaca, NY: Cornell University Press, 1989.

Evans, Carolyn, Freedom of Religion Under the European Convention On Human Rights, Oxford European Human Rights Series, Oxford, 2000.

Fluehr-Lobban, Carolyn, ed., Against Islamic Extremism, 'The Writing of Muhammed Sa'id al-'Ashmawy', University Press of Florida, Gainesville, 1998.

Geaves Ron, Gabriel Theodore, Haddad Yvonne, and Smith Jane I., Editors, Islam & The West 'Post 9/11', Ashgate Publishing Limited, England, 2004.

Gottschalk Peter & Greenberg Gabriel, Islamophobia Making the Muslims the Enemy, Rowman & Littlefield Publishers, INC., Lanham, 2008.

Haddad-Yazbek, Yvonne, (ed.), Muslims in the West, from Sojourners to Citizens, Oxford University Press, Oxford, 2002.

Haddad-Yazbek, Yvonne (ed.), The Muslims of America, Oxford University Press, Oxford, 1991.

Halliday, Fred, Nation and Religion in the Middle East, Lynne Rienner Publisher, USA, 2000.

Haviland, W.A., Cultural Anthropology, Belmont, CA: Wadsworth, 2002.
Hobsbawm, E., J., Nations and Nationalism Since 1780, Program, Myth, Reality, University Press, Cambridge, 1990.
Hopkins, Nicholas S.& Ibrahim, Saad Eddin, Ed., Arab Society 'Social Science Perspective', The American University Cairo Press, Cairo, 1985.
Huntington, Samuel P., The Clash of Civilizations 'And the Remaking of World Order', Simon and Schuster UK ltd, 1997& 2002.
Ibrahim, Saad Eddin, Egypt, Islam, and Democracy, Critical Essays, The American University of Cairo Press, Cairo, 2002.
Jong, Cornelis D. de, The Freedom of Thought, Conscience and Religion or Belief in the United Nations (1946–1992), Intersentia, Oxford, 2000.
Kälin Walter, Grundrechte im Kulturkonflikt "Freiheit und Gleichheit in der Einwanderungsgesellschaft, Verlag Neue Zürcher Zeitung, Zürich, 2000.
Kymlicka, Will, Multicultural Citizenship, A Liberal Theory of Minority Rights, Clarendon Press, Oxford 1995.
Liebesny, Herbert J., The Law of the Near and Middle East: Readings, Cases, and Materials, State University of New York Press, Albany, 1975.
Lindholm Tore, Durham, W. Cole Jr., & Tahzib-Lie Bahia G., (eds.), Facilitating Freedom of Religion or Belief: A Deskbook, Koninklijke Brill NV. Netherlands, 2004.
Little D., Kelsay, J. and Sachedina, A.A., eds. Human Rights and the Conflict of Cultures: Western and Islamic Perspectives on Religious Liberty, University of South Carolina, Columbia, 1988.
Maalouf Amin, On Identity, Harvill Panther, Great Britain, 2000.
Mahmassani, S., The philosophy of Jurisprudence in Islam, Leiden 1961.
Mamdani, Mahmood, Good Muslim, Bad Muslim 'America, the Cold War, and the Roots of Terror, Pantheon Books, New York, 2004.
Manea, Elham, Regional Politics in the Developing World: The Case of the Arabian Peninsula, Yamen, Saudi Arabia, Oman, Zürich, 2001.
Mayer Anne E., Islam and Human Rights 'Tradition and Politics', Westview Press, United States, 2007.
Mittleman, Alan, Religion As A Public Good, Jewish and Other Americans on Religion in the Public Square, Rowman & Littlefield Publishers, INC., United States of America, 2003.
Müller Lars, Kälin Walter, Wyttenbach Judith eds., The Face of Human Rights: What are Human rights?, Lars Müller Publishers, Baden, 2004.
Munoz, Gema Martin, Ed., Islam, Modernism and the West, 'Cultural and political relations at the End of the Millennium, I. B. Tauris Publisher, London, 1999.
Muscroft, Sarah, Ed., Children's Rights: Equal Rights?, The International Save the Children Alliance, United Kingdom, 2000.
Nielson, Jorgen S., *Muslims in Western Europe*, 2nd ed., Edinburgh University Press, Edinburgh, 1995.

Nolan R. W., Communication and Adapting Across Cultures: Living and Working in the Global Village, Westport, CN: Bergin and Barvey, 1999.
Poggi, Gianfranco, The Development of the Modern State, A Social Introduction, Stanford University Press, Stanford, 1978.
Saeed Abdullah and Saeed Hassan, Freedom of Religion, Apostasy and Islam, Ashgate Publishing Limited, England, 2004.
Samovar Larry A., Porter, Richard E., Communication Between Cultures, 5th edition, Thomson Wadsworth, Canada, 2004.
Smith, Jane I., Islam in America, Columbia University Press, New York, 1999.
Tahzib, Bahiyyih G, Freedom of Religion or Belief, Ensuring Effective International Legal protection, The Hague, 1995.
Yamani, Mai, Cradle of Islam, The Hijaz and the Quest for an Arabian Identity, I. B. Tauris & CO Ltd, London, 2004.

Arabic Books

Al Fanjiri Ahmed Shawaqi, Mafahim Kad Toakher al Muslemeen, Mktabat Dar el Helal, 2005.
Al hajj youssef kamal, Hoqoq Al insane, Mouasassat Renee Mouawad, Beirut, 1999.
Al Hassan, Youssef, Al bouad al dini fi al syasa al Amricyia, Derassa fi Al harrkah Al massehiyah al Aosoulyia Al amricyia, Markaz Derassat Al wahada Al Arabia, Beirut, 2000.
Al-Banna Gamal, Freedom of belief in Islam, Dar al-Ansar, Cairo, 1977.
Al-Banna Gamal, Our first Demand is Freedom of Belief, Dar AL-Fikr Al-Islami, Cairo, 2000.
'Ashmawy Mohammed Said, Ma'alm Al-Islam, Sina Publication, Cairo, 1989,
'Ashmawy Mohammed Said, *Usûl al-Shari'a (Roots of Islamic law)*, Sina for publication, Cairo, 1992.
Mahfoudh, Mohammad. Al huria wa al islah fi al 3alm Al islami, Arab Scientific Publishers, Beirut, 2005.
Naif Arab Academy for Security Sciences, Hoquq Al insane bean al Shari'a al Islamia wa al Qanoun Al wadh'ai, part I, Riyadh, 2001.
Qaradawi, youssef, al Hallal wa al Haram fi al Islam, Al maktab al islami, 7th edition, Beirut, 1973.
Sakneni Issam, aL-Abassiuon Fi Sannoate Al-Tassis, Al-mo'asasa al-Arabia L'lderrasat wa Al-nashr, Beirut,1998.
Shaltout, Mahammod, al-Islam 'Aqida wa *Shari'a*, (no other informations available).
Sharour, Mohammed. al kitab wa Al Qur'an, Derrassat Islamia Mo'aasserh, Al ahali, Syria, (Publishing date not available).
Shatnawi, Fisal, Hoquq al Insane wa al Qanoun al Douali al Insani, Dar wa Mktabat al Hamed Ll'nasher, Amman, 2001.

Articles

Alves Lindgren Jose A., The Declaration of Human Rights in Post modernity, *Human Rights Quarterly*, 22.2 (2000), pp. 478–500.

An-Na'im, Na'im, Abdullahi A., Human Rights in the Arab World: A Regional Perspective, *Human Rights Quarterly*, 23.3 (2001), pp. 701–32.

An-Na'im Abdullahi A., "The Islamic Law of Apostasy and its Modern Applicability: A Case from the Sudan," *Religion*, Vol. 16, 1986, pp. 197–223.

An-Na'im, Abdullahi A., Human Rights and Islamic Identity in France and Uzbekistan: Mediation of the Local and Global, *Human Rights Quarterly*, 22.4 (2000), pp. 906–941.

Anthony F. Heath, James R. Tilley, British National Identity and Attitudes towards Immigration, International Journal on Multicultural Societies (IJMS), 7. 2, 2005, pp. 82–89.

Aral Berdal, The Idea of Human Rights as Perceived in the Ottoman Empire, *Human Rights Quarterly*, 26.2 (2004), pp. 454–482.

Baderin Mashood A., Dialogue Among civilization as a Paradigm Achieving Universalism in International Human Rights: A Case Study With Islamic Law, *Asia-Pacific on Human Rights and the Law*, 2. 2, 2001, pp. 1–41.

Barrington, Lowell W., "Nation" and "Nationalism": The Misuse of Key Concepts in Political science, *Political Science and Politics*, 30. 4, Dec. 1997, pp. 712–16.

Bassam Tibi, "Islamic law / Shari'a, Human Rights, Universal Morality and International Relations", *Human Rights Quarterly*, 16.2 (1994), pp. 73–102.

Beckley, Gloria; Burstein, Religious Pluralism, Equal Opportunity and the State, *the Western Political Quarterly*, 44.1, Mar. 1991, pp. 185–208.

Berger, Maurits S., Apostasy and Public Policy in Contemporary Egypt: An Evaluation of Recent Cases from Egypt's Highest Courts, *Human Rights Quarterly*, 25.3 (2003), pp. 720–740.

Bielefeldt, Heiner, Muslim Voices in Human Rights Debate, *Human Rights Quarterly*, 17.4 (1995), pp. 587–617.

Chris L. Coryn, James M. Beale & Krista M. Myers, Response to September 11: Anxiety, Patriotism, and Prejudice in the Aftermath of Terror, *Social Psychology*, 9.12, March 9, 2004, pp. 165–84.

Chris L. S. Coryn, Catherine Borshuk, The Scope of Justice for Muslim Americans: Moral Exclusion in the Aftermath of 9/11, The *Qualitative Report*, 11. 3, Sept. 2006, pp. 586–604.

Dirk Haubrich, September 11, Anti-Terror Laws and Civil Liberties: Britain, France and Germany Compared' Government and Opposition, 38 (1), 2003, pp. 3–31.

Fagan Andrew, Between God and Democracy, Human Rights & Human Welfare, 2.2. (Spring /Summer), 2002, pp.15–22.

Freeman Michael, The Problem of Secularism in Human Rights Theory, *Human Rights Quarterly*, 26.2, May 2004, pp. 375–400.

Ghanea, Nazila, Human Rights of Religious Minorities and of Women in the Middle East, *Human Rights Quarterly*, 26.3 (2004), pp. 705–729.

Goodhart, Micheal, Origins and Universality in the Human Rights Debates: Cultural Essentialism and the Challenge of Globalization, *Human Rights Quarterly*, 25.4 (2003), pp. 935–964.

Gunn, T. Jeremy " Religious Freedom and Laïcité: A Comparison of the United States and France", Brigham Young University Law Review, 2004, pp. 419–506.

Gunn, T. Jeremy, The Complexity of Religion and the Definition of "Religion" in International Law, *Harvard Human Rights Journal*, 16, Spring 2003, pp. 190–215.

Herland Christopher, The Status of the International Covenant on Civil and Political Rights (ICCPR) in the Domestic Law of State Parties: An Initial Global Survey Through UN Human Rights Committee Documents, *Human Rights Quarterly*, 22.1 (2000), pp. 257–260.

Hicks, Neil, Does Islamist Human Rights Activism Offer a Remedy to the Crisis of Human Rights Implementation in the Middle East?, *Human Rights Quarterly*, 24.2 (2002), pp. 361–381.

Hoffman Paul, Human Rights and Terrorism, *Human Rights Quarterly*, 26.4 (2004), pp. 932–955.

Hugh B. Urban, America, Left Behind 'Bush, the Neoconservatives, and Evangelical Christian Fiction, *Journal of Religion & Society*, Vol. 8, 2006, pp. 1–15.

Huntington Samuel P., The religious Factors in World Politics, Religion and Politics, Schweizerisches Institutes fur Auslandforschung, Zurich, 2001, pp. 147–159.

Ismail, Salwa, Confronting the Other: Identity, Culture, Political, and Conservative Islamism in Egypt, International Journal Middle East Studies, 30 (1998), pp. 25–29.

Jason Morgan-Foster Third Generation Rights: What Islamic Law Can Teach the International Human Rights Movement, *Yale Human Rights & Development, L.J.*, Vol. 8, pp. 67–116.

Jovanović, Miodrag A. Recognizing Minority Identities Through Collective Rights, *Human Rights Quarterly*, 27.2 (2005), pp. 625–651.

Kabasakal Arat, Zehra F. Forging A Global Culture of Human Rights: Origins and Prospects of the International Bill of Rights, *Human Rights Quarterly*, 28.2, May 2006, pp. 123–160.

Kälin, Walter, "Human Rights and the Integration of Migrants", Ch. 16, in Aleinikoff, T. Alexander & Chetail, Vincent, Ed., Migration and International Legal Norms, T.M.C. Asser press, The Hague, 2003, pp. 271–287.

Kanev, Krassimir, Muslim religious freedom in the OSCE area after September 11, *Helsinki Monitor*, No. 4, 2004, pp. 233–243.

Katz, Wilber G., Freedom of Religion and State Neutrality, University of Chicago, *Law Review*, 20 (1952–1953), pp. 426–440.

Lanser, Thomas R., Rights, Respect and 'Asian Values', Freedom Reviewer, Jul-Aug 95, Vol. 26, Issue 4, pp. 42–45.

Lyon Dawn & Spini Debora, Unveiling the Headscarf Debate, Legislative note, Feminist Legal Studies, Kluwer Academic Publishers, Netherlands, 12, 2004, pp. 333–345.
Mashhour, Amira, Islamic Law and Gender Equality: Could There be a Common Ground?: A Study of Divorce and Polygamy in Shari'a Law and Contemporary Legislation in Tunisia and Egypt, *Human Rights Quarterly*, 27.2, May 2005, pp. 562–596.
Mohamed Talbi, Religious Liberty: A Muslim Perspective, in: Conscience and Liberty, 3rd year, No. 1 (Spring 1991), pp. 23–31.
Monshipouri, Mahmood, Promoting Universal Human Rights: Dilemmas of Integrating Developing Countries, *Yale Rights & Development L.J.*, Vol. 4, 2001.
Moosa, Ebrahim, The Dilemma of Islamic Rights Schemes, *Journal of Law and Religion*, Vol. 15, No. 1/2, 2000–2001, pp. 25–61.
Muhammad Zafrullah Khan, 'Punishment of Apostasy in Islam' (London Mosque, no date given), 8.
Oestreich Joel E., Liberal Theory and Minority Group Rights, The Johns Hopkins University Press, *Human Rights Quarterly*, 21.1 (1999), pp. 108–132.
Pejic Jelena, Minority Rights in International Law, *Human Rights Quarterly*, 19.3 (1997), pp. 666–685.
Price, Daniel (2002). "Islam and Human Rights: A Case of Deceptive First Appearances", *The Journal for the Scientific Study of Religion*, 41(2), pp. 213–225.
Price, Daniel, "Islam and Human Rights: A Case of Deceptive First Appearances", *The Journal for the Scientific Study of Religion*, 41.2, 2002, 213–225.
Ramraj, Victor M., The Emerging Security Paradigm in the West: A Perspective from Southeast Asia, Asia-Pacific, *Journal on Human Rights and the Law*, 1, 2003, pp. 1–20.
Rehman, Javaid, Accommodating Religious Identities in an Islamic State: International Law, Freedom of Religion and the Rights of Religious Minorities, International Journal on Minority and Group Rights, Vol. 7, Kluwer Law International, the Netherlands, 2000, pp. 375–376.
Rodley, Nigel S., Conceptual Problems in Protection of Minorities: International Legal Departments, *Human Rights Quarterly*, 17.1 (1995), pp. 48–71.
Sachedina Abdulaziz, The Nature of Scriptural Reasoning in Islam, *The Journal of Scriptural Reasoning*, Number 5.1, April 2005, pp. 1–12.
Sawitri Saharso, "Culture, Tolerance and Gender," *The European Journal of Women's Studies*, 10.1 (2003), pp. 7–27.
Sebastian Poulter, "Muslim Headscarves in School: Contrasting Legal Approaches in England and France," *Oxford Journal of Legal Studies*, Vol. 17, 1997, pp. 43–74.
Sethre Ian, The Great Game for the Twenty-first Century: Islamic Extremism and central Asia, *Human Rights & Human Welfare*, Volume 3, 2003, pp. 103–110.
Shah, Niaz, A., Freedom of Religion: Koranic and Human Rights Perspectives, *Asian-Pacific Journal on Human Rights and the Law*, 1&2 (2005), pp. 69–88.

Shaikh Abdur Rahman, Punishment of Apostasy in Islam (New Delhi: Kitab Bhavan, 1996), The International Journal of Human Rights, Vol. 5, No. 3, Autumn 2001, pp. 45–70.
Sullivan, Donna J., Advancing the Freedom of Religion or Belief Through the UN Declaration on the Elimination of Religious Intolerance and Discrimination, *The American Journal of International Law*, Vol. 82, 1988, pp. 487–520.
Walker, Scott; Poe, Steven C., Does Cultural Diversity Affect Countries' Respect for Human Rights?, *Human Rights Quarterly*, 24.1 (2002), pp. 237–263.
Waltz, Susan, Universal Human Rights: The Contribution of Muslim States, Johns Hopkins University Press Human Rights Quarterly 26.4 (2004), pp. 799–844.
Weiler, J. H. H., European Law of Religion – organizational and institutional analysis of National Systems and their Implications for the Future European Integration Process, Jean Monnet Working Paper, Lasia Bloß, NYU School of Law, New York, 2003.

UN Reports

Annual report of the Independent Expert on minority issues (Ms. Gay McDougall), E/CN.4/2006/74.
Report Submitted by Special Rapporteur (Amor Abdelfattah) in accordance with Commission on Human Rights resolution 1994/18, E/CN.4/1995/91.
Report Submitted by Special Rapporteur (Amor Abdelfattah) on the implementation of the Declaration on the elimination of all forms of intolerance and of discrimination based on religion belief: visit to the Islamic Republic of Iran, E/CN.4/1996/95/Add.2.
Report Submitted by Special Rapporteur (Amor Abdelfattah) in accordance with Commission on Human Rights resolution 1996/23, E/CN.4/1997/91.
Report by the Special Rapporteur on contemporary forms of racism (Diène, Doudou), Situation of Muslim and Arab peoples in various parts of the world in the aftermath of the events of 11 September 2001 – E/CN.4/2003/23.
Report submitted by Special Rapporteur on freedom of religion or belief (Amor Abdelfattah), pursuant to Commission on Human Rights resolution 2002/40 Addendum Visit to Algeria (16–26 September 2002), E/CN.4/2003/66/Add.1.
Report of the High Commissioner for Human Rights, Combating Defamation of Religion, 19 February\2004 E/CN.4/2004/16.
Report submitted by Special Rapporteur on freedom of religion or belief (Amor Abdelfattah,) on Civil and Political Rights, Including Religious Intolerance, E/CN.4/2004/63.
Report submitted by Special Rapporteur on freedom of religion or belief (Jahangir Asma,) on Civil and Political Rights, Including the Question of Religious Intolerance, Corrigendum, E/CN.4/2005/61/Corr.1.

Report of the High Commissioner for Human Rights on combating defamation of religions, E/CN.4/2006/12.
Report of the Chairperson-Rapporteur of the Working Group on Arbitrary Detention; the Special Rapporteur on the independence of judges and lawyers; the Special Rapporteur on torture and other cruel, inhuman or degrading treatment or punishment; the Special Rapporteur on freedom of religion or belief; and the Special Rapporteur on the right of everyone to the enjoyment of the highest attainable standard of physical and mental health on the situation of detainees at Guantánamo Bay, E/CN.4/2006/120, 27 February 2006.
Report on Racism, Racial Discrimination, Xenophobia and all Forms of Discrimination, submitted by the Special Rapporteur on Contemporary forms of racism, racial discrimination, xenophobia and related intolerance (Doudou Diène), E/CN.4/2006/16.
Report of the Special Rapporteur on Contemporary forms of racism, racial discrimination, xenophobia and related intolerance (Doudou Diène), Summary of cases transmitted to Governments and replies received, E/CN.4/2006/16/Add.1.
Report of the Special Rapporteur on Contemporary forms of racism, racial discrimination, xenophobia and related intolerance (Doudou Diène), Racism, Racial Discrimination, Xenophobia and all Forms of Discrimination: Situation of Muslims and Arab People in Various Part of the World, E/CN.4/2006/17.
Report of the Special Rapporteur on freedom of religion or belief (Ms. Asma Jahangir), E/CN.4/2006/5.
Addendum to the Report of the Special Rapporteur on freedom of religion or belief (Ms. Asma Jahangir), to Communications to and from Governments (Egypt), E/CN.4/2006/5/Add.1.
Addendum 2, to the Report of the Special Rapporteur on freedom of religion or belief (Ms. Asma Jahangir), Mission to France (18 to 29 September 2005), E/CN.4/2006/5/Add.4.
Updated study the Special Rapporteur on Contemporary forms of racism, racial discrimination, xenophobia and related intolerance (Doudou Diène), Political platforms which promote or incite racial discrimination, E/CN.4/2006/54.
Report of the Special Rapporteur on the right to freedom of opinion and expression (Mr. Ambeyi Ligabo), E/CN.4/2006/55.
Study of the Current Dimensions of the Problems of Intolerance and of Discrimination on Grounds of Religion or Belief (E Odio Benito), UN Doc. reprinted in Human Rights Study Series No.2, UN Sales No. E.89.XIV.3, 1989, E/CN.4/Sub.2/ 1987/26 (1986).
Study of Discrimination in the Matter of Religious Rights and Practices, (A. Krishnaswami), E/CN.4/Sub.2/ 200/Rev.1, page 1 n. 1, UN Sales No. 60.XIV.2 (1960).
Elimination of All Forms of Intolerance and Discrimination Based on Religion or Belief, (T C Van Boven), UN Doc., E/CN.4/Sub.2/1989/32 1989.

G. A. Res. 36/55, U.N. GAOR, 36th Sess., Supp. No. 51, at 171, U.N. Doc. A/36/684 (1981).
Implementation of the Declaration on the Elimination of All Forms of Religious Intolerance and of Discrimination Based on Religion or Belief, (GA/SHC/3763), Note by the Secretary-General, A/51/542/Add.2.
The Human Rights Committee, eighty-Seventh Session, July 2006, CCPR/C/USA/Q/3/CRP.4.
Models of National or Local Action to Prevent or Combat Intolerance of Religion or Belief, United Nations Seminar on the Encouragement of Understanding, Tolerance and Respect in Matters Relating to Freedom of Religion or Belief, Chapter III: (Boyle Kevin), Geneva, Switzerland 3–14 Dec. 1984, HR/Geneva/1984/CRP.
Seminar on the Encouragement of Understanding, Tolerance, and Respect in Matters Relating to Freedom of Religion or belief, Special Rapporteur of the Sub-Commission on Prevention of Discrimination and Protection of Minorities, (Beneito Odio E.,), 3–14 December, HR/GENEVA/1984/BP.
Elimination of All Forms of Intolerance and Discrimination Based on Religion or Belief,(T C Van Boven), UN Doc. E/CN.4/Sub.2/1989/32 1989.
Proposals concerning a definition of the term minority, (Jules Deschênes), E/CN.4/Sub.2/1985/31 .
Definition of minorities (Stanislav Chernichenko), E/CN.4/Sub.2/AC.5/1996/WP.1 and E/CN.4/Sub.2/AC.5/1997/WP.1.
Classification of minorities and differentiation in minority rights, (Mr. Asbjørn Eide), E/CN.4/Sub.2/AC.5/1996/WP.2.
Human Rights Committee, General Comment 23, Article 27 (Fiftieth session, 1994), Compilation of General Comments and General Recommendations Adopted by Human Rights Treaty Bodies, U.N. Doc. HRI\GEN\1\Rev.1 at 38 (1994).
Annual report of the Independent Expert on minority issues, specific Groups and Individuals: *Minorities*,(Gay McDougall), E/CN.4/2006/74.
Sub-Commission on Prevention of Discrimination and Protection of Minorities (first session) – E/CN.4/52 (certain articles), E/CN.4/52, Section V. in Fact Sheet No. 18.
Working Paper, United Nations Seminar on the Encouragement of Understanding, tolerance and Respect in Matters Relating to freedom of religion or Belief, (Boyle Kevin), Geneva, Switzerland, 3–14, 1984, HR/Geneva/1984/WP.5.
Report of the Special Rapporteur on the promotion and protection of human rights and fundamental freedoms while countering terrorism, (Martin Scheinin), A/HRC/4/26, 29. January 2007.
Report of the Special Rapporteur on the promotion and protection of human rights and fundamental freedoms while countering terrorism, (Martin Scheinin), Mission to the United States of America, A/HRC/6/17/Add.3, 22 November 2007.
Report of the Special Rapporteur on the promotion and protection of human rights and fundamental freedoms while countering terrorism, (Martin Scheinin), A/HRC/6/17, 21 November 2007.

United Nations Development Programme, Arab Human Development Report 2004 –Towards Freedom in the Arab World" New York, April 2005.

Articles Online[1]

A History of Backlash Attacks Against Arabs and Muslims in America, <http://www.hrw.org/reports/usahate.usa1102-03.htm# P22_31469>.

Abou El Fadl, Khaled, *The Place of Tolerance in Islam On reading the Qur'an – and misreading it.* Available online at: <http://www.bostonreview.net/khaled-abou-el-fadl-the-place-of-tolerance-in-islam>.

Abu Zayd Nasr H., The Qur'anic Concept of Justice, <http://them.polylog.org/3/fan-en>.

Al-Banna Gamal, The Hijab, <http://www.islamiccall.org>.

Alfred de Zayas, *The International Judicial Protection of the Rights of People and Minorities.* Viewed in his personal website available online at: <http://alfreddezayas.com/Chapbooks/AMSTERDAM.shtml#N_1_>.

Amnesty International USA, Threat and Humiliation *(Racial Profiling, Domestic Security and Human Rights in the United States)*, Amnesty International USA Publications, 2004.

An-Na'im Abdullahi A., The Islamic Counter-Reformation, 2002, <http://www.digitalnpq.org/archive/2002_winter/an_naim.html>.

Arab American Institute, Healing the Nation: The Arab American Experience after September 11, AAI's first-anniversary report, <http://www.newsu.org/course_files/wsu_islam_11/pdf/ArabAmericanExperience.pdf>.

Azadpur Mohammad, Interpreting Political Violence in Islamic Philosophy, <http://them.polylog.org/5/fam-en.htm>.

Barnett, Laura, Freedom of Religion and Religious Symbols in the Public Sphere, Law and Government Division, *14 March 2006, Library of Parliament, Canada,* <http://www.parl.gc.ca/information/library/PRBpubs/prb0441-e.htm>.

Bowling Benjamin and others, Policing Discrimination, Xenophobia, Intolerance and the Abuse of Power from Police Work, United Nations Research Institute for Social Development Program on Identities, Conflict and Cohesion, May 2004. <http://www.unrisd.org/80256B3C005BCCF9/(httpAuxPages)/B26DCF2059E2F3E5C1256EC300495016/$file/bowling.pdf>.

Bryan Ronald Wilson, Apostates and New Religious Movements, Oxford, England, 1994. <http://www.neuereligion.de/ENG/Wilson/>.

Cairo Institute for Human Rights Studies (2005) Why Did the Islamic State Fail in the Modern Age?, <http://www.cihrs.org/IbnRoshd>.

1 All entries without other mention were last retreived in October 2010.

Canadian Council on American-Islamic Relations, *Presumption of Guilt: A National Survey on Security Visitations of Canadian Muslims*, June 2005, <http://www.caircan.ca/downloads/POG-08062005.pdf>.

Carter, Terrence S., and Carter, Sean S., Worldwide Implications of America's Emerging Policies Concerning NGOS, *Nonprofits and, Anti-terrorism and Charity Law*, No. 5, Carter & associates, Nov. 30, 2004, pp. 1–7. See article: <http://www.carters.ca/pub/alert/atcla/atcla05.pdf>.

Carter, Terrence S., Claridge, Nancy E., Carter, Sean S., Due Process and Anti-Terrorism Initiatives Worldwide-Recent Developments, Anti-Terrorism and Charity Law alert No. 16, 26 Feburary 2009, pp. 1–4. See article: <http://www.carters.ca/pub/alert/ATCLA/index.htm>.

Césari, Jocelyne, American and European Muslims After 9/11: What is Different? French and U.S. Approaches to Understanding Islam, Stanford University, September 12–14, 2004. <http://francestanford.stanford.edu/sites/francestanford.stanford.edu/files/Cesari.pdf>.

Césari, Jocelyne, Caeiro Alexandre, Hussain Dilwar, Islam and Fundamental Rights in Europe, Final report, École Pratique des Hautes Etudes Groupe de Sociologie des Religions et de la Laïcité European Commision, Oct. 2004. <http://w3.uniroma1.it/jmobservatory/eu_document/eu_doc_rapporti/2004islam_fundamental_rights.pdf>.

Clinton Bennett, Religious Minorities: Challenge or Threat, Westminster College, Oxford, delivered at the International Coalition on Religious Freedoms, Conference on "Religious Freedom and the New Millennium" Berlin, Germany, May 29–31, 1998, <http://www.religiousfreedom.com/index.php?option=com_content&view=article&id=154&Itemid=57>.

Council of Europe, "Freedom of religion and religious minorities in France," Resolution No. 1309/2002, <http://www.cesnur.org/2002/fr_council.htm>.

Dankowitz A., Accusing Muslim Intellectuals of Apostasy, MEMERI No. 208, February 18, 2005, <http://www.memri.org/report/en/0/0/0/0/0/0/1321.htm>.

Dankowitz, A., Egyptian Sheikh Dr. Abd Al-Sabour Tantawi – Islamic Reformist: A Religious and Intellectual Profile, MEMRI, No. 287, 13 July 2006. Available online at: <http://www.memri.org/report/en/0/0/0/0/0/0/1741.htm>.

Delanty, G. (1996) 'Beyond the Nation-State: National Identity and Citizenship in a Multicultural Society – A Response to Rex', Sociological Research Online, vol. 1, no. 3, <http://www.socresonline.org.uk/socresonline/1/3/1.html>.

Democracy in the Arab World, Challenges, Achievements and Prospects <http://www.hks.harvard.edu/fs/pnorris/Acrobat/stm103%20articles/IDEA%20arabworld.pdf>.

Deshmukh, Fiona, *Legal secularism in France and Freedom of Religion in the United States: A Comparison and Iraq as a Cautionary Tale*, Houston Journal of International Law, 2007, <http://www.questia.com/library/1G1-175629987/legal-secularism-in-france-and-freedom-of-religion>.

Diana Ayton-Shenker, The Challenge of Human Rights and Cultural Diversity, <www.un.org/rights/dpi 1627e.htm>.
ECRI General Policy Recommendation N° 5 on combating intolerance and discrimination against Muslims, <http://www.coe.int/t/dghl/monitoring/ecri/activities/gpr/en/recommendation_n5/Rec5%20en21.pdf>.
Esposito John L., *Conversations with History*; Institute of International Studies, UC Berkeley, <http://globetrotter.berkeley.edu/people3/Esposito/esposito-con2.html>.
European Monitoring Center on racism and xenophobia Report "Muslims in the European Union: Discrimination and Islamophobia", 2006, <http://eumc.europa.eu/eumc/index.php>.
European Monitoring Centre on Racism and Xenophobia, Anti-Islamic reactions in the EU after the terrorist acts against the USA, 12th September to 31st December 2001, <http://www.pedz.uni-mannheim.de/daten/edz-b/ebr/05/Spain.pdf>.
Evans, Carolyn, "Religious freedom and religious hatred in democratic societies", Monash University, 2006, <http://www.law.monash.edu.au/castancentre/events/2006/conf-06-evans-paper.html>.
Ferrari, Silvio, New Religious Movements in Westerrn Europe, Research and Analysis – No. 9 – October 2006, <http://religion.info/pdf/2006_10_ferrari_nrm.pdf>.
Freedom of Thought and Belief: Between the State's Anvil and the Islamic Groups' Hammer," speech opening EOHR's Third Intellectual Seminar on Freedom of Thought, Belief and Expression," Cairo, May 1–2, 1992, <http://freecopts.net/english/index.php?option=com_content&task=view&id=237>.
Geisser, Vincent, Intellectual and Ideological Debates on Islamophobia: A 'French Specificity' in Europe? "French and US Approaches to Understanding Islam", September 2004, <http://francestanford.stanford.edu/sites/francestanford.stanford.edu/files/Geisser.pdf>.
Geldenhuys Deon and Rossouw Johann, The International Protection of Minority Rights, A special report complied for the F W de Klerk Foundation, August 2001, <http://www.changing-europe.org/download/Summer_School_2008/Sata.pdf>.
Gilles Ivaldi, *Extreme Right Parties in France, An overview*, 8 July 2002, <http://www.politik.uni-mainz.de/ereps/download/france_overview.pdf>.
Gunn, T. Jeremy. "Under God but Not the Scarf: The Founding Myths of Religious Freedom in the United States and *Laïcité* in France," *Journal of Church and State*, Vol. 7, 2004, <http://digitalcommons.law.byu.edu/do/search/?q=Gunn%2C%20T.%20Jeremy.%20%E2%80%9CUnder%20God%20but%20Not%20the%20Scarf%3A%20The%20Founding%20Myths%20of%20Religious%20Freedom%20in%20the%20United%20States%20and%20La%C3%AFcit%C3%A9%20in%20France&start=0&context=4277457>.
Heiko Henkel, The Danish Cartoon Controversy and the Self-Image of Europe (2006), Radical philosophy, <http://www.radicalphilosophy.com/commentary/%E2%80%98the-journalists-of-jyllands-posten-are-a-bunch-of-reactionary-provocateurs%E2%80%99>.

Human Right Watch Report, The Road to Abu Ghraib, June 8, 2004, <http://www.hrw.org/en/node/12123/section/1>.
Juan-Diez Medrano and Matthias Koenig, "Nationalism, Citizenship and Immigration in 82, Social Science Research – Editorial Introduction" International Journal on Multicultural Societies (IJMS), Vol. 7, No. 2, 2005, <http://unesdoc.unesco.org/images/0014/001425/142588E.pdf>.
Judge Tulkens dissenting Opinion, <http://slomanson.tjsl.edu/SahinTurk.pdf>.
Kay Guinane, *Muslim Charities and the War on Terror, Top Ten Concerns and Status*, March 2006, <http://www.foreffectivegov.org/files/npadv/PDF/MuslimCharities TopTenUpdated.pdf>.
Kenneth W. Dam – Deputy Secretary of the Treasury, *"The Financial Front of the War on Terrorism: The Next Phase,"* delivered to the Council on Foreign Relations New York, New York. June 8, 2002.Viewed online: <http://www.treas.gov/press/releases/po3163.htm>.
Leavitt, Noah, A Review of Elaine Cassel's "The War on Civil Liberties: How Bush and Ashcroft have Dismantled the Bill of Rights, <http://writ.findlaw.com/books/reviews>.
Legomsky Stephen H., The Ethnic and Religious Profiling of Noncitizens: National Security and International Human Rights, Boston College, Boston College, *Third World Law Journal* No. 1, Volume 25, 2005, <http://lawdigitalcommons.bc.edu/cgi/viewcontent.cgi?article=1092&context=twlj>.
Leonard, Karen. "American Muslims: South Asian Contributions to the Mix, "French and US Approaches to Understanding Islam", September 2004, <http://france stanford.stanford.edu/sites/francestanford.stanford.edu/files/Leonard.pdf>.
Linda Feldmann and Warren Richey, "Has post-9/11 dragnet gone too far?" The Christian Science Monitor, September 12, 2003, <http://www.csmonitor.com/2003/0912/p01s04-uspo.html>.
Mehmet Aydin, *Fighting Intolerance and Discrimination against Muslims: facilitating integration and respecting Cultural Diversity*, OSCE Conference on Anti-Semitism and on Other Forms of Intolerance, Cordoba, 8 and 9 June 2005, <http://www.osce.org/cio/15477>.
Memorandum in Support of the US's Assertion of States Secret Privilege, 18 January 2005, <http://www.fas.org/sgp/jud/arar-memo-011805.pdf>.
Nimrod, Raphaeli, Demands for Reforms in Saudi Arabia MEMRI's Middle East Economic Studies Program, No. 247, October 13, 2005, <http://www.memri.org/report/en/0/0/0/0/0/0/1502.htm>.
O'Sullivan, Declan, The Death Sentence for Mahmoud Muhammad Taha: Misuse of the Sudanese Legal System and Islamic Shari'a Law? <http://www.alfikra.org/article_page_view_e.php?article_id=35&page_id=1>.
Ömür Orhun, Dealing With Intolerance and Discrimination Against Muslims: Social and Political Solution, International Conference on Islamophobia, Istanbul, 8–9 December 2007) CIO.GAL/29/08, 8 February 2008 <https://www.google.com/

#q=%C3%96m%C3%BCr+Orhun%2C+Dealing+With+Intolerance+and+Discrimination+Against+Muslims%3A+Social+and+Political+Solution%2C+International+Conference+on+Islamophobia%2C+Istanbul%2C+8%E2%80%93+9+December+2007%29>.

Parekh Bhikhu, Unity and Diversity in Multicultural Societies, International Institute for Labour Studies, Geneva, March 2005. <http://test-red.pucp.edu.pe/ridei/wpcontent/uploads/biblioteca/Parekh_multiculturalismo.pdf>.

Parker Laura, "The ordeal of Chaplain Yee." USA Today, May 16 2004, <http://www.usatoday.com/news/nation/2004-05-16-yee-cover_x.htm>.

Parliament of the World's Religions, Barcelona, July 7th–13th 2004, International Association of Religious Freedom Panel, 9 July 2004, "Freedom of Religion for All", Presentation by Professor Kevin Boyle, Human Rights Centre, University of Essex, United Kingdom. <http://www.iarf.net/PWR04%20report/Boyle%20PWR%20lecture.PDF>.

Pastor, Eugenia Relaño, " Flawed Implementation of International Religious Freedom Act of 1998: A European Perspective", Brigham Young University Law Review. 2005, online: <http://digitalcommons.law.byu.edu/cgi/viewcontent.cgi?article=2242&content=lawreview>.

Patricia Crone, professor of Islamic history at the Institute for Advanced Study, Princeton, What do we actually know about Mohammed? <http://www.opendemocracy.net/faitheurope_islam/mohammed_3866.jsp>.

Perumalil Augustine, Does Religion Promote Violence?, <http://them.polylog.org/5/fpa-en.htm#s1#s1>.

Pippa Norris & Ronald Inglehart, Islam & the West: Testing the "Clash of Civilizations" Thesis, Harvard University and the University of Michigan, available online:<http://www.hks.harvard.edu/fs/pnorris/Acrobat/Clash%20of%20Civilization.pdf>.

President Issues Military Order: Detention, Treatment, and Trial of Certain Non-Citizens in the War Against Terrorism, November 13, 2001, <http://www.whitehouse.gov/news/releases/2001/11/20011113-27.html>.

Public Law 107–56, 107th Cong., 1st sess. (26 October 2001), *USA Patriot Act,* sec. 507(j) (2)(A). Full text available at: <http://thomas.loc.gov/cgibin/query/D?c107:4:./temp/~c107CatuiX>.

Report of OSCE-ODIHR Roundtable: The Representation of Muslims in Public Discourse, Warsaw, 9 May 2006, <http://www.osce.org/odihr/23561>.

Report on Torture and Cruel, Inhuman, and Degrading Treatment of Prisoners at Guantánamo Bay, Cuba, Center for Constitutional Right July 2006, 25. <http://www2.ohchr.org/english/bodies/hrc/docs/ngos/ccr.pdf>.

Report on USA Human Rights After September 2001: Report 6.4: US Muslims Feeling a "Chilling Effect", Meikele John Civil Liberties Institute to the UN Human Rights Committee, August 29, 2005, <http://www.ohchr.org/english/bodies/hrc/docs/ngos/liberties.doc>.

Rex John, (1996) 'Contemporary Nationalism, Its Causes and Consequences for Europe – A Reply to Delanty' Sociological Research Online, vol. 1, no. 4, <http://www.socresonline.org.uk/socresonline/1/4/rex.html>.

Roy, Oliver, Muslim Minorities in Europe – Questions of Culture, Ethnicity, and Religion, OSI – New York, March 29, 2006, <http://theamericanmuslim.org/tam.php/features/articles/interview_with_olivier_roy_full_equality_before_the_law_for_all_religions>.

Safi, Louay M., Human Rights and Cultural Reform in Contemporary Muslim Society: From the Hegemonic Discourse to Cross-Cultural Dialogue, <http://www.law.emory.edu/ihr/publics/lsafi1.pdf>.

Secretary-General, Addressing Headquarters Seminar on Confronting Islamophobia, Stresses Importance of Leadership, Press Release SG/SM/963, HR/4802, PI/1627. Available at: <http://www.un.org/News/Press/docs/2004/sgsm9637.doc.htm>.

Seminar on the Encouragement of Understanding, Tolerance, and Respect in Matters Relating to Freedom of Religion or belief, 3–14 December 1984, HR/GENEVA/1984/BP. 2, <http://www.euro-islam.info/PDFs/silentrev.pdf>.

Stahnke Tad; Blit Robert C., The Religion –state Relationship and the Right to Freedom of Religion or Belief: A Comparative textual Analysis of the Constitutions of Predominantly Muslim Countries. <http://www.uscirf.gov/images/stories/pdf/Comparative_Constitutions/Study0305.pdf>.

Taylor,Gray, Freedom of religion in America, Contemporary review, June, 2003, <http://www.findarticles.com/p/articles/>.

The "Taguba Report" On Treatment Of *Abu Ghraib* Prisoners In Iraq, Article 15–6 Investigation of the 800th Military Police Brigade, <http://news.findlaw.com/wsj/docs/iraq/tagubarpt.html>.

The 1978 UNESCO Declaration on Race and Racial Prejudice, Adopted and proclaimed by the General Conference of the United Nations Educational, Scientific and Cultural Organization at its twentieth session, on 27 November 1978, Article 5 (3), <http://www.unesco.org/education/nfsunesco/pdf/RACE_E.PDF>.

The American Civil Liberties Union, *Sanctioned Bias: Racial Profiling Since September 11*, 2001, Feb. 2004, 5, <https://www.aclu.org/sites/default/files/FilesPDFs/racial%20profiling%20statement%20for%20un.pdf>.

The answer by Ibn Khaldoun Center to Sheik Al Azahr is available online in Arabic at: This Translation is by Dankowitz A., Accusing Muslim Intellectuals of Apostasy, MEMERI No. 208, February 18, 2005. <http://memri.org/bin/articles.cgi?Page=archives&Area=ia&ID=IA20805#_edn12#_edn12>.

The FIDH and the Egyptian Organisation for Human Rights (EOHR), THE EMERGENCY LAW IN EGYPT, 3 February 2011, <http://www.fidh.org/THE-EMERGENCY-LAW-IN-EGYPT>.

The Egyptian Organization on Human Rights, The Situation of Human Rights in Egypt Annual Report 2003, Cairo, Egypt, 2004.

The International Commission of Jurists ("ICJ"), Counter-Terrorism and Human Rights: *Assessing Damage, Urging Action,* the Eminent Jurists Panel on Terrorism Report, 16, February, 2009, p. 213, <http://digitalcommons.wcl.american.edu/cgi/viewcontent.cgi?article=1190&context=hrbrief>.

The Pew Global Attitudes Project, The Great Divide: How Westerners and Muslims View Each Other, Europe's Muslims More Moderate, 2006, <http://pewglobal.org/reports/display.php?ReportID=253>.

The September 11 Detainees: A Review of the Treatment of Aliens Held on Immigration Charges in Connection with the Investigation of the September 11 Attacks, U.S. Department of Justice Office of the Inspector General, April 2003. Available online <http://www.justice.gov./oig/special/0306/press.pdf>.

The Status of Muslim Civil Rights in the United States in 2002: Stereotypes and Civil Liberties, <http://cair.com/civil-rights/civil-rights-reports/12-civil-rights/11728-2002-civil-rights-report-stereotypes-and-civil-liberties.html>.

The U.S. Department of Justice, Office of the Inspector General, Supplemental Report on September 11 Detainees' Allegations of Abuse at the Metropolitan Detention Center in Brooklyn, New York, December 2003, <http://www.justice.gov/oig/special/0312/final.pdf>.

The Vatican Report: Sects or New Religious Movements: A Pastoral Challenge, this report, originally released on June 11, 1986, Reprinted from: Cultic Studies Journal, Vol. 3, No. 1, 1986, <http://www.csj.org/infoserv_articles/vatican_report_sects.htm>.

Third report on France, Adopted on 25 June 2004 and made public on 15 February 2005, European Commission against Racism and Intolerance, Council of Europe, CRI (2005) 3, 'Necessity of moving towards an integrated society', <http://www.coe.int/t/e/human_rights/ecri/1-ECRI/2-Country-by country approach/France/France_CBC_3.asp#TopOfPage>.

U.S. General Accounting Office, Report to Congressional Committees, Homeland Security: Justice Department's Project to Interview Aliens after September 11, 2001, 8 (2003), viewed online at: <http://www.gao.gov/new.items/d03459.pdf>.

U.S. Supreme Court Should Review and Reject Secret Detentions, Human Rights Watch press release, September 30, 2003, <http://www.hrw.org/press/2003/09/us093003.htm>.

Violence, Politics, and Human Rights, Shirin Ebadi in Dialogue with Nermeen Shaikh, <http://them.polylog.org/5/des-en.htm>.

Vorkink Mark W. & Scheick Erin M., *The "War on Terror" and The Erosion of the Rule of Law: The U.S. Hearings of the ICJ Eminent Jurist Panal,* Human Rights Brief, Volume 14 Issue 1, Winter 2006 Convention Against Torture, art. 3, Dec. 10, 1984, <http://www.unhchr.ch/html/menu3/b/h_cat39.htm>.

White House Press Secretary announcement of President Bush's determination re legal status of Taliban and Al Qaeda detainees (February 7, 2002), <http://www.state.gov/s/l/38727.htm>.
Workshop on "Islam and Reform," held in Cairo on October 5–6, 2004, (translated) in Yehoshua, Y., A Cairo Conference Calling for Reform Raises the Ire of the Egyptian Religious Establishment, MEMRI, October 22, 2004, No. 192. <http://freerepublic.com/focus/f-news/1252556/posts>.
Yousaf Ali's Translation of the Qur'an, <http://www.usc.edu/dept/MSA/quran/>.

International Documents

Charter of the United Nations, June 26, 1945, 59 Stat. 1031, T.S. 993, 3 Bevans 1153, entered into force Oct. 24, 1945.
Declaration on the Elimination of All Forms of Intolerance and of Discrimination Based on Religion or Belief, G.A. res. 36/55, 36 U.N. GAOR Supp. (No. 51) at 171, U.N. Doc. A/36/684 (1981).
Declaration on the Rights of Persons Belonging to National or Ethnic, Religious or Linguistic Minorities, G.A. res. 47/135, annex, 47 U.N. GAOR Supp. (No. 49) at 210, U.N. Doc. A/47/49 (1993).
Human Rights Committee, General Comment 11, Article 20 (Nineteenth session, 1983), Compilation of General Comments and General Recommendations. Adopted by Human Rights Treaty Bodies, U.N. Doc. HRI/GEN/1/Rev.1 at 12 (1994).
International Convention on the Elimination of All Forms of Racial Discrimination, G.A. res. 2106 (XX), Annex, 20 U.N. GAOR Supp. (No. 14) at 47, U.N. Doc. A/6014 (1966), 660 U.N.T.S. 195, *entered into force* Jan. 4, 1969.
International Covenant on Civil and Political Rights, G.A. res. 2200A (XXI), 21 U.N. GAOR Supp. (No. 16) at 52, U.N. Doc. A/6316 (1966), 999 U.N.T.S. 171, entered into force Mar. 23, 1976.
International Covenant on Economic, Social and Cultural Rights, G.A. res. 2200A (XXI), 21 U.N.GAOR Supp. (No. 16) at 49, U.N. Doc. A/6316 (1966), 993 U.N.T.S. 3, entered into force Jan. 3, 1976.
Optional Protocol to the International Covenant on Civil and Political Rights, G.A. res. 2200A (XXI), 21 U.N. GAOR Supp. (No. 16) at 59, U.N. Doc. A/6316 (1966), 999 U.N.T.S. 302, entered into force March 23, 1976.
Second Optional Protocol to the International Covenant on Civil and Political Rights, aiming at the abolition of the death penalty, G.A. res. 44/128, annex, 44 U.N. GAOR Supp. (No. 49) at 207, U.N. Doc. A/44/49 (1989), entered into force July 11, 1991.
United Nations, Economic and Social Council, Siracusa Principles on the Limitation and Derogation Provisions in the International Covenant on Civil and Political Rights, U.N. Doc. E/CN.4/1985/4, Annex (1985).

Universal Declaration of Human Rights, G.A. res. 217A (III), U.N. Doc A/810 at 71 (1948).
World Conference Against Racism, Racial Discrimination, Xenophobia and Related Intolerance, Programme of Action, Agenda item 9, adopted on September 8, 2001 in Durban South Africa, U.N. Doc. A/CONF.189/5 (2001).
U.N. Doc and regional documents and others <http://www1.umn.edu/humanrts/>.

WELTEN DES ISLAMS
WORLDS OF ISLAM
MONDES DE L'ISLAM

Herausgegeben von / Edited by / Edité par

SILVIA NAEF, ULRICH RUDOLPH & GREGOR SCHOELER

Ziel der Reihe „Welten des Islams" der Schweizerischen Asiengesellschaft ist es, repräsentative, qualitativ hochstehende Forschungsarbeiten zu den islamischen Kulturen und Gesellschaften in Gegenwart und Vergangenheit vorzustellen. Sie nimmt Studien zu verschiedenen Bereichen wie Kunst, Literatur und Philosophie sowie Übersetzungen und Interpretationen von Quellentexten auf. Sie will aber auch Arbeiten zu relevanten Themen und aktuellen Fragen anbieten, die neben dem wissenschaftlichen Zielpublikum einer breiter interessierten Leserschaft zugänglich sind.

Die Reihe versteht sich als Forum für geistes- und sozialwissenschaftliche Arbeiten aus der Schweiz. Ausserdem werden Beiträge aus der internationalen Forschung aufgenommen. Die Hauptpublikationssprachen für die Monographien, Sammelbände und Übersichtswerke sind Deutsch, Französisch und Englisch.

Die Reihe wird von einem Herausgebergremium geleitet, das von führenden Fachvertretern aus den jeweiligen akademischen Disziplinen beraten wird.

Vol. 1 Dorothea Krawulsky
Eine Einführung in die Koranwissenschaften. ʿUlūm al-Qurʾān
2006, 205 S. ISBN 3-03910-753-4

Vol. 2 Alessandro Monsutti, Silvia Naef & Farian Sabahi (Eds)
The Other Shiites. From the Mediterranean to Central Asia.
2007, 266 p. ISBN 978-3-03911-289-0

Vol. 3 Tobias Heinzelmann & Henning Sievert (Hrsg.)
Buchkultur im Nahen Osten des 17. und 18. Jahrhunderts.
2010, 266 S. ISBN 978-3-0343-0451-1

Vol. 4 Hana Sadik El-Gallal
Islam and the West. The Limits of Freedom of Religion.
2014, 340 S. ISBN 978-3-0343-0578-5